# IBM WebSphere Application Server 8.0 Administration Guide

Learn to administer a reliable, secure, and scalable environment for running applications with IBM WebSphere Application Server 8.0

**Steve Robinson**

BIRMINGHAM - MUMBAI

# IBM WebSphere Application Server 8.0 Administration Guide

Copyright © 2011 Packt Publishing

First published: September 2011

Production Reference: 1150911

Published by Packt Publishing Ltd.
Livery Place
35 Livery Street
Birmingham B3 2PB, UK.

ISBN 978-1-84968-398-2

www.packtpub.com

Cover Image by Sandeep Babu (sandyjb@gmail.com)

# Credits

**Author**
Steve Robinson

**Reviewers**
Dave Hay

Jacek Laskowski

Meenakshi Verma

**Acquisition Editor**
Stephanie Moss

**Development Editor**
Hyacintha D'Souza

**Technical Editors**
Arun Nadar

Pallavi Kachare

Priyanka S

**Copy Editors**
Brandt D'Mello

Leonard D'Silva

Laxmi Subramanian

Kriti Sharma

**Project Coordinator**
Kushal Bhardwaj

**Proofreader**
Linda Morris

**Indexer**
Monica Ajmera Mehta

**Graphics**
Geetanjali Sawant

**Production Coordinator**
Arvindkumar Gupta

**Cover Work**
Arvindkumar Gupta

# About the Author

**Steve Robinson** is an independent WebSphere specialist and consultant. He has been consulting in the IT field since 1997 and has been involved in client projects around the globe; many of which are for Fortune 500 companies.

Steve started out originally as a consultant in the IBM Lotus Notes/Domino product suite, where he excelled in middleware integration technologies to ensure that homogenous environments could exist in the new heterogeneous world. Having worked for many different industries, Steve has had a plethora of experience in the integration of most technologies across many different systems and cultures. He is also an accomplished programmer in C, Java, and the Microsoft .NET development tools.

Steve has gleaned a lot of insight due to the amount of large enterprise projects he has been involved with and his passion for documentation and process improvement is recognized by all those he works with.

Steve is married and lives with his family in England. He spends his time either writing or researching new products and technologies for client projects along with investigating new ways to automate processes where possible.

Steve is also known for his contribution to the WebSphere Internet community through one of his many top-ranking WebSphere knowledge portals: www.webspheretools.com.

# Acknowledgement

To my loving wife and "bestest buddy" Jacqui; without you I would not be the person I am today. You keep me grounded, while I dream my biggest dreams. To my family; thanks for all your continued encouragement and belief in me and for constantly reminding me that not everything in life is work.

I thank the reviewers for their contributions. Thanks guys, you helped me ensure that the content was accurate.

I would also like to thank the staff at Packt Publishing who helped me keep my writing in form and to the point.

# About the Reviewers

**Dave Hay** is a Portal and Collaboration Architect with IBM Software Services for Lotus (ISSL). He has been responsible for the design and delivery of IT solutions for some of IBM's major UK customers. Dave's work is mainly focused on the role of the Infrastructure Solution Architecture, and he has experience with many of the core components that would comprise a portal or collaboration solution.

Dave has worked in a variety of roles with IBM since 1992, and has been with IBM Software Group since 2000. He has worked with WebSphere Application Server for much of that time, starting with v3 and covering a number of platforms, including AIX, OS/400, Linux, and Windows.

**Jacek Laskowski** has over 15 years of IT experience having focused on software development and architecture design in open source and commercial projects. He's interested in Service Oriented Architecture with Java Enterprise Edition, Business Process Management, and Business Rule Management System solutions. He is a seasoned technology professional with a strong software development and advisory track record. His interests revolve around Java Enterprise Edition (Java EE) and supportive solutions, be them runtime environments or specifications, like Enterprise OSGi, Service Component Architecture (SCA), WS-BPEL, and WS-BPMN, to name a few.

He is a leader of the Warszawa Java User Group and has been a speaker at local and international conferences. He has been organizing Confitura (formerly Javarsovia) and Warsjawa conferences for the Polish Java community. He contributes to open source projects such as Apache OpenEJB and Apache Geronimo. He envisages himself using functional languages in projects and the decision to learn Clojure (possibly JRuby and Scala) influences his current self-learning activities.

Sharing knowledge is his passion. He mentors students in the IBM Education Student Internship (ESI) program. He is an author of IBM Redbooks publications and has contributed to a few others as a technical reviewer. While supporting business partners and customers with their use of IBM WebSphere BPM products, he regularly runs courses and workshops in Poland and abroad. He is a member of the NetBeans Dream Team–highly-skilled and motivated NetBeans users.

He actively blogs at `http://blog.japila.pl` and `http://blog.jaceklaskowski.pl`. You can also follow him at `@jaceklaskowski` on Twitter.

I'd like to thank my family–my wife, Agata, and 2 kids, Iweta and Patryk – for their constant support, encouragement and patience. It was them who kept me considering other activities, besides spending time hacking, reading computer books or blogging.

Love you all so much!

**Meenakshi Verma** has been part of the IT industry since 1998. She is experienced in putting up solutions across multiple industry segments using SAP BI, SAP Business Objects, and Java/J2EE technologies. She is currently based in Toronto, Canada and is working with a leading utility company.

Meenakshi has been helping with technical reviews for books published by Packt Publishing across varied enterprise solutions. Her earlier work includes *JasperReports for Java Developers*, *Java EE 5 Development using GlassFish Application Server*, *Practical Data Analysis and Reporting with BIRT*, *EJB 3 Developer's Guide*, *Learning DOJO*, and *WebSphere Application Server*.

I'd like to thank my father (Mr. Bhopal Singh) and mother (Mrs. Raj Bala) for giving me a strong foundation and their unconditional love and support. I am also grateful to my husband (Atul Verma) for his encouragement and support throughout the review of this book and many others, my four year old son (Prieyaansh Verma) for giving me the warmth of his love, despite my hectic schedules, and my brother (Sachin Singh) for always being there for me.

# www.PacktPub.com

## Support files, eBooks, discount offers and more

You might want to visit www.PacktPub.com for support files and downloads related to your book.

Did you know that Packt offers eBook versions of every book published, with PDF and ePub files available? You can upgrade to the eBook version at www.PacktPub.com and as a print book customer, you are entitled to a discount on the eBook copy. Get in touch with us at service@packtpub.com for more details.

At www.PacktPub.com, you can also read a collection of free technical articles, sign up for a range of free newsletters and receive exclusive discounts and offers on Packt books and eBooks.

http://PacktLib.PacktPub.com

Do you need instant solutions to your IT questions? PacktLib is Packt's online digital book library. Here, you can access, read and search across Packt's entire library of books.

## Why Subscribe?

- Fully searchable across every book published by Packt
- Copy and paste, print and bookmark content
- On demand and accessible via web browser

## Free Access for Packt account holders

If you have an account with Packt at www.PacktPub.com, you can use this to access PacktLib today and view nine entirely free books. Simply use your login credentials for immediate access.

## Instant Updates on New Packt Books

Get notified! Find out when new books are published by following @PacktEnterprise on Twitter, or the *Packt Enterprise* Facebook page.

# Table of Contents

# Preface

I have been lucky enough during my career to have worked as a developer, a consultant, and for many years as a **WebSphere Application Server (WAS)** administrator. I have also held senior architecture roles. One thing I have learned is that it is difficult for one person to know everything about a complex product such as **WAS 8**. More often than not, we find ourselves struggling to find the right amount of time and patience, to learn all the intricacies of a new product.

WAS has now become a highly in-depth product, as has **JEE (Java Enterprise Edition**, formerly known as **J2EE)** on which **WebSphere 8** is based. During this foray into WebSphere Application Server 8, I have kept in mind that some readers are new to WAS and require an overview which gives them a complete view of what the product entails, while others are seasoned and are looking for insights that are not so easily understood, or available through IBM's standard documentation.

It is a challenge for any author to provide detail and at the same time convey and allow for simple understanding. I believe that throughout this book you will be able to read and understand the topics presented with minimal effort. As you try the exercises and examples, you will gain more in-depth understanding and experience to support your administration of WebSphere Application Server 8.

## What this book covers

*Chapter 1, WebSphere Application Server 8 Product Overview* covers the new capabilities of WebSphere and provides an overview of the underlying WAS architecture and how it relates to JEE 6. Explanations of important WAS concepts and terminology are also covered.

*Chapter 2, Installing WebSphere Application Server* covers how to plan and prepare your WAS installation, and shows how to manually install WebSphere using the graphical installer, and how to use a response file for automated silent installation. The fundamentals of application server profiles are described and the administrative console is introduced. In this chapter we also introduce the IBM Installation Manager which is new to WAS 8 and facilitates the management of WAS installations.

*Chapter 3, Deploying your Applications* explains the make-up of Enterprise Archive (EAR) files, how to manually deploy applications, and how the **Java Naming and Directory Interface (JNDI)** is used in the configuration of resources. Connecting to databases is explained via the configuration of **Java Database Connectivity (JDBC)** drivers and data sources used in the deployment of data-aware applications. This chapter also covers how to use managed deployments, a new feature of WebSphere 8 that allows applications to be deployed using monitored folders.

*Chapter 4, Security* demonstrates the implementation of global security and how to federate **Lightweight Directory Access Protocol (LDAP)** and file-based registries for managing WAS security. Roles are explained, where users and groups can be assigned different administrative capabilities. Security domains and SSL configurations are also explained.

*Chapter 5, Administrative Scripting* introduces ws_ant, a utility for using Apache Ant build scripts to deploy and configure applications. Advanced administrative scripting is demonstrated by using the wsadmin tool with Jython scripts, covering how WAS configuration and application deployments can be automated using the extensive WAS Jython scripting objects.

*Chapter 6, Server Configuration* explains the WAS installation structure and key XML files, which make up the underlying WAS configuration repository. Logging is covered showing the types of log files and log settings which are vital for administration. Also included in this chapter is the new feature of WAS 8, known as **High Performance Extensible Logging (HPEL)**, which provides an efficient binary file approach to logging. Application server Java Virtual Machine JVM settings and class loading are also explained.

*Chapter 7, WebSphere Messaging* explains basic **Java Message Service (JMS)** messaging concepts, and demonstrates both JMS messaging using the default messaging provider and **WebSphere Message Queuing (MQ)** along with explanations of message types. Use of Queue Connection Factories, Queues, and Queue Destinations are demonstrated via a sample application. MQ Link is explained, demonstrating how to connect WAS to foreign WebSphere MQ networks. The new WAS 8 feature of disabling WebSphere MQ process is also covered in this chapter.

*Chapter 8, Monitoring and Tuning* shows how to use **Tivoli Performance Monitor (TPV)**, request metrics, and JVM tuning settings to help you improve WAS performance and monitor the running state of your deployed applications. Analysis of Java heap and core dumps is also explained.

*Chapter 9, Administrative Features* covers how to enable the administrative agent for administering multiple application servers with a central administrative console. The IBM HTTP Server and the WebSphere plug-in are explained along with how to implement SSL between the IBM HTTP Server, the WebSphere plug-in and the WebSphere Application Server.

*Chapter 10, Administration Tools* demonstrates some of the command line utilities vital to the WebSphere administrator for debugging and problem resolution. Also in the chapter the **IBM Support Assistant (ISA)** is introduced and an example given on how to analyze WAS log files, using one of the many ISA add-ons.

*Chapter 11, Product Maintenance* shows how to maintain your WebSphere Application Server by keeping it up-to-date with the latest fix packs and feature packs. Locating the fix pack on IBM's web and the process of how to download the latest fix packs is covered. Backing up WebSphere configurations is also explained.

# What you need for this book

Below is a list of the software applications used in this book:

- Your preferred operating system choice of either an IBM supported version of Windows or Linux. Note: For Linux users it is recommended that you use a supported Linux OS such as Red Hat Enterprise Linux 5.6; however it is possible to use Centos 5.6.
- You will need your favorite text editor for editing scripts.
- For shell access from Windows to Linux you will need an SSH client such as PuTTY.
- For Linux based GUI installs, you will need an X11 server running. If you are connecting from Windows to Linux you can use a Windows X11 server such as Xming.
- WebSphere Application Server 8 Trial.
- WebSphere MQ 7 Trial.
- IBM Installation Manager.
- IBM Support Assistant.

Sample applications and scripts are also required.

Visit http://www.packtpub.com/files/code/3892_Code.zip to directly download the example code.

# Who this book is for

If you are a system administrator or an IT professional who wants to learn about IBM WebSphere Application Server v8.0, this book will walk you through the key aspects of installation and administration of a WAS environment. You do not need any previous experience in WebSphere Application Server, but some understanding of Java Enterprise Edition (JEE) technologies will be helpful. In addition, JEE application developers and architects who want to understand how WebSphere manages JEE applications will find this book useful.

# Conventions

In this book, you will find a number of styles of text that distinguish between different kinds of information. Here are some examples of these styles, and an explanation of their meaning.

Code words in text are shown as follows: "Login to the DefaultApplication using the username waslocal and the password waslocal, and the snoop servlet will load".

A block of code is set as follows:

```
#Uninstall the application
deployEAR="<deploy_home>/HRListerEAR.ear"
appName="HRListerEAR"
AdminApp.uninstall(appName);
#save
AdminConfig.save();
```

Any command-line input or output is written as follows:

```
AdminTask.extractConfigProperties('[-propertiesFileName c:\temp\hrLister.
props -configData Application=HRlisterEAr]')
```

**New terms** and **important words** are shown in bold. Words that you see on the screen, in menus or dialog boxes for example, appear in the text like this: "To access the repository table, click **File | Preferences... | Repositories**".

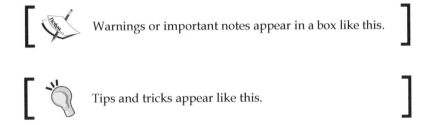

Warnings or important notes appear in a box like this.

Tips and tricks appear like this.

# Reader feedback

Feedback from our readers is always welcome. Let us know what you think about this book—what you liked or may have disliked. Reader feedback is important for us to develop titles that you really get the most out of.

To send us general feedback, simply send an e-mail to feedback@packtpub.com, and mention the book title via the subject of your message.

If there is a book that you need and would like to see us publish, please send us a note in the **SUGGEST A TITLE** form on www.packtpub.com or e-mail suggest@ packtpub.com.

If there is a topic that you have expertise in and you are interested in either writing or contributing to a book, see our author guide on www.packtpub.com/authors.

# Customer support

Now that you are the proud owner of a Packt book, we have a number of things to help you to get the most from your purchase.

# Downloading the example code

You can download the example code files for all Packt books you have purchased from your account at http://www.PacktPub.com. If you purchased this book elsewhere, you can visit http://www.PacktPub.com/support and register to have the files e-mailed directly to you.

# Errata

Although we have taken every care to ensure the accuracy of our content, mistakes do happen. If you find a mistake in one of our books—maybe a mistake in the text or the code—we would be grateful if you would report this to us. By doing so, you can save other readers from frustration and help us improve subsequent versions of this book. If you find any errata, please report them by visiting http://www.packtpub.com/support, selecting your book, clicking on the **errata submission form** link, and entering the details of your errata. Once your errata are verified, your submission will be accepted and the errata will be uploaded on our website, or added to any list of existing errata, under the Errata section of that title. Any existing errata can be viewed by selecting your title from http://www.packtpub.com/support.

# Piracy

Piracy of copyright material on the Internet is an ongoing problem across all media. At Packt, we take the protection of our copyright and licenses very seriously. If you come across any illegal copies of our works, in any form, on the Internet, please provide us with the location address or website name immediately so that we can pursue a remedy.

Please contact us at copyright@packtpub.com with a link to the suspected pirated material.

We appreciate your help in protecting our authors, and our ability to bring you valuable content.

# Questions

You can contact us at questions@packtpub.com if you are having a problem with any aspect of the book, and we will do our best to address it.

# 1
# WebSphere Application Server 8.0: Product Overview

WebSphere Application Server, often referred to simply as **WAS**, is a JEE-compliant application server platform. JEE stands for Java Enterprise Edition and was previously referred to as J2EE. JEE application servers provide functionality to deploy fault-tolerant, distributed, and multi-tier Java software. They also provide the runtime environment and management interface to manage the many modular components that make up JEE applications. Before we begin to look into the specifics of WebSphere Application Server 8 administration, it is important to understand what the product is, why it is often the product of choice to provide a base for an enterprise JEE **SOA (Service Oriented Architecture)** along with support for the many Java-based standards, and how an organization can benefit from using WAS. We also need to cover some specific WAS terminology and concepts used throughout the book.

In this first chapter, we will cover the following:

- What is WebSphere Application Server
- Why choose WAS
- Previous versions
- Enhancements and capabilities
- WebSphere Application Server architecture
- WAS concepts and terminology
- WebSphere Application Server products

# What is WebSphere Application Server?

**IBM WebSphere Application Server**, is IBM's answer to the JEE application server. WAS first appeared in the market as a Java Servlet engine in June 1998, but it wasn't until version 4 (released in 2001) that the product became a fully JEE 1.2-compliant application server.

Over the last 10 years, since version 1.2 was released, IBM has invested heavily in WAS and it is developed with open industry standards in mind such as Java EE, XML, and Web Services. WebSphere Application Server is now IBM's flagship for the WebSphere brand and forms the base of many of IBM's extended product range.

The latest release of WebSphere Application Server version 8, is a JEE 6-compliant application server. Every new version is required to provide improved efficiency and continued compliancy with standards, allowing customers who invest in WAS to make use of the new Java capabilities of each new JEE release.

When choosing an application server platform on which to run applications and services, architects and developers need to know that WAS will support new JEE features and improved coding practices. WAS has evolved as a product with each new update of the JEE standard, and IBM has continued to provide new versions of WAS to support available features of each new JEE release.

The following table shows a simple comparison of current and previous WAS versions and its compliancy to JEE specifications:

| Version | Compliancy | | | |
|---|---|---|---|---|
| | **JEE** | **EJB** | **Servlet** | **JSP** |
| WebSphere 8 | 6 | 3.1 | 3.0 | 2.2 |
| WebSphere 7 | 5 | 3.0 | 2.5 | 2.1 |
| WebSphere 6.1 | 1.4 | 2.1 | 2.4 | 2.0 |
| WebSphere 6 | 1.4 | 2.1 | 2.4 | 2.0 |
| WebSphere 5.1 | 1.3 | 2.0 | 2.3 | 1.2 |
| WebSphere 5 | 1.3 | 2.0 | 2.3 | 1.2 |
| WebSphere 4 | 1.2 | 1.1 | 2.2 | 1.1 |
| WebSphere 3.5 | 1.2 | 1.0 | 2.1 | 1.0 |

# Why choose IBM WebSphere Application Server?

JEE is an ever-changing world, and as soon as a new application server is released by IBM, new standards and approaches become available, or they become the preferred method of choice by the JEE community. Organizations who have invested in JEE technology require an application server platform that allows them to extend their existing legacy systems, and provide services-based frameworks on which their enterprise applications and systems can be based. So there is a continuing need for IBM to facilitate all the facets of the new JEE enterprise features, namely **JMS**, **Web Services**, **Web Applications**, and **Enterprise JavaBeans**, ensuring their product continues to innovate and provide the ability for their customers to extend their own core systems.

IBM is committed to ensuring WAS negates the need for complex architectures, while at the same time providing a platform for servicing business applications, process automation/workflow, and complex bus topologies as required. The WAS product is continually being updated and improved to bring in new technologies as they are released or accepted by the community as a whole.

WAS can be considered the base of your enterprise JEE application service provisioning toolbox, and can be extended with custom business solutions as required. Developers and architects want to ensure that their application designs use the latest JEE standards and programming models. Reading through the WAS product specification sheet, which can be downloaded from `http://www.ibm.com/developerworks/downloads/ws/was/`, you can see that there are many new features in WebSphere Application Server version 8 supporting many industry **JEE API's (Application Programming Interfaces)** and standards.

Let's now turn to a quick, but not so brief, overview of the new capabilities under WebSphere 8.

 Not all new JEE features are chosen by IBM to be fully supported in the new versions of WAS. IBM assesses every new specification, and determines the features they will implement. Sometimes their decision can be entirely commercial, that is how they can implement an IBM-specific solution within the bounds of WebSphere; other times they are influenced by their customers and/or industry needs.

# Enhancements and capabilities

Improving WebSphere Application Server's capability offering is something that IBM is very good at. Each new release offers more support for the ever changing JEE specification and industry/community-provided Java APIs. IBM evaluates customer and industry feedback when building new versions of the WAS. These considerations influence how WebSphere supports JEE applications.

Details of new capabilities have been included in this chapter as it is important to have knowledge of what WebSphere actually supports. This is not a book on architecture; it is about administering WebSphere Application Server. However, in your job as a WebSphere administrator, you will need to provide a WebSphere environment designed by architects to support applications built by developers, who will have incorporated new JEE features in the application(s) requiring deployment. You will find yourself setting up resources to support these new APIs. You will also often find yourself debugging applications, which may not be running correctly due to conflicts of APIs packaged in the application with those already provided by WebSphere within its internals.

> If you require an in-depth view of what's new in WAS 8, it is recommended you visit the official WAS 8 features page at the following URL: http://www-01.ibm.com/software/webservers/appserv/was/features/. It is also good practice to review the product data sheet, which can be downloaded from the aforementioned URL.

# Support for industry standards

Architects require common standards. Because IBM continually welcomes and supports new development and design approaches within the JEE application community, it gives architects the confidence that any inter-communicating systems they design for WAS 8 will communicate and work with external systems with much less effort.

An enterprise will contain many third-party systems and interfaces. By using WAS 8, companies can feel confident that their design approach will be consistent with other industry solutions, standards, and practices. This allows for quicker integration due to the fact that systems will require less design and development to interface the third-party products and systems, that is fewer barriers to integration and interconnectivity.

The following table gives a summary of key standards that WebSphere 8 supports:

| Standard | Description |
| --- | --- |
| **Java EE 6 programming model** | Compliance with the latest Java EE specification, which delivers ease of use and productivity enhancements. Updates also include performance, security, and reliability enhancements delivered by the IBM Java SDK 6.0 (J9 2.6). |
| **OSGi (Open Services Gateway initiative)** | WAS 8 has updated optimized support for applications, which are designed to use OSGi, and it supports integrated bundle support.<br><br>OSGi is a module system and service platform for the Java programming language. It implements a complete and dynamic component model allowing application components to be remotely installed, started, stopped, updated, and uninstalled without requiring a reboot. It also allows an application to be dynamically extended. WebSphere implements the OSGi framework within the installation process and internal configuration. |
| **Web 2.0** | WAS 8 provides Web 2.0 to SOA connectivity allowing Ajax-based clients and mash-ups to leverage external web services, internal SOA services, and JEE assets across the enterprise.<br><br>Web 2.0 in itself is not a technology, rather a change in the approach in which software developers implement standards, models, and APIs, and the way in which end-users use web-based applications. It is hard to get exact agreement on the definition of Web 2.0, but we see it every day in the rich applications coming forth and making our web experience more dynamic. JEE vendors provide features and APIs that make Web 2.0 programming easier by removing some of the hard boundaries between web-based systems and APIs; hence, Web 2.0 is often mentioned as part of the feature set of an application server like WebSphere. |
| **Java batch** | Reuse existing skills to quickly and cost-effectively develop, deploy, and manage batch applications. |
| **IBM SDK** | Security, performance, and reliability enhancements to IBM SDK 6.0. |

| Standard | Description |
|---|---|
| **Service Component Architecture (SCA)** | As part of the larger **SOA (Service-Oriented Architecture)** Foundation which is incorporated into all of the IBM software brands, **SCA (Service Component Architecture)** capable products, such as the WebSphere Application Server, allow architectures to benefit from the decoupling of service implementation from the details of the infrastructure. Put simply, SCA is a set of specifications which describe a model for building applications and systems using a Service-Oriented Architecture. SCA extends and complements previous approaches to implementing services, and builds on open standards such as Web Services. What this means to larger organizations is that their **Enterprise Service Bus (ESB)** implementations can leverage SCA with WebSphere since its design adheres to and supports industry-recommended best practice. |
| **Communications Enabled Applications (CEA)** | CEA provides a new style of application to the community. It leverages the JSR 289 standard for **SIP (Session Initiation Protocol)** support and provides template JavaScript widgets out-of-the-box, which are fully customizable via CSS and can be embedded into existing web and Java applications. |
| **Session Initiation Protocol (SIP)** | **SIP** is an industry standard suite of protocols that can be used to establish, modify, and terminate voice sessions, and is often seen in **call-me now** applications. Simply put, it is a standard by which voice and video media services are incorporated into JEE applications running on WAS. |
| **JPA (Java Persistence API)** | **JPA** provides a **POJO (Plain Old Java Object)** standard and **ORM (Object Relational Mapping)** for data persistence among applications. |
| | JPA was defined as part of the EJB 3.0 specification as a replacement for the EJB 2 CMP Entity Beans specification. Most of the persistence vendors have released implementations of JPA, confirming its adoption by the industry and users, including **Oracle TopLink**, **Oracle Kodo**, **JDO (Java Data Objects)** and of course the well-known **Spring Hibernate**. |
| **SAM (Simple Asynchronous Messaging)** | **SAM**, otherwise known as "extension" provides interfaces to the IBM Messaging and Queuing middleware products using a set of libraries and some client-side code referred to as **XMS**. The IBM Message Service Client is an **Application Programming Interface (API)** that is consistent with the **Java Message Service (JMS)** API and is often used with client technologies like PHP. |
| | Applications using SAM can exchange messages between other Message Service Client applications with minimal effort, which allows Open Source web-based programs to benefit and easily co-exist with IBM messaging. |

| Standard | Description |
|---|---|
| **SDO (Service Data Objects)** | Service Data Objects is a newer model for data access developed jointly by IBM and BEA (now Oracle), and standardized with the JSR235 standard, providing a common framework for data application development. Developers no longer need to be familiar with technology-specific APIs. By employing SDO, they can access data from multiple data sources, including relational databases, entity EJB components, XML pages, Web services, the **Java Connector Architecture (JCA),** and JavaServer Pages (via Java Servlet API). |

# New features

There have been many internal product improvements for efficiency in both resource management and administration time saving. The following table gives an overview of new enhancements to WAS realized in version 8:

| Feature/Capability | Description |
|---|---|
| Monitored deployments | New monitored directory-based application install, update, and uninstall of Java EE application. |
| HPEL | New High Performance Extensible Logging (HPEL) problem determination tools and enhanced security and administration features to improve administrator productivity and control. |
| Updated installation process | New simplified install and maintenance through IBM Installation Manager to improve efficiency and control. |
| Workload efficiency | Run the same workload on fewer servers, creating savings of 30 percent due to updates in the performance for EJB and web services. |
| Improved performance and high availability with WebSphere MQ | Messaging is a key part of any enterprise both in Java's JMS and IBM's specific messaging platform called WebSphere MQ. WAS continues to provide ease of integration with MQ. |

| Feature/Capability | Description |
| --- | --- |
| Security hardening | Security domains have been improved to offer more secure protection for services provided by WAS. |
| | Simplified exchange of user identity and attributes in Web Services using **Security Assertion Mark-up Language (SAML)** as defined in the OASIS Web Services Security SAML Token Profile Version 1.1. |
| | SAML assertions represent user identity and user security attributes, and optionally to sign and to encrypt SOAP message elements. |
| | The **Organization for the Advancement of Structured Information Standards (OASIS)** is a global consortium that drives the development, convergence, and adoption of e-business and web service standards. |
| | Web Services Security API (WSS API) and WS-Trust support in JAX-WS to enable customers building single sign on Web services-based applications. |
| | The WSS API supports Security token types and deriving keys for signing, signature and verification, encryption, and decryption. |
| Security auditing enhancements | Auditable security events are security events that have audit instrumentation added to the security run time code to enable them to be recorded to logs for review. |
| | Enhanced cookie support to reduce cross-site scripting vulnerabilities and also better support for security, for example, SSO (Single Sign On) and LPTA (Lightweight Third Party Authentication). |
| | Enhanced security configuration reporting, including session security and Web attributes. |
| | Additional security features enabled by default. |
| | Security enhancements required by Java Servlet 3.0. |
| | Java Authentication SPI for Containers (JSR 196) support, which allows third-party authentications for requests or responses destined for web applications. |
| | Configure federated repositories at the domain level in a multiple security domain environment. |

| Feature/Capability | Description |
|---|---|
| Performance improvements | JPA L2 cache and JPA L2 cache integration with the DynaCache environment. |
| | New caching features functionality for servlet caching, JSP, web services, command cache, and so on. |
| Improved migration support | Better support for migrating applications deployed to WebSphere Application Server 6.0, 6.1, and 7.0. |
| | The command line tools and GUI wizard have been improved. |
| **JDBC (Java Database Connectivity)** | New and upgraded providers for database connectivity support for **JDBC**. |

# Reference table for supported standards

The following table is a quick reference, listing the new standards mentioned previously as adhered to, or provided, by WebSphere Application Server v8:

| Standard | Level | Description |
|---|---|---|
| JEE | 6.0 | Java Platform, Enterprise Edition, or Java EE. |
| EJB | 3.1 | Enterprise JavaBeans (EJB) technology is the server-side component architecture for the JEE Platform. |
| Servlet | 3.0 | Servlet is a Java class in Java EE that conforms to the Java Servlet API and often generates HTML from Java code. |
| JCA | 1.6 | Java EE Connector Architecture (JCA) for connecting to legacy systems outside of JDBC. |
| JSP | 2.0 | Java Server Pages (JSP) allows HTML pages to have Java code embedded for dynamic HTML generation. |
| JSF | 2.0 | Java Server Faces and uses Apache MyFaces 2.0 implementation. |
| JPA | 2.0 | Apache OpenJPA 2.0 implementation of the Java Persistence API (JPA). |
| JTA | - | Java Transaction API (JTA) is one of the Java Enterprise Edition (Java EE) APIs. |
| SIP | 1.1 | Voice and video calls over Internet Protocol (IP). |
| JMS | - | Java Message Service (JMS) is one of the Java Enterprise Edition (Java EE) APIs. |
| JMX | - | The Java Management Extensions (JMX) API is one of the Java Enterprise Edition (Java EE) APIs. |

| Standard | Level | Description |
|---|---|---|
| JDBC | - | Java Database Connection (JDBC) is one of the Java Enterprise Edition (Java EE) APIs. |
| RMI | - | Remote Method Invocation (RMI) is one of the Java Enterprise Edition (Java EE) APIs. |
| JavaMail | 1.4 | JavaMail APIs provide a framework for building mail client applications. |
| JAF | 1.4 | JavaMail API requires the JavaBeans Application Framework (JAF). |
| SSL | 3.0 | Secure Sockets Layer. |
| SOAP | 1.2 | SOAP is a specification for the exchange of XML-based information in distributed environments. |
| XPath | 2.0 | XPath is a language for addressing parts of an XML document. |
| XSLT | 2.0 | XSLT stands for XSL Transformations. XSL is a style sheet language for XML. |
| XQuery | 1.0 | Intelligent XML search API. |
| JAX-WS | 2.2 (partial) | Java programming language API for creating web services. |
| JAX-B | 2.2 | Java Architecture for XML Binding (JAXB) is a Java technology that provides an easy and convenient way to map Java classes and XML schema for simplified development of web services. |
| CDI | JSR 299 | Support for Contexts and Dependency Injection (CDI) . |
| JAX-RS | - | API for RESTful Web Services (JAX-RS) is one of the Java Enterprise Edition (Java EE) APIs. |

# Architecture and internals

We have mentioned that WebSphere Application Server 8 has been developed to adhere to the new JEE 6 specification. We will now quickly look at what JEE 6 is made up of, so we can see how WAS maps out.

# JEE 6 Server architecture model

It is important for a WAS 8 administrator to have a good awareness of the JEE 6 server architecture model. Let's look at Java EE 6 and quickly run though the internal JEE containers. This should give you an insight and understanding into what WebSphere 8 has to offer in the way of JEE 6 support for these containers. We cannot delve into every API/Standard of JEE 6 as we are here to learn WebSphere Application Server, but I think the overview of the containers will help provide context for the specific features of the JEE specification.

## Java EE containers

The JEE specification outlines four types of container, as shown in the following diagram. These containers form the guidelines of the services, which are to be provided by a JEE application server as implemented by a software vendor like IBM:

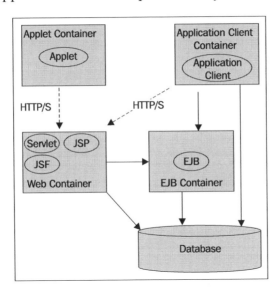

A JEE application will use one or more of the previous four components, that is an application can simply be a web application running in the Web Container alone, or a JEE application can be more complex and contain both Web components and EJB components, and so more than one container can be used in serving an application.

# Applet container

The **Applet container** manages Java applets. An Applet is a Java program that can be embedded into a web page. Most web pages are rendered using HTML/XML-based technology. By embedding the tags <APPLET> and </APPLET> a browser will load a Java applet, which can use the Java AWT/Swing interface APIs, allowing a traditional client-like application to run within the browser. The Applet container manages the execution of the applet, and contains the web browser.

# Web container

The **Web container**, also known as a **Servlet container,** provides web-related services. In a nutshell, this is the component of a web-server which serves web content, web-services, facilitates web-security, application deployment, and other key services. The following diagram shows the availability of the Java EE 6 APIs in the web container:

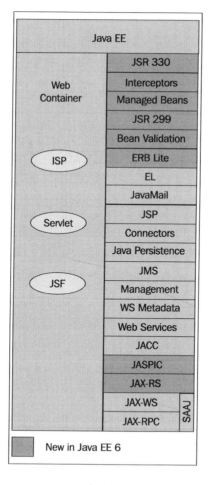

# EJB container

The **EJB (Enterprise JavaBean) container** manages the services of the EJB API and provides an environment for running the enterprise components of a JEE application. Enterprise JavaBeans are used in distributed applications, and facilitate transaction services and appropriate low-level implementations of transaction management and coordination, as required by key business processes. They are essentially the business components of an application.

The EJB container also manages database connections and pooling, threads, and sockets on behalf of enterprise beans, as well as state and session management. The following diagram shows the availability of the Java EE 6 APIs in the EJB container:

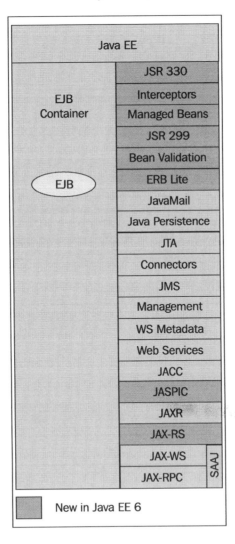

## Application client container

An application client runs on a user's client machine and provides a traditional rich Graphical User Interface **(GUI)** created from the Swing or the **Abstract Window Toolkit (AWT)** API. Application client's access enterprise beans running in the business tier—which we explained earlier—run in the EJB container. An application client can use **RMI (Remote Method Invocation)** or other protocols, such as **SOAP (Simple Object Access Protocol)**, over HTTP **(Hypertext Transfer Protocol)**. The following diagram shows the Java EE 6 APIs within the application client container:

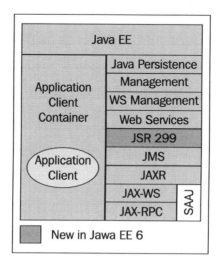

If you would like to know more about the Java 6 API, this link has a great walkthrough of the Java EE 6 Tutorial: `http://download.oracle.com/javaee/6/tutorial/doc/index.html`.

Now that we have seen the various APIs contained within the four component containers for the JEE 6 platform, we can now look at the internal architecture of WebSphere with some context established.

# Inside WebSphere Application Server

Before we look at installing WAS and deploying an application, we will quickly run over the internals of WAS. The anatomy of WebSphere Application Server is quite detailed so, for now, let's briefly outline some of the more important parts, discovering more about the working constituent parts as we work through each of the remaining chapters.

The following diagram shows the basic architecture model for a WebSphere Application server JVM:

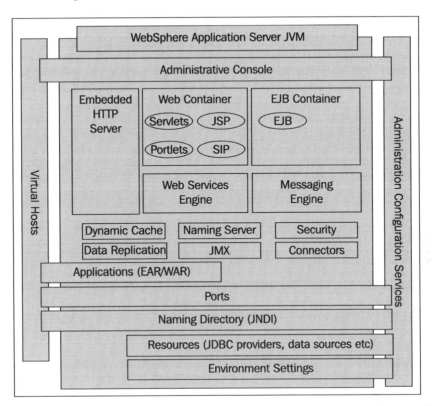

# JVM

All WebSphere Application Servers are essentially **Java Virtual Machines (JVMs)**. IBM has implemented the JEE application server model in a way that maximizes the JEE specification, and also provides many enhancements creating specific features for WAS. JEE applications are deployed to an Application Server.

# Web container

A common type of business application is a web application. The WAS web container is essentially a Java-based web server contained within an application server's JVM, which serves the web component of an application to the client browser.

# EJB container

Applications need not only comprise of web components. In a more complex enterprise-based application, business objects are created to provide a layer of abstraction between a web application and the underlying data. The EJB container provides the services required to manage the business components as implanted with EJBs.

# Virtual hosts

A virtual host is a configuration element that is required for the web container to receive HTTP requests. As in most web server technologies, a single machine may be required to host multiple applications and appear to the outside world as multiple machines. Resources that are associated with a particular virtual host are designed not to share data with resources belonging to another virtual host, even if the virtual hosts share the same physical machine. Each virtual host is given a logical name and assigned one or more DNS aliases by which it is known. A **DNS alias** is the TCP/ host name and port number that is used to request a web resource, for example, `<hostname>:9080/<servlet>`.

By default, two virtual host aliases are created during installation. One for the administration console called `admin_host` and another called `default_host`, which is assigned as the default virtual host alias for all application deployments, unless overridden during the deployment phase. All web applications must be mapped to a virtual host, otherwise web browser clients cannot access the application that is being served by the web container.

# Environment settings

WebSphere uses Java environment variables to control settings and properties related to the server environment. WAS variables are used to configure product path names, such as the location of a database driver, for example, `ORACLE_JDBC_DRIVER_PATH`, and environmental values required by internal WAS services and/or applications.

# Resources

Configuration data is stored in XML files in the underlying configuration repository of the WebSphere Application Server. Resource definitions are a fundamental part of J2EE administration. Application logic can vary depending on individual business requirements, and there are several resource types that can be used by an application. The following table shows a list of some of the most commonly used resource types:

| Resource types | Description |
|---|---|
| JDBC (Java database connectivity) | Used to define providers and data sources. |
| URL providers | Used to define end-points for external services, for example, web services. |
| JMS providers | Used to define messaging configurations for Java Message Service, **Message Queuing (MQ)** connection factories and queue destinations, and so on. |
| Mail providers | Enable applications to send and receive mail, typically using the **SMTP (Simple Mail Transfer Protocol)**. |

# JNDI

The **Java Naming and Directory Interface (JNDI)** is employed to make applications more portable. JNDI is essentially an API for a directory service, which allows Java applications to look up data and objects via a name. Naming operations, such as lookups and binds, are performed on contexts. All naming operations begin with obtaining an initial context. You can view the initial context as a starting point in the namespace. Applications use JNDI lookups to find a resource using a known naming convention. You can override the resource the application is actually connecting to without requiring a reconfiguration or code change in the application. This level of abstraction using JNDI is fundamental and required for the proper use of WAS by applications.

# Application file types

There are four main file types we work with in Java applications. An explanation of these file types is shown in the following table:

| File Type | Description |
| --- | --- |
| **JAR file** | A JAR file (or Java ARchive) is used for organizing many files into one and employ the `.jar` file extension. |
| | The actual internal physical layout is much like a ZIP file. A JAR is generally used to distribute Java classes and associated metadata. In JEE applications, the JAR file often contains utility code, shared libraries, and EJBs. An EJB is a server-side model that encapsulates the business logic of an application and is one of the several Java APIs in the Java Platform, Enterprise Edition with its own specification. You can visit `http://java.sun.com/products/ejb/` for information on EJBs. |
| **RAR file** | A **RAR (Resource Adapter Archive)** is a special Java archive (JAR) file that is used to package a resource adapter for the Java 2 Connector (J2C) architecture and has the `.rar` file extension. |
| | Stored in a RAR file, a resource adapter may be deployed on any JEE server, much like the EAR file of a JEE application. A RAR file may be contained in an EAR file or it may exist as a separate file. WebSphere supports both. |
| | A resource adapter is analogous to a JDBC driver. Both provide a standard API through which an application can access a resource that is outside the JEE server. For a resource adapter, the outside resource is an **EIS (Enterprise Information system)** and allows a standard way for EIS vendor's software to be integrated with JEE applications; for a JDBC driver, it is a **DBMS (Database Management System)**. Resource adapters and JDBC drivers are rarely created by application developers. In most cases, both types of software are built by vendors who sell products such as tools, servers, or integration software. |

| File Type | Description |
|---|---|
| **WAR file** | A WAR file (Web Application) is essentially a JAR file used to encapsulate a collection of JavaServer Pages (JSP), Servlets, Java classes, HTML, and other related files, which may include XML and other file types depending on the web technology used. For information on JSP and Servlets, you can visit `http://java.sun.com/products/jsp/`.<br><br>Servlet can support dynamic web page content; they provide dynamic server-side processing and can connect to databases.<br><br>**JavaServer Pages (JSP)** files can be used to separate HTML code from the business logic in web pages. Essentially, they too can generate dynamic pages; however, they employ Java beans (classes), which contain specific detailed server-side logic.<br><br>A WAR file also has its own deployment descriptor called `web.xml`, which is used to configure the WAR file and can contain instructions for resource mapping and security. |
| **EAR file** | An Enterprise Archive file represents a JEE application that can be deployed in a WebSphere Application Server. EAR files are standard Java archive files (JAR) and have the file extension `.ear`. An EAR file can consist of the following:<br><br>One or more web modules packaged in WAR files.<br><br>One or more EJB modules packaged in JAR files.<br><br>One or more application client modules.<br><br>Additional JAR files required by the application.<br><br>Any combination of the above.<br><br>The modules that make up the EAR file are, themselves, packaged in archive files specific to their types. For example, a web module contains web archive files and an EJB module contains Java archive files. EAR files also contain a deployment descriptor (an XML file called `application.xml`) that describes the contents of the application and contains instructions for the entire application, such as security settings to be used in the runtime environment. |

 When an EJB module or web module (WAR) is installed as a standalone application, it is automatically wrapped in an Enterprise Archive (EAR) file by the WebSphere deployment process, and is managed on disk by WebSphere as an EAR file structure. So, if a WAR file is deployed, WebSphere will convert it into an EAR file.

# WebSphere Application Server terminology

Throughout this book we will be referring to WAS-specific terminology. There are some key points and terms we need to clarify to aid in understanding WAS as we discuss the finer points of WAS administration. The following section outlines important keywords and terminology, referred to in later chapters.

## Runtime binaries

The core product files are the actual product binary files, and can be shared by many profiles. The directory structure for the product has two major divisions of files in the installation root directory for the product. One division is the runtime binaries and the other is for profiles. We will discuss this in detail in *Chapter 2, Installing WebSphere Application Server.*

## Profiles

A profile is an 'instance' of a WebSphere Application Server configuration. A profile contains its own set of administration scripts, its own environment, its own repository, and its own node agent. Many profiles can be created from a single install. Profiles can be installed to share runtime binaries allowing multiple profiles to benefit from a single maintenance update. It is also possible to allow each profile to have its own copy of the runtime binaries allowing profiles to update independently.

An example of using multiple profiles might be that a developer needs to create separate profiles of the product in order to segregate development and testing, each profile being based on a different fix-pack level, and/or containing specific configuration settings. In the following chapters, we will explain profiles in more detail.

## Cells

A unit of management is a **Cell**. The entire administrative configuration data is stored in XML files containing the master configuration of the Cell. It is also a grouping of nodes into a single administrative domain. For WebSphere Application Server, it means you group (federate) several servers within a Cell, then you can administer them with a single administrative console. Federating multiple application servers into a single administrative console is covered in *Chapter 9, Administrative Features.*

The following diagram outlines the components of a Cell:

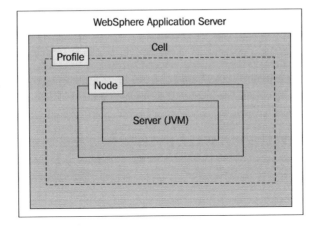

# Nodes

A **node** is the term which can be given to the physical OS instance on which the WebSphere process will run. Another important term related to nodes is the **Node Agent**. Node Agents are responsible for spawning or killing server processes and also configuration synchronization between the Deployment Manager and the Node in the WebSphere Network Deployment product.

When using WebSphere Application Server, there is no node agent process available for a standalone application server node, unless you decide to federate the application server node with a Deployment Manager for a given Cell of an existing WebSphere Network Deployment installation. In short, a standalone installation of a WebSphere is in fact a single Cell, Node, Node Agent, and Server all in one.

It can be quite confusing at times, because WAS is designed for scalability and extension, so depending on the version of WAS purchased, you can extend its architecture and infrastructure footprint. Some of these terms come into their own once you upgrade to WebSphere Network Deployment and other extended variants of WAS.

Since version 7, the administrative agent has become **available**. This provides a single interface to administer multiple standalone application servers. Multiple servers may exist for development, test, staging, pre-production, and so forth, thus having a single administration console to manage many servers provides administrators with new capability.

# Servers

Each standalone Application Server node needs to run a JVM in which a deployed JEE application will run. With WAS base, each profile will have a single JVM. In WAS ND, we can have multiple JVMs per node, which is part of the highly-available design architecture of WAS ND. You could say an installation of a standalone WebSphere application server is a cell, a node, and a server with a single JVM all in one along with an administration console.

# WebSphere Application Server products

WebSphere Application Server also forms the base of WebSphere Application Server 8 Network Deployment (WAS-ND) Edition, which is designed for the more complex enterprise, with support for high availability such as clustering, failover, load balancing and work load management, and so on.

Other products in the WebSphere range include WebSphere Portal, WebSphere ESB, WebSphere Process Server, and many others. The following table provides a quick review of WebSphere Application Server products:

## Product editions

| Product Edition | Description |
| --- | --- |
| Application Server | Build, deploy, and manage SOA business applications and services of all types. Application Server also known as Application Server Base is the foundation of the WebSphere Application Server suite. |
| Application Server – Express | An affordable solution at a reduced cost. |
| Application Server Community Edition | Lightweight Java EE application server based on open source Apache Geronimo. |
| Application Server Network Deployment | Provides high-availability with near-continuous availability along with advanced performance and management capabilities, for mission-critical applications. |
| | ND provides JVM clustering, data replication services, and advanced workload management. |
| Application Server for Developers | WebSphere Application Server for Developers provides simplified access to enable developers to build and test in the same environment that will ultimately support their applications. |

| Product Edition | Description |
| --- | --- |
| Application Server for z/OS | Takes advantage of the qualities of service of IBM z/OS, by harnessing the full capabilities of the z/OS. |

# Related Product editions

| Product Edition | Description |
| --- | --- |
| Application Server Hypervisor Edition | Optimized to instantly run in VMware and other server virtualization environments. |
| WebSphere Virtual Enterprise | Consolidate application servers and maximize utilization while monitoring application health. |
| WebSphere eXtreme Scale | Provides distributed object caching for elastic scalability and cloud environments. |
| WebSphere Extended Deployment Compute Grid | Enable practical reuse of on-line Java™ assets in the batch workloads. |

# Supported OS

WebSphere is supported on the following OS (Operating System) platforms:

- Windows
- AIX
- Linux
- Solaris
- i/OS
- z/OS

Beginning with Version 6.1 and now with Version 8, IBM is supporting open standard specifications and have aligned WAS with a view to a more common approach across all the platforms, to the extent that WAS now works with a large number of Web servers including Apache HTTP Server, Netscape Enterprise Server, Microsoft Internet Information Services (IIS), IBM HTTP Server for i5/OS, IBM HTTP Server for z/OS, and IBM HTTP Server for AIX/Linux/Microsoft Windows/Solaris.

Following is a table of Platforms and recommended versions of OS:

| OS | Supported Version |
|---|---|
| Linux 32 | • Red Hat Enterprise Linux (RHEL) 5.0 Advanced Platform (32- and 64-bit kernels) |
| | • Red Hat Enterprise Linux 5.0 Desktop editions (32- and 64-bit kernels) |
| | • SUSE Linux Enterprise Desktop (SLED) 10.0 (32- and 64-bit kernels) |
| | • SUSE Linux Enterprise Desktop 11.0 (32- and 64-bit kernels) |
| | • SUSE Linux Enterprise Server (SLES) 10.0 (32- and 64-bit kernels) |
| | • SUSE Linux Enterprise Server 11.0 (32- and 64-bit kernels) |
| Linux 64 | • Red Hat Enterprise Linux 5.0 Advanced Platform (64-bit kernels only) |
| | • Red Hat Enterprise Linux 5.0 Desktop editions Platform (64-bit kernels only) |
| | • SUSE Linux Enterprise Desktop 10.0 (64-bit kernels only) |
| | • SUSE Linux Enterprise Desktop 11.0 (64-bit kernels only) |
| | • SUSE Linux Enterprise Server 10.0 (64-bit kernels only) |
| | • SUSE Linux Enterprise Server 11.0 (64-bit kernels only) |
| HP-UX | • HP-UX 11iv2 with Patch Bundle dated December 2007 (64-bit kernel support) |
| | • HP-UX 11iv3 with Patch Bundle dated September 2009 (64-bit kernel support) |
| Solaris 32 | • Oracle Solaris Version 10 with a patch cluster dated October 2009 or later (32- and 64-bit kernel support) |
| Solaris 64 | • Oracle Solaris Version 10 with a patch cluster dated October 2009 or later (64-bit kernel support) |

| OS | Supported Version |
|---|---|
| Windows 32 | • Microsoft XP Professional with SP2 |
| | • Microsoft Windows Server 2003, Datacenter with SP2 (32- and 64-bit editions) |
| | • Microsoft Windows Server 2003, Enterprise with SP2 (32 and 64-bit editions) |
| | • Microsoft Windows Server 2003, Standard with SP2 (32- and 64-bit editions) |
| | • Microsoft Windows Server 2003 R2 (32- and 64-bit editions) |
| | • Microsoft Vista Business |
| | • Microsoft Vista Enterprise |
| | • Microsoft Vista Ultimate |
| | • Microsoft Vista Ultimate SP1 |
| | • Microsoft Windows 7 Enterprise (32- and 64-bit editions) |
| | • Microsoft Windows 7 Professional (32- and 64-bit editions) |
| | • Microsoft Windows 7 Ultimate (32- and 64-bit editions) |
| | • Microsoft Windows Server 2008, Datacenter with SP1 (32- and 64-bit editions) |
| | • Microsoft Windows Server 2008, Enterprise with SP1 (32 and 64-bit editions) |
| | • Microsoft Windows Server 2008, Standard with SP1 (32- and 64-bit editions) |
| | • Microsoft Windows Server 2008 R2, Standard (64-bit edition only) |
| | • Microsoft Windows Server 2008 R2, Enterprise (64-bit edition only) |
| | • Microsoft Windows Server 2008 R2, Datacenter (64-bit edition only) |

| OS | Supported Version |
|---|---|
| Windows 64 | • Microsoft Windows Server 2003 Enterprise with SP2 (64-bit edition only) |
| | • Microsoft Windows Server 2003 Datacenter with SP2 (64-bit edition only) |
| | • Microsoft Windows Server 2003 Standard with SP2 (64-bit edition only) |
| | • Microsoft Windows Server 2003 R2 (64-bit editions only) |
| | • Microsoft Windows Server 2008 Enterprise with SP1 (64-bit edition only) |
| | • Microsoft Windows Server 2008 Datacenter with SP1 (64-bit edition only) |
| | • Microsoft Windows Server 2008 Standard with SP1 (64-bit edition only) |
| | • Microsoft Windows Server 2008 R2, Standard (64-bit edition only) |
| | • Microsoft Windows Server 2008 R2, Enterprise (64-bit edition only) |
| | • Microsoft Windows Server 2008 R2, Datacenter (64-bit edition only) |
| AIX 32 | • AIX 6.1 with Recommended Maintenance package 6100-00-04 |
| AIX 64 | • AIX 6.1 with Recommended Maintenance package 6100-00-04 |
| z/OS 32 | • z/OS: V1.10, 1.11, or 1.12 |
| z/OS 64 | • z/OS: V1.10, 1.11, or 1.12 |

# Summary

In this chapter, we have been introduced to WebSphere Application Server v8 capabilities and features to be compliant with JEE version 6. We had a look at the four main components of the JEE 6 platform to provide some context for understanding the WAS 8 internals.

We have explained key terms relating to WAS and explained WebSphere Application Server profiles. We learned that WebSphere Application Server base is the base product on which a suite of extended business products are offered by IBM, which include Application Server, and we briefly covered these products.

Understanding WAS is critical to understanding all the other products in the WebSphere brand. Becoming familiar with WAS is important to anyone who works in the Java enterprise community whether he/she is a programmer, administrator, or an architect. In the remaining chapters of this book, we will cover installing, configuring, administering, and maintaining WAS, and in the next chapter we will learn two different methods of installing WAS. One method will cover a **GUI (Graphical User Interface)** based install using the IBM Installation Manager. The other method is a demonstration of how to use command-line tools, which are designed for scripting automated installations.

# 2
# Installing WebSphere Application Server

To learn how to administer IBM WebSphere Application Server (WAS), we first need to know how to install the product. As we discussed in *Chapter 1, WebSphere Application Server 8.0: Product Overview* WAS v8 is based on JEE 6 and can run on many platforms from Windows through to UNIX and even mainframes.

For the remainder of this book, we will discuss WAS Administration mostly from a Linux/Unix standpoint using Red Hat Enterprise Linux (RHEL) 5.0 Update 6 as our Linux distribution. By learning to install and administer WAS using Linux, you will be well-prepared and equipped to work with WAS. The skills learned in this book are useful for all WAS installations and configurations on all certified versions of Unix; for example, Solaris, AIX and HP-UX, the SUSE Linux distribution and also Windows.

Since you may have a requirement to install WAS in a Windows environment, equivalent Windows commands are included for reference throughout the book.

[   It is possible to install WAS on the CentOS 5.6 Linux distribution. CentOS is based on rebuilt RedHat source packages, and is free to download; however, running WAS on CentOS is not officially supported by IBM. ]

This chapter explains the topics in detail, so if you want to read this chapter in one sitting, you may want to get comfortable. We have many topics to cover, as mentioned in the following list:

- Planning an application server install
- Installation scenarios
- Preparation and prerequisites
- Graphical installation

- Installing base binaries
- Understanding profile types
- Installing profiles
- Verifying an installation
- Administration console
- Uninstalling WAS
- Silent installs

# Installation planning

Before beginning any WAS installation, it is recommended you answer the following three questions to help prepare and plan for an installation:

1. What version of WAS is required to support your applications?

   ○ Investigations are made to ensure that your application(s) will run in the version of WAS you intend to install. A good WAS version compatibility matrix can be found at the following URL: http:// en.wikipedia.org/wiki/Websphere. You can also consult the summary table titled *Reference table for supported standards* which was presented in *Chapter 1, WebSphere Application Server 8.0: Product Overview*. It is also recommended you speak to your application developers or application vendors to accurately assess (Java Virtual Machine (JVM) requirements.

2. Are there any OS tweaks for the platform required for the chosen version of WAS?

   ○ It is important to understand what version of **Operating System (OS)** you are going to use. First, decide which platform you are going to install on and then research what the prerequisites are for that platform. Each platform may have certain OS changes or optimizations, which are stipulated for correct installation of WAS. For detailed OS requirements, you can refer to the WAS product documentation at the following URL: http://publib.boulder.ibm. com/infocenter/wasinfo/v8r0/index.jsp.

3.  What version of OS and fix packs are required to support the chosen version of WAS?

    ○   Not only do you need to understand the base installation version, you may also want to understand what the latest fix packs are to ensure that your version of WAS is fully up-to-date to the level required. You can go to IBM Support Fix Central located at the following URL to find the latest WebSphere fix pack versions `http://www-933.ibm.com/support/fixcentral/`. We will cover more about maintenance and fix packs in *Chapter 11, Product Maintenance*.

# Installation scenarios

Before beginning an installation, it is advised that you think about the type of WAS install you wish to perform. There are several installation scenarios and knowing which components are available might influence your chosen installation path. You may also wish to think about coexistence or interoperability with other WAS implementations or helper services. Helper services are other applications and/or technologies that may be required for your applications to run correctly on WAS and function as per their design. This means you may have to consider other installation requirements in addition to those of WAS.

The WAS installation process requires two main actions:

1.  Installation of base binaries (which are the core executables).
2.  Profile creation.

The base binaries are the product mechanics made up of executables and shell scripts, and can be shared by one or many profiles. Profiles exist so data can be partitioned away from the underlying core runtime. Simply put, a profile contains an Application Server. When an Application Server is running, the server process may read and write data to the underlying configuration files and logs. So, by using profiles, transient data is kept away from the base product. This allows us to have more than one profile using the same base binaries, and also allows us to remove certain profiles without affecting other profiles. Another reason for separating the base binaries is that we can upgrade the product with maintenance updates and fix packs without having to re-create all profiles. Sometimes you do not want a specific profile to be updated. WAS profile management has been designed for flexibility.

A conceptual diagram of the WAS installation components is shown next:

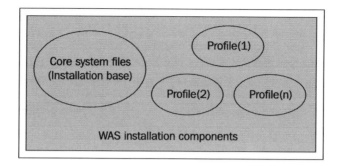

## Profile types

During the installation process, you can decide to install different profile types. There are two main profile types: application server profiles and management profiles. Your installation scenarios will determine the combination of profile types you will be selecting throughout the installation wizard.

The following table explains the different profile types:

| Profile type | Description |
| --- | --- |
| Application server | WAS has the ability to have multiple application server definitions using the same underlying base binaries. Each profile defines the attributes and configurations for a given application server. |
| | Each standalone application server can optionally have its own administrative console application, which you use to manage the application server. |
| | We will cover how to install a profile later in the chapter. |
| Management profile | A Management profile defines an administrative agent, which provides a single interface (administrative console) to administer multiple application servers. |
| | We will cover the administrative agent in *Chapter 9, Administrative Features*. |

## Preparation and prerequisites

Before we start with the WebSphere Application Server installation, we need to ensure the correct installation media is available and that the operating system prerequisites have been met.

It is also important to ensure that there is enough free disk space on your filesystem, and that you also have a large enough folder or /tmp, c:/temp for Windows. A recommended size for the tmp folder is 1 Gigabyte; this will also cater for the deployment of large JEE applications. The installer program checks for required space before calling the WAS installation wizard and will inform you if there is not enough disk space; however, it is good to be prepared upfront to minimize such issues.

 It is recommended best practice that you refer to the IBM documentation for installation prerequisites, which can be found at the following URL: http://www-01.ibm.com/ support/docview.wss?uid=swg27021246.

# Windows installation prerequisites

There are no specific prerequisites for this book, except that it is recommended that you install using a user with Administration privileges. To give a user, the required administrator privileges is as simple as adding the desired user to the Windows *administrators* group.

# Linux installation prerequisites

If you are not using Linux, then you can skip this section and move onto the *Graphical Installation* section. If you are considering running WAS 8 on a Linux platform visit the following IBM URL to locate and read up on the prerequisites for installing WebSphere Application Server 8 on Linux platforms: http://publib. boulder.ibm.com/infocenter/wasinfo/v8r0/topic/com.ibm.websphere. installation.nd.doc/info/ae/ae/tins_prepare.html.

## Installing as root on Linux

When installing WAS on a UNIX-like platform, Linux, you should install using the root user or appropriate sudo access. After the installation is complete, the ownership of the installation binaries should be changed to an appropriate non-root user.

It is often company policy for production environments not to allow products such as WAS as the Linux root user for reasons, such as security and the configurability of shell environment variables and shell profiles. Another very good reason to use a non-root user is that you can apply settings to the Linux profile for the user account assigned to WAS, thus segregating WAS or application-specific settings away from other systems, which may also be running on the same machine.

While learning WAS and to keep things simple, without getting sidetracked by security and folder permission errors, it is recommended that you install and run WAS instances as the root user on Linux. Using root will ensure WAS installations will work with all the third-party products that we will install throughout this book.

## Filesystem preparation for Linux

Before running the WAS installation, we need to check the **umask**. The umask setting controls the permissions that will be masked (not set) for any newly created files, for example, 022. By using the Linux command umask, we can check the current umask. It needs to be set to 022. We can set this by typing the following command in a secure shell:

```
umask 022
```

Using the umask command ensures that all new files will be set with the 8-bit inverse permission of 755.

# Graphical installation

For our first installation, we are going to use the new **IBM Installation Manager (IIM)** in graphical mode to install and configure WAS. We will install WAS in two parts. Part 1 will be installation of the base binaries and part 2 will be an installation of an application server profile. In each part, we will list the actions as a set of steps. Later in the chapter, we will cover command-line installs often called silent installs.

# Part 1—Installing the base binaries

The WAS v8 installation GUI has been changed since WAS v7. IBM has updated many of its products to use a common Java-based installation tool called the **IBM Installation Manager (IIM)**. A major benefit is that **IIM** provides a common installation interface for many products, with transferrable knowledge, allowing you to learn how to use IIM for one product and pick it up quickly in another. It also lends to a common approach to scripted installs for all products which incorporate IIM. Scripting installations save both time and expense and can dramatically reduce human error. Another important evolution of the WAS install process is that IIM uses installation repositories which employ a single set of downloads for all WAS versions and OS variants. Prior to the WAS 8 release, each OS version of WAS required separate downloads. Using a repository system now saves many hours of download and also disk space and simplifies the management of different installation packages.

# Downloading WAS 8

Traditionally, installation media for WAS used to be obtained on CD; however, this is now a fading method due to organizations moving to Internet-based downloads often referred to as *software by wire*. IBM provides the official WAS software downloads using an online system called **Passport Advantage**. If your organization has a passport advantage account, then media CDs can still be requested to be delivered as part of your license agreement. For our WAS installation, we are going to use the IBM WebSphere Application Server for Developers Trial version 8; however, we need to first download the IBM installation manager, which will be used to install this particular version in WAS.

# Downloading IBM Installation Manager

At the time of writing, the latest version of IIM (version 1.4.4) can be downloaded from IBM at the following location: `https://www-304.ibm.com/support/docview.wss?uid=swg24029226`.

> If you would like to understand more about IIM you can consult the online documentation located at the following URL: `http://publib.boulder.ibm.com/infocenter/install/v1r4/index.jsp`.

# Installing IIM

You should have downloaded one of the following files:

| Description | Download filename |
| --- | --- |
| IBM Installation Manager 1.4.4 Linux | `agent.installer.linux.gtk.x86_1.4.4000.20110525_1254.zip` |
| IBM Installation Manager 1.4.4 Windows | `agent.installer.win32.win32.x86_1.4.4000.20110525_1254.zip` |

The following steps will help you run the installer:

1. **For Linux:**
   - Copy the downloaded `agent.installer.linux.gtk.x86_1.4.4000.20110525_1254.zip` file to a suitable location on your Linux server and unzip it. Take note of this location for future reference.
   - Decompress the ZIP file.

- ° Ensure you have an **X Window System** (**X11** for short) session running.
- ° Run the installer using the following command:

```
./install
```

2. **For Windows:**

- ° Copy the downloaded `agent.installer.win32.win32.x86_1.4.4000.20110525_1254.zip` file to a suitable location on your Windows server. Take note of this location for future reference.
- ° Decompress the ZIP file.
- ° Run the installer using the following command:

```
install.exe
```

Once the installer is loaded, follow the steps mentioned next:

1. The IIM installer will begin an installation wizard. The following screen is presented detailing the version of IIM that is going to be installed. You are also given an option to **Check for other Versions, Fixes, and Extensions**. If you choose this option, IIM will contact the IBM online repositories and scan for IIM updates. Click **Next** to continue:

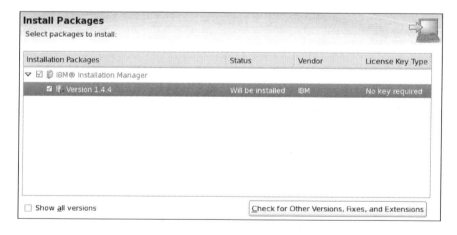

2. Read the license agreement, and then select the **I accept the terms in the license agreement** radio option, and click **Next**.

3. In the following screen you will be given an option to change the location where the IBM Installation Manager will be installed. Either accept the default location or alter it as per your requirement. We will refer to this path as `<iim_root>`. Click **Next** to continue:

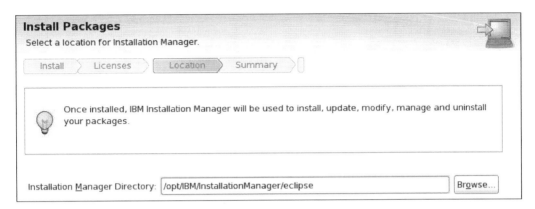

 The default installation path for IIM on Windows is: `C:\Program Files (x86)\IBM\Installation Manager\eclipse`.

4. Review the installation summary information that is presented and click **Install** to perform the installation.

5. Once the IIM installation has completed, click the **Restart Installation Manager** button to restart IIM.

# Installing WAS using IBM Installation Manager

In this section, we detail the steps required to install WAS using the IIM:

1. If IIM is not already running, launch IIM. You can use the following commands to launch IIM:

    ○ **For Linux:**

    `<iim_root>/IBMIM`

    ○ **For Windows:**

    `<iim_root>\IBMIM.exe`

2. Once IIM is loaded, you will be presented with the workbench screen:

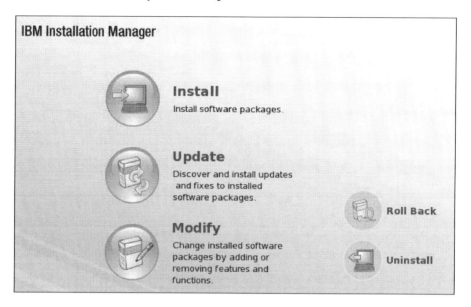

3. Before we can install WAS, we need to set the repository location preferences. This will inform IIM where the WAS repository components are located. Using the **File** menu, select the **Preferences** option.

In the **Preferences** page, you can select the location of your WAS binary repositories. If you have a Passport Advantage account, you can set the appropriate authentication settings for downloading the commercial versions of IBM products and install from a local repository.

4. To add a repository location, click the **Add Repository** button located at the top right-hand corner of the preferences screen.

5. In the **Add a repository** pop-up dialog, type the following URL in the **Repository** field: `http://www.ibm.com/software/repositorymanager/V8WASDeveloperILAN`.

6. Click **OK** to add the URL to the **Repositories** list. You will be prompted by IIM to supply your IBM username and password (**IBM ID**). If you do not have an IBM ID, click the **IBM ID and FAQ** link to register. Once you have entered your IBM ID username and password, click **OK**. A new entry will appear in the Repositories list:

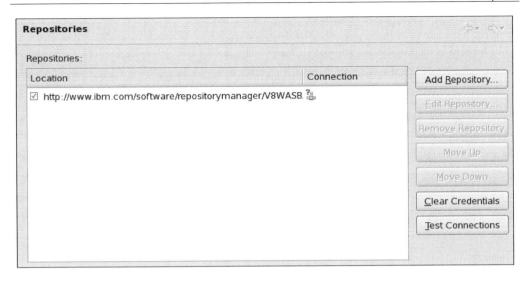

7.  Click **OK** again to close and return to the main workbench screen.

8.  From the main workbench screen, locate and click the **Install** button, as shown in the following screenshot:

9.  IIM will check online for the availability of the latest downloads and fix packs for the trial. Once the process has been completed, a list of installation packages will be presented.

10. Ensure that all the installation packages are selected. Click the **Check for other Versions, Fixes and Extensions** button and IIM will re-verify the available downloads online. Once the verification is complete, click **Next**.

11. In the following screen you will be presented with details of the actual WAS binaries and latest fixes that need to be downloaded from the online IBM repository. Click **Next** to continue.

12. You will now be presented with another license screen, this time for WAS. Read the license agreement, then select the **I accept the terms in the license agreement** radio option, and click **Next**.

13. On the next screen, you will be asked to fill out a questionnaire detailing your reason for evaluating WAS. Answer the questions as required and click **Next** to continue.

14. The next screen defines where the IIM will create the WAS-shared resources folder. This folder contains the files that make up what is known as the installation repository. Accept the default location suggested by the IIM installer, or enter a different one. In the following example, we have used the default provided location **/opt/IBM/IMShared.** We will refer to the location as `<iim_shared_resources>`. Click **Next** to move on to the next screen where you will be asked to supply the location to install the WAS binaries:

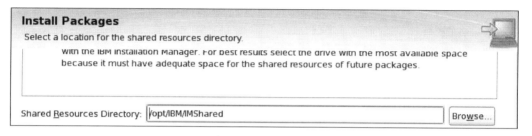

15. You will now be given an opportunity to decide where you want to install this instance of WAS. Once again, you can decide on a file path that is convenient to your needs. It may be useful to shorten the folder names, which will make it easier for administration later when we need to navigate through the WAS filesystems. For our purposes, we are going to accept the default location in the **installation directory** field as shown in the following screenshot. Take note of this path. Throughout the book it will be referred to as the `<was_root>` path:

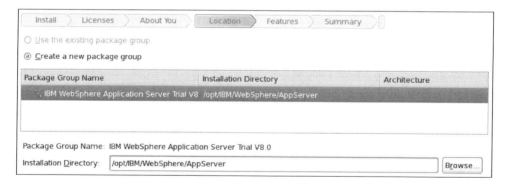

16. On the next page, select your preferred language, and click **Next** again, to move onto the features screen.

17. Within the features screen, you will have the option to install the sample applications provided by IBM for testing JEE concepts and features of WAS. We will not be using the sample applications within this book, so this is an optional choice. You may wish to install the samples for later exploration. There are two other options, which we will leave checked:

    - EJBDeploy tool for pre-EJB 3.0 modules:

      Provided for backwards compatibility for generating EJB 2.0 deployment code.

    - Standalone clients and resource adapters:

      Provides a set of clients for a variety of technologies, such as JAX-WS, JAX-RPC, JAX-RS, XML, EJB, JPA, JMS, and others.

18. Consult with your application development team to understand whether you need to incorporate these two options, or not.

> Installing the sample applications will add extra logging information to your installation and clutter the admin console, so it is recommended not to install these applications until you need them. They can be installed using IIM at a later date.

19. Also within the features screen, IIM will have already detected your **Operating System (OS)** architecture and pre-selected either the 32-bit or 64-bit **IBM Software Development Kit** option. Ensure this is correct for your OS. Click **Next** to continue.

20. Click **Next** to proceed to the final summary screen and review the options you have chosen in the previous steps.

21. Click the **Install** button to begin the actual WAS installation. Once the installation is complete, you will be given an option to run the **Profile Management Tool (PMT)** to create a WAS profile. At this stage, we do not want to launch the PMT tool. We will cover how to create profiles after we have verified the binaries have been installed.

22. Select the option labeled **None** and exit the IBM Installation Manager.

# Verifying the installed binaries

Previously, we chose to defer the running of the Profile Management Tool, so we could demonstrate the manual creation of a profile later on in the chapter. All we have installed at this point is the base binaries into the location we specified.

By looking at the files installed by the installer, you will see what makes up the base binaries. You will also notice that the folder permissions are `rwxr-xr-x (755)`, which is a result of the `022` `umask` that we set before we ran the installation wizard.

The presence of the **Uninstall** folder contains an uninstaller, which we can use to uninstall WAS.

We will now do a quick check to see if the base binaries have installed correctly by running the WAS command script `versionInfo.sh` (which is found in the `<was_root>/bin` folder). We can generate a report that will identify the state of the installation.

From now on, we will refer to folders as relative to the base install folder; for example, using the syntax `<was_root>/<folder_path>` would refer to the WAS base installation folder, plus the path we are working with. Since you may have chosen not to follow the default WAS convention during installation, you can substitute the base folder with the appropriate naming convention.

Run the following command:

1. **For Linux:**

   ```
   <was_root>/bin/versionInfo.sh
   ```

2. **For Windows:**

   ```
   <was_root>\bin\versionInfo.bat
   ```

The result of running the previous command will be a report similar to the following screenshot:

```
-------------------------------------------------------------------
IBM WebSphere Product Installation Status Report
-------------------------------------------------------------------


Report at date and time July 7, 2011 10:55:00 AM BST

Installation
-------------------------------------------------------------------
Product Directory        /opt/IBM/WebSphere/AppServer
Version Directory        /opt/IBM/WebSphere/AppServer/properties/version
DTD Directory            /opt/IBM/WebSphere/AppServer/properties/version/dtd
Log Directory            /var/ibm/InstallationManager/logs

Product List
-------------------------------------------------------------------
BASETRIAL                installed

Installed Product
-------------------------------------------------------------------
Name                     IBM WebSphere Application Server
Version                  8.0.0.0
ID                       BASETRIAL
Build Level              n1118.03
Build Date               5/3/11
Architecture             x86-64 (64 bit)
Installed Features       IBM 64-bit SDK for Java, Version 6
                         EJBDeploy tool for pre-EJB 3.0 modules
                         Embeddable EJB container
                         Stand-alone thin clients and resource adapters

-------------------------------------------------------------------
End Installation Status Report
-------------------------------------------------------------------
```

# Installation logs

The IIM logs events as it is installing the WAS product. If there is a problem with your installation, you can consult the logs. The IIM logs files are located at the following location:

1. **For Linux:**

   `/var/logs`

2. **For Windows non-administrator**:

   `C:\Documents and Settings\All Users\Application Data\IBM\Installation Manager\logs`

3. **For Windows administrator**:

   `C:\Documents and Settings\<user id>\Application Data\IBM\Installation Manager\logs`

A really nice feature of the IIM logging style is that it produces a set of XML files that can opened in a web Brower. In the root of the IIM log location will be a file called `index.xml`. If you open this main index file in your favorite web browser, you can navigate through the logs as if they were web pages.

Log files are the life blood of WAS. They are used for problem solving and runtime status. We will delve more into server logging in *Chapter 6, Server Configuration*, where we formerly cover WAS logs.

## Agent data location

Previously in WAS 7 the installer stored application registry information in a file called `vdp.properties` (`Vital Produt properfiles file`), which is now no longer the case. IIM will store data in the agent data location, or `appDataLocation`, and it is this directory that IIM uses for data that is associated with an application. Associated data includes the state and history of operations that the Installation Manager completes.

Changing the content, files, or directories in the agent data location directory or subdirectories is not supported. Changes to the content might prevent IIM from working.

There is a file called the `cic.appDataLocation` property, which is set in the `config.ini` file and can be located at:

1. **For Linux:**

   `<iim_root>/eclipse/configuration`

2. **For Windows:**

   `<iim_root>\eclipse\configuration`

By editing the `cic.appDataLocation` property within the `config.ini` file, you can choose the specific location where you want IIM to store the agent data location.

## Part 2—Creating a WAS profile

By themselves, the base binaries serve no purpose. We must create a profile which is essentially an application server definition.

We use the **Profile Management Tool (PMT)** to create WAS profiles using a GUI. The tool is Java-based. To manually run it, type the following command:

1. **For Linux:**

   ```
   <was_root>/bin/ProfileManagement/pmt.sh
   ```

2. **For Windows:**

   ```
   <was_root>\bin\ProfileManagement\pmt.bat
   ```

3. Once the PMT has loaded, the option to **Create** a profile will be available. Click the **Create** button to start the actual profile-creation wizard:

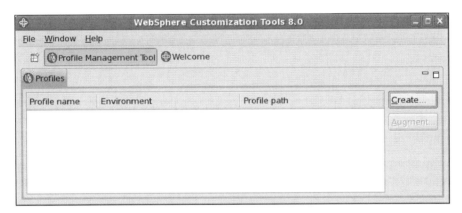

4. In the environment screen you will be asked to either create a Management profile or an Application server profile. The two profile types are explained in the following table:

| Profile Option | Description |
| --- | --- |
| Management | A management profile includes an administrative agent server and services for managing multiple application server environments. An administrative agent manages application servers that are on the same machine. We will cover the Administrative agent in *Chapter 9, Administrative Features*. |
| Application server | A standalone application server environment runs your enterprise applications. The application server is managed from its own administrative console and functions independently of all other application servers. |

WebSphere Application Server requires at least one profile to be functional as an actual server.

5. Ensure the **Application server** option is selected and click **Next** to continue:

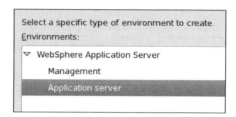

6. In the **Profile Creation options** screen as shown in the following screenshot, select **Advanced profile creation**. Choosing this option allows for greater choice, flexibility, and control of our profile creation as opposed to using a default configuration. Default configurations are set by the wizard, and use naming conventions and settings that you may not wish to use, but are useful if you are needed to quickly build a test/development environment:

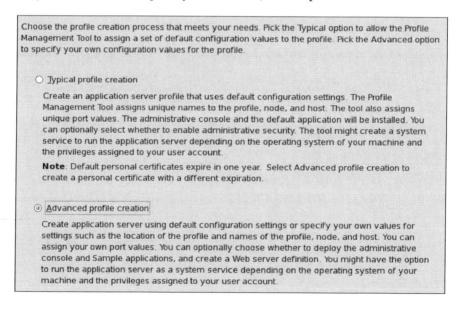

7. On the next screen, we can see that the there are some optional choices. The **Deploy the administrative console (recommend)** option will install a special web application allowing an administrator to configure WAS using a web-based UI. Please ensure the **Deploy the administrative console (recommend)** option is selected before continuing.

8. There is also an option to **Deploy the default application**. The default application contains some very useful testing features, which we will cover in *Chapter 9, Administrative Features* when we look at IBM HTTP Server (IHS). For now, uncheck this option. Click on **Next** to continue to the profile name and location screen:

Select the applications to deploy to the WebSphere Application Server environment being created.

☑ Deploy the administrative console (recommended).

    Install a Web-based administrative console that manages the application server. Deploying the administrative console is recommended, but if you deselect this option, the information center contains detailed steps for deploying it after the profile exists.

☐ Deploy the default application.

    Install the default application that contains the Snoop, Hello, and HitCount servlets.

9. In the **Profile name and location** screen we determine the actual name for our first profile and the location within the filesystem where it will be created. The profile will make up our application server definition. Enter `appsrv01` in the **Profile name** field and `<was_root>/profiles/appsrv01` in the **Profile directory** field, as shown in the following screenshot:

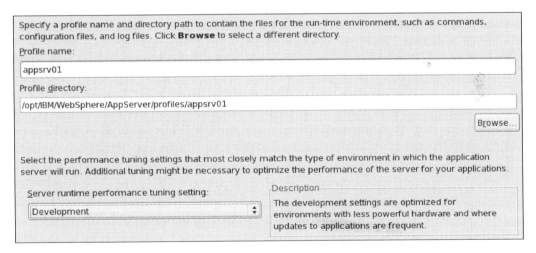

Specify a profile name and directory path to contain the files for the run-time environment, such as commands, configuration files, and log files. Click **Browse** to select a different directory.

Profile name:

appsrv01

Profile directory:

/opt/IBM/WebSphere/AppServer/profiles/appsrv01

Browse...

Select the performance tuning settings that most closely match the type of environment in which the application server will run. Additional tuning might be necessary to optimize the performance of the server for your applications.

Server runtime performance tuning setting:

Development

Description

The development settings are optimized for environments with less powerful hardware and where updates to applications are frequent.

 Using lowercase for all folder names prompted in a wizard makes it easier to remember especially when typing folder paths in Linux, as Linux is case-sensitive.

In the previous example, the **Server runtime performance tuning** option is set to **Development**, which speeds up server start-up. Since we will be starting and stopping the server many times during the course of our learning, it is recommended that we turn this option ON to save time when waiting for server restarts.

The following table describes the three runtime-performance options:

| Option name | Description |
|---|---|
| Standard | The **Standard** option invokes conservative settings optimized for general purpose usage. The performance monitoring infrastructure service is enabled to gather statistics so you can further tune the server. We will learn more about tuning in *Chapter 8, Monitoring and Tuning*. |
| Development | The **Development** option sets settings to ensure WAS is optimized for performance when updates to applications are requested as would be for a development and/or testing environment. |
| Production | The **Production** option sets settings to ensure WAS is optimized for performance when updates to applications are infrequent. |

1. Click **Next** to move on to the next screen.

2. The next screen is the **Node and Host Names** screen. The **Node name** is an important part of the installation process. It is recommended to keep this name as short as possible. We will cover the administration of WAS nodes in later chapters. The **Server name** is the actual name of the application server's JVM. This name will be referred to in logging and configuration, which again we will address in later chapters. The **Host name** will automatically be taken from the OS host's file and can be changed in the wizard at this point to suit your requirements. You can use a hostname, or **Fully Qualified Domain Name (FQDN)**. If you decide to change the hostname in the wizard, ensure that the change is reflected in your host file or DNS as required.

If you use an FQDN, first test that it is resolvable. In our examples, we will be using a manually-derived hostname for simplicity. Our hostname will be **node01** and our domain name is **waslocal. com**. The FQDN will be **node01.waslocal.com**. (This is not a real Internet domain.)

We are running on a private network so we can call it whatever we like, as long as our OS host file is configured correctly.

3. Enter the values listed in the following table into the fields on the **Nodes and Host Names** screen:

| Field Name | Field Value |
|---|---|
| Node name | **node01** |
| Server name | **server01** |
| Host name | In the examples, we have used **node01.waslocal.com,** which has been added to the local host file and points to 127.0.0.1 (localhost) |

4. You can see the application of these values in the following screenshot.

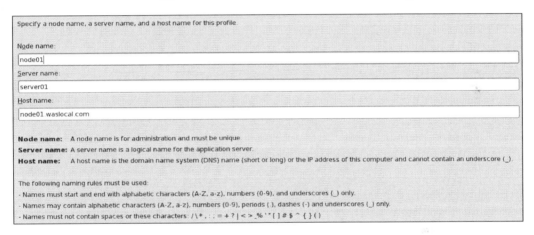

5. Click **Next** to move on to the **Administrative Security** screen.

6. In the **Administrative Security** screen, we will disable administrative security for now and re-enable it in *Chapter 4, Security*. It is recommended for production environments that you enable administrative security right from the start to secure against unwanted changes being made to your server configuration by non-administrators. Leave the option **Enable administrative security** unchecked and click **Next** to move on to the security certificate screens.

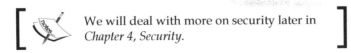

We will deal with more on security later in *Chapter 4, Security*.

7. The next screen is the **Security Certificate (Part 1)** screen. This is a new feature of the WAS installation wizard available since version 7. In previous versions of WAS, the security certificate screens were not available. The options available are: to use default certificates, use an existing keystore, or create one from another **Certificate Authority (CA)**. For now, we will use the default keystore as generated by the installer. Certificates that are used for SSL are beyond the scope of this book. We will accept the default settings. Click **Next** to go to the **Security Certificate (Part 2)** screen.

8. The next screen is the **Security Certificate (Part 2)** screen. When a browser connects to a page using SSL, it presents the hostname of the URL used to gain access to that page. If the SSL certificate within WAS doesn't match this hostname, then an exception will be displayed. The reason for this is that SSL provides a secure connection. If you connect to a host and the actual hostname doesn't match the hostname associated with the SSL certificate presented by the server, then you need to be informed whether to trust the site or not. The wizard will generate a self-signed certificate as part of the installation process. By updating the distinguished name of the self-signed certificate that WAS generates, we can stop browser exceptions.

   In the **Issued to distinguished name** field, type the following:

   ```
   cn=node01.waslocal.com,ou=Node01Cell,ou=node01,o=IBM,c=US
   ```

   In the **Issued by distinguished name** field type the following:

   ```
   cn=node01.waslocal.com,ou=RootCertificate,ou=Node01Cell,ou=node
   01,o=IBM,c=US
   ```

9. Click **Next** to move on to the **Port Value Assignment** screen.

10. WAS requires the use of several ports during runtime. It is wise to ensure that no other application is already using the ports that you wish to use. The wizard is quite clever and will detect port usage, even including older versions of WAS, and recommend free ports; however, it is good practice to use the Linux/Windows command `netstat -an` to ensure that no other processes are using these ports. Use the following steps to check for used ports:

    ° Open a secure shell to your Linux server, or for Windows simply open a command prompt.

    ° Type the following command:
      ```
      netstat -an
      ```

    ° Within the report that is generated, you are looking to see if ports have already been used.

The following table shows the default ports that WAS will use:

| Port Name | Default Port Value |
| --- | --- |
| Administrative console | 9060 |
| Administrative console secure | 9043 |
| HTTP transport | 9080 |
| HTTPS transport | 9443 |
| Boostrap | 2809 |
| SIP | 5060 |
| SIP secure | 5061 |
| SOAP connector | 8880 |
| Administrative inter-process communication | 9633 |
| SAS SSL ServerAuth | 9401 |
| CSIV2 ServerAuth listener | 9403 |
| CSIV2 MultiAuth listener | 9402 |
| ORB listener | 9100 |
| High availability-manager communication | 9353 |
| Service integration | 7276 |
| Service integration secure | 7286 |
| Service integration MQ interoperability | 5559 |

11. Since this is our first WAS profile, we will use the defaults recommended by the wizard. If you see different ports than the default ones, then it means you must have other processes running on these ports, or another version of WAS is already installed.

The administrative console port is very important. We will use this port to gain access to the administration console. Please take note of the **Administrative console port (Default 9060)**, before you move on to the next step.

12. Click **Next** to go to the next step of the installation, where we choose whether we want WAS to automatically restart on reboot. If you wish to have WAS automatically start up again when a server is rebooted, then you can enable this option. In our examples, we don't require WAS to start on reboot, so we will leave the **Run the application server process as a Linux service** checkbox unchecked.

   ○ **Linux users**: If enabled, the wizard will generate an automatic start and stop script in the `init.d` directories as required by the Linux run levels. We will not be discussing Linux run levels in this book; please consult your Linux distribution's documentation.

   ○ **Windows users**: For those of you who have chosen to install WAS on Windows, the equivalent screen will provide an option to install Windows service. You will require administrative privileges to ensure that the service can start and stop WAS correctly.

Automatic start and stop scripts are recommended for production environments. However, Linux administrators may wish to craft their own start-up scripts. If you wish to learn how these start-up scripts work, then enable the creation of the **Linux Service Definition** to view the resulting script and it is also recommended that you consult how Linux run levels work.

If you wish to add a service definition post-install and have appropriate access, you can run the WAS Linux command script `<was_root>/bin/wasservice.sh` or the Windows command script `<was_root>\bin\wasservice.bat`, which will create the appropriate start and stop scripts.

13. Click **Next** to enter the **Web Server Definition** screen. We will be covering Web Server definitions in *Chapter 9, Administrative Features*. For now, we will skip this screen, leaving the **Create a Web server definition** checkbox unchecked. Click **Next** to move on to the **Profile Creation Summary** screen.

14. The final step of the wizard is **Profile Creation Summary**. The wizard presents a summary of your configuration options. If you are not happy with your configuration, you can go back and change your settings. If your settings are correct, click **Create**, which will start the profile creation.

# First steps console

Once the profile creation is complete, you can choose to run the **First steps** console, which offers a few checks that you can run to verify that the installation and profile creation was successful. To verify your GUI-based installation, it is best to ensure that you run all the checks within, and ensure that your installation and profile creation was successful and get quick proof that WAS is actually functional.

1. Launch the **First steps** console by selecting the on-screen option labeled **Launch the First steps console**, and click **Finish** which will trigger the console to load. You can see the console in the following screenshot:

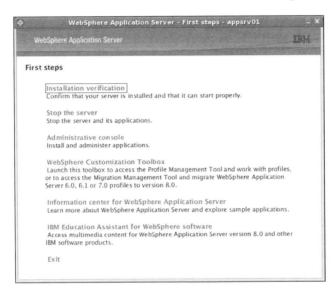

2. Click on the **Installation verification** option in the **First steps** console as shown in the previous screenshot. If there were no problems with the installation, WAS will be started and a report similar to the following screenshot will be generated:

3. Now that we have proven the application server was able to start, we can now stop the server by clicking on **Stop the server**. The **First steps** console should now report that **server01** has stopped. This is shown in the following screenshot:

4. You can now close down the First steps console window. When you exit the **First steps** console and return back to the Profile Management Tool, you will see that the new profile is listed in the profile list, as shown in the following screenshot:

5. You have now successfully installed the WebSphere Application Server. You can close the PMT.

# Profile Manager Tools (PMT) logs and files

Similar to the installation logs, the **Profile Management Tool (PMT)** also leaves a small footprint of logs detailing the profile creations.

## Logs

During the creation of a profile, the PMT logs to a file called `pmt.log` in the `<was_root>/logs/manageprofiles` folder. This log file can be used to help diagnose causes of issues when a profile creation fails. This file most probably will not need to be consulted very often.

## Files

After a profile is created, a useful file called `AboutThisProfile.txt` is created in the profile's logs folder; for example, `<was_root>/profiles/appsrv01/logs`.

This file can be useful to determine basic information about the profile-like ports and general settings.

 Also located in the logs folder is a file called `ivtClient.log`, which contains the logging information, reported previously in the First steps console..

# Administrative console

To test our application server is functioning correctly, we will log in to the administration console. The administration console is a web application, which is used to configure the WebSphere Application Server. You can use it to perform tasks such as:

- Add, delete, start, and stop application servers
- Deploy new applications to a server
- Start and stop existing applications, and modify certain configurations
- Add, delete, and edit resource providers
- Configure security, including access to the administrative console
    - Details are covered in *Chapter 4, Security*.
- Collect data for performance and troubleshooting purposes
    - Details are covered in *Chapter 8, Monitoring and Tuning*.

Currently, the application server is in a stopped state. Before we can log in to the admin console, we must start the newly created application server. To start the application server, we can use a special command script. Command scripts are found in the `<was_profile_root>` directory.

There are two scripts that we will use often throughout the book to start and stop WAS.

| Script Name | Description |
| --- | --- |
| startServer.sh (Linux) | Used to start a given application server. |
| StartServer.bat (Windows) | Example usage: startServer.sh <servername> |
| stopServer.sh (Linux) | Used to stop a given application server. |
| StopServer.bat (Windows) | Example usage: stopServer.sh <servername> |

To start our application server, we will use the startServer.sh command as follows:

```
<was_profile_root>/bin/startServer.sh server01
```

Once you run the script, you will see the following output in the Linux SSH session or command-line console if you are using Windows:

```
ADMU0116I: Tool information is being logged in file
           /apps/was8/profiles/appsrv01/logs/server01/startServer.log
ADMU0128I: Starting tool with the appsrv01 profile
ADMU3100I: Reading configuration for server: server1
ADMU3200I: Server launched. Waiting for initialization status.
```

When the server has actually started, you will see an extra line mentioning that the server has started and its associated UNIX **Process ID (PID)**.

```
ADMU3000I: Server server01 open for e-business; process id is 3813
```

Now that the application server has started, we can navigate to the admin console URL.

We can craft the URL as follows:

```
http://<hostname>:<port>/ibm/console.
```

We noted earlier that an important port was the **admin_default port**, which in our case is 9060. By using this port and the IP address/hostname/FQDN of our server, we can access the admin console with our favorite web browser using a URL similar to the following URL:

```
http://node01.waslocal.com:9060/ibm/console.
```

If you made a host-file modification on our desktop machine, we would be able to use a hostname or FQDN to access the admin console from your workstation as by default, the hostname on the server will not be known to a client machine unless you use DNS.

If you are able to browse from the local server machine where the application server is running, you can use `http://localhost:9060/ibm/console`.

When we navigate to the admin console URL, we see the following login screen:

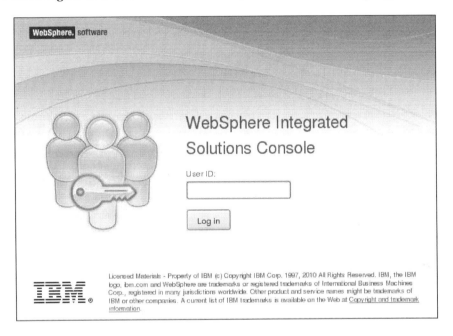

During the installation, we opted not to turn on global security, and so we can log in using any username and no password is required. For the purpose of this book, we will log in using **wasadmin** for the **User ID** field.

Once logged in, we can see the administration console welcome screen and the main navigation panel on the left-hand side (LHS). Looking at the LHS panel shown in the following screenshot, we can see a list of all the configuration items, that is features and resources that are available for WAS administration:

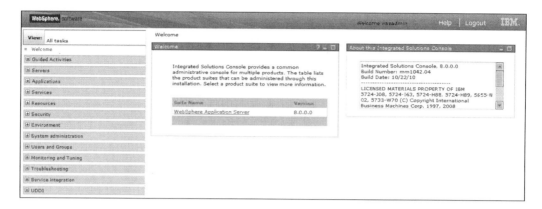

The administration panel provides a GUI that allows administrators to administer WAS. There is also an interactive command-line interface called wsadmin.sh for Linux or wsadmin.bat for Windows, which is used for administering WAS without using the admin console. We will cover administrative scripting in *Chapter 5, Administrative Scripting*.

# Uninstalling WAS

Before we move on and cover how to do a **silent (no GUI)** installation of WAS, we need to cover how to uninstall WAS. It is important to know how to uninstall WAS correctly because if you don't, residual folders and files can be left behind. If you try to install WAS over an existing WAS installation, the wizard will exit in error. So if you purposely want to re-install again into the same folder path, you need to ensure that WAS is removed correctly before you do so.

What we will do is remove the installation we created earlier and then re-create the same setup using a command-line based silent installation.

First we need to stop the WAS process using the stop server command located in the following folder `<was_root>/<profile_root>/bin`

1. **For Linux:**

   `<was_profile_root>/bin/stopServer.sh server01`

2. **For Windows:**

   `<was_profile_root\bin\stopServer.bat server01`

# Manually deleting profiles

Before uninstalling WAS binaries it is good practice to remove profiles ahead of uninstalling WAS. To delete a profile, you can use the `manageprofiles.sh` command-line script. Using a SSH/Terminal session for Linux (or command prompt in the case of Windows), navigate to `<was_profile_root>/bin` and then type the following command:

1. **For Linux:**

   `./manageprofiles.sh -listProfiles`

2. **For Windows:**

   `manageprofiles.bat -listProfiles`

The result will be:

**[appsrv01]**

To delete the appsrv01 profile, run the following command:

1. **For Linux:**

   `./manageprofiles.sh -delete -profileName appsrv01`

2. **For Windows:**

   `manageprofiles.bat -delete -profileName appsrv01`

 You can use the help switch of the `manageprofiles.sh`/`manageprofiles.bat` command to list the available command-line arguments.

# Uninstalling WAS using IIM

You can use the IIM GUI to uninstall WAS using the following steps:

1. Load IIM and click on the **Uninstall** button, as shown in the following screenshot:

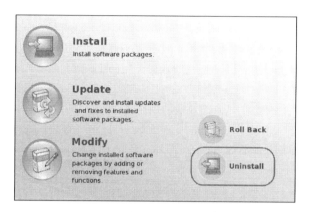

2. In the **Uninstall Packages** screen, select the **IBM WebSphere Application Server Trial v8.0** package, as shown in the following screenshot and click **Next** to continue:

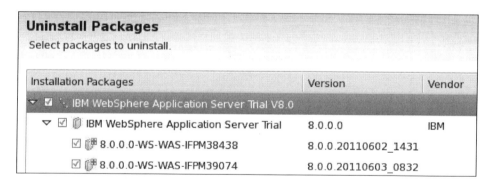

3. The wizard will then provide a summary screen; click **Uninstall** to continue. IIM will then remove all WAS profiles for that particular WAS package, and then remove the WAS binaries. The entire repository located in the `<iim_ shared_resources>` folder will also be deleted. Once the uninstall process is complete, a screen will be presented giving you the option to view the uninstall logs:

4. Click **Finish** to return to the IIM workbench. You can now close the IIM.

5. Delete the `<was_root>` installation folder.

# Uninstalling WAS using command line

IIM has some new features for uninstalling WAS. You can work with response files and Installation Manager to uninstall the product silently in a variety of ways. You can use a response file by:

- Recording a new response file and using the GUI
  - The process of recording a response file is the same as recording an installation response file. We cover this later on in the chapter.

- Using a response file
  - IIM provides a simple sample-response file called `uninstall.xml`, which can be used as part of a silent uninstall. We will cover how to do this in the following paragraph.

 Running the uninstaller script with no parameters will automatically launch the IIM, and then you will be provided with the same process as mentioned previously. However, if you need to run the install in headless mode (with no GUI) you can use the commands which follow.

To uninstall via the command line using the default sample `response.xml` file as created by IIM during the installation, navigate to the `<iim_root>/eclipse` directory and run the following command:

1. **For Linux:**

```
./IBMIM --launcher.ini silent-install.ini -input <was_root>/
uninstall/uninstall.xml -log /var/tmp/uninstall_log.xml
```

2. **For Windows:**

```
IBMIM.exe --launcher.ini silent-install.ini -input <was_root>\
uninstall\uninstall.xml -log c:\temp\uninstall_log.xml
```

 Following a successful uninstall you will need to remove the original folder where you installed WAS, as contained within are the logs from the installation process. You cannot install WAS into the same location a second time if it is not empty.

The uninstaller will now unregister the WebSphere 8.0.0.0 package group we installed earlier and then it will delete the WAS binaries from the filesystem. Once the uninstall process has completed, you can delete the `<was_root>` folder and all its contents, allowing you to re-install into the same location at a later stage. We will now move onto how to install WAS silently using IIM in headless mode.

# Silent installation

So far, we have covered using the GUI approach to install WAS. The IIM installation process can also be run silently in headless mode. By using special response files, we can preset installation settings which do not require any user input.

Using response files is the technique used in automatic installations where servers are built to a known standard and naming convention. This ensures that each new WAS is installed exactly the same way each time. This is critical for production environments to ensure each server is configured the same way. This lends to easier support and fewer errors are introduced into environments, which is a key factor in supporting production systems. Another vital reason to use silent installations is that some organizations do not install X11 on production servers for security reasons.

# Installing packages silently using Installation Manager

To install product packages silently using the Installation Manager, you must first create a **response file**. A response file can contain many different settings and they can often change as product packages are updated, and so being able to get a list for all available settings along with the correct syntax can be difficult and time consuming. To solve this problem, IBM has added a feature to the IIM to record installations, as such automatically creating a response file with the correct settings. You can then use a record response file with the silent command-line option and install WAS in an automated non-GUI fashion.

## Recording a response file

You can use the IBM Installation Manager to record installation actions into a response file. When you record a response file, the selections that you make in Installation Manager are stored in an XML file. When you use the recording option of IIM, you do not actually install WAS, you are just recording a set of instructions that will be used to generate a response file. The resulting response file can be used in silent mode, instructing IIM to use the data in the XML response file to install packages without user intervention.

You cannot record a response file to install Installation Manager. To install both Installation Manager and an IBM product, you must modify a response file to add the commands to install IIM; however, it is beyond the scope of this book.

## Command-line options for recording

There are three important command-line options which can be used to instruct IIM to record a response file:

- responseFile
  - The <responseFile> is a file path and filename of the response XML-based file you want to generate. The response file is used in a silent installation.
- -skipInstall
  - The -skipInstall argument requires that the <agentDataLocation> is a directory that you can write to.
- agentDataLocation
  - The <agentDataLocation> is a folder where you want IIM to store the recorded installation data. You can use the same <agentDataLocation> in another subsequent recording session to record updates or modifications to the IBM product. These changes are recorded in the <agentDataLocation> directory. For more information about the -skipInstall argument, see Installation Manager help and look up command-line arguments.

## Running a recording

Use the following steps to instruct the IIM to record a GUI installation into an XML response file:

1. On a command line, change to the eclipse subdirectory in the <iim_root> directory where you installed Installation Manager earlier in the chapter. Run the following command:
   - **For Linux:**
     ```
     cd <iim_root>/eclipse
     ```
   - **For Windows:**
     ```
     cd <iim_root>\eclipse
     ```

2. Run the following command to record a response file for the IBM product installation. This command uses the `-skipInstall <agentDataLocation>` argument, which records the installation commands without installing the IBM product. Substitute your own filename and location for the response file. Verify that the file paths that you enter exist. Installation Manager does not create directories for the response file.

 Using the `-log` option is not supported when recording a response file.

- ○ **For Linux:**

  ```
  ./IBMIM -record /var/tmp/was8_install.xml -skipInstall /var/
  tmp/was8
  ```

- ○ **For Windows:**

  ```
  ./IBMIM -record c:\temp\was8_install.xml -skipInstall c:\
  temp\was8
  ```

 On Windows, use `IBMIM.exe` for installations that are not silent and when recording a response file. The `IBMIM.exe` command is not supported for silent installations. Use `IBMIMc.exe` for silent installations.

Do not use the command `IBMIMc` on Linux and UNIX operating systems.

3. Follow the on-screen instructions as required by the IIM wizard. You will need to set the repository location again. You can set the location of the repository in the repository table. To access the repository table, click **File | Preferences... | Repositories**. The text **(Recording...)** is displayed in the IIM title bar when you are recording a response file.

4. Click **Finish**, and then close Installation Manager to finish the recording of the response file.

The result of running the command will be an XML response file, which is created and saved in the location that you specified in the command-line options outlined previously.

# Installing in silent mode using a response file

Now we have a response file prepared, we can run a silent install. Before we do so, we need to cover the IIM command-line options available to the recording process.

## Command-line options for installing

To run IIM in record mode, there are several command-line parameters which can be used to instruct IIM to silently install using a response file:

- `--launcher.ini`: Indicates that an install preferences ini-file is being used to set IIM settings. Settings which can be included here are JVM to use, JVM memory size, no splash screen, and so on. You can read the IIM help to learn more about ini-file settings.

- `<silent-install.ini>`: The filename and file path to the install ini-file you have configured. There is a sample file called `silent-install.ini` located in the `<iim_root/eclipse>` folder.

- `-input`: The input option is used when a response file is being used.

- `<responseFile>`: The actual filename and file path of the XML response file to use in the silent install.

- `-log`: Specifies that a log file should be generated containing information about the installation and installation results.

- `<logFile>`: The actual filename and file path of the log file that will be generated.

## Running the silent install

To run IIM in silent mode, run the following command from the eclipse subdirectory in the directory where you installed Installation Manager, that is, `<iim_root>/eclipse`.

1. **For Linux:**

   ```
   ./IBMIM --launcher.ini silent-install.ini -input /var/tmp/was8_
   install.xml -log /var/tmp/was8/silent_install_log.xml
   ```

2. **For Windows:**

   ```
   IBMIMc.exe --launcher.ini silent-install.ini -input c:\ temp\was8_
   install.xml 1 -log c:\temp\was8\silent_install_log.xml
   ```

When the installation is successful, it returns a status of **0**. An unsuccessful operation returns a non-zero number.

When the Installation Manager installer is run, it reads the response file and (optionally) writes a log file to the directory specified. If you specified a log file and directory, the log file is empty when the operation is successful. The log file contains error elements if the operation was not completed successfully.

# Silent profile creation

Now we have installed WAS silently, we need to cover how to create profiles using the profile management command-line script. The script is located in the `<was_root>/bin` folder with the following name:

1. **For Linux:**

   `./manageprofiles.sh`

2. **For Windows:**

   `manageprofiles.bat`

The following table explains the valid command-line modes for the `manageprofiles` script:

| Command-line option | Description |
| --- | --- |
| augment | The augment parameter is used to make changes to an existing profile with an augmentation template. The augment parameter causes the `manageprofiles` command to update or augment the profile identified in the `-profileName` parameter using the template in the `-templatePath` parameter. |
| create | Creates the profile. You can Specify `manageprofiles -create -templatePath <fully_qualified_file_ path_to_template>`. Use `-help` for specific information about creating a profile. Available templates include: Management – Used in conjunction with the `-serverType` parameter to indicate the type of management profile; Default – A standard application server profile. |
| delete | Deletes the profile. Deleting a profile does not delete the profile directory. You must specify the `-profileName` parameter with the `-delete` parameter. |

| Command-line option | Description |
| --- | --- |
| unaugment | Augmentation is the ability to change an existing profile with an augmentation template. To unaugment a profile that has been augmented, you must specify the -unaugment parameter and the -profileName parameter. |
| unaugmentAll | Unaugments all profiles. |
| deleteAll | Deletes all profiles for the current WAS instance. |
| listProfiles | Lists all the profiles set for the current instance of WAS. |
| listAugments | Lists the registered augments on a profile that is in the profile registry. You must specify the -profileName parameter with the -listAugments parameter. |
| backupProfile | Performs a compressed filesystem backup of a profile folder and the profile metadata from the profile registry file. Any servers using the profile that you want to back up must first be stopped prior to invoking the manageprofiles command with the -backupProfile option. The -backupProfile parameter must be used with the -backupFile and -profileName parameters. |
| restoreProfile | Restores a profile backup. Must be used with the -backupFile parameter. |
| getName | Gets the name for a profile registered at a given -profilePath parameter. Commonly used in automation scripting. |
| getPath | Gets the filesystem location for a profile of a given name. Requires the -profileName parameter. Commonly used in automation scripting. |
| validateRegistry | Checks all of the profiles that are listed in the profile registry to see if the profiles are present on the filesystem. Returns a list of missing profiles. |
| validateAndUpdateRegistry | Checks all of the profiles that are listed in the profile registry to see if the profiles are present on the filesystem. Removes any missing profiles from the registry. Returns a list of the missing profiles that were deleted from the registry. |
| getDefaultName | Returns the name of the default profile. |
| setDefaultName | Sets the default profile to one of the existing profiles. Must be used with the -profileName parameter. |
| response | The name of the response file that can be used to pass options to the manageprofiles script as opposed to using lengthy command-line options. |

| Command-line option | Description |
| --- | --- |
| help | For each of the commands mentioned earlier, you can request contextual help. For example:<br><br>For Linux:<br><br>`<was_root>/bin/manageprofiles.sh -create -help`<br><br>For Windows:<br><br>`<was_root>\bin\manageprofiles.bat -create -help` |

To automatically create a profile, we will now craft a command-line script complete with command-line options to create a profile, with the same settings we used in our manual IIM profile creation earlier.

Please run the following command from the `<was_root>/bin` directory.

1. **For Linux:**

```
./manageprofiles.sh -create -profileName appsrv01 -profilePath
  <was_root>profiles/appsrv01 -templatePath
  <was_root>/profileTemplates/default -cellName appsrv01node01
-hostName
  node01.waslocal.com -nodeName node01
```

2. **For Windows:**

```
manageprofiles.bat -create -profileName appsrv01 -profilePath
  <was_root>\profiles\appsrv01 -templatePath
  <was_root>\profileTemplates\default -cellName appsrv01node01
-hostName
  node01.waslocal.com -nodeName node01
```

The result will be as follows:

**INSTCONFSUCCESS: Success: Profile appsrv01 now exists. Please consult /var/ apps/was8/profiles/appsrv01/logs/AboutThisProfile.txt for more information about this profile.**

Now that we have demonstrated how to create a profile using a command-line script, it is recommended that you experiment with the -help command to drill down into all the available subcommands of each mode of the manageprofiles command script. It may also be pertinent to read up on how to use the -response mode option, which allows a profile response file to be used instead of using such a lengthy command line. Response files are very useful in automation when you want to have a master script to manage many different profile creation types. Each different profile type can be specified by different response files.

# Summary

In this chapter, we covered how to install an application server and learned that there are different optional installation scenarios. Depending on requirements, there are multiple ways to install WAS.

The manual techniques shown previously have given a cross-section of possible install variations and demonstrated how flexible the installation process is. We also covered the ability to use a silent installation by using a response file that is used to direct IIM for silent installs. Silent installs dramatically speed up an installation. When installations are frequent, a response file approach ensures less installation errors due to the fact that it requires no human intervention. Once configured and tested, they can be run again and again without introducing errors that are often introduced when information needs to be typed into fields as required by a GUI-like IIM.

We were also introduced to a few command-line scripts such as start, stop, and other commands to manage profiles. We also had a brief look at the administration console.

A reoccurring theme in this chapter was the use of evaluating logs to ensure our installations were successful and error-free. Ensuring we have a stable set of binaries and correctly configured profile(s) ensures an application server is less likely to contain errors related to the actual installation process. In the next chapter, we will cover the process of deploying and configuring applications, including how to configure Java Database Connectivity (JDBC). We will also introduce a new WAS 8 feature known as **monitored deployments**. Monitored deployments allow a drag-and-drop approach to application deployments.

# 3
# Deploying your Applications

Now that we have installed an application server, we want to be able to deploy applications. Applications can be installed both manually and in an automated fashion using scripts. In this chapter, we will cover how to manually deploy a **JEE (Java Enterprise Edition)** application, later covering automated deployments in *Chapter 5, Administrative Scripting.* As we walk through this chapter, we will show you how to deploy two applications. One application does not require database connectivity, while the second is a database-aware application which requires some **WebSphere Application Server (WAS)** configuration to provide database connectivity to the application. We will also cover a new feature of WAS 8, where an application can be deployed simply by placing the application in a special monitored directory.

In this chapter, we will cover the following topics:

- Deploying an application
- Starting and stopping applications
- Data sources
- JDBC providers
- J2C aliases
- Deploying database-aware applications
- Business-Level Applications (BLA)
- Monitored deployments

# Deploying an application

As WebSphere Application Server administrators, we are asked to deploy applications. These applications may be written in-house or delivered by a third-party vendor. Either way they will, most often, be provided as an EAR file for deployment into WAS. You may remember this from *Chapter 1, WebSphere Application Server 8.0: Product Overview*, where we created a profile and opted not to install an EAR file called the "default application". For the purpose of understanding a manual deployment, we are going to install the default application EAR file.

The default application can be located in the `<was_root>/installableApps` folder. The following steps will show how we deploy the EAR file.

1. Open the Administration console and navigate to the **Applications** section and click on **New Application**, as shown in the following screenshot:

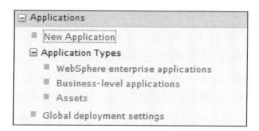

2. You now see the option to create one of the following three types of applications:

| Application type | Description |
| --- | --- |
| **Enterprise Application** | An EAR file on a server configured to hold installable Web Applications, WAR, Java archives, library files, and other resource files. |
| **Business-level Application** | A business-level application is an administration model, similar to a server or cluster. However, it lends itself to the configuration of applications as a single group of modules. More about this topic is covered at the end of this chapter. |
| **Asset** | An asset represents one or more application binary files that are stored in an asset repository, such as Java archives, library files, and other resource files. Assets can be shared between applications. We cover managing assets as part of BLAs later on in this chapter. |

3. Click on **New Enterprise Application**.

4. As seen in the following screenshot, you will be presented with the option to either browse locally on your machine for the file, or remotely on the Application Server's filesystem. Since the EAR file we wish to install is on the server, we will choose the **Remote file system** option.

> It can sometimes be quicker to deploy large applications by first using **Secure File Transfer Protocol (SFTP)** to move the file to the application server's file system and then using the **remote file system option**. Using the **Local file system** option is slower, as it will require an HTTP file transfer from your local machine to the server.

5. The following image depicts the path to the new application. Click **Browse**:

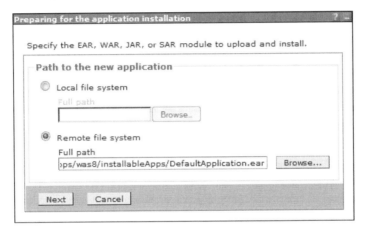

6. You will now see the name of the application server node. If there is more than one profile, select the appropriate instance. You will then be able to navigate through a web-based version of the application server's filesystem, as shown in the following screenshot:

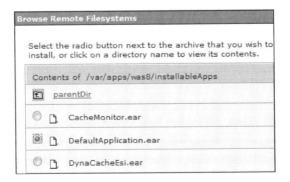

7. Locate the `DefaultApplication.ear` file. It will be in a folder called `installableApps` located in the root WAS install folder, for example, `<was_root>/installableApps,` as shown in the previous screenshot.

8. Click **Next** to begin installing the EAR file.

On the **Preparing for the application installation** page, there are two options to choose from:

| Install option | Description |
| --- | --- |
| **Fast Path** | The deployment wizard will skip advanced settings and only prompt for the absolute minimum settings required for the deployment. |
| **Detailed** | The wizard will allow, at each stage of the installation, the user to override any of the J2EE properties and configurations available to an EAR file. |

The **Choose to generate default bindings and mappings** setting allows the user to accept the default settings for resource mappings or override with specific values. Resource mappings will exist depending on the complexity of the EAR. Bindings are JNDI to resource mappings, which have been preset in the application. Not all applications will contain XML-based binding files. Binding files are generated by developers using IBM development tools such as **Rational Application Developer (RAD)**. EAR files also contain pre-configured XML descriptors which specify the JNDI name that the application resource uses to map to matching (application server) provided resources. An example would be a JDBC data source name which is referred to as `jdbc/mydatasource,` whereas the actual data source created in the application server might be called `jdbc/datasource01.` By choosing the **Detailed** option, you get prompted by the wizard to decide on how you want to map the resource bindings. By choosing the **Fast Path** option, you are allowing the application to use its pre-configured default JNDI names, which can also be pre-set using the aforementioned binding files.

1. We will cover the details of resources in later chapters. For now, select **Fast Path.** Click on **Next**:

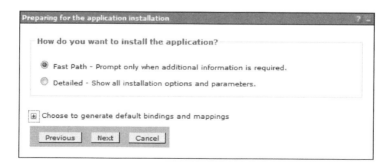

2. In the **Path to the new application** screen, browse the remote filesystem and select `DefaultApplication.ear` from the `<was_root>/installableApps` folder. Click **Next**:

| Contents of /opt/IBM/WebSphere/AppServer/installableApps |
| --- |
| ⬆ <u>parentDir</u> |
| ◎ 🗋 CacheMonitor.ear |
| ◉ 🗋 DefaultApplication.ear |

3. In the next screen, we are given the ability to fill out some specific deployment options.

   Following is a list of options presented on this page:

| Option value | Description/Values |
| --- | --- |
| **Precompile JavaServer Pages files** | Specify whether to precompile **JavaServer Pages** (**JSP**) files as a part of the installation. The default is not to precompile JSP files. |
| **Directory to install application** | Specifies the directory to which the **Enterprise Application Resource** (**EAR**) file will be installed.<br><br>You can change this if you want the application to be physically located outside of the WebSphere Application Server file structure. |
| **Distribute application** | The default is to enable application distribution. You can override this and choose not to distribute the application across multiple nodes. |
| **Use Binary Configuration** | Specifies whether the application server uses the binding, extensions, and deployment descriptors located within the application deployment document, the `deployment.xml` file (default), or those located in the EAR file. |
| **Deploy enterprise beans** | The tool generates the code needed to run the Enterprise JavaBean (EJB) files. You must enable this setting when the EAR file is assembled and the EJBDeploy is not run during packaging.<br><br>Its default value is false. |
| **Application name** | A logical name for the application. The default name is the same as the EAR file. An application name must be unique within a cell. |

| Option value | Description/Values |
| --- | --- |
| **Create MBeans for resources** | Specifies whether to create MBeans for resources, such as servlets or JSP files, within an application when the application starts. |
| | The default is to create MBeans. |
| **Override class reloading settings for Web and EJB modules** | Specifies whether the WebSphere Application Server runtime detects changes to application classes when the application is running. |
| | If this setting is enabled and if application classes are changed, then the application is stopped and restarted to reload updated classes. |
| | The default is not to enable class reloading. |
| **Reload interval in seconds** | Specifies the number of seconds to scan the application's filesystem for updated files. |
| **Process embedded configuration** | Specifies whether the embedded configuration should be processed. An embedded configuration consists of files such as `resource.xml` and `variables.xml`. When selected or true, the embedded configuration is loaded to the application scope from the `.ear` file. |
| **File Permission** | Allows all files to be read but not written to. |
| | Allows executables to execute. |
| | Allows HTML and image files to be read by everyone. |
| **Application Build ID** | A string that identifies the build version of the application. Once set, it cannot be edited. |
| **Allow dispatching includes to remote resources** | Web modules included in this application are enabled as remote request dispatcher clients that can dispatch remote includes. |
| | Default = `true`. |
| **Allow servicing includes from remote resources** | Web modules included in this application are enabled as remote request dispatcher servers that are resolved to service remote includes from another application. Default = `true`. |
| **Business level application name** | Specifies whether the product creates a new business-level application with the enterprise application that you are installing or makes the enterprise application a composition unit of an existing business-level application. |

| Option value | Description/Values |
|---|---|
| **Asynchronous Request Dispatch Type** | Specifies whether web modules can dispatch requests concurrently on separate threads. |
| **Allow EJB reference targets to resolve automatically** | Specifies whether the product assigns default JNDI values for EJB reference targets, or automatically resolves incomplete EJB reference targets. |

4.  For most applications, you will not have to change these previous settings. However, in this deployment, we will override the EAR application name to be:

    ```
    Default Application
    ```

    as opposed to:

    ```
    DefaultApplication.ear
    ```

5.  Click on **Next** to move on to the **Map modules to server** page and map the application to the appropriate server.

    At this stage, we only have one application server profile. However, we discussed in *Chapter 1, WebSphere Application Server 8.0: Product Overview* that we can administer several application servers. We are going to look at managing multiple server nodes in *Chapter 9, Administrative Features*. For this application, we will see two resources contained in the application, namely, an EJB and a WAR file. We want to ensure that both of these are mapped to the same server, **server01**, which we created in *Chapter 1, WebSphere Application Server 8.0: Product Overview*.

6.  Select both checkboxes and click **Apply** to ensure the application modules are bound to **server01**, and then click **Next**:

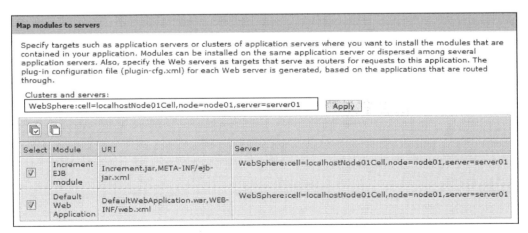

7. You will now be presented with a summary of the options chosen during the configuration of the deployment. Click **Finish** and the wizard will expand the uploaded EAR file into a temporary folder and override any files as required.

Up until now, all the work that has been done by the wizard has been in a temporary folder called `wstemp`, found at the root of the application server's profile. Here is an example of what that might look like:

```
<was_profile_root>/wstemp/anonymous1231468782776/workspace/cells/
websphereNode01Cell/applications/DefaultApplication.ear.
```

Once the EAR file has been deployed, a summary report will be given confirming the installation that has occurred. You must save the changes when prompted, otherwise the installation will be discarded. Saving will store the EAR file to the `installedApps` folder, which is in the following location:

```
<was_profile_root>/appsrv01/installedApps/websphereNode01Cell.
```

The EAR file is written to the `installedApps` folder and is expanded on-disk and is the runtime version of the application, meaning that this is what WebSphere Application Server considers to be the actual application.

There is another important area known as the **application registry** and an EAR file will exist there too, containing the actual EAR file which was uploaded. The application's registry is located at:

```
<was_profile_root>/config/cells/websphereNode01Cell/applications.
```

1. Click **Save** to continue. The application has now been deployed.
2. Navigate to the **Applications** section of the administration console and click **WebSphere enterprise applications**. You will get a list of installed applications.

# Starting and stopping your applications

In the **WebSphere enterprise applications** screen, we have the ability to start and stop installed applications. Below is a table explaining the actions that can be performed against one or more selected applications:

| Option | Description |
| --- | --- |
| **Start** | When an application is stopped, you will see an icon which is a green arrow representing a start button.<br><br>To start, select one or more applications and click on the **Start** button. |
| **Stop** | When an application is started, you will see a red-cross shape icon representing a stop button.<br><br>To stop, select one or more applications and click the **Stop** button. |
| **Install** | As a part of deploying an application, you install application files on a server. Depending on EAR/WAR complexity, the deployment wizard will dynamically produce a guide of steps which requires user input. |
| **Uninstall** | Select applications you wish to uninstall. It is recommended you stop applications first. |
| **Update** | Used to apply delta updates. Only the application code elements that have been changed in the application since last deployment are updated while the application continues running. |
| **Rollout Update** | If an application is deployed across multiple nodes, you can use the **Rollout Update** option which replaces the application one node at a time. Using this method reduces the amount of time that any single node member is unavailable for service during application deployment. |
| **Remove File** | Deletes a file of the deployed application or module. **Remove File** deletes a file from the configuration repository and from the filesystem of all the nodes where the file is installed. |
| **Export** | Allows the application to be exported as an EAR file. Can be used to back up an application version. |
| **Export DDL** | By using the Export DDL option, you can export DDL (Data Definition Language) files located within database-aware EJB modules. |
| **Export File** | Allows the exporting of a specific file from an enterprise application or module. |

1. We are going to start the default application. Select **DefaultApplication** and click on the **Start** action, as shown in the following screenshot:

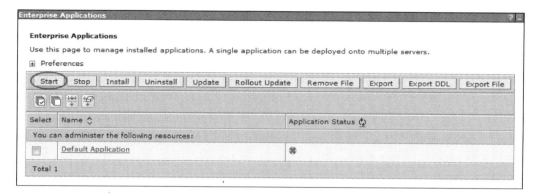

2. When an application has successfully started, you will get a message similar to the one shown in the following screenshot:

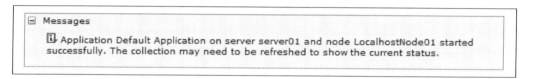

3. Now that **DefaultApplication** is started, we can use a web browser to navigate to the URL `http://<host_name>:9080/snoop`.

4. A page will load, similar to the following screenshot:

## Snoop Servlet - Request/Client Information

**Requested URL:**

http://node01.waslocal.com:9080/snoop

**Servlet Name:**

Snoop Servlet

**Request Information:**

| | |
|---|---|
| Request method | GET |
| Request URI | /snoop |
| Request protocol | HTTP/1.1 |
| Servlet path | /snoop |
| Path info | <none> |
| Path translated | <none> |
| Character encoding | <none> |
| Query string | <none> |
| Content length | <none> |
| Content type | <none> |
| Server name | node01.waslocal.com |
| Server port | 9080 |

The default application contains a very useful administration Servlet called snoop. The **snoop** servlet is an excellent tool to use in testing. Snoop reports on the following attributes:

- Servlet context initialization parameters
- URL invocation request parameters
- Preferred client locale
- Context path
- User principal
- Request headers and their values
- Request parameter names and their values
- HTTPS protocol information
- Servlet request attributes and their values
- HTTP session information
- Session attributes and their values

The snoop application will be used later in *Chapter 9, Administrative Features*, when we look at the configuration of SSL SSL between IBM HTTP Server (IHS) and the WebSphere plugin.

# Data access applications

We have just deployed an application that did not require database connectivity. Often, applications in the business world require access to an **Relational Database Management System** (RDBMS) to fulfill their business objective. If an application requires the ability to retrieve information from, or store information in, a database then you will need to create a data source which will allow the application to connect and use the database (DB).

Looking at the following image, we can see the logical flow of the sample data access application that we are going to install. The basic idea of the application is to display a list of tables that exist in a database schema. Since the application requires a database connection, we need to configure WAS before we can deploy the application. We will now cover the preparation required, before we install our DB-aware application (HR Lister):

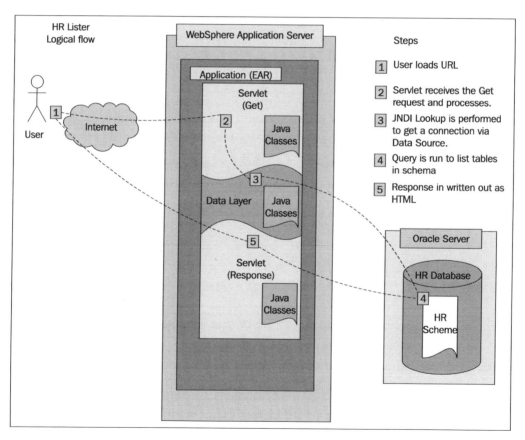

# Data sources

There are many RDBMS vendors in the market place and WAS provides several native JDBC providers for connecting databases. Traditionally, organizations use RDBMS such as Oracle, IBM DB/2, and Microsoft SQL server. In most cases, JEE-based systems running in WAS will use either Oracle or IBM DB/2 as these two RDBMS products are enterprise ready, extremely scalable, and are best suited for Unix-based systems. Recently, there have been many advances in open source Java-based RDBMS which are capable of being embedded within an application. What this means, is that an application can use a file-based Java DB without the need to implement a full-blown RDBMS architecture. Your WAS configurations for data access will depend on the application data storage needs, and the type of data management structure you have in place. Since we cannot demonstrate connecting to all RDBMS types and data usage scenarios, we will cover two scenarios. The first scenario will demonstrate how to connect to an enterprise product from a vendor, such as Oracle. The second scenario will explain how to use the new Derby JDBC provider available in WAS v8.

Detailing these two scenarios will give you the information required to connect to other DB implementations via JDBC.

# Preparing for Oracle

Before you create a data source to connect your application to Oracle, we need to ensure that the appropriate client database driver software is installed. For our demonstration, we are going to use **Oracle Express Edition** (**Oracle XE**), which is the free (limited) version of the commercial Oracle database product. There are many open source databases to choose from. Oracle's free RDBMS has been used in this chapter because JDBC with Oracle XE is quite easy to configure and represents a true enterprise environment. Many organizations choose to use Oracle as their enterprise RDBMS. By following these steps, you will be able to apply the same logic to any of the major vendors' full RDBMS products, that is, DB/2, Oracle RAC, SQL Server, and so on. Another reason why I chose Oracle XE is that it is an enterprise-ready DB and is administered by a simple web-based interface. I have used the Linux version of Oracle XE 10g in my example and the download size is about 211MB, so it does take time to download. For those who wish to use Oracle XE for Windows, this is possible as well, and I have included a few Windows instructions if you choose this option.

# Installing Oracle XE

To install Oracle XE, you can use the following steps:

1. Download Oracle XE from Oracle's website using the following URL:
   `http://www.oracle.com/technetwork/database/express-edition/ downloads/index.html`.

   Locating the installers:

   ° **For Linux:**

      Transfer the `oracle-xe-10.2.0.1-1.0.i386.rpm` (221,136,869 bytes) file to an appropriate directory on your Linux server using WinSCP (Secure Copy) or your chosen Secure FTP client.

   ° **For Windows:**

      Transfer the `OracleXE.exe` (165,332,312 bytes) file to your Windows desktop or server, as required.

   Running the installers:

   ° **For Linux:**

      Since the Linux XE installer uses X Windows, ensure that you have Xming running, if using an SSH session to install. Then install Oracle XE by using the `rpm` command, as shown here: rpm-ivh `oracle-xe-10.2.0.1-1.0.i386.rpm`.

   ° **For Windows:**

      Simply run the `OracleXE.exe` by double-clicking in Windows Explorer.

2. Follow the installer steps as prompted:

   ° HTTP port = 8080
   ° Listener port = 1521
   ° SYS & SYSTEM / password = oracle
   ° Autostart = y

Oracle XE was installed using the default install option for installing an RPM. If you require support, the administration process is fully documented on Oracle's website.

3. Ensure that Oracle XE is running. You can now access the web interface via a browser from the local machine; by default, XE will only accept a connection locally.

   As shown in the following image, we have a screenshot showing Firefox being used to connect to OracleXE using the URL `http://localhost:8080/apex`.

 The reason we use Firefox on Linux is that this is the most commonly installed default browser on the newer Linux distributions. If you have chosen to install OracleXE on Windows, you can use **Windows Remote Desktop (RDP)** to access the Oracle web-based administration interface.

4. When the administration application loads, you will be presented with a login screen as you can see below. You can log in using the username **SYSTEM** and password `oracle`, as set by your installation process:

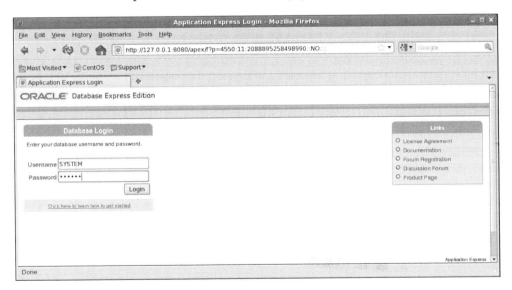

5. Oracle XE comes with a pre-created user called HR, which is granted ownership to the HR Schema. We want to use these schemas in our example. However, the account is locked by default, for security reasons, and so we need to unlock the HR user account. To unlock an account, we need to navigate to the **Database Users | Manage Users** screen:

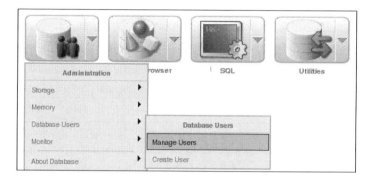

6. You will notice that the icon for the **HR** user is locked. You will see a small padlock on the HR icon that looks like this:

7. Click on the **HR** user icon and unlock the account, as shown in the following screenshot. You need to reset the password and change **Account Status** to **Unlocked**, and then click **Alter User** to set the new password. Set the new password to be HR:

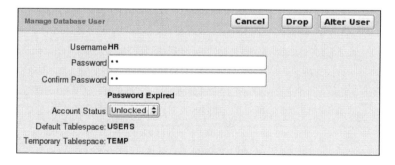

8. The following figure shows that the HR account is unlocked:

9. Now that the HR account is unlocked, log out and log back into the administration interface using the HR user to ensure that the account is now open for service and is accessible.

10. Another good test to ensure connectivity to Oracle is to use an Oracle admin tool called **sqlplus**, which is a command-line tool that DBAs can use to administer Oracle. We are going to use sqlplus to perform a simple query to list the tables in the HR schema. To run sqlplus, we need to set up an environment variable called $ORACLE_HOME, which is required to run sqlplus.

   - **For Linux:**
     - ○ To set $ORACLE_HOME, type the following command in a Linux shell:

       ```
       export ORACLE_HOME=/usr/lib/oracle/xe/app/oracle/
       product/10.2.0/server
       ```

 If you have installed Oracle XE in a non-default location, then you may have to use a different path.

   - **For Windows:**
     - ○ Create an environment variable by right-clicking **My computer** within Windows and selecting the **Properties** option.
     - ○ Within the **System-properties** window, click the **Environment Variable** button.
     - ○ Add a user or system variable called ORACLE_HOME that points to the root of your local windows Oracle installation.

11. To run `sqlplus`, type the following command in a shell or command-prompt:

    - **For Linux:**

      `$ORACLE_HOME/bin/sqlplus`

    - **For Windows:**

      `%ORACLE_HOME\bin\sqlplus`

12. The result will be a login screen showing the screen output below:

    **SQL*Plus: Release 10.2.0.1.0 - Production on Mon Mar 14 23:29:54 2011**

    **Copyright (c) 1982, 2005, Oracle.  All rights reserved.**

    **Enter user-name**

13. You will be prompted for a username. Type the following command:

    `HR@xe<enter>`

14. For the password, type the following command:

    `HR<enter>`

15. When you have successfully logged in, you can type the following commands in the SQL prompt:

    `SELECT TABLE_NAME FROM user_tables<enter>`
    `/<enter>`

16. The / command indicates to execute the command buffer. The result will be a list of tables in the HR schema, as shown in the following screen output:

    **TABLE_NAME**

    `-----------------------------`

    **REGIONS**

    **LOCATIONS**

    **DEPARTMENTS**

    **JOBS**

    **EMPLOYEES**

    **JOB_HISTORY**

    **COUNTRIES**

    **7 rows selected.**

17. We have now successfully verified that Oracle works from a command line, and thus, it is very likely that WAS will also be able to communicate with Oracle. Next, we will cover how to configure WAS to communicate with Oracle.

# JDBC providers

Deployed applications use JDBC providers to communicate with RDBMS:

- The JDBC provider object provides the actual JDBC driver implementation class for access to a specific database type, that is Oracle, SQL Server, DB/2, and so on.

- You associate a data source with a JDBC provider. A data source provides the connection to the RDBMS.

- The JDBC provider and the data source provide connectivity to a database.

# Creating a JDBC provider

Before creating a JDBC provider, you will need to understand the application's resource requirements, that is the data sources that the application references. You should know the answer to the following questions:

- Does your application require a data source? Not all applications use a database.

- What are the security credentials required to connect to the database? Often databases are secured and you will need a username and password to access a secure database.

- Are there any web components (Servlets, JSP, and so on) or EJBs that need to access a database?

Answering these questions will determine the amount of configuration required for your database connectivity configurations.

1. To create a JDBC provider, log into the WAS administrative console and click on the **JDBC Provider** link in the **JDBC** category of the **Resources** section, located in the left-hand panel of the administration console, as shown below:

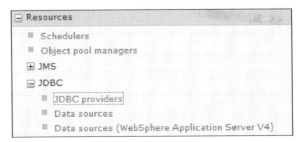

2.  Choose an appropriate scope from the **Scope** drop-down pick list. Scope determines how the provider will be seen by applications. We will talk more about scope in the JNDI section. For now, please choose the **Cell** scope, as seen in the following screenshot:

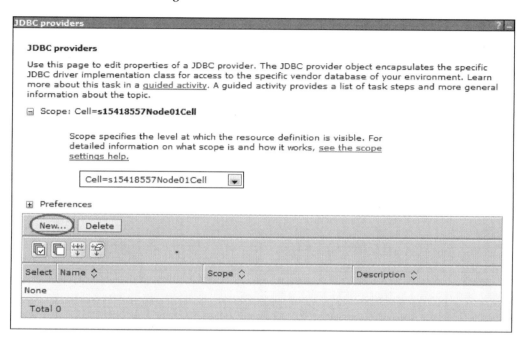

3.  Click **New** and the new JDBC provider wizard is displayed, as shown in the following screenshot:

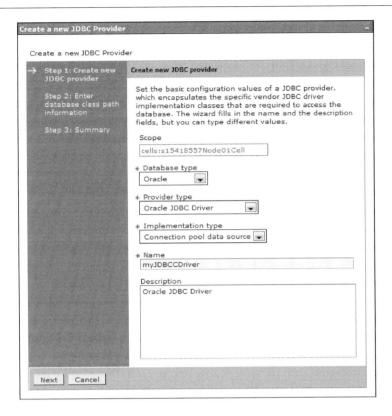

4. Select the **Database type** as **Oracle**, **Provider type** as **Oracle JDBC Driver**, **Implementation type** as **Connection pool data source**, and **Name** for the new JDBC provider. Enter **MyJDBCDriver** as the provider name, as seen in the previous screenshot. We also need to choose an **Implementation type**. There are two implementation types for Oracle JDBC Drivers. The following table explains them:

| Implementation type | Description |
| --- | --- |
| Connection pool data source | Use **Connection pool data source** if your application does not require a connection that supports two-phase commit transactions. |
| XA Datasource | Use **XA Datasource** if your application requires two-phase commit transactions. Two-phase commit transactions allow a transaction to be rolled back in the event of a failure, allowing an application to handle this event and act accordingly. |

5.  Click **Next** to go to the database **class path** screen.

    As shown in the following screenshot, enter the database class path information for the JDBC provider. It is important to note that, by default, WAS has used a JAR file called `ojdbc6.jar`.

6.  Change the **Class path** field to read `${ORACLE_JDBC_DRIVER_PATH}/ojdbc14.jar`. The reason we need to do this is because WAS 8 knows about the latest version of the JDBC driver used in communicating with the full version of Oracle and it is preset as such. We have used OracleXE, which provides an older version of the JDBC provider and so we need to change the default JDBC driver, as suggested by the wizard.

7.  Click **Apply** to ensure that WAS remembers the driver **Class path** field change:

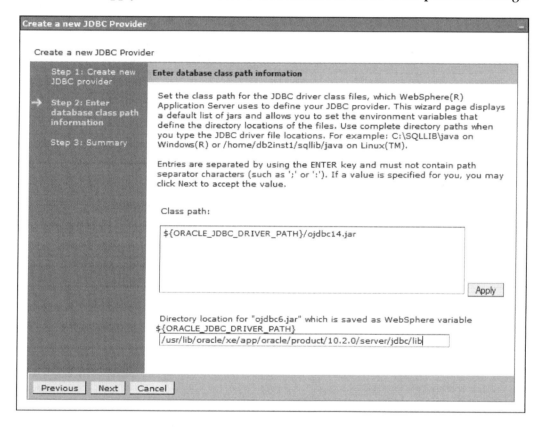

8.  As long as you have installed Oracle XE using the default paths, you will be able to use the following path in the **Directory location** field: `/usr/lib/oracle/xe/app/oracle/product/10.2.0/server/jdbc/lib`.

9.  Click **Next** to proceed to the next step, where you will be presented with a summary, as shown in the following screenshot. Review the JDBC provider information that you have entered and click **Finish**.

> Since WAS 8.0 is the latest version of WebSphere Appication Server, the wizard already knows about the new version of the Oracle 11g JDBC Driver. We are connecting to Oracle XE 10g and the driver for this is `ojdbc14.jar`. The `classpath` file can contain a list of paths or JAR filenames which, together, form the location of the resource provider classes. Class path entries are separated by using the *Enter* key and must not contain path separator characters (such as ; or :). Class paths can contain variable (symbolic) names that can be substituted using a variable map. Check your driver installation notes for specific JAR file names that are required.

10. You will now be prompted to save the JDBC provider configuration. Click **Save**.

> When configuration changes are saved, WAS updates the underlying XML files which contain configuration settings. We will cover more on the WAS filesystem and key XML configuration files in *Chapter 6, Server Configuration*, where we delve more into administrative configuration.

11. Once you have saved the JDBC provider configuration we have just run through, you will be returned to the **JDBC providers** screen where you will see the new provider listed, as shown in the following screenshot:

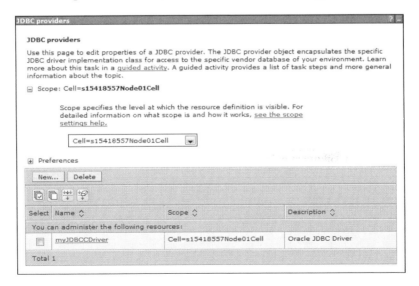

We now need to set up an authentication alias which will contain the username and password for communicating with the Oracle Schema.

## Creating a J2C alias

If a database has security enabled, which is the case for most RDBMS, we will need to somehow provide the username and password for the connection. By creating a J2C alias, we can create an authentication resource, independent from the provider and data source. Using this approach, we can change the alias if the database username and password are changed without reconfiguring the provider or data source. This is a key concept and WAS provides levels of abstraction to allow the configuration of resources independently from each other. So, it can be said that the JDBC Provider, data source, and J2C alias are loosely coupled. This concept also allows the application to access a database though a JNDI lookup and the application does not need to know the database username and password.

1.  To create a J2C alias, navigate to the **Security** section in the left-hand navigation panel and click on the **Global security** link:

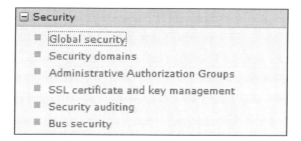

2.  Expand the **Java Authentication and Authorization Service** category in the **Authentication** section, found in the bottom right-hand side of the **Global security** screen.

3.  Click on **J2C authentication data**, as shown in the following screenshot:

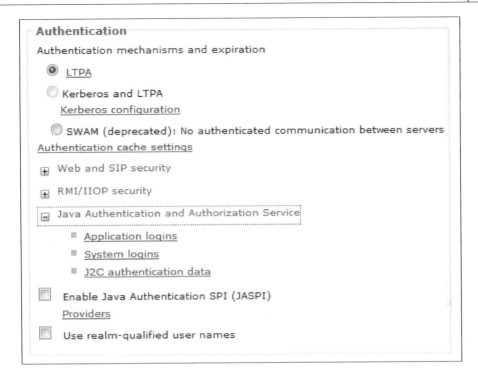

4. You will be presented with a screen where you can click **New** to create a new J2C authentication alias. Enter **HR** for the **Alias**, enter **HR** for the **User ID**, and **HR** for **Password**, as shown in the following screenshot:

> Oracle usernames and passwords are not case sensitive.

5. Click **Apply** and then **Save**. A new alias will be created, as shown in the following screenshot:

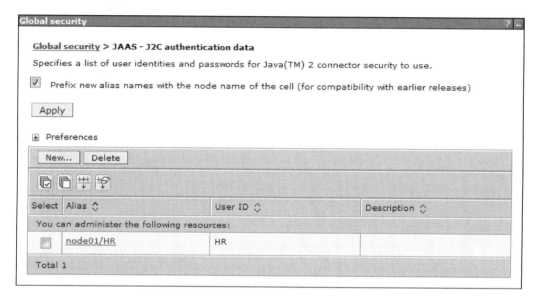

We will reference this J2C authentication alias when we create our data source in the following steps.

## Creating a data source

Now that we have created a provider and authentication alias, we need to create an actual JDBC data source which an application will use via JNDI to access the HR database. In the next steps, we will use the administrative console to create a new data source.

1. Open the Administrative console and navigate to the **JDBC** section in the left-hand side panel and click on **Data sources**, as shown in the following screenshot:

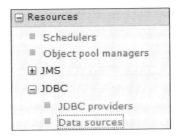

2. We will be looking at the **JNDI (Java Naming and Directory Interface)** scope in later chapters. For now, select the **Cell** scope and click **New**, as demonstrated in the next screenshot:

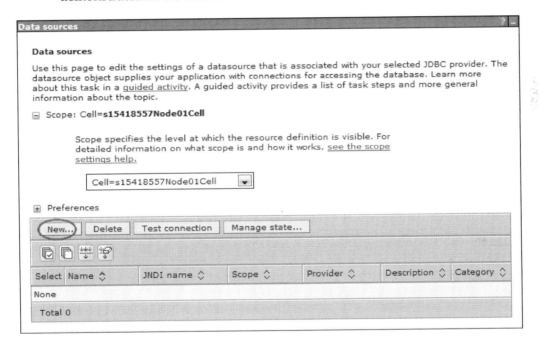

3. You will now be asked to fill out the data source information.

4. Enter the value **HRDataSource** in the **Data source name** field and the value **jdbc/hrdatasource** in the **JNDI name** field, as shown in the following screenshot:

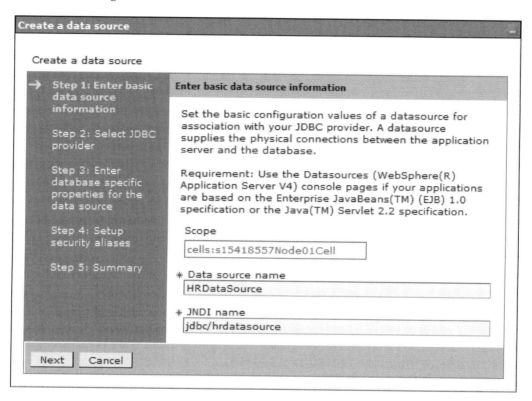

5. The JNDI name provides a naming context for the data source, as used in resource lookups by application code. Click **Next** to move on to the next screen where you will be asked to select a JDBC provider for your data source. Select the JDBC provider that we created previously, as seen in the following screenshot:

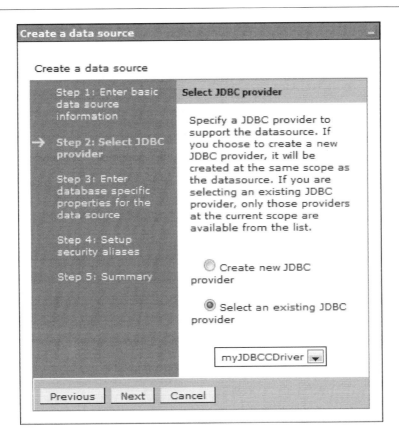

6. Click **Next**, and in the following screen, enter into the **URL** field the following connection string, `jdbc:oracle:thin:@<host_name>:1521/xe`. Please replace the `<host_name>` component with your appropriate server's IP address or hostname.

7. The JDBC connection string we are using in our example is an Oracle thin client URL. This allows WAS to connect to Oracle via a URL, which is made up of the following syntax: `<driver_type>:@<host>:<port>/<service_name>`. It can be broken up as follows:

   `<driver_type>` = `jdbc:oracle:thin`

   `<host>` = `node01waslocal.com` (the IP address or host name of your Linux machine; it could even be localhost, if Oracle is installed on the same machine as WAS)

   `<port>`=`1521` (default Oracle listener port)

   `<service_name>` = `xe` (the Oracle instance and service name)

8. Click **Next** to set up a security alias. In this screen, there are several fields.

9. There are two options for applying the J2C alias. They are listed as follows:

| Authentication alias | Description |
|---|---|
| Component-managed | Use when the resource configured in the EJB's deployment descriptor res-auth property is set to `Application`. |
| Container-managed | Use when the resource configured in the EJB's deployment descriptor res-auth property is set to `Container`. |

10. Since our application is controlling access to the database, we are going to use a **Component-managed authentication alias**. We will now select our J2C authentication alias, mapping our user ID and password to the data source, as shown in the following screenshot:

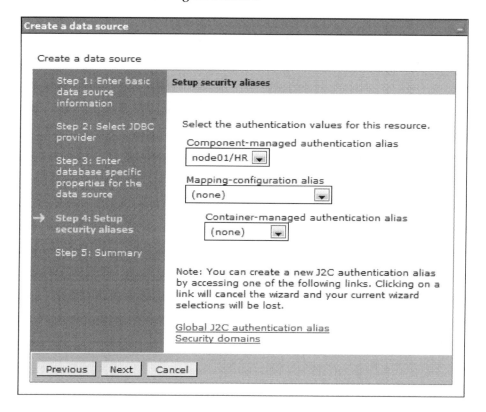

11. Click **Next** to view the summary screen, click **Finish**, and then **Save**. You will now see the data source listed in the data sources panel.

If you choose to re-edit the HRDataSource you just created, you will find a section called **Related Items** where you will see a link to the JAAS—J2C authentication data we created earlier.

12. Test the data source by selecting the required data source and click **Test Connection**. If the data source is configured correctly, you will see a message similar to the one below:

```
⊟  Messages
     ⓘ The test connection operation for data source MyDataSource on server server01 at node
     node01 was successful.
```

# Deploying a data access application

Now that we have created a JDBC provider and a data source which uses the Oracle provider, we are now ready to deploy a data access application. Our application comes in the form of an EAR file called HRLister.ear, which can be downloaded from the Packt Publishing website at the following location: http://www.packtpub.com.

The HRLister EAR file contains a single web application which, in turn, contains a **servlet** called listtable. The application is used to show how to deploy an application which uses a resource reference. The resource reference uses a JNDI lookup to find the data source and allows the application to connect to the HR database.

Our application contains several deployment descriptors; one is called application.xml and the other is called web.xml. The two descriptors detail certain configuration information which will be used by WAS at deployment.

1. To begin the deployment, click the **Install** button in the **Enterprise Applications** section, as seen in the main panel.

2. If you have not already done so, download the HRLister.ear file onto c:/temp on your desktop. Click on the **Browse** button to browse for the EAR file in c:/temp and click **Next** to continue.

3. On the next page, select the **Detailed-Show all installation options and parameters** radio option button, which will force the wizard to ask for information during the deployment steps. The wizard is dynamic and will contain more steps, depending on the contents of the EAR file. The workings of the sample HRListerEAR EAR file are quite simple. However, some EAR files can contain many JEE artifacts which result in a greater number of steps to complete the deployment process.

We will now cover the steps we will be presented with by the installation wizard during the installation process.

4.  Click **Next** to enter the **Select installation options** screen and change the **Application name** from **HRListerEAR** to **HR Lister**.

 The application name is a logical name change and does not affect the running of the application. In environments which contain multiple streams of development, it may be prudent to name each application with a standard naming scheme to determine which version of the application is at what stage of the development process.

# Mapping modules to servers

Leave all other options as default and click **Next** to enter the **Map modules to servers** screen. Because we have a web application, we need to ensure that the application can map to the appropriate virtual host. A virtual host already exists by default, as explained earlier, and is allowing HTTP connections to port 9080, which is the default HTTP port as set by WAS.

If we have more than one virtual host, we can choose at this stage to map the web application(s) contained in the EAR file to separate ports. Since our application only contains one web application, we do not wish to change it and will use the default host. If we did wish to change it, we would select the web module and map it to an available virtual host and click **Apply** which would store the mapping. Leave the screen set as it is and click **Next** to move on to the next screen, where we will set some loading options.

# Providing JSP reloading options for web modules

In the **Provide JSP reloading options for Web modules** screen, we can once again leave the defaults. The **JSP reloading** option allows the web server to reload JSPs, which allow for hot deployment of artifacts. This means that we can replace JSPs on the filesystem, and WAS will automatically pick up those which have been changed. JSPs are compiled into servlets to work inside the web container and these options decide whether they are cached after the first compile or not. Click **Next**.

# Mapping shared libraries

The **Map Share Libraries** section allows the configuration of shared libraries. A shared library is a JAR file that is used by more than one module in an EAR file. An EAR file can contain many web modules and EJB modules, and they can be designed to share common code routines. We do not have any other modules in the applications and no shared JARS, so we do not need to worry about shared libraries in this deployment. Therefore, we can proceed by clicking **Next** to move on to the share libraries page. If your application needed to reference a shared library, this is where you would assign shared libraries to the application. Once again, we have no shared libraries in our application, so we need not worry about this page. Click **Next** to go to the **Map resource references to resources** page.

# Mapping resource references to resources

On the **Map resource references to resources** page, we can see that there is a field called **Target Resource JNDI Name** as shown in the next screenshot, and it already has the JNDI name **jdbc/mydatasource**. If you recall from our data source creation, this was not the JNDI name that we gave to our JDBC data source. The reason is that the wizard is presenting an option to override the JNDI name of the data source defined as a resource reference in the application's web.xml.

The idea here is about decoupling the application from the data source. This level of abstraction means that an administrator can choose which data source is to be used, as opposed to the application deciding what resource it wishes to use. There might be a requirement to change the database and move the data to a different data source. This can be done via the wizard at deployment time, as well as post-deployment by changing the application settings in the administrative console. As long as the application resources are designed to be overridden, an administrator can override the application's named resource with the resource name he/she has configured within WAS.

Though this is best practice for application design, not all applications will be designed this way. Sometimes you will be forced to use the name given by the application and you will have no choice but to declare a resource using the name the application has hardwired within its code.

The `web.xml` file contained in the web module defines an internal name that the application uses for the data source. In this application example, the HR application uses the JNDI name of `jdbc/mydatasource`. However, we configured our WAS data source JNDI name to be `jdbc/hrdatasource`. The **Map resource references to resources** screen of the installation wizard is used to map the two together. This is a very powerful concept of JEE application design and allows for deployment time changes based on administration decisions, which do not affect the application code, thus providing flexibility of deployment:

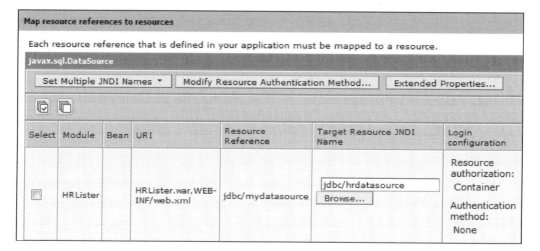

You may notice, in the **Map resource references to resources** screen, a new WebSphere Application Server 8 feature allowing the ability to browse for the correct JNDI resource name, as opposed to typing in manually which can be prone to human error.

Click **Next** to open the **Map virtual hosts for Web modules** page.

# Mapping virtual hosts for web modules

Here, we leave the default settings and use the `default_host`, which will assign the web module to port 9080. Click **Next**.

# Mapping context roots for web modules

The next page of the wizard is where we set the application context root. The context root is used to calculate the base path of the application. All URIs should be relative to the context root; this allows for the applications runtime URL to be changed as required. Each application URI must be unique. If multiple web applications exist in an EAR, or multiple web applications across multiple EARs are installed on the server, then the context root can be overridden by the administrator. The `application.xml` file contains the default context root and we can override it here if we wish. At this time, we will leave it set to `hrlister`.

# Reviewing the deployment steps

Click **Next** to review the summary of the wizard's deployment steps, and click **Finish** when you are happy that the summary correctly lists the configuration you have made. If there are no errors shown in the summary, you can click **Save** to persist the application deployment. If there are errors found at this point, you will need to review the logs to see what the problem could be. If you were to find a problem, you can choose not to save the configuration. A typical problem at this point could be that the application has been packaged incorrectly and WAS cannot install it, or maybe the application refers to versions of Java APIs unknown to WAS. After saving to the master configuration, you will be redirected back to the main **Enterprise Applications** screen, where you will see the HR Lister application currently in the stopped state, as seen in the following screenshot. A red x means that an application is in a stopped state.

# Using the application

Select the **HRLister** application, as shown in the following screenshot, and click **Start** to start the application:

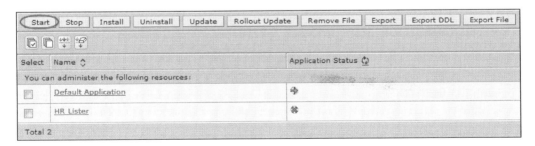

Once the HR Lister application has started, open a browser and navigate to the following URL: `http://<host_name>:9080/hrlister/listtable?dbtype=oracle`.

The URL can be broken up as follows:

`<host_name>:<port>/<context_root>/<URL>`

`<host_name>` = IP address or hostname

`<port>` = 9080, the default host port for WAS

`<URI>` = the resource name, that is, the `ListTable` servlet

`<Querystring Paramter>` = dbtype?<derby or oracle>

As it loads, the `ListTable` servlet will connect to the HR database and list the tables in the HR schema, as shown in the following screenshot:

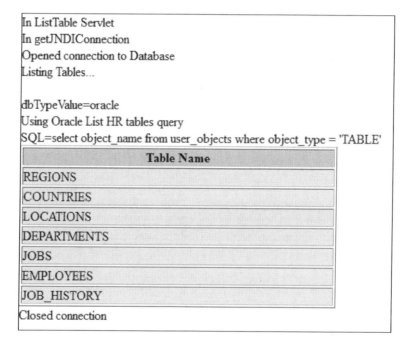

Congratulations! You have now successfully installed and configured a data access application using an enterprise RDBMS product from Oracle.

# Overview of Derby

Apache Derby is a Java relational database management system that can be embedded in Java programs. Apache Derby is developed as an open source project under the Apache 2.0 license. Derby was previously distributed as **IBM Cloudscape** in previous versions of WAS.

 It is interesting to note that Sun (now Oracle) distributes the same Derby binaries as Java DB.

WebSphere Application Server supports the use of the Apache Derby database in test environments only. The product does not support the use of the Apache Derby database in production environments, and so this scenario is really only suitable for test or for **Proof of Concept (POC)** environments.

# Derby JDBC

The Derby JDBC Provider 40 provides JDBC access to the Apache Derby database by using the framework that is already embedded in the application server. An installation of Derby 10.5 is installed as part of the WAS installation and can run in two modes. The first mode is embedded, which is used by WAS to manage locally-persisted data storage for features of WAS 8, such as JMS (Java Message Service) high-availability. We cover JMS in *Chapter 7, WebSphere Messaging*. The second mode is a network mode where we can run Derby much like a traditional DB where the client application process connects to the DB using JDBC.

For our example, we will be configuring Derby to run as a network server, then we will re-configure the HR Lister application to use a different JDBC provider, that is, the Derby provider. A simple verification to test the HR Lister application will use Derby as its data source for the listing of all the tables in the default Derby SYS-schema.

# Managing Derby

Derby is located in `<was_root>/derby`, which we will refer to as `<derby_root>`. In a directory called `<derby_root>/bin/ networkServer` is a set of commands for managing Derby as a network server, which is listed in the following table. We will use some of these scripts in the following example:

| Command script | Description |
|---|---|
| dblook | Dumps DDL information. |
| networkServerControl | Controls the networkServer process (can be used for functions such as ping and trace). |
| startNetworkServer | Starts the networkServer process. |
| stopNetworkServer | Stops the networkServer process. |
| ij | Starts a command line tool for executing SQL statements. |

## Starting Derby

To start Derby as a network server allowing applications to connect locally, use the following command:

- **For Linux:**

  ```
  nohup <derby_root>/bin/networkServer/startNetworkServer.sh -h
  0.0.0.0 &
  ```

- **For Windows:**

  ```
  <derby_root>\bin\ networkServer\startNetworkServer.bat -h 0.0.0.0
  ```

## Stopping Derby

To stop the Derby network server, use the following command:

- **For Linux:**

  ```
  <derby_root>/bin/ networkServer /stopNetworkServer.sh
  ```

- **For Windows:**

  ```
  <derby_root>\bin\ networkServer\stopNetworkServer.bat
  ```

# Creating tables in Derby

For our example, we need to verify that we can list the system tables contained within the SYS schema. To run the `ij.sh` command-line tool and allow the execution of SQL to select all the system tables within the default SYS schema, carry out the following steps:

1. Navigate to `<derby_root>/bin/networkServer` and start Derby using the start command, as listed previously. You will see the following screen output:

   **Apache Derby Network Server - 10.5.3.1 - (957402) started and ready to accept connections on port 1527**

2. Once the service is running, you can run the `ij.sh` tool using the following command:

    ○ **For Linux:**

      `./ij.sh`

    ○ **For Windows:**

      `ij.bat`

3. The result will be a Derby command prompt, similar to the following screen output:

   **./ij.sh ij version 10.5**
   **ij>**

4. From within the `ij` command prompt, type the following command to connect to the Derby network server and create a database called HR:

   ```
   CONNECT 'jdbc:derby:
     //localhost:1527/hr;create=true;user=SYS;password=SYS';
   ```

5. Next, execute the following SQL command to select all the system tables:

   ```
   SELECT tablename FROM SYSTABLES;
   ```

The screen result will be as follows:

**TABLENAME**

---------------------------------------------------------------------------------------

**SYSALIASES**

**SYSCHECKS**

**SYSCOLPERMS**

**SYSCOLUMNS**

**SYSCONGLOMERATES**

**SYSCONSTRAINTS**

**SYSDEPENDS**

**SYSDUMMY1**

**SYSFILES**

**SYSFOREIGNKEYS**

**SYSKEYS**

**SYSROLES**

**SYSROUTINEPERMS**

**SYSSCHEMAS**

**SYSSTATEMENTS**

**SYSSTATISTICS**

**SYSTABLEPERMS**

**SYSTABLES**

**SYSTRIGGERS**

**SYSVIEWS**

Now we are ready to re-configure the HR Lister application to use Derby instead of Oracle to list tables within a given schema.

# Adding a Derby JDBC data source

To configure a Derby JDBC data source, we will need to create a JDBC provider and then create a data source associated with the new provider.

## Creating a Derby JDBC provider

1.  To configure a new JDBC provider for Derby, we will need to follow similar steps as outlined for the Oracle JDBC provider we created earlier. Then select **JDBC providers** from the **JDBC** section on the left-hand navigation panel of the admin console. Select **Cell** scope and then click **New**, as shown in the following screenshot:

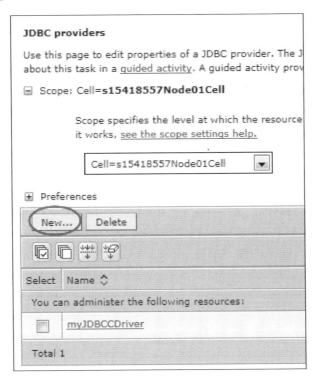

2. You will now be presented with the **Create new JDBC provider** screen. Select **Derby** from the **Database Type** select-list. Select **Derby Network Server using Derby client 40** from the **Provider Type** select-list. For the **Implementation type** field, choose **Connection pool data source**. We do not choose an XA Data source, as this application does not have transactional management. Please type in **MyDerbyJDBCProvider** in the **Name** field. You can use the default value for the **Description** field, as shown in the following screenshot:

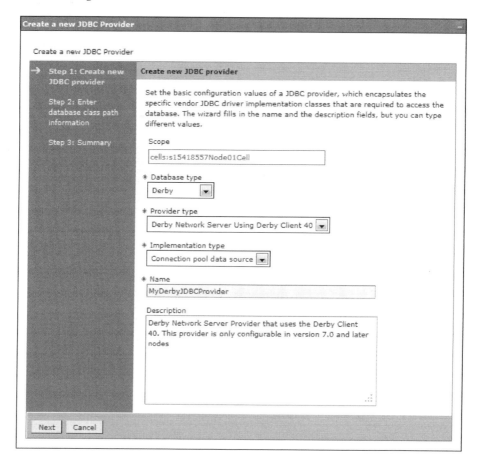

3. Click **Next** to continue on to the summary screen and click **Finish** and then **Save**. You will then be taken back to the JDBC Drivers list and you will now see the new Derby JDBC Provider.

# Creating a Derby JDBC data source

1. To create a new JDBC data source, click on the **Data sources** link located in the **JDBC** section of the left-hand side navigation panel of the admin console. Select **Cell** scope and you should see the existing HR data source called **HRDatasource**. Click **New** to begin the wizard to define a new data source which the HR Lister application will use to connect to Derby instead of Oracle.

2. In the Create Data source screen, type HRDerbyDataSource in the **Data source name** field, type jdbc/hrderbydatasource in the **JNDI Name** field, and then click **Next**.

3. In the next screen, you will be prompted to select a JDBC provider. Choose **Select an existing JDBC provider**, select the Derby provider you created as an example MyDerbyJDBCProvider, and then click **Next**.

4. On the next screen, you will be asked to fill in the **Database name** field. Type hr and click **Next**.

5. On the Setup security aliases page, click **Next**, click **Finish**, and then **Save**.

# Creating a new JAAS for Derby data source

For a Derby JDBC data source, we need to provide an authentication alias just like we did for the Oracle JSBD data source. To create a new J2C authentication alias and assign to the new data source we just created, use the following steps:

1. Click on the **Data sources** link located in the **JDBC** section of the left-hand side navigation panel of the admin console. Select the **Cell** scope and you should see the existing HR data source for Derby called **HRDerbyDatasource**. Select the data source and then click on the link called **JAAS - J2C authentication data**, located in the section titled **Related Items**.

2. Click **New** to create a new J2C authentication alias and type SYS in the name field and SYS for both the username and password fields. The value SYS is the default username and password that the Derby network server uses for the default SYS schema.

3. Click **OK**. Navigate to the data source's list, re-open the **HRDerbyDatasource** configuration, and set the **Component-managed authentication alias** to the SYS alias you have just created, as shown in the following screenshot:

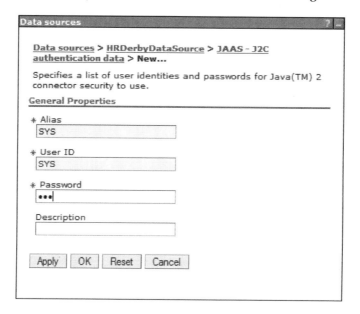

4. Click **OK** and then **Save** to ensure the configuration is set. You have now configured a Derby data source with a JAAS username and password alias.

It is good practice to test your data source using the test button located in the data source's list screen. This ensures that the data source can connect. It is better to resolve connection issues at this stage, before involving an application.

# Changing an application's data source

Now that we have created a new JDBC data source, we need to re-configure the HR Lister application to use the JNDI name jdbc/hrderbydatasource, as opposed to the current name of jdbc/hrdatasource, which is a data source bound to an Oracle JDBC provider.

1. To change an application resource mapping, such as a JDBC data source binding, select **WebSphere enterprise applications** from the **Applications** section of the left-hand side navigation panel of the Administrative console.

2. Locate the HR Lister application (it should be called **HRListerEar** unless you have changed the name) and click on the link to open the **Enterprise Applications** settings page.

3. Within the **Enterprise Applications** settings page, click the link named **Resource references**, located within the **References** section, as shown in the following screenshot:

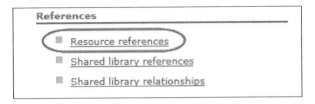

4. You will now be presented with a list of resource references. The HR Lister application only has one resource reference, and as shown in the following screenshot, it will show a binding `jdbc/hrdatasource` which we know is the application's data source for communicating with Oracle:

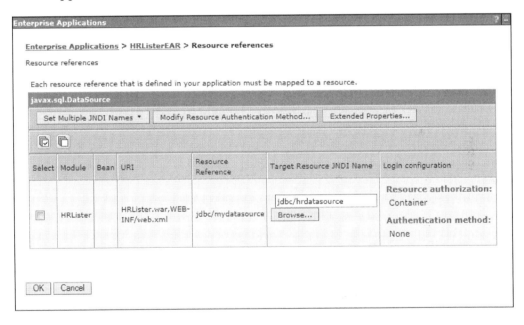

5. Click **Browse** and select the resource reference called **HRDerbyDataSource** from the available list of resource references and click **Apply**. The HR Lister application will now be using a data source that communicates with a Derby DB instead of Oracle. When prompted, click **Save** to ensure that the configuration is set and then restart the application server.

To test that the application is functioning correctly, open the following URL in a browser: `http://<host_name>:9080/hrlister/ listtable?dbtype=derby`

6. The HR application will now list all the system tables of the HR database, as defined by the SYS schema, as seen in the following screenshot:

```
In ListTable Servlet
In getJNDIConnection
Opened connection to Database
Listing Tables...

dbTypeValue=derby
Using Derby List System tables query
SQL=SELECT tablename FROM SYSTABLES
```

| Table Name |
|---|
| COUNTRIES |
| SYSALIASES |
| SYSCHECKS |
| SYSCOLPERMS |
| SYSCOLUMNS |
| SYSCONGLOMERATES |
| SYSCONSTRAINTS |
| SYSDEPENDS |
| SYSDUMMY1 |
| SYSFILES |
| SYSFOREIGNKEYS |
| SYSKEYS |
| SYSROLES |
| SYSROUTINEPERMS |
| SYSSCHEMAS |
| SYSSTATEMENTS |
| SYSSTATISTICS |
| SYSTABLEPERMS |
| SYSTABLES |
| SYSTRIGGERS |
| SYSVIEWS |

```
Closed connection
```

Congratulations, you are now able to connect an application to Derby via JDBC.

# Business-level applications

A business-level application is a logical administration model that provides a definition of an application, as it makes sense to the business. BLAs are stored in the product configuration repository, just like standard JEE applications. A business-level application can contain artifacts such as Java Platform, Enterprise Edition (Java EE) applications or modules, shared libraries, data files, and other business-level applications. You might use a business-level application to group related components or to add capability to an existing application. For example, suppose you want to add new capability to a Java EE application already deployed on a product server. You can add that capability by creating a new business-level application and grouping several JEE artifacts. Each artifact may be an independently-working application and when coupled with another, can extend functionality of the BLA as a whole. In some cases, you do not even need to change the deployed Java EE application configuration to add the capability. However, this will depend on the application design. Another use of BLAs is to manage shared libraries which contain common code. JEE artifacts such as JAR files can be shared as assets between multiple applications.

Before creating a business-level application, you must develop the artifacts to go in the application and configure the target server or cluster. To demonstrate how to configure BLA applications, we will use a sample application called BLAApp, which is a simple web application (WAR). BLAApp.war requires the use of functions contained within a shared library called ServletUtilities.jar. We will create a BLA definition and add the BLAApp.war and ServletUtilities.jar as assets which will be used by the BLA to produce a working web application.

The creation of the BLAs requires these high-level steps:

- Import assets to a repository
- Create a business-level application

# Importing assets

Before creating BLAs, you need to import the assets which will be referenced by the BLS definition. In the following steps, we will import the BLAApp.war and SevletHelpers.jar files for us in our BLA. Both of these files can be downloaded from http://www.packtpub.com.

1. Click on **Applications | Application Types | Assets** from the left-hand navigation panel in the Administrative console:

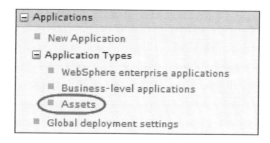

2. Click **New Asset**:

3. Locate the Path to the asset section and click **Browse** to select the BLAApp.war file. Click **Next**.

4. On the **Select options for importing an asset** page, we do not need to specify any settings for our deployment, so click **Next** to continue.

 It is possible to create asset relationships at this stage of the wizard, if other assets have already been uploaded. We will learn how to modify BLA assets in the next section.

5. Review the summary on the **Import an asset to the asset repository** page and click **Finish** to complete the import.

6. Save the changes.

7. Using the same steps mentioned above, import the SevletUtilities.jar file, and click on **Save**.

# Creating a BLA

Once assets have been uploaded to the repository, you can create BLAs which reference one or more assets. The steps below explain how to create a new BLA definition and assign existing assets to the BLA:

1.  Select **Applications | New Application** from the left-hand navigation panel in the Administrative console.

2.  Click **New Business Level Application** to begin the BLA creation wizard:

3.  Enter myBLA in the **Name** field and click **Apply** and **Save** changes.

4.  To view the new BLA, click **Applications | Application Types | Business-level Applications** to be presented with a list of existing BLAs:

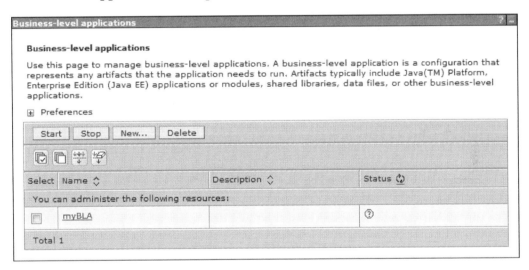

5.  Click on **myBLA**, as shown previously, to enter the BLA properties screen.

6.  Locate the **Deployed assets** section, click **Add**, and then select **Add Asset** from the drop-down list:

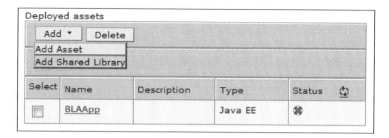

7.  Select the **BLAApp.war** radio option and click **Continue**:

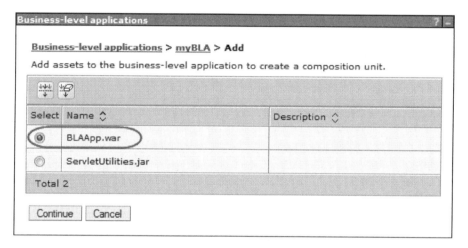

8.  We will now be presented with the standard application deployment wizard. Choose the **Fast Path - Prompt only when additional information is required** option and click **Next** to continue.

9.  On the **Select installation options** screen, you can alter application settings. We have no need to change any of these settings. Leave the default options presented and click **Next**.

10. On the **Map modules to servers** page, ensure that the application is mapped to server01 and click **Next** to continue.

11. On the Map virtual hosts for Web modules page, ensure that the **default_ host Virtual Host** is selected and click **Next**.

12. On the **Metadata for modules** screen, accept the default settings and click **Next** again.

13. Review the summary information presented, click **Finish**, and then click **Save**.

14. You will then be returned to the BLA list screen. This time you will notice that a red cross now appears in the **Status** column, indicating that the **myBLA** application is currently stopped:

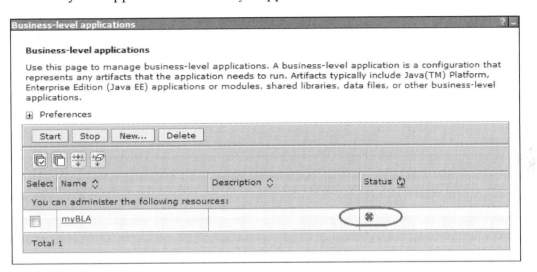

15. Click on the **myBLA** application again to add the SharedUtilities.jar asset to the BLA.

16. Locate the **Deployed assets** section and click **Add**. From within the drop-down list, select **Add Shared Library**:

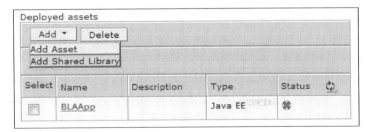

17. Select the **ServletUtilities.jar** radio option and click **Continue**:

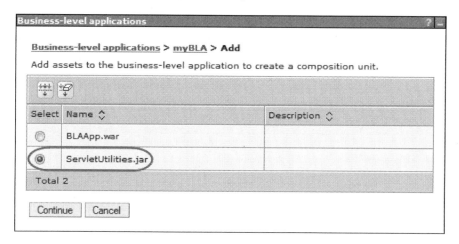

18. On the **Set options settings** screen, you will notice that the name assigned
to this asset is now **ServletUtilities_0001.jar**. WAS does this to create
an internal reference copy for the BLA's class loader management. This
reference copy is known as a **Composition Unit**. Note, we will discuss
more about class loaders in *Chapter 6, Server Configuration*. Click **Next**
to continue:

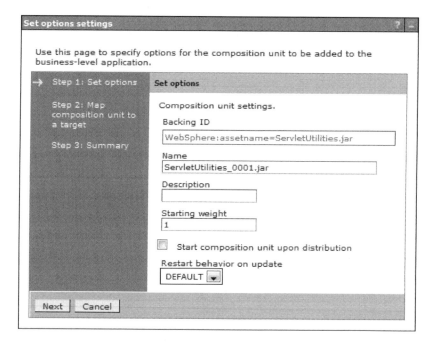

19. The following screen is where we map the BLA's asset to a server. You will notice that the wizard has already selected server01 as the target for the composition unit. Automatic target selection only occurs when there is a single target. At this stage, we only have a target, namely, server01. In *Chapter 9*, *Administrative Features*, we will discuss web server definitions, which are also targets. Click **Next**:

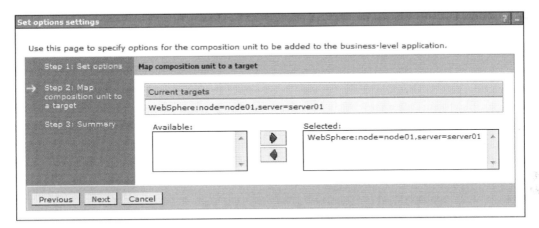

20. On the final screen, review the **Summary**, click **Finish**, and then **Save**.

21. We have added both the BLAApp.war and ServletUtilities.jar as assets to the BLA. Now we need to inform the BLA about the dependency of BLAApp.war to reference the ServletUtilities.jar shared library asset. Click on the **myBLA** link to enter the BLA configuration screen.

22. Click on the **BLAApp.war** link to enter its application configuration screen.

23. Locate the **References** section and click on the **Shared library relationships** link:

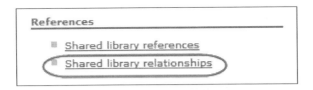

24. The **Assign asset or composition unit IDs as shared libraries to the application or each module screen** is where you can specify asset or composition unit IDs as shared libraries that the application or individual modules reference. If a composition unit ID is specified, it must be part of the business-level application that this enterprise application belongs to. If an asset ID is specified, a composition unit is created from the asset. When editing an application, only composition unit IDs can be specified as shared libraries. Check the entry titled **BLA Application** (Web Module) and click the **Reference shared libraries** button:

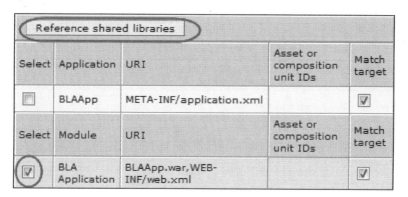

25. In the next screen, ensure that the **ServletUtilities_0001.jar** composition unit is selected, as shown in the following screenshot, and then click **OK**:

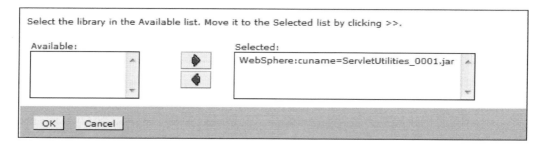

26. The wizard will return to the previous screen where you will notice that the **ServletUtilities_0001.jar** is now related to the BLA Application's web module:

| Select | Module | URI | Asset or composition unit IDs | Match target |
|---|---|---|---|---|
| ☐ | BLA Application | BLAApp.war, WEB-INF/web.xml | WebSphere:cuname=ServletUtilities_0001.jar | ☑ |

27. Click **OK** and **Save** to complete the relationship wizard.

28. You will now be returned to the BLAApp's configuration screen. Click **OK** and then **Save** to return to the BLA listing screen.

29. Before we start the application, we need to ensure that the BLAApp.war (Web Module) has the correct context root.

30. Open the myBLA application and click on the BLAApp link, which is located in the **Deployed assets** list:

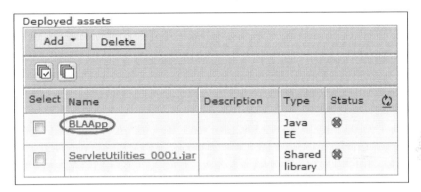

31. Within the BLAApp's configuration screen, locate the **Web Module Properties section** and click on the **Context Root For Web Modules** to set the context root.

32. In the **Context Root For Web Modules** screen, enter the value /bla into the **Context Root** field, as shown in the following screenshot:

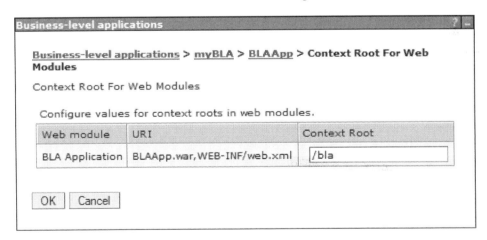

33. Click **OK** and **Save**, and then **Apply** and **Save** to return to the **Business Level Applications** list screen.

34. To start the configured BLA, select **myBLA** and click **Start**:

35. A message will appear stating the myBLA application has started successfully and the **Status** column will contain a green arrow indicating the application was successfully started:

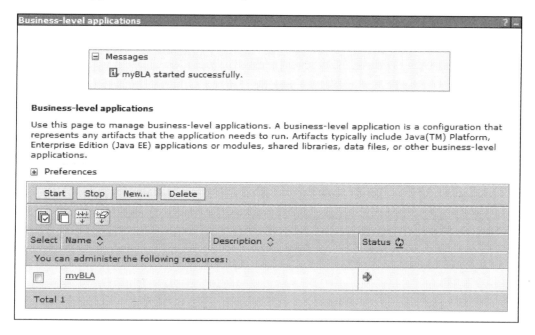

36. To access the running BLA application, open the following URL in a browser:
```
http://<host_name>:9080/bla/getsession
```

37. The result will be a snoop-like application that displays information about your browser's web session:

**Welcome, Newcomer**

**Information on Your Session:**

| Info Type | Value |
|---|---|
| JSESSIONID | AeERDBnezLfeh000kJ8xOu_ |
| Creation Time | Fri Jul 08 04:49:00 BST 2011 |
| Time of Last Access | Fri Jul 08 04:49:00 BST 2011 |
| Number of Previous Accesses | 0 |

Congratulations, you have now successfully installed a Business-level Application and learned how to configure shared library in the process.

# Monitored deployments

IBM has added a great new feature for WAS 8 known as **monitored deployments**. Within the administrative console, it is now possible to set a global deployment setting which allows an administrator to specify a monitored directory. A monitored directory allows an administrator to simply drop an Application EAR file into a monitored folder and WAS will automatically install it. This saves you time, especially in development environments where many deployments may be made in a single day as part of testing new versions of an application. WAS will poll the monitored directory for any new application artifacts that appear and automatically install them. Since we have already installed the DefaultApplication.ear earlier, we will first uninstall it and then re-install it using a monitored directory. You cannot install an application again using the same assigned name if it already exists as an installed application. If you wish to re-install an application and use the same logical name of an application version that is already installed, you must first remove the installed application version before you can install the new version. It is possible, however, to install an application many times, as long as you assign a different logical name to each application during its deployment.

# Uninstalling the DefaultApplication.ear file

To uninstall the DefaultApplication.ear file, carry out the following steps:

1. Click on the **WebSphere enterprise applications** link in the **Application Types** category of the **Applications** section, located in the left-hand side navigation panel of the Administrative console.

2. Within the **Enterprise Applications** screen, select `DefaultApplication.ear`, click the **Uninstall** action button, and click **OK** to confirm.

3. Click **Save** to complete the configuration change.

# Global deployment settings

1. To set the monitored directory which WAS will poll to pick up applications to automatically install, click on the link labeled **Global deployment settings**. This is located in the **Application Types** category of the **Applications** section, as seen in the following screenshot:

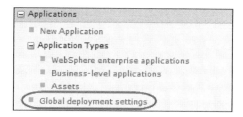

2. You will then be presented with a screen where you will define the location of the monitored directory. Check the option labeled **Monitor directory to automatically deploy applications** and leave the polling interval field set to five seconds, as shown in the following screenshot:

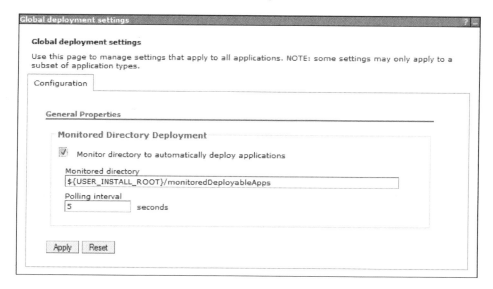

3. Click **Apply** to save the change.

As you can see in the previous screenshot, the default location is a folder called **${USER_INSTALL_ROOT}/monitoredDeployableApps**. You can override this field with any location that you want. Note the use of a WAS environment variable. Using a WAS environment variable means that the configuration knows where the root of the WAS installation is. This is particularly useful in automated scripting where a script can refer to a location as specified by an administrator, as opposed to a pre-specified (hardcoded) location in a deployment script.

A server restart is required. To restart the server, you can use the `startServer` and `stopServer` scripts we covered in *Chapter 1, WebSphere Application Server 8.0: Product Overview*. Once the application server has been restarted, a new folder will appear in the root of your application server's profile directory `<was_profile_root>/monitoredDeployableApps`, for example `<was_root>/profiles/appserv01/monitoredDeployableApps`.

# The MonitoredDeployableApps folder structure

Once monitored deployment has been turned on and the server restarted, there is a set of subfolders created in the `monitoredDeployableApps` folder. The following table explains these subfolders:

| Folder name | Description |
| --- | --- |
| `deploymentProperties` | This folder contains deployment property files which are used by the monitoring process. There needs to be one for every application that requires the use of overriding configuration settings. If no property file(s) contains a reference to an application being installed, then a default install will take place. |
| `servers` | Within the `servers` folder is a folder for each application server instance being monitored. Each folder has the same name for each server. Note, at this stage we have not covered management of multiple application server instances. We cover multi-application server management using the administrative agent in *Chapter 9, Administrative Features*. |

# Drag and drop deploy

To install the `DefaultApplication.ear` file automatically, simply copy the `DefaultApplication.ear` file into the appropriate subfolder which has been configured for your server. An example folder could be similar to the following:
`<was_profile_root>/monitoredDeployableApps/servers/server01`

WAS will automatically detect the new file and install the application. In case you have forgotten, the `DefaultApplication.ear` file is located in the `<was_root>/installableApps` folder.

Looking at the `SystemOut.log`, we can see the effect of a monitored deployment, as shown in the example `SystemOut.log` output below.

**[14/03/11 22:37:07:802 GMT] 0000001d AppManagement I CWLDD0015I: Event id 317949289-1. Application DefaultApplication is installed successfully.**

**[14/03/11 22:37:07:802 GMT] 0000001d AppManagement I CWLDD0020I: Event id 317949289-1. Starting application DefaultApplication...**

**Content removed...**

**[14/03/11 22:37:08:174 GMT] 0000001d webcontainer I com.ibm.ws.webcontainer. VirtualHostImpl addWebApplication SRVE0250I: Web Module Default Web Application has been bound to default_host[*:9080,*:80,*:9443,*:5060,*:5061,*:443].**

**[14/03/11 22:37:08:182 GMT] 0000001d ApplicationMg A WSVR0221I: Application started: DefaultApplication**

**Content removed...**

**[14/03/11 22:37:08:218 GMT] 0000001d WatchService I CWLDD0008I: Event id 317949289-1. End of processing.**

When we next look in the administrative console, we can see that the `DefaultApplication.ear` file has been deployed and started automatically by WAS.

# Controlling monitored deployments

As explained earlier, there is a folder called `deploymentProperties` within the root of the `monitoredDeployableApps` directory. It is possible to create a property file to tell WAS how we want the application deployed, thus giving us the flexibility to change deployment options, which we would normally be offered during a manual console-based install.

# Creating a template properties file

Since creating a properties file is quite involved, it is possible to extract the properties file of an existing deployed enterprise application to use as a template for learning how to correctly craft a property file. The property file can then be used to instruct WAS during monitored deployments. Since we have not yet covered administration scripting, we will defer automatic generation until *Chapter 5, Administrative Scripting*, where we will cover administrative scripting using the Jython language and then re-visit monitored deployment configuration using a properties file.

# Summary

In this chapter, we learned about deploying applications. We deployed two types of applications, one being a simple web application and the other being a data access application which was connected to a database. In this chapter, we focused on Oracle and Derby. However, we know that we could use any other database vendor and WAS can be easily configured to talk to other RDBMS types.

Business-level applications were explained and demonstrated by example. We also learned how to deploy shared libraries as BLA composition units. BLAs allow multiple applications to share common JEE artifacts via the BLA asset management function.

In this chapter, we focused on manual deployments for the installation of an application. Later, in *Chapter 5, Administrative Scripting*, we will cover how to automate deployments using administrative scripting. We also learned about a new feature of WebSphere Application Server 8, which allows a drag and drop style of deployment by simply placing an application artifact in a monitored directory. We will cover more about pre-configuring monitored deployments using scripting at the end of *Chapter 5, Administrative Scripting*. In the next chapter, we will cover WAS security, where we will learn how to secure the WAS environment.

# 4
# Security

Security is an important part of any application server configuration. In this chapter, we will cover how to secure the WebSphere Application Server's Administrative console as well as how to configure different types of repositories containing the users and groups of authorized users that are given different levels of access to administer a WebSphere server.

In this chapter, we will cover the following topics:

- JEE security
- Global security
- File-based standalone custom repository
- Local **Operating System (OS)** repository
- Standalone **Lightweight Directory Access Protocol (LDAP)** repository
- Federated repositories
- Administrative roles
- Security domains
- **Lightweight Third-Party Authentication (LTPA)**
- Managing SSL

# JEE security

WebSphere security is based on the JEE application programming model. The JEE security model is designed to separate the application's need for security and administration of security, allowing applications to be portable between vendors who have a slightly different implementation of the JEE security model. There are two aspects of security that need to be explained:

1. **Authentication** is essentially asking, "Are you who you say you are?"
2. **Authorization** is simply, once we know who you are, "What are you allowed to do?"

WebSphere employs repositories to register and store users and groups. Groups organize users together for a common action and users are assigned as members of groups. Knowing this, we will now move on to learn how to secure our WebSphere server.

# Global security

In *Chapter 1, WebSphere Application Server 8.0: Product Overview*, during the installation process of the WebSphere Application Server, we opted not to turn on global security and thus did not have to supply a password to log in to the Administrative console. We logged in using the username **wasadmin** and we were not prompted for a password. The truth of the matter is that we could have actually used any name, as the console wasn't authenticating us at all. To protect our WAS from unauthorized access, we need to turn on global security.

> It is important to secure the administration of WebSphere, even if the applications being installed are not using security. It is paramount to ensure we have control of our WebSphere environments. The larger your team is, the more important this becomes. In time, other people in your organization will get to know the URLs of your WebSphere servers and, if they are not secured, you cannot really know who is making changes without your approval. Securing the console stops inadvertent access and can ensure that only trained administrators are sanctioned to access and make configurations to environments. This is integral to keeping your WebSphere environment stable.

Here is a brief list of the steps required to implement global security:

1. Verify which supported registries are available for your operating system.

2. Acquire the information required to connect to the user registry.

3. Define the users and groups that will be given administrative access within the selected registry.

4. Define which users will be assigned administrative privileges.

# Global security registry types

Global security is enabled to secure your WAS server, however, to do so requires a user registry. A user registry contains the user and group names for authentication and authorization purposes. Once configured, an application server will connect to the registry and perform lookups to acquire user credentials used in areas where authorization is required.

There are four types of registry which are explained in the following table:

| Registry Type | Description |
| --- | --- |
| **Standalone LDAP registry** | Only uses LDAP-defined users and groups and requires LDAP configuration. |
| **Local operating system** | Specifies the registry for the local OS. |
| **Standalone custom registry** | Allows a custom registry that is essentially based on Java code implementation. |
| **Federated repositories** | Manages users and groups across multiple repositories using a virtual realm. The registries can also be made up of the combinations of the other registry types. |

First, we are going to demonstrate the creation and configuration of a file-based standalone custom repository, then cover use of the local operating system as a repository, followed by our preferred method of using an LDAP repository. For LDAP, we will cover both a standalone LDAP repository and a federated repository which includes an LDAP repository.

# Turning on global security

The following steps will guide you through enabling Global security:

1. To turn on global security, log in to the Admin console and navigate to the **Security** section of the left-hand-side navigation panel and click **Global security**:

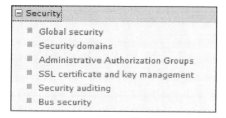

You will now be taken to the main **Global security** configuration page as shown in the following screenshot:

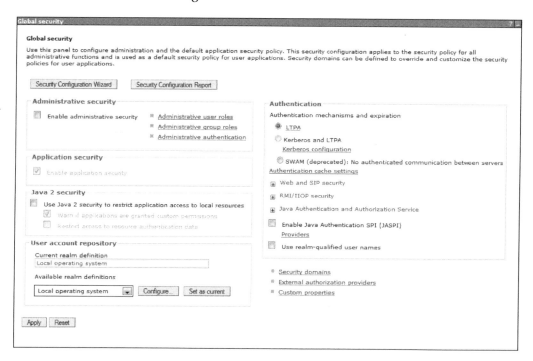

WebSphere provides a wizard to set up basic security using an internal repository. What we are going to do is run the wizard to secure our Admin console.

2.  Click the **Security Configuration Wizard** button, as shown in the previous screenshot. You will be presented with an option to decide on the extent of your security protection. Leave the screen options set to their default and click **Next** to move on to the next page, where you will select which type of repository you wish to use.

> The **Use Java 2 security to restrict application access to local resources** option, as seen in the **Security Configuration Wizard**, is used when you do not trust the application's code. Since, in most cases, you trust the code you are installing in your EAR/WAR files, you do not need to turn this option on.

3.  On the **Select user repository** page, you have four types of repository to choose from, as described previously.

> The default repository is built into WebSphere and is based on the platform you are running on.

The simplest way to provide administrative security is to use a file-based standalone custom registry. In our first example, we are going to start by selecting **Standalone custom registry** during our use of the Global security wizard, as shown in the following screenshot:

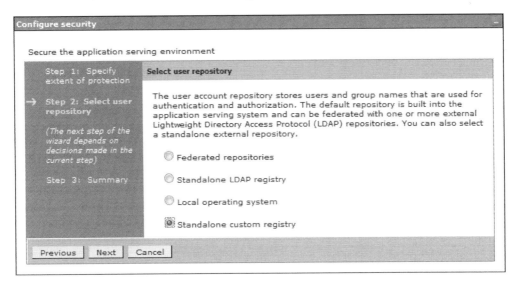

4. Select **Standalone custom registry** in the **Select user repository** screen and click **Next**.

   Before we continue with the wizard we need to set up two property files—one for users and one for groups. These properties files will contain authorized users and groups. Our custom registry will use these two files.

5. We need to create a folder within the WebSphere filesystem called `<was_root>/fileRegistry`. In this folder, we will create a file called `user.props`, with the following contents:

```
# Format:
# name:passwd:uid:gids:display name
# where name    = userId/userName of the user
#       passwd = password of the user
#       uid    = uniqueId of the user
#       gid    = groupIds of the groups that the user belongs to
#       display name = a (optional) display name for the user.
wasadmin:wasadmin:101:101:WebSphere Administrator
```

6. We will then create a second file named `group.props`; the contents of the file will be as follows:

```
# Format:
# name:gid:users:display name
# where name    = groupId of the group
#       gid    = uniqueId of the group
#       users  = list of all the userIds that the group contains
#       display name = a (optional) display name for the group.
admins:101:wasadmin:Administrative group
```

 You need to ensure that any new files you create are assigned appropriate rights using chmod and chown on Linux to ensure WebSphere processes can read the file. This is not a requirement in Windows as files are accessible by default.

7. In the **Configure standalone custom registry** page, type **wasadmin** in the **Primary administrative user name** and add two properties. The **usersFile** property will point to the `user.props` file and the **groupsFile** property will point to the location of the `group.props` file, as seen in the following screenshot:

**Custom registry class name** is already filled in with a Java class that exists in the internals of WebSphere and which contains the code for WebSphere to use the `user.props` and `group.props` files. We will not go into detail as to how this class is internally coded; it is beyond the scope of this book as it involves discussing Java programming.

8. Click **Next** to view the summary, and then click **Finish** to complete your file-based repository, while remembering to **Save** your configuration when prompted to do so.

9. For the security configuration change to take effect, you will now need to restart WAS. When you next try to log in to the Administrative console, you will be prompted for a username and password.

Now that you have enabled global security, you will also notice that your application server will have issues while starting and stopping via the command line; this is because, once Global security is enabled, a username and password is required to stop an application server.

Let's say you are trying to stop the application server using the stop shell script we learned in *Chapter 1, WebSphere Application Server 8.0: Product Overview*:

- **For Linux:**

  `<was_profile_root>/bin/stopServer.sh server01`

- **For Windows:**

  `<was_profile_root>\bin\stopServer.bat server01`

You will now be presented with a pop-up dialog that requires you to enter a username and password before you can stop the server. An example of what the dialog looks like is shown in the following screenshot:

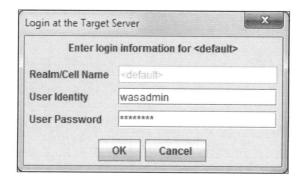

It can be very annoying having to continuously type in a username and password every time you bounce your server. To stop this, we can alter a file called `soap.client.props`.

The `soap.client.props` file is located in the `<was_profile_root>/properties` folder, as shown in the following screenshot:

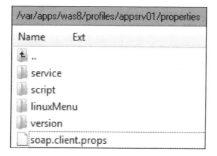

10. Edit the file using the `vi` command (if using Linux, or your preferred text editor if using Windows) and change the `com.ibm.SOAP.securityEnabled` setting's value from `false` to `true`. Change the `com.ibm.SOAP.loginUserid` setting's value to `com.ibm.SOAP.loginUserid=wasadmin` and the `com.ibm.SOAP.loginPassword` setting value to `wasadmin`.

The changes just made can be seen in the following code:

```
com.ibm.SOAP.securityEnabled=true
com.ibm.SOAP.authenticationTarget=BasicAuth
com.ibm.SOAP.loginUserid=wasadmin
com.ibm.SOAP.loginPassword=wasadmin
```

11. Save the `soap.client.props` file. Now when you stop and start WAS, you will no longer be prompted for a username and password. We will cover encoding the administrative password in *Chapter 10, Administrative tools.*

Linux users may see the following error:

**ADMU0116I: Tool information is being logged in file**

**/apps/was8/profiles/appsrv01/logs/server01/stopServer.log**

**ADMU0128I: Starting tool with the appsrv01 profile**

**ADMU3100I: Reading configuration for server: server01**

**X connection to localhost: 10.0 broken (explicit kill or server shutdown).**

If you do get an **X connection** error while trying to stop a server, it means that a login pop-up dialog cannot be displayed for the user to authenticate with, as X Windows is not running. One solution could be to simply run XMing, the X11 server we used in *Chapter 1, WebSphere Application Server 8.0: Product Overview.* Once X11 is running, the next time you try to stop a server, a login pop-up dialog will allow you to type in the username and password.

12. Once global security is enabled, when you try to log in to the standard login URL `http://<host_name>:9060/ibm/console`, you will be presented with a screen informing you that you are being redirected to a secure site. A warning that you have received a **Secure Sockets Layer (SSL)** certificate from an unknown **Certificate Authority (CA)** will be shown in the browser.

If you have problems getting to the port 9060, then it might be because the console wants to redirect to port 9043 (the secure HTTP port for the Admin console), now that we have global security enabled. You might need to change your firewall configuration or temporarily turn off your firewall while you are trying the exercises.

You may need to alter both your workstation and server firewall settings.

13. If you are using Internet Explorer, click **Continue to this website (not recommended)**; if you are using Firefox, click **I Understand the Risks** and then add and confirm a security exception.

 Browser versions change and each vendor might show different SSL certificate warnings, worded in different ways, with slightly different recommendations, to solve the problem. Be aware, all they are trying to do is alert you to the fact that the SSL certificates come from an un-trusted certificate authority and you have the choice to continue or not.

14. After you have opted to continue, trusting the SSL certificate, you will then be redirected to the administrative login screen, as shown in the following screenshot. However, it will now be using the following secure administrative URL. Note the use of the HTTPS protocol and the port **9043**, as shown in the following screenshot:

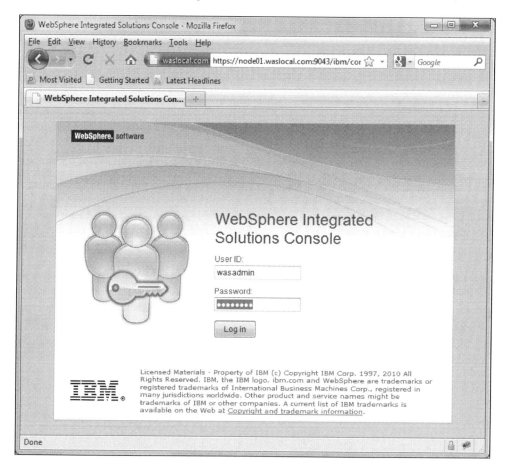

15. Type **wasadmin** for the username and **wasadmin** for the password, and click **Log in** to gain access to the Administrative console.

Implementing a file-based repository requires the least effort and can often seem the best way to secure WebSphere. However, being a file-based repository, it means that anyone who has access to the operating system can gain access to the props files containing your usernames and groups and alter the files. Using a file-based repository is not recommended for production. In our next example, we are going to discuss how to use the local operating system as our security manager for users and groups.

# Local operating system

We are now going to turn on global security with the **Local operating system** option, which is the default option in the security configuration wizard. We mentioned in *Chapter 2, Installing WebSphere Application Server* that installing WAS to run as root on Linux platforms is not ideal and not the most secure way to run WebSphere in Linux. However, to use the local Linux operating system as a user registry, we need to have WebSphere running as root.

For Windows users, WebSphere must be running under a user with administrative privileges. Since root/administrative access is required for local operating system usage, it means it is not the best method for production environments, because it requires a lower level of administration and is not easily managed. This method can be a good way to secure a local desktop version of WebSphere when you are testing configurations.

Using a federated LDAP repository is a better method and more suitable to production-like environments. LDAP repositories will be covered after this section.

This time, in the **Global security** wizard, select **Local operating system** on the **Secure the application serving environment** page and click **Next** to configure the local operating system. Type `wasadmin` into the **Primary administrative user name** field and click **Next** to review the **summary** page. Click **Finish** on the summary page to complete the wizard.

You should now receive the following error message:

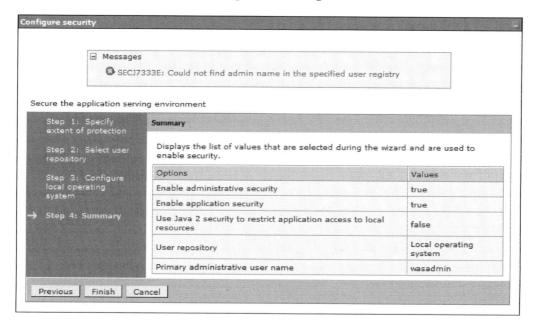

The reason for this error is that the `wasadmin` user does not exist as a user in the local operating system, and so we cannot complete the wizard. We need to create a user in our chosen operating system. The following sections provide details specific to both Linux and Windows.

# Creating a Linux user and group

By using the `addUser` Linux command, we can add a new user and password. To create a new user, we must also create an associated group that the user must belong to. The `groupadd` command is used to create a new group account. The new group will be entered into the system files as required, with appropriate configuration files being updated.

 There are two types of groups: a **primary user group** and a **secondary group**. All user account- related information is stored in `/etc/passwd`, `/etc/shadow`, and `/etc/group` files. Consult the Linux documentation for use of groups.

All Linux OS user accounts must belong to a group. So first, we are going to create a group called was by typing the following command into an SSH session to our Linux box:

```
/usr/sbin/groupadd was
```

To create a user, use the useradd command to add a new user and automatically add the user to an existing group (or create a new group and then add the user).

If the group does not exist, create it. The syntax for creating a group is useradd -g {group-name} username. Please note that the small -g option means adding the new user to the initial login group (primary group). The group name must exist. Type the following command to create a new user called wasadmin and add wasadmin to the was group:

```
/usr/sbin/useradd wasadmin -g was
```

We can check to see that the user is created by typing the following command:

```
cat /etc/passwd | cut -d":" -f1
```

You will find the user wasadmin listed at the end of the screen output, as a result of executing the previous command.

You now need to run the following command as root, to assign a password to the user named wasadmin:

```
passwd
```

The command will prompt you to enter a password; enter wasadmin. The user wsadmin now has this set as their password.

For the WebSphere Application Server Local OS security registry to work on Linux, a shadow password file must exist. The shadow password file is named shadow and is located in the /etc directory. If the shadow password file does not exist, then an error occurs while trying to complete the local OS global security option.

To create the shadow file, run the following Linux command:

```
pwconv
```

A /etc/shadow file will be created from the /etc/passwd file. After creating the shadow file, you can continue with the wizard to configure the local operating system security.

# Creating a Windows user

If you have chosen to use Windows, the process of creating a user is much simpler. To create a user called `wasadmin`, open **Windows Computer Management**. You can load the Computer Management console by simply right-clicking on the computer icon available in Windows Explorer as shown in the following screenshot:

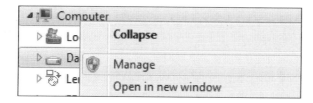

One you have loaded the **Computer Management** applet, you can right-click the **Users** folder which is located in the **Users and Group** category on the left-hand-side of the applet as shown in the following screenshot:

In the **New User...** dialog, enter **wasadmin** in the **User Name** field and `wasadmin` in the **Password** and **Confirm password** fields, as shown in the following screenshot, and check the **Password never expires** checkbox. Click **Create** and then **Close**:

You have now added a local user to the Windows operating system that WAS can use for authentication. Carry on with the security wizard.

 Avoid trouble: On Windows, the application server must be started with Administrator privileges if you chose to start WAS using a command prompt. If you start WAS as a service then this is not an issue.

## Completing the security wizard

Once you have created a local user and a shadow file using the basic Linux user/group administration, or simple Windows user administration, as outlined previously, we can use this new user's name in the security wizard and we will be able to complete the wizard's process.

 You may have to start the wizard again if you took too long and the console timed out. If so, restart the local OS global security process using the wizard and remember to save your configuration once you have completed the wizard.

Once the **Global security** wizard is complete, you need to stop and start (bounce) the application server for security to take effect. Once WAS has started backup, we will now be presented with a login screen, which will be the same as in the file-based example previously shown.

We have now learned how to secure a WebSphere Application Server using the local operating system. However, this means that the user will only exist on this physical machine and, in reality, this is not practical in an environment where there are many Linux/Unix or Windows machines running WAS.

Also, you may wish to allow many different types of users to access the console with different rights, and so administration becomes difficult with many users. Using an OS-based authentication method would mean you would be continually updating your local OS with the required user accounts for each separate machine on your network on which WAS is installed.

For security reasons, most Linux/Unix administrators rarely permit processes to run as root. Since most production WAS server processes are not running as the root user, the local OS approach is not practical. It is recommended best practice for WAS Administrators to employ a user directory which can be shared by all WAS servers. This is why WAS should primarily be configured to use an LDAP (Lightweight Directory Access Protocol) directory.

LDAP provides the ability to have a centrally-administrated user and group directory independent from WAS. Using a central user directory allows administration of passwords without worrying about how many server machines have to be updated to allow user management. It can be tedious if you have to go around and update each server's local user accounts when you want to change your WAS administration password. Common sense dictates that you also don't want a different password each time you log in to a different instance of WebSphere Application Server.

WebSphere Application Server distinguishes between the user identities for administrators who manage the environment, and server identities for authenticating server-to-server communications. In most cases, server identities are automatically generated and are not stored in a repository.

# Standalone LDAP

LDAP registries can handle the large scale and high performance needs of enterprise applications. For production environments, an LDAP registry is the recommended approach for user and group management. What we will cover in the next few pages is how to configure WAS to use an LDAP registry, as opposed to the less secure file-based security option.

Using LDAP requires the use of an LDAP directory. There are many products in the marketplace and your organization will most probably have a solution from one of the more well-known vendors. Two commonly-used LDAP products are Microsoft's **ADAM**, which is a light-weight implementation of Active Directory, and IBM's **Tivoli Directory Server**. Both of these products are examples of commercially available LDAP directory servers. There are also open source products such as **ApacheDS LDAP** and **OpenLDAP**. Using open source LDAP implementations is not officially supported by IBM, however, they can be useful for proof-of-concept environments.

# Sample directory tree

To implement a standalone LDAP registry, you will need to install and configure an appropriate LDAP directory server of your choice. You must also configure appropriate users and groups required for WAS to implement global security using the LDAP directory. For the purpose of describing how to configure a standalone LDAP registry we will be referring to an example directory tree representing a set of fictitious users and groups. The following directory tree represents a made-up organization's directory tree:

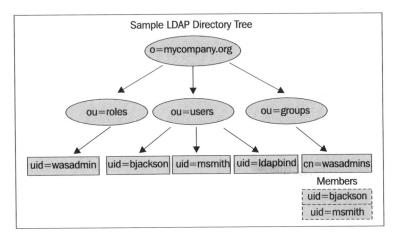

In the following section, we will refer to user identities from the sample directory tree seen previously.

# LDAP object classes

There are many ways in which LDAP directory trees can be organized and what you go with will depend on your company's naming standards and requirements. Each directory tree contains entries representing entities such as users and groups. Object classes serve as an attribute template. The object classes assigned to an entity specify a collection of required or optional attributes, which define the entity within the LDAP directory.

The LDAP standard provides these basic types of object classes:

- People in the directory
- Groups in the directory, including unordered lists of individual objects or groups of objects
- Locations, such as the country name and description
- Organizations in the directory

An example list of attributes and object classes to define a user called Bob Jackson are as follows:

```
dn: cn=Bob Jackson,ou=users,o=mycompany.org

cn: cn=Bob Jackson

uid: bjackson

mail: bjackson@mycompany.org

objectclass: top

objectclass: person

objectclass: organizationalPerson

objectclass: inetOrgPerson

userpassword: password

sn: Jackson

givenname: Bob

telephonenumber: 123456789

title: WebSphere Administrator
```

It is important that you understand the attributes and object classes used in your LDAP directory to correctly configure LDAP connection settings and LDAP filters for WAS. Configuring the LDAP connection and LDAP filters settings will become clear in the next section.

# Configuring an LDAP registry in WebSphere

Before we continue, we need to explain the primary administrator user ID. One of the details common to all user registries or repositories is the primary administrative username. This ID is a member of the chosen repository, but also has special privileges on the WebSphere Application Server. The privileges for this ID and the privileges that are associated with the administrative role ID are the same. The primary administrative username can access all of the protected administrative methods of WebSphere.

For Windows users: The primary administrator ID must not be the same name as the machine name of your system because the repository sometimes returns machine-specific information when querying a user of the same name.

When configuring standalone LDAP registries, as we are about to, it is important to verify that the Primary administrative username is a member of the repository and not just the LDAP administrative role ID. The Primary administrative username does not run WebSphere Application Server processes. Rather, the process ID runs the WebSphere Application Server processes. As discussed in *Chapter 2, Installing WebSphere Application Server*, a process ID is determined by the way the process starts. For example, if you use a command line to start processes, the user ID that is logged in to the system is the process ID. If running as a service, the user ID that is logged in to the system is the user ID running the service. If you choose the local operating system registry, the process ID requires special privileges to call the operating system APIs. The process ID must be assigned the platform-specific privileges on the OS where WebSphere is installed.

Standalone LDAP repositories must contain the primary administrative user ID; otherwise, you will not be able to log in to the administrative console.

Now that we have covered a few formal points about the primary administrator we can configure WebSphere to use a standalone LDAP repository.

## LDAP security settings

In our examples, we have chosen to use a pre-configured Tivoli Directory Server as our LDAP server. If you wish to follow these steps exactly, an LDIF file is available from download from `http://www.packtpub.com`. You can import this LDIF file into your own LDAP server to re-create the sample directory tree seen in the previous section.

Follow these steps to configure WAS to use a stand-alone LDP repository:

1. Navigate to the **Security** section of the left-hand-side panel in the Administrative console and click on **Global security**.

2. In the **Security** page, under the **User account repository** section, select **Standalone LDAP registry** from the **Available realm definitions** list and click **Configure** to enter the **Standalone LDAP registry** settings page. Here, you can configure all the appropriate settings for WAS to use an LDAP repository. As shown in the next screenshot, type **wasadmin** in the **Primary administrative user name** field. This is the primary user WebSphere will use for the server identity.

 For users using the sample LDIF tree, the password for wasadmin is `wasadmin`.

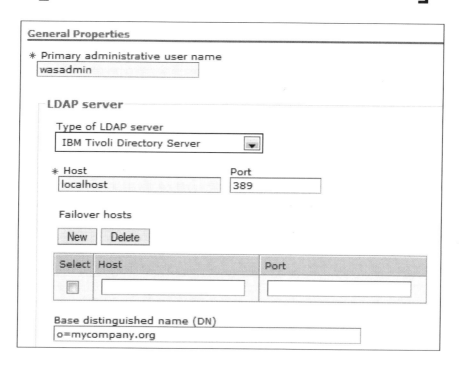

3. In the LDAP server section, choose an appropriate LDAP server type from the **Type of LDAP server** list. There are several pre-configured LDAP server types which are tuned for common LDAP servers. If you are not sure of the type of LDAP server you are using, you can choose the custom option. In our examples, we have chosen the **IBM Tivoli Directory Server** option because we are using Tivoli Directory Server as our LDAP directory. If you decide not to use Tivoli Directory Server, ensure that you modify settings appropriately.

4. Next, specify the **Host** and **Port** of the LDAP server and an optional **Base Distinguished Name (DN)**. The Base distinguished name (DN) indicates the starting point for LDAP searches within the LDAP directory tree.

Following is a table of settings used in the example:

| Field name | Value entered |
| --- | --- |
| Host | **localhost** |
| | (We can use localhost because the LDAP server is installed on the same machine as WebSphere. If this is not the case in your setup, then change accordingly) |
| Port | **339** |
| | (Default LDAP port) |
| **Base distinguished Name (DN)** | **o=mycompany.org** |
| | (The base DN is where the LDAP bind will start searches) |

5. Next, we need to complete the **Security** section located on the right-hand side of the page. In this section, we have two fields to fill in. **Bind distinguished name (DN)** is the name which WebSphere will use to connect to LDAP for name searches. The **Bind password** is the password for this user. If you have chosen to import the sample LDIF file, fill in these fields with the appropriate values shown in the following screenshot. If you have not chosen to use the sample directory tree, then modify it according to your needs:

In production systems, you would use a non-LDAP administration user as your bind username. Normally, a separate LDAP user is used for WebSphere connection binding.

The following table lists the values used in the example:

| Field name | Value entered |
| --- | --- |
| **Bind distinguished name (DN)** | `cn=ldapbind,ou=users,o=mycompany.org` |
| **Bind password** | `ldapadmin` |

 If no name is specified for the **Bind distinguished name (DN)**, the application server binds anonymously. The LDAP server must be setup to allow anonymous binding.

6. Once you have completed filling in the required fields, click **Apply** and you will then be prompted with the following message:

---

⊟ Messages

⚠ After changing the active user registry settings, click Apply on the Global security panel.

⚠ Changes have been made to your local configuration. You can:

- <u>Save</u> directly to the master configuration.

- <u>Review</u> changes before saving or discarding.

⚠ The server may need to be restarted for these changes to take effect.

---

7. Click **Save**.

8. Before we can complete our LDAP configuration, we need to look at the default LDAP search filters. To edit the advanced LDAP settings, click on **Advanced Lightweight Directory Access Protocol (LDAP) user registry settings** in the configuration page for a **Standalone LDAP Registry**, as shown in the following screenshot:

---

**Additional Properties**

▦ <u>Advanced Lightweight Directory Access Protocol (LDAP) user registry settings</u>

---

9. Within the **Advanced Lightweight Directory Access Protocol (LDAP) user registry settings** screen, you will now be presented with the option to change LDAP attributes:

```
General Properties
  User filter
  (&(uid=%v)(objectclass=inetOrgPerson))

  Group Filter
  (&(cn=%v)(|(objectclass=groupOfNames)(objectclass=groupOfUniqueNames)))

  User ID map
  *:uid

  Group ID map
  *:cn

  Group member ID map
  ibm-allGroups:member;ibm-allGroups:uniqueMember;groupOfNames:member;gro
```

10. A default set of predefined filters exists, which are provided for each LDAP server that the WAS supports. You can modify these filters to fit your LDAP configuration. The **User filter** field contains an LDAP string, which provides the LDAP search filter that is used to obtain information about users and groups from an LDAP directory server. If you are using the sample directory tree, you will need to change the **User filter** field from **(&(uid=%v)(objectclass=ePerson))** to **(&(uid=%v)(objectclass=inetOrgPerson))** as shown in the previous screenshot, to ensure that WAS queries the Tivoli Directory Server's LDAP tree correctly. If you have not used the sample LDAP tree, you will need to ensure that the LDAP filters are correctly set for your LDAP directory. Click **OK** to return to the **Global security** screen.

11. Once again, you are informed that the server needs restarting for the repository to take effect. Click **Save** but, before you restart, it is wise to click the **Test connection** button located at the top of the screen, just above the **General properties** section, to ensure that your LDAP bind settings are correct. If your configuration is correct, a message is displayed at the top of the page, similar to the one shown in the next screenshot.

 If an error occurs, a corresponding message will be displayed. Common cause(s) of connection failure are the ports being incorrect or blocked by a firewall, and/or bind name and password details are incorrect:

```
Messages
  The test connection operation for LDAP host node01.waslocal.com on port 10389 was successful.
```

12. From within the current **Standalone LDAP registry** settings page, click **OK** to accept all the settings. You will be returned to the **Global security** page.

13. Within the **Global security** page, ensure that **Standalone LDAP registry** is selected from the **Available realm definition** pick-list and click the **Set as current** button, as shown in the following screenshot:

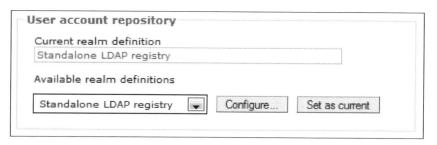

14. Click **Apply** and you will be prompted to save the configuration. Click **Save** to save the security changes to the master configuration.

15. Restart WAS for the LDAP settings to take effect.

# Security.xml

So where are the LDAP security settings stored? Before we continue, it is a good time to quickly understand where the LDAP repository configuration is located within the WAS filesystem. The reason we need to know where the LDAP settings are stored is because if you enable LDAP and something goes wrong, you will not be able to log in to the control panel any longer. Knowing what file contains the LDAP settings will allow you to correct mistakes by editing this file. The file to take note of is called `security.xml`. This is an important file because it is where WAS will store security information for user registries. This file is located in the following folder path:
`<was_profile_root>/config/cells/<cell_name>`.

**Downloading the example code**

You can download the example code files for all Packt books you have purchased from your account at `http://www.PacktPub.com`. If you purchased this book elsewhere, you can visit `http://www.PacktPub.com/support` and register to have the files e-mailed directly to you.

Looking at the **userRegistries** stanza contained within security.xml, you will see the LDAP **baseDN**, **bindDN**, and **userFilter** settings specified. The following is a snippet of XML from security.xml showing the configuration from the previous section.

```
<userRegistries xmi:type="security:LDAPUserRegistry"
  xmi:id="LDAPUserRegistry_1" serverId="" serverPassword="{xor}"
  realm="localhost:389" ignoreCase="true" useRegistryServerId="false"
  primaryAdminId="wasadmin" useRegistryRealm="true" type="CUSTOM"
  sslEnabled="false" sslConfig=""baseDN="o=mycompany.org "
  bindDN="cn=ldapbind,ou=users,o=mycompany.org"
  bindPassword="{xor}Mzs+Lz47MjYx" searchTimeout="120"
  reuseConnection="true">
<searchFilter xmi:id="LDAPSearchFilter_1"
  userFilter="(&amp;(uid=%v)(objectclass=inetOrgPerson))"
  krbUserFilter="(&amp;(krbPrincipalName=%v)(objectclass=person))"
  groupFilter="(&amp;(cn=%v)(|(objectclass=groupOfNames)
  (objectclass=groupOfUniqueNames)))" userIdMap="*:uid"
  groupIdMap="*:cn" groupMemberIdMap="ibm-allGroups:member;
  ibm-allGroups:uniqueMember;groupOfNames:member;
  groupOfUniqueNames:uniqueMember" certificateMapMode="EXACT_DN"
  certificateFilter=""/>
<hosts xmi:id="EndPoint_1300479955511" host="localhost"
  port="10389"/>
</userRegistries>
```

 Be careful while editing files such as security.xml and do not do so unless you are certain about the outcome. A rule of thumb is to never edit these files manually.

# Administrative roles

Once LDAP is configured, we need a way to assign different levels of privileges to different users, thus controlling what groups of people can do within the Administrative console. You may want some people to have only the ability to start and stop applications; others you may wish to allow full configuration access. WAS implements delegating privileges through the use of administrative roles. There are eight predefined roles in WebSphere Application Server 8, as outlined in the following table, which the users are mapped to:

| Administrative Role | Description |
| --- | --- |
| Monitor | A user or group with the monitor role can do the following:<br><br>• View the WebSphere Application Server configuration<br>• View the current state of the Application Server |

| Administrative Role | Description |
|---|---|
| Configurator | Assigned monitor privilege plus the ability to configure. For example, a user assigned the configurator role can do the following:<br><br>• Create a resource<br><br>• Map an application server<br><br>• Install and uninstall an application<br><br>• Deploy an application<br><br>• Assign users and groups to role mapping for applications<br><br>• Set up Java 2 security permissions for applications |
| Operator | Assigned monitor privileges and can stop and start the server and monitor the server status in the Administrative console. |
| Administrator | An individual or group assigned this role will have the operator and configurator privileges, plus additional privileges that are granted for administration. |
| Iscadmins | Available to Administrative console users. Users who are granted this role have administrator privileges for managing users and groups in the federated repositories. |
| Deployer | Use this role to grant users the ability to completely deploy an application and configure application runtime settings. |
| Admin Security Manager | By using the Admin Security Manager role, you can assign users and groups to the administrative user roles and administrative group roles. |
| Auditor | This role allows users to modify the configuration settings for security auditing and the role includes the monitor role. This allows the auditor to view but not change the rest of the security configuration. |

 Users and groups can be added or removed from administrative roles using the WebSphere Application Server Administrative console by a user given the appropriate authority. The administrator role is for this purpose.

# Mapping users and groups to administrative roles

In the following examples we are using fictitious users as defined in the sample LDAP tree earlier. If you have not imported the sample LDIF then replace the example user names with the appropriate usernames used within your own LDAP directory tree.

In this example scenario, we wish to give some basic administrative access to a user known as Bob Jackson. To do this, we must assign him a user role. We are going to use the Operator role, which limits many of the administrative options available to Bob.

To manage administrative user roles, log in to the Administrative console and follow these steps:

1. Locate the **Administrative security** section of the **Global security** page, where we started our global security configuration.

2. Clicking the **Administrative user roles** link will take us to a configuration page, which will allow us to assign administrative roles to our LDAP users. As seen in the following screenshot, we already have a role assigned to wasadmin because it was set to be the primary administrative user in our global security configuration:

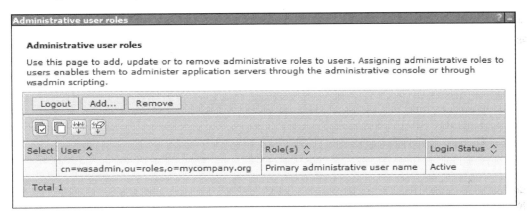

3. To add a new role mapping, click **Add** and you will be directed to a screen where you can assign other LDAP users to other roles. We want to assign the **Operator** role to the LDAP user named **Bob Jackson**.

4. Within the **Administrative user roles** screen select **Operator** from the **Role(s)** pick-list and type **bjackson\*** in the **Search string** field. When you click **Search**, a query will be made to the LDAP directory using the wildcard filter to look for any user whose uid starts with bjackson. The result of the search will return matches. The users found in LDAP that match the find will be listed in the **Available** field. Note the reason why uid is used is because the current LDAP user filter is set as follows:
   (&(uid=%v)(objectclass=inetOrgPerson))

5.  Select the user **Bob Jackson** from the **Available** field and click the arrow pointing right to assign **Bob Jackson** the **Operator** role. You will see the user move from the **Available** list to the **Mapped role** list:

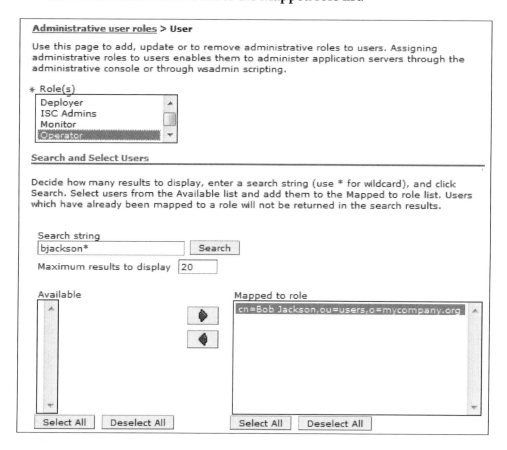

6.  Click **OK** to return to the **Administrative user roles** screen. You will see the new user role mapping as follows:

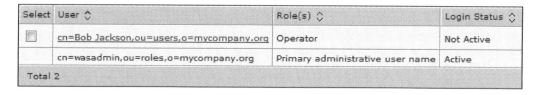

| Select | User ◇ | Role(s) ◇ | Login Status ◇ |
|---|---|---|---|
| ☐ | cn=Bob Jackson,ou=users,o=mycompany.org | Operator | Not Active |
| | cn=wasadmin,ou=roles,o=mycompany.org | Primary administrative user name | Active |
| Total 2 | | | |

7.  Click **Save** to save the new role-mapping to the master configuration. Bob Jackson can now log in to the Administrative console as a user who has the ability to only start and stop applications, as explained by the operator definition earlier in this section.

8. Click the **Logout** link located in the top section of the Admin console and log back in as Bob. Note, for readers who are using the sample LDIF tree, Bob's password will be `password`. Once logged in, the **Welcome** screen will show a message stating that this user has limited administrative rights.

> The login User ID in our examples uses the `uid` attribute, as defined in our LDAP configuration. So, for Bob, his `uid` is bobjackson, so this is his User ID for logging into the Admin console. By using this knowledge, you can configure your LDAP by adding your own custom objects and WebSphere LDAP settings in order to ensure the configuration filters use these settings, and control what style of User ID are required for login names. Often, large organizations employ a global directory, which is used for both desktop logins and e-mail; it is possible to federate your organization's global directory if it supports LDAP being used by WAS.

9. Navigate to the **WebSphere enterprise applications** screen and you will see that there are only three options available—**Start**, **Stop**, and **Rollout Update**. If you navigate to the Global security section, which we were editing earlier, you will notice that Bob does not have privileges to alter security settings.

You can now log the Bob Jackson user out and log in again using `wasadmin`, to gain full administration capabilities.

# Federated repositories

In WebSphere it is possible to federate repositories allowing a single virtual repository from which to query user accounts. What we are now going to do is federate the internal file-based repository and a newly-created LDAP repository.

This technique is often used for adding a default set of administrative users to the internal file-base repository so, if the LDAP server is not available, administrators can still log in to WAS. Another application of federated repositories is separating administrative users and application users. An example could be that you can have one repository dedicated for admin users and another repository for your corporate users, that is, the users who will actually use applications deployed to WebSphere.

The following steps demonstrate how to configure a federated repository:

1. To begin the process of creating our federated repository, navigate to the **Global security** and click on the Security Configuration wizard:

2. In the **Step 1** of the security wizard, accept the default settings and click **Next**.

 At the least, this task provides for secure administration. However, administrative security alone does not provide full security. In most production environments, it is recommended that you also enable application and resource security.

3. On the **Select user repository** screen, choose **Federated repositories** from the list of available options:

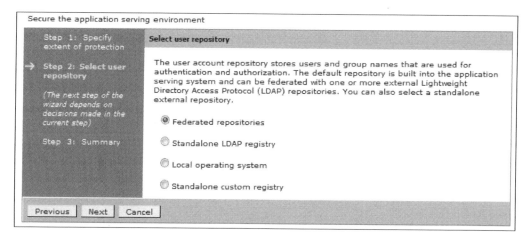

4.  On the **Configure federated repository** screen, enter `wasadminlocal` in the **Primary administrative user name** field and enter `wasadminlocal` for the password. We use `wasadminlocal` because we have wsadmin defined as a user in LDAP. We need a different user identity for the internal file-based registry to stop principal name clashes.

5.  Click **Next** and then **Finish** and **Save**. Global security has now been enabled for federated security configuration.

6.  Locate the **User account** section. **Federated repositories** should already be set in the **Available realm definition** pick-list. Click the **Configure** button as shown in the following screenshot:

7.  Locate the **Related Items** section at the bottom of the **Federated repositories** screen and click **Manage respositories**:

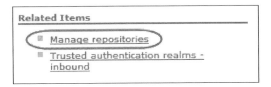

8.  You will now be presented with a list of managed repositories. Click **Add** and select **LDAP repository** from the list:

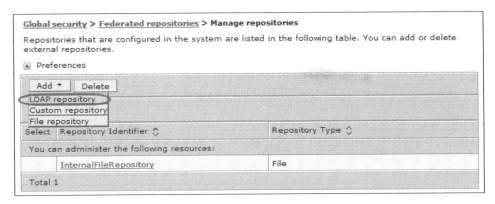

9. When the **New** LDAP repository screen appears, fill in the following fields and values as listed in the following table:

| Field name | Value entered |
|---|---|
| **Repository identifier** | LDAP |
| **Directory type** | Custom |
| **Primary host name** | localhost |
| **Port** | 389 |
| **Bind distinguished name** | cn=ldapbind,ou=users,o=mycompany.org |
| **Bind password** | ldapbind |
| **Login properties** | cn (if you require other properties then separate with a semicolon, for example, cn;uid) |

 These settings are derived from the previous section on configuring a standalone LDAP repository explained earlier in the chapter.

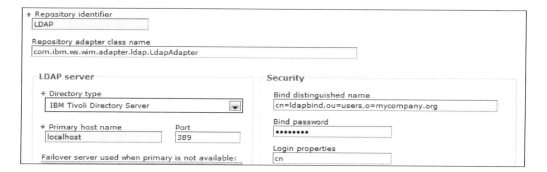

10. Once you have entered all the previous values, click **OK**, and then **Save**. You will be redirected to the **Manage repositories** screen. You will now see an entry for the LDAP repository:

| | InternalFileRepository | File |
|---|---|---|
| ☐ | LDAP | LDAP:IDS |

11. Click the **Federated repositories** link located at the top of the **Manage repositories** screen to return to the Federated repositories screen:

> Global security > Federated repositories > **Manage repositories**

12. We are now going to add an LDAP realm to include the new LDAP repository. Click **Add base entry to Realm** then, on the **Repository reference** screen, click on the **Add Repository** pick-list and select **LDAP** from the **Repository** list. Enter o=mycompany.org in the **Distinguished name of a base entry that uniquely identifies this set of entries in the realm** field. This assigns an internal DN to uniquely identify entries in this realm. Click on **OK** and then **Save**. You will be returned to the **Federated repositories screen**:

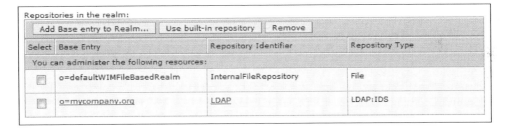

13. On the **Federated repositories** screen, you will see the new **LDAP** repository listed in the **Repositories in the realms** table, as shown in the following screenshot:

| Select | Base Entry | Repository Identifier | Repository Type |
|--------|-----------|----------------------|-----------------|
| \[Add Base entry to Realm...\] \[Use built-in repository\] \[Remove\] | | | |
| You can administer the following resources: | | | |
| ☐ | o=defaultWIMFileBasedRealm | InternalFileRepository | File |
| ☐ | o=mycompany.org | LDAP | LDAP:IDS |

14. To complete, click **Apply** and **Save**.

15. Return to the main **Global security** screen and set the **Current realm definition** to be **Federated repositories**, by clicking **Set as current**:

16. Click **Apply** and **Save** to ensure that all settings are saved. At this point, WAS will validate all the repository settings and present errors accordingly. If the settings are all validated, you will see the following detailed message:

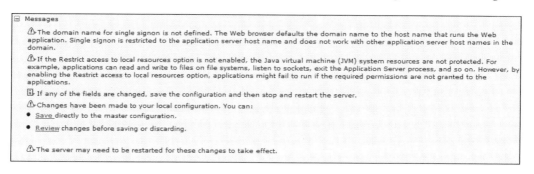

17. As instructed by the wizard, restart WAS for the federated repository to take effect.

# Adding new users to a realm

Now that WAS has a virtual realm created, it is possible to add administrative users via the Administrative console. As mentioned earlier, an advantage of using a federated repository is the fact that LDAP and locally defined WAS users can coexist. This feature allows the WAS administrative users to be administered independently from the main LDAP repository.

Separating WAS admin users and LDAP users means that administrative user security and application user security can be independently managed. It is important to note that more than one LDAP repository can be created so you could configure different LDAP servers for different application requirements where application users' registries may need to be separately managed.

Follow the ensuing steps to add new administrative users to the internal file-based repository identified as `defaultWIMFileBasedRealm`:

1. Log in to the Administrative console using the username `wasadminlocal` and password `wasadminlocal`.

2. To add new users, click on the **Manage Users** link located in the **Users and Groups** section within the left-hand-side navigation panel of the Administrative console:

3. Within the **Manage Users** screen, we are going to create a new fictitious person to be assigned administrative rights. Click the **Create** button to add a new user. Enter the value `swilliams` in the **User ID** field, the value `Sally` in the **First Name** field, and the value `Williams` in the **Last Name** field. Finally, enter the value `password` for both of the password fields:

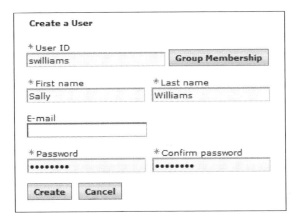

4. Click **Create** to save the new user and then click **Close**. Sally Williams will now show up as a user within the **Manage Users** table:

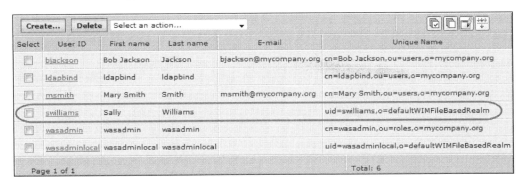

You can now optionally assign a role to Sally Williams, allowing her to login and administer WAS, just like we did with Bob Jackson earlier.

You can also create groups within the default `WIMFileBasedRealm` and assign users to groups. Groups can then be assigned to roles, making it easier to add and remove access to specific users as required for administration purposes. Now that we have a federated repository that also references LDAP, we can add and assign roles to users from either of the repository realms contained within the federated repository.

# Security domains

As we learned earlier in the chapter, WebSphere Application Server security settings are defined in the global security section within the Administrative console. By default global security is specific to one cell and is applicable cell-wide. Since WebSphere Application Server V7, we now have the ability to define more than one security domain. Security domains allow segregation of security settings and can override a subset of the global security settings for a given domain. Domains can be used to provide customized security settings for applications and service integration buses. Each security domain is assigned a level of scope that defines where its settings are applicable. Settings that are not explicitly defined in a security domain, will default to the global security settings.

Since WAS provides a single-domain configuration by default, making administration easier for most security requirements. However, a single domain might not be the ideal configuration for certain situations that need settings customized for specific applications or the segregation of security for different groups of users. By applying security settings, that is, creating multiple domains provides administration flexibility. This flexibility allows security settings to be configured, allowing spate domains to offer different settings from those that are specified by the default global security settings.

# Security domain attributes

With the creation of a new security domain, it is possible to define attributes at the security domain level. By setting attributes, it is possible to differentiate specific domain settings from those at the global level. An administrator decides what different settings need to be applied to the new security domain and he/she only needs to specify the attributes that will not be common. Any attributes that are not specifically set in the new domain are obtained from the default global configuration.

The following table shows a comparison of the security features that can be specified in the global security settings and those that a new security domain can override:

| Global security configuration | Security domain overrides |
| --- | --- |
| • Enablement of application security | • Enablement of application security |
| • Java 2 security | • Java 2 security |
| • User realm (registry) | • User realm (registry) |
| • Trust Association Interceptor (TAI) | • Trust Association Interceptor (TAI) |
| • SPNEGO Web authentication | • SPNEGO Web authentication |
| • RMI/IIOP Security (CSIv2 protocol) | • RMI/IIOP Security (CSIv2 protocol) |
| • JAAS | • JAAS |
| • Authentication mechanism attributes | • Authentication mechanism attributes |
| • Authorization provider | • Authorization provider |
| • Custom properties | • Custom properties |
| • Web attributes (single sign-on) | |
| • SSL | |
| • Audit | |
| • LTPA authentication mechanism | |
| • Kerberos authentication mechanism | |

## Creating a security domain

To demonstrate security domains, we will now create a new security domain and set specific security attributes for the domain. Once the domain is configured, we will test access using the snoop servlet. As part of the domain creation, we will use the local operating system to provide the user/group registry for the realm.

## Preparing a local operating system registry

Before we can create the domain we need to prepare a new user so that we can test authentication. Please use the following steps to prepare for the new security domain:

1. Set WAS to use the local operating system registry. You can follow the instructions for creating a registry using the local operating system, as discussed earlier in the chapter.

2. Create a new user called `waslocal` in your local operating system with the password `waslocal`.

3. Once you have set the global security to use the local operating system registry, you will need to ensure that you set the **Primary administrative user name** in the **General Properties** section of the local operating system registry:

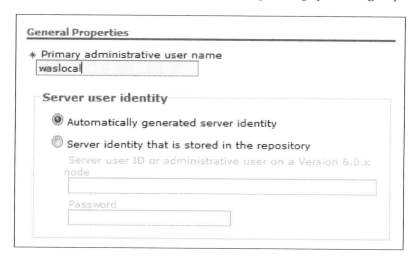

4. Save and apply your changes, and remember that you need to restart WAS for the changes to take effect.

Now that we have assigned a new user as the primary administrative username, when we next try to login to the Administrative console using `wsadmin`, access will be denied as shown in the next screenshot:

You will now need to log in as `waslocal`, using the password `waslocal` to log in to the Administrative console.

# Creating a security domain

Now that we have configured WAS to, once again, use a local operating system registry, with a new user, we can create the new security domain. Follow the following steps to create a security domain:

1. To create a new security domain, click on the **Security domains** link located in the **Security** section of the left-hand-side of the Administrative console.

2. Once presented with the security domains panel, click **New**.

3. In the new security domain details page, type `MySecurityDomain` in the **Name** field. Optionally, you can add a description. Click **Apply** or **OK** to complete.

Immediately, you will be presented with a security attributes panel for the **MySecurityDomain**, as seen in the next screenshot. The **Assigned Scopes** section contains a list of available scopes for which security will be applied. It is possible to assign the security domain to a Cell, SiBus, or a server. If this product was **WebSphere Application Server Network Deployment (WAS ND)**, then cluster scope would be available for clustered servers. In our example, we are going to use server scope. We define server scope as we want the security domain applied to applications installed on this server. Please select **server01**. This will bind the security domain to the server:

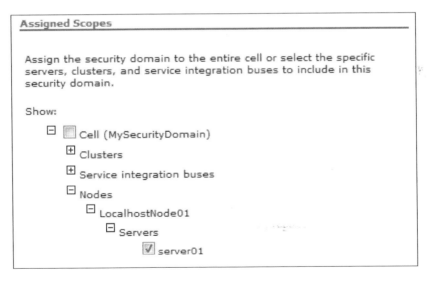

4. Next, we need to decide on the attributes that we want to override with this domain. Expand the **Application Security** attribute, select **Customize for this domain**, and ensure that the **Enable application security** checkbox is checked as shown in the following screenshot:

5. Now, we are going to define a new realm for a new local operating system-based repository. We will use this realm to provide a specific user, who will be given authorization, to access the secured application. From the attribute tree list, expand the node called **User Realm** and select **Local operating system** for the list of **Realm types**, as shown in the next screenshot. Click **Configure** to begin configuring the realm:

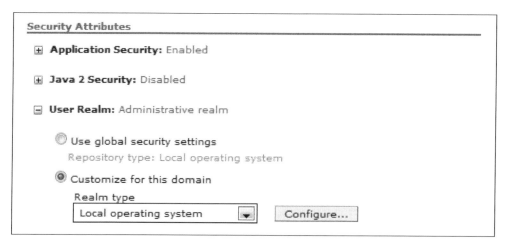

6. Once you have entered the registry realm configuration screen, locate the **General Properties** section and select the **Provide a realm name** option and type **MyRealm** as the realm's name:

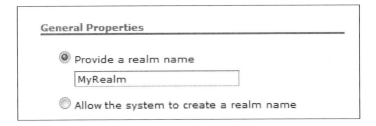

7. Click **OK**. You should be returned to the security domain's configuration screen. Click **OK** to apply and **Save** to ensure that all configurations are saved.

Now that we have configured the domain, we need to assign security rights to the snoop application so that the `waslocal` user can browse the snoop servlet. Before we apply security rights, open the following URL: `http:<host_name>:9080/snoop`.

As you can see, if you try to access the snoop servlet, the following error will occur:

 If you have not installed the `Default Application`, then the snoop servlet will not be available. Please deploy the application using instructions in *Chapter 3, Deploying your Applications* on how to deploy an application.

What we will do now is configure the user rights to gain access to the snoop servlet. The following steps outline the process to enable `waslocal` to access the snoop servlet:

1. Within the Administrative console, navigate to **Applications | Application Types | WebSphere Enterprise applications** to list the installed applications.

2. Click on the **Default Application** to drill down into the applications details configuration screen.

3. Locate the **Detailed properties** section and click on the **Security role to user/group mapping** link.

4. You will now be presented with a list of roles and mappings. Click the **All role** checkbox and then click the **Map Users** button to map the `waslocal` user to the **All role**. Note that the **All role** has been defined in the applications deployment descriptor (`web.xml`) as per the applications security design.

5. Select the realm called **MyRealm** from the **User Realm** listbox, then click **Search**. The result will be a list of users available to assign to the role. This list of users comes from the local operating system registry.

6. Select the **waslocal** user from the **Available** list of users and click the right-arrow button to select the user and move that user to the **Selected** list.

7. Click **OK** to return to the previous screen, which will show that **waslocal** is now mapped to the **All role**.

8. Click **OK** and **Save** to complete the security configuration of the **DefaultApplication**.

9. Restart WAS for the changes to take effect.

We have now completed the creation of a new security domain, the local operating system registry configuration, and the mapping of a local user to the **All role**. The next time you open the `snoop servlet` URL, you will be prompted with a realm-based login screen, as shown in the following screenshot:

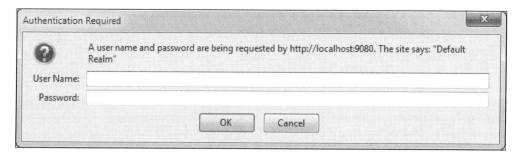

Login to the `DefaultApplication` using the username `waslocal` and the password `waslocal` and the snoop servlet will load. This concludes our example of using a separate security domain. This was just one example of using security domains; however, as outlined in the security domain section previously, there are many attributes that can be applied for specific security needs to a given domain, as required by applications within that security domain.

# LTPA overview

Lightweight Third-Party Authentication (LTPA) is an IBM proprietary security protocol which provides authentication technology used in WebSphere and Lotus Domino products. When accessing web servers that use LTPA, it is possible for a web user to re-use their login across different physical servers. It is important to note that LTPA uses tokens, which are issued to support single sign-on (SSO) in the application server product across multiple application server domains (cells). SSO is a mechanism that establishes trust across two or more applications located on different OS hosts using forwarded credentials. When a user authenticates against one enterprise application, the user is guaranteed access to another application running on a different WAS instance without having to re-authenticate, as long as the applications they are using share the same LTPA keys and their realm is also the same. An example could be a Lotus Domino server or an IBM WebSphere Application Server that is configured to use the LTPA authentication and will challenge the web user for a name and password. When the user has been authenticated, their browser will have received a session cookie, which is only available for one browsing session. This cookie contains the LTPA token and forms the basis of the forwarded credentials. When a user tries to access a server that is a member of the same authentication configuration as the first server, and the session is still valid, the user is automatically authenticated and will not be challenged for a username and password, hence the term single sign-on.

An administrator's responsibility, if the need arises, is to share the LTPA keys and the password among domains. Sharing LTPA tokens allows multiple WAS instances to communicate using a single sign-on approach. One example I was recently challenged with was a situation where developers using remote desktop development machines with local instances of WAS, required communication with a shared server-based version of WAS. The shared version of WAS was running a common application providing a set of services that each developer's instance of WAS needed to communicate with. This same scenario could also be realized in the situation where two WAS instances in different cells are required to communicate with each other.

It is now a good time to discuss authentication in a little more detail. The following diagram shows the authentication flow in a single sign-on situation, including the authorization data which contains LTPA tokens:

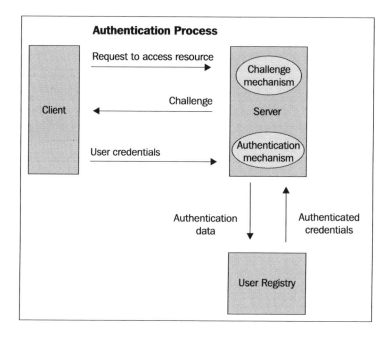

The following table explains the components in the previous diagram:

| | |
|---|---|
| **Client** | A web-browser or application client or WAS server acting as a client, requests access to a resource. If the resource is secured, then a challenge is made. |
| **Challenge mechanism** | A challenge mechanism will request authentication data of various types, depending on the security being implemented. This could be a client certificate or a token (cookie); it could also be some basic authentication data like username/password or a more complex form-based, application-driven login. |
| **Authentication mechanism** | The authentication mechanism decides on how authentication data is passed to a user registry. In WebSphere, this is primarily via an LTPA token (cookie). |
| **User registry** | Associates user credentials with the principal. The principal is the actual entity in the appropriate configured user registry. |

# LTPA configuration

When you turn on administrative (Global) security, you must configure Lightweight Third-Party Authentication (LTPA) or Kerberos. When we enabled administrative security, the LTPA authentication mechanism was selected as the default authentication mechanism. If you wish for different WebSphere application servers to facilitate single sign-on, you will need to share LTPA keys. Sharing of keys is done by exporting and importing keys.

## Steps for importing and exporting LTPA keys

1. Click on the **Global security** link located in the **Security** section at the left-hand-side navigation panel of the Administrative console. You will then be presented with the **Global security** page. Locate the section titled **Authentication mechanisms and expiration** and then click the **LTPA** link. You will then be presented with the **LTPA** screen, as shown in the following screenshot:

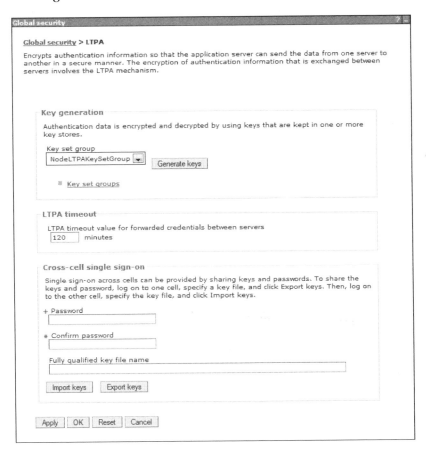

2. Optionally, locate the **Key generation** section and select the appropriate group from the **Key set group** field that contains your public, private, and shared LTPA keys. These keys are used to encrypt and decrypt data that is sent between servers. We use the default key set group. Note, it is possible to create other key set groups if you require producing different key sets for different LTPA keys for multiple single sign-on configurations across multiple WAS cells.

3. Set the **LTPA timeout** value as required. This value refers to how long the server credentials from another server are valid before they expire. The default value is **120 minutes**.

4. Enter a password in the **Password** field. This password is used to protect the generated keys that are used to encrypt and decrypt the LTPA keys from the SSO properties file.

5. To share the keys and password, log on to one cell, specify a key file, and click **Export keys**. Then, log on to the other WebSphere cell, specify the key file, and click **Import keys**.

6. Click **Apply** or **OK**.

# Managing SSL

**SSL (Secure Sockets Layer)** is the industry standard for encrypting communication between clients and servers. WAS utilizes the SSL protocol to provide a secure transport layer allowing a secure connection between a client and server and provides a full set of features for managing SSL configuration.

SSL works via a series of handshakes, which are exchanged at the start of an SSL session. The handshake uses asymmetric keys that consist of a public key and a private key. The public key can be distributed widely, but the private key is never distributed; it is always kept secret. When an entity encrypts data using a public key, only entities with the corresponding private key can decrypt that data. The client and server work together to ensure a secure communication.

As an administrator, it is your job to ensure that the SSL certificates used by WAS are managed. An administrator may need to update certificates that have expired or add new certificates. In previous versions of this product, it was necessary to manually configure each endpoint for SSL. In WAS 8, you can define a single configuration for the entire application-serving environment. This capability enables you to centrally manage secure communications. It is now much easier to manage SSL certificates and key/trust stores.

# Certificates and Certificate Authorities

**Certificate Authorities (CA)** providers are the official organizations that guarantee that an SSL certificate is genuine. CA root certificates refer to the certificates created by these organizations and such certificates are included by software vendors in browsers and client applications. For a browser to trust a server certificate, the signer (CA) must already exist in the client (browser) certificate vault, or key store. All public SSL-based websites will have SSL certificates that have been signed by these organizations and so a trust relationship can occur. However, if your WebSphere Application Server infrastructure is internal and you still want SSL enabled, then you can use personal self-signed certificates. When WAS is installed, a set of self-signed certificates are generated to allow SSL transports. These certificates however are not known by the browser. As far as the browser is concerned these certificates cannot be verified as trusted because they are signed with an unknown root CA.

In a nutshell, self-signed certificates make your data safe from eavesdroppers, but say nothing about who the recipient of the data is. This is common for intranet websites that aren't available publicly. This is why we get a browser error, similar to the following when we first log in to the Admin console when global security has been enabled:

**This Connection is Untrusted**

You have asked Firefox to connect securely to  Node01.waslocal.com:9043,  but we can't confirm that your connection is secure.

Normally, when you try to connect securely, sites will present trusted identification to prove that you are going to the right place. However, this site's identity can't be verified.

**What Should I Do?**

If you usually connect to this site without problems, this error could mean that someone is trying to impersonate the site, and you shouldn't continue.

Get me out of here!

▸ **Technical Details**

▸ **I Understand the Risks**

You can see that the browser doesn't trust the signer certificates that has been presented by WAS. This is because it is self-signed. The user can optionally choose to trust the certificate. When the user creates an exception, the certificate will be added to the browser's local trust vault, alternatively known as a key store. This action will inform the browser to not raise an exception the next time this domain is revisited.

# Key stores and trust stores

WAS uses certificates that reside in key stores to establish trust for SSL connections. A **Keystore** is a key database file that contains both public keys and private keys. Public keys are stored as signer certificates while private keys are stored in the personal certificates. The keys are used for a variety of purposes, including authentication and data integrity. They are located in:

```
<was_profile_root>/config/cells/<cell_node_name>/nodes/<node_name>
  /key.p12
```

A trust store file is a key database file that contains the public keys for target servers. The public key is stored as a signer certificate. If the target uses a self-signed certificate, extract the public certificate from the server Keystore file. Add the extracted certificate into the trust store file as a signer certificate. For a commercial certificate authority (CA), the CA root certificate is added. The trust store file can be a more publicly accessible key database file that contains all the trusted certificates. it is located in:

```
<was_profile_root>/config/cells/<cell_node_name>/nodes/<node_name>
  /trust.p12
```

# Managing Key stores and certificates

1.  To view Key stores and certificates, log into the Administrative console and then click on the **SSL certificate and key management** link located in the **Security** section of the left-hand-side navigation panel, as shown in the following screenshot:

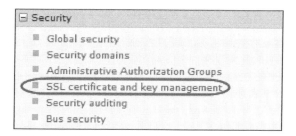

2.  Within the **SSL certificate and key management** screen, locate the **Related Items** section and click the **Keystores and certificates** link. As shown in the next screenshot, the **Keystore usages** option is set to **SSL keystores** and the default node key store and trust store will be listed:

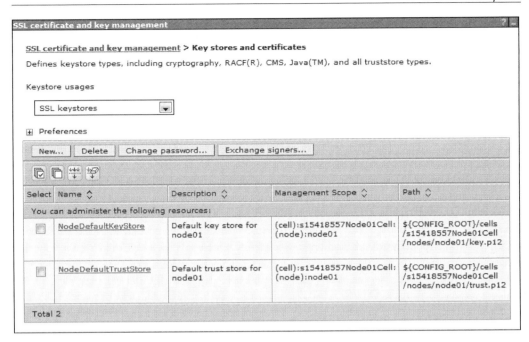

3. Click on the **NodeDefaultKeyStore** link to view the Keystore properties screen.

4. Locate the **Additional Properties** section and click the **Personal certificates** link; you will be presented with the **Personal certificates** screen, which lists the current self-signed certificates as generated during the WebSphere installation process:

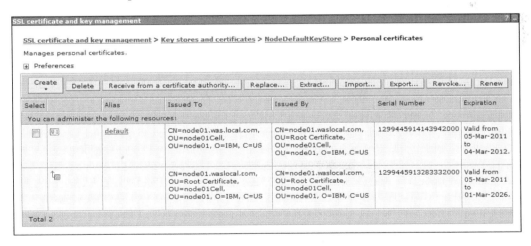

Within the **Personal certificates** screen there is an array of management options. The **Personal certificates** page lists all personal certificates in the selected key store. You can perform most certificate management operations in this panel, including creating a new self-signed certificate, deleting a certificate, receiving one generated from a CA, replacing a certificate (simultaneous delete-and-create, replacing references across all key stores), extracting the signer, and importing or exporting a personal certificate.

The following table outlines each button as shown previously:

| Button name | Description |
| --- | --- |
| **Create** (drop-down list) | Enables the application server to create the following certificates:<br><br>• Self-signed Certificate<br><br>• A-signed Certificate<br><br>• Chained Certificate |
| **Delete** | Specifies to delete a certificate from the key store. Be careful that the certificate alias is not referenced elsewhere in the Secure Sockets Layer configuration. |
| **Receive from a certificate authority** | Enables the application server to receive a certificate authority (CA)-generated certificate from a file to complete a certificate request. |
| **Replace** | Replaces a personal certificate with another personal certificate. Any place in the security configuration where the certificate alias is referenced will be replaced with the new certificate alias. |
| **Extract** | Extracts the signer part of a personal certificate from the key store and stores it in a file. The file can then be used to add the signer to another key store. |
| **Import** | Imports a certificate, including the private key, from a key store file or managed key store. |
| **Export** | Exports a certificate, including the private key, to a specified key store file or managed key store. |
| **Revoke** | Revokes a CA-signed certificate. Use this option if you wish to revoke trusted certificates. |
| **Renew** | Renews a self-signed or chained certificate. This option is used if you wish to manually renew a certificate. |

As you can see in the previous screenshot, detailing the **Personal certificates** screen, there are two certificates. The certificate with the **default** label has been signed with the internal default root certificate. The default certificate is stored within the server's `key.p12` file and has a life span of one year. The root certificate will have a lifespan of 20 years. Both certificates were created during the server's profile creation in *Chapter 2, Installing WebSphere Application Server*. The server's default certificate is chained to the root certificate.

## Chained certificates

Chained certificates are personal certificates that have been signed by another personal certificate. An example of a personal certificate is when you create a self-signed certificate for use in your WebSphere infrastructure.

## Monitoring certificate expiration

Since the default personal certificate expires every year, WAS will automatically renew the default personal certificate.

Certificate monitoring ensures that the default chained certificate for each node is not allowed to expire. The certificate expiration monitoring function issues a warning before certificates and signers are set to expire. Those certificates and signers that are located in key stores managed by the WebSphere Application Server configuration can be monitored.

You can configure the expiration monitor to automatically replace a certificate. A chained certificate will be recreated based on the same data used for the initial creation and sign it with the same root certificate that signed the original certificate. A self-signed certificate or chained certificate is also recreated based upon the same data that is used during the initial profile creation.

Steps to configure expiration monitoring:

1. Click **Security | SSL certificate and key management | Manage certificate expiration** from within the Admin console
2. Type the number of days in the **Expiration notification threshold** field. The WebSphere Application Server will issue an expiration warning (n) showing the number of days before expiration. When a certificate is within the expiration threshold, and automatic replacement is enabled, certificates are replaced.
3. Type the number of days in the **Certificate pre-notification threshold** field. This value specifies the time period before the threshold when warnings are issued by the certificate monitor concerning upcoming replacement dates.

4.  Enable checking. If you do not want to have certificate monitoring enabled, clear the checkbox.

5.  Optionally, enter the time of day in the **Scheduled time of day to check for expired certificates** field to specify when you want certificate monitoring to take place to schedule the running of the certificate expiration monitor.

6.  Optionally, set the **Check by calendar** field to **Weekday** and enter the day of the week that you want to run the certificate expiration monitor on. For **Repeat Interval**, specify the frequency for running the certificate monitor.

7.  Optionally, set the **Check by number of days** field by entering a number for how frequently the monitor runs, in number of days.

8.  **Automatically replace expiring self-signed certificates**. If you do not want to recreate the self-signed certificate, clear the checkbox.

9.  **Delete expiring certificates and signers after replacement**. If you do not want to delete the expired certificates and signers, clear the checkbox.

10. Click **Apply** to save your changes.

# Creating certificate requests

When WAS is required to service a production environment requiring SSL, you will need to import SSL certificates. These certificates come from your trusted certificate authority. You must first generate a certificate request from WAS. The request process creates the appropriate public and private keys required. The **Certificate Signing Request (CSR)** will contain the public key that has been certified by the CA provider. The CSR is then manually sent to our CA provider and a certificate is generated for you. Once you receive the CSR signed with your new certificate, it needs to be imported into WAS.

Steps to create a CSR are as follows:

1.  Click **Security | SSL certificate and key management | Key stores and certificates | keystore** from within the Admin console.

2.  Click **Personal certificate requests | New**.

3.  Type the full path of the certificate request file destination in the **File for certificate request field**. The certificate request is created in this location.

4.  Type an alias name in the **Key label** field. The alias identifies the certificate request in the key store.

5.  Select a **Key size** value. The valid key size values are 512, 1024, 2048, 4096, and 8192. The default key size value is 2048 bits.

6. Type a common name (CN) value in the **Common name** field. This value is the CN value in the certificate distinguished name (DN).

7. Optionally, type an organization value in the **Organization** field. This value is the O value in the certificate DN.

8. Optionally, type an organizational unit value in the **Organizational unit** field. This organizational unit value is the OU value in the certificate DN.

9. Optionally, type a locality value in the **Locality** field. This locality value is the L value in the certificate DN.

10. Optionally, type a state or province value in the **State or province** field. This value is the ST value in the certificate DN.

11. Optionally, type a zip code value in the **Zip code** field. The zip code value is the POSTALCODE value in the certificate DN.

12. Optionally select a country value from the **Country or region** field. This country value is the C= value in the certificate request DN.

13. Click **Apply** to generate the CSR.

14. Send the CSR to your Certificate Authority provider for signing.

# Receiving a certificate request

Steps to receive a certificate-request (CSR) which has been certified by your CA provider:

1. Click **Security | SSL certificate and key management | Manage endpoint security configurations | {Inbound | Outbound} | ssl_configuration | Key stores and certificates | [keystore]**.

2. Under **Additional Properties**, click **Personal certificates**.

3. Select a personal certificate.

4. Click **Receive a certificate from a certificate authority**.

5. Type the full path and name of the certificate file.

6. Select a data type from the list.

7. Click **Apply** and **Save**.

# Setting Cell or Node SSL aliases

The SSL configuration for each certificate will have no default SSL alias set. Once you have received your certificate, you need to set the SSL configuration for the cell or nodes as required. Setting the SSL alias will inform WAS which SSL certificate to use for the SSL transports.

For SSL, Nodes are certified independently from Cells. For Nodes, follow the Cell process outlined below.

Following are the steps to assign an SSL alias to a Cell:

1. Open **Security | SSL certificate and key management**.
2. Click on the **CellDefaultSSLSettings**.
3. Ensure the **Default client certificate alias** matches the SSL certificate name you imported earlier.
4. Click **Apply** and **Save**.

# Summary

In this chapter, we learned that for global security to work, we need a repository of users, and groups of users, who are authorized to access the Administrative console. WAS uses three main types of registries, which can be used to store the users and groups that are given access to log in and configure the server. On large systems used by businesses and other organizations, there will likely be several system administrators and application servers dispersed across more than one machine and, if you use a local OS user registry, each machine would have its own user registry and it would be hard to keep them all up-to-date and secure. Hence LDAP is a better option. We also learned that it is possible to federate multiple repositories together, allowing user searches to be done across multiple mixed repositories. We covered security domains that allow different security attributes configured to separate security concerns as might be required in a real-world WAS installation. LTPA keys, and their part in single sign-on, was also discussed as well as how to administer importing and exporting LTPA keys between WAS cells.

We covered how to manage SSL and understood how to generate and import CSR requests for when you require certificates signed by an external certificate authority provider to be imported into WAS.

There are many parts to security administration, too many to be covered in one chapter. It is recommended to have some further reading on the subject. There are several great PDF's detailing WAS security available at the IBM Red Books site `http://www.redbooks.ibm.com/` and I also think the book titled *IBM-WebSphere-Application-Server-v7.0-Security*, also available from Packt Publishing, is a good read for a more detailed overview of both application and server security and covers extended topics such as Kerberos, Java 2 security, JAAS, Realms, and also Security Domains.

In the next chapter, we will cover administrative scripting. Monitored deployments were introduced in *Chapter 3, Deploying your Applications*. In this next chapter, we will learn how to extend monitored deployment configurations to allow automatic drag and drop deployments, by employing administrative scripting techniques, covered in *Chapter 6, Server Configuration*.

# 5

# Administrative Scripting

As a **WebSphere Application Server (WAS)** administrator, you will soon find that doing administration manually becomes laborious when you have a large number of administration tasks to perform. Whether you work for a large organization or not, you will need to deploy many applications into your WAS environments. Sometimes the same deployment will be repeated time and time again. In *Chapter 3, Deploying your Applications*, we learned how to manually deploy an EAR file using the Administration console. We found that, depending on the type of application being deployed, there could be many configuration elements involved before an application is considered ready for runtime use. To speed up deployments and make them more consistent and controllable, we need to look at how we can automate our deployments. It is also important that we are able to automate the configuration of WAS, which can save many hours of manual administrative efforts. In this chapter, we will cover the following topics:

- Automation
- ws_ant (Ant)
- wsadmin tool
- Jython scripting
- Configuring applications using property files
- Command assistance

# Automation

Automation doesn't come for free; it requires some effort from the administrator, yet the rewards are great. Being able to automate an application deployment allows for the control of naming standards and ensures consistency each time applications are deployed or WAS configurations are made. Scripting also lends to auditing and version control and the ability to do in minutes what could take a human hours, without human-induced errors. As administrators, our key goals are to deploy new applications and update existing applications and administrative configurations rapidly without error. WAS comes with administration tools that can run automation scripts. There are two main tools used for automation—one is called **wsadmin**, which uses the **Jython** or **JACL (Java Application Control Language)** languages and the other is **ws_ant**, which uses Ant an XML-based Java build language. The wsadmin tool can be used for both deployment and configuration of all areas of WAS, whereas ws_ant is mainly used for non-production application deployments. We will cover ws_ant first, then move on to wsadmin.

# The ws_ant tool

The ws_ant tool is based on Apache Ant. **Apache Ant** is a Java library and command-line tool whose mission is to drive processes described in build files as targets and extension points dependent upon each other.

 If you wish to learn more about Ant, you can read up about it on the Apache website located at http://ant.apache.org/.

Ant XML-based configuration files contain sequential commands as groups of tasks. These XML files reference a tree of task groups called targets in which various tasks are specified to run in a particular order. Each task is run by an object that implements a particular task interface. WAS utilizes Ant via the ws_ant utility, which provides specific Ant tasks designed to make application deployment easier. It is not recommended that ws_ant be used in production servers as it is strongly linked to development. In enterprise systems, developers will not have access to live systems. ws_ant is not scalable unlike wsadmin-based scripting, which is more suitable for enterprise WAS designs and production configurations.

The ws_ant tool can be found within the WAS file-system at the location <was_root>/bin/ws_ant.

By combining the WAS tasks listed in the table below with those provided by Ant, you can create build scripts that compile, package, install, and test your application on the application server.

| ws_ant task name | Description |
| --- | --- |
| com.ibm.websphere.ant.<br>tasks.ListApplications | Lists all the applications installed on a WebSphere application. |
| com.ibm.websphere.ant.<br>tasks.InstallApplication | Allows you to deploy an application in to a WebSphere Application Server. |
| com.ibm.websphere.ant.<br>tasks.UninstallApplication | Allows you to uninstall an existing application from a WebSphere Application Server. |
| com.ibm.websphere.ant.<br>tasks.ServerStatus | Reports on Server status. |
| com.ibm.websphere.ant.<br>tasks.StartServer | Allows you to start a standalone server instance. |
| com.ibm.websphere.ant.<br>tasks.StopServer | Allows you to stop a standalone server instance. |

New ws_ant tasks have been introduced in **WebSphere 8(WAS 8)**, as outlined in the following table:

| ws_ant task name | Description |
| --- | --- |
| com.ibm.websphere.ant.tasks.<br>StartApplication | Allows ws_ant to start an application. |
| com.ibm.websphere.ant.tasks.<br>StopApplication | Allows ws_ant to stop an application. |

The Apache Ant tasks for the product reside in the Java package com.ibm.websphere.ant.tasks. API documentation is available from the IBM Information Centers and contains detailed information about all of the Ant tasks that are provided by this package and how to use them. You can find the API at the following URL, within the library section: https://www14.software.ibm.com/iwm/web/cc/earlyprograms/websphere/wsasoa/library.shtml

# Uninstalling the HR application

To demonstrate the ws_ant tool, we will automate a deployment of the HR application we manually installed in *Chapter 3, Deploying your Applications*.

If the HR application EAR file is installed in WAS, please uninstall it. If you have not yet uninstalled an EAR file from WAS, go through the following steps:

1. Log in to the Administartion console and navigate to the **Application Types** section of the **Applications** panel located on the left-hand side of the Administartion console and click the **WebSphere enterprise applications** link.

2. In the **Enterprises Applications** panel, which lists the current-installed applications, select the **HRListerEAR** application and click **Uninstall**.

3. You will be prompted to confirm your choice. Click **OK** to continue and, once the application has been uninstalled, you will need to click **Save** to save the configuration.

# Deploying an application using ws_ant

We will now demonstrate the use of the ws_ant task called `wsInstallApp`. Before we can run a ws_ant automated application deployment, we need to create an XML file which will contain the ws_ant tasks we wish to run to deploy the application. Traditionally, Ant-based utilities look for a default XML file called `build.xml`. However, any XML filename can be used as long as you pass the name of the file on the command line when you run ws_ant.

> We could use the name `build.xml` for the XML file to keep in line with the common use of Ant, but by using a different file we immediately know what the script is used for by just looking at its name.

Before we create our first script you need to reference a few folders from within the scripts. The folders you will need to create or reference for the scripts to work are explained as follows:

| Folder reference | Description |
| --- | --- |
| `<scripts_home>` | The root location on your server where you will locate all your scripts.<br><br>(In the examples, I have used `/root/was8book` on Linux as my script location) |

| Folder reference | Description |
|---|---|
| `<deploy_home>` | The root location where you will store all EAR files used in these exercises. EAR files are downloaded from www.packtpub.com. |
| | (In the examples, I have used `/root/was8book/deploy` on Linux as my EAR file location). |
| `<was_root>` | The root of your WAS installation. |
| `<was_profile_root>` | The root of your Application Server profile. |

> For all scripting exercises please ensure that you replace all place-holder folder names with the correct equivalent locations on your system.
>
> In some example file paths, I will use a Linux notation using the / (forward slash) separator. If you are using WAS make sure you use \ (backslash) as your folder separator.

The steps to create the script are as follows:

1. Create a file called `deployHR.xml` in a folder called `<scripts_home>/ws_ant`.

2. Copy the following code into `deployHR.xml`, ensuring you replace appropriate paths variables and save the XML file:

```xml
<?xml version="1.0" encoding="UTF-8"?>
<project name="HR Lister Application Depoyment" default="build-all" basedir=".">
  <!-- global properties -->
  <property name="hostName" value="localhost" />
  <property name="connType" value="SOAP" />
  <property name="port" value="8880" />
  <property name="userId" value="wasadmin" />
  <property name="password" value="wasadmin" />
  <property name="deployEar.dir" value="<deploy_home>" />
  <property name="deployEar" value="HRListerEAR.ear" />
  <property name="wasHome.dir" value="<was_root>" />

  <!-- mbean declaration" -->
  <taskdef name="wasInstallApp" classname="com.ibm.websphere.ant.tasks.InstallApplication" />

  <!-- installation Target-->
  <target name="installEar">
```

```
        <echo message="Deployable EAR File found at: ${deployEar.
dir}/${deployEar}" />
        <wasInstallApp ear="${deployEar.dir}/${deployEar}"
        wasHome="${wasHome.dir}"
        conntype="${connType}"
        port="${port}"
        host="${hostName}"
        user="${userId}"
        password="${password}" />
    </target>

    <target name="build-all" depends="installEar">
        <!--Main Target-->
    </target>
</project>
```

3. To run the ws_ant script, navigate to the `<was_root>/bin` folder and type the following command:

    ○  For Linux:

    ```
    ./ws_ant.sh -f <scripts_home>/ws_ant/deployHR.xml
    ```

    ○  For Windows:

    ```
    ws_ant.bat -f <scripts_home>\ws_ant\deployHR.xml
    ```

4. The result of running the `deployHR.xml` ws_ant script will be displayed in stdout (the shell scripts console). A sample of the output you would expect to see is as follows:

```
installEar:

    [echo] Deployable EAR File found at: /root/was8book/deploy/
HRListerEAR.ear

[wasInstallApp] Installing Application [/root/was8book/deploy/
HRListerEAR.ear]...

    [wsadmin] WASX7209I: Connected to process "server01" on
node node01 using SOAP connector;  The type of process is:
UnManagedProcess

    [wsadmin] ADMA5016I: Installation of HRListerEAR started.

    [wsadmin] ADMA5058I: Application and module versions are
validated with versions of deployment targets.

    [wsadmin] ADMA5005I: The application HRListerEAR is configured
in the WebSphere Application Server repository.

    [wsadmin] ADMA5053I: The library references for the installed
optional package are created.
```

```
[wsadmin] ADMA5005I: The application HRListerEAR is configured
in the WebSphere Application Server repository.

[wsadmin] ADMA5001I: The application binaries are saved in /
var/apps/was8/profiles/appsrv01/wstemp/Script12edf1052fc/
workspace/cells/s15418557Node01Cell/applications/HRListerEAR.ear/
HRListerEAR.ear

[wsadmin] ADMA5005I: The application HRListerEAR is configured
in the WebSphere Application Server repository.

[wsadmin] SECJ0400I: Successfully updated the application
HRListerEAR with the appContextIDForSecurity information.

[wsadmin] ADMA5005I: The application HRListerEAR is configured
in the WebSphere Application Server repository.

[wsadmin] ADMA5113I: Activation plan created successfully.

[wsadmin] ADMA5011I: The cleanup of the temp directory for
application HRListerEAR is complete.

[wsadmin] ADMA5013I: Application HRListerEAR installed
successfully.

[wasInstallApp] Installed Application [/root/was8book/deploy/
HRListerEAR.ear]


build-all:


BUILD SUCCESSFUL
Total time: 15 seconds
```

# Managing an application using ws_ant

We have seen how to use ws_ant to install an application. We will now create another script called manageHR.xml, which will contain several ws_ant tasks. The manageHR.xml script is designed so we can call tasks individually or as a complete set from beginning to end. These Ant targets can be called individually by specifying a particular target to the ws_ant command line.

1. Create a file called manageHR.xml in the same folder you created earlier, for example, <scripts_home>/was_ant/manageHR.xml.

2. Copy the following code into the manageHR.xml file:

```
<?xml version="1.0" encoding="UTF-8"?>

<project name="Manage HR Lister Application Deployment"
default="build-all" basedir=".">
    <!-- global properties -->
    <property name="hostName" value="localhost" />
```

```
      <property name="connType" value="SOAP" />
      <property name="port" value="8880" />
      <property name="userId" value="wasadmin" />
      <property name="password" value="wasadmin" />
      <property name="appName" value="HRLister" />
      <property name="deployEar.dir" value="="<deploy_home>" />
      <property name="deployEar" value="HRListerEAR.ear" />
      <property name="wasHome.dir" value="<was_root>" />

      <!-- mbean declarations" -->
      <taskdef name="wsUninstallApp" classname="com.ibm.websphere.
ant.tasks.UninstallApplication" />
      <taskdef name="wsInstallApp" classname="com.ibm.websphere.ant.
tasks.InstallApplication" />
      <taskdef name="wsListApplications" classname="com.ibm.
websphere.ant.tasks.ListApplications" />

      <!-- List Target-->
      <target name="listApplications">
         <wsListApplications
         wasHome="${wasHome.dir}"
         conntype="${connType}"
         port="${port}"
         host="${hostName}"
         user="${userId}"
         password="${password}" />
    </target>

     <!-- Uninstall Target-->
     <target name="uninstallEAR">
         <wsUninstallApp application="${appName}"
         wasHome="${wasHome.dir}"
         conntype="${connType}"
         port="${port}"
         host="${hostName}"
         user="${userId}"
         password="${password}" />
    </target>

    <!-- installation Target-->
    <target name="installEAR">
         <echo message="Deployable EAR File found at: ${deployEar.
dir}/${deployEar}" />
         <wsInstallApp ear="${deployEar.dir}/${deployEar}"
         options="-appname ${appName}"
```

```
                wasHome="${wasHome.dir}"
                conntype="${connType}"
                port="${port}"
                host="${hostName}"
                user="${userId}"
                password="${password}" />
    </target>

    <target name="build-all" depends="listApplications,
uninstallEAR, listApplications, installEAR, listApplications">
        <!--Main Target-->
    </target>

</project>
```

Using the following table, you can see the syntax of the different types of command lines required to run the individual targets:

| Target name to run | Command-line syntax |
|---|---|
| listApplications | For Linux: |
| | `<was_root>/bin/ws_ant.sh listApplications -f <scripts_home>/ws_ant/manageHR.xml` |
| | For Windows: |
| | `<was_root>\bin\ws_ant.bat listApplications -f <scripts_home>\ws_ant\manageHR.xml` |
| uninstallEAR | For Linux: |
| | `<was_root>/bin/ws_ant.sh uninstallEAR -f <scripts_home>/ws_ant/manageHR.xml` |
| | For Windows: |
| | `<was_root>\bin\ws_ant.bat uninstallEAR -f <scripts_home>\ws_ant\manageHR.xml` |
| installEAR | For Linux: |
| | `<was_root>/bin/ws_ant.sh installEAR -f <scripts_home>/ws_ant/manageHR.xml` |
| | For Windows: |
| | `<was_root>\bin\ws_ant.sh installEAR -f <scripts_home>\ws_ant\manageHR.xml` |

| Target name to run | Command-line syntax |
|---|---|
| `<No target specified>` (Runs all targets) | For Linux:<br><br>`<was_root>/bin/ws_ant.sh install -f <scripts_ home>/ws_ant/manageHR.xml`<br><br>For Windows:<br><br>`<was_root>\bin\ws_ant.sh install -f <scripts_ home>\ws_ant\manageHR.xml` |

3. Feel free to experiment with the `manageHR.xml` file and try our different target combinations. If you choose to run the `manageHR.xml` file with no specific target mentioned, the build-all target will run. The build-all target calls named targets in a particular order.

```
<target name="build-all" depends="listApplications, uninstallEAR,
listApplications, installEAR, listApplications">
        <!--Main Target-->
        </target>
```

4. Since the `manageHR.xml` file has a project declaration, which specifies the default target as `build-all`, the `build-all` target will be called if no target name is specified on the command line. This is shown as follows:

```
<project name="Manage HR Lister Application Deployment"
default="build-all" basedir=".">
```

IBM maintains that ws_ant is not suited for production system configurations, though this does not stop anyone from using Ant as such. A better tool for administrative scripting in WAS is the wsadmin tool. The reason is that administration scripting using Jython is far more powerful than ws_ant. It is interesting to note that ws_ant is in fact an Ant wrapper which calls some wsadmin commands internally.

On the Apache Ant website you can also find sample Ant projects to give you insights into Ant commands. Knowing more about Ant can be helpful to give you ideas how Ant commands can be used in your ws_ant XML files. For more detailed information about Ant commands, refer to the Apache organization website at http://ant.apache.org/.

# The wsadmin tool

WebSphere Application Server supports the use of both JACL and Jython languages for administrative scripting. For the purposes of this book, we will only refer to Jython.

**Jython** is an implementation of the high-level, dynamic, object-oriented Python language written in pure Java, and is employed by WAS. By using Jython scripts, we can readily craft administrative tasks and run them in an automated fashion using the WAS administration command-line tool. By creating scripts, we can automate both configurations and application deployments .The scripts are shown as follows:

- **For Linux/Unix:**

  `wsadamin.sh`

- **For Windows:**

  `wsadmin.bat`

The wsadmin tool acts as an interface to WAS Java objects for access by scripts. Internally, WAS employs the JMX API to create MBeans (JMX management objects) that are exposed as an API of internal WAS objects, which wsadmin can utilize to configure WAS.

If you wish to learn more about MBeans, go to `http://java.sun.com/docs/books/tutorial/jmx/mbeans/index.html`.

In WAS 8, the wsadmin tool (`wsadmin`) supports five top-level scripting objects: the `AdminConfig`, `AdminControl`, `AdminApp`, `AdminTask`, and the `Help` objects. Scripts use these objects for application management, configuration, control, and communicating with the internal MBeans that run in the WAS product.

The following table explains the scripting objects:

| Scripting Object | Description |
|---|---|
| **AdminConfig** | Communicates with the `config` service and is used to modify, remove, or display WebSphere internal configuration data. The object essentially supports making changes to the configuration WAS product. |
| **AdminControl** | Used to run commands that affect the server runtime. This object works with the running MBeans objects within the WAS process. MBeans represent internal components of the runtime, which can be manipulated by scripted calls. |

| Scripting Object | Description |
|---|---|
| **AdminApp** | Used to administer configurations and settings of deployed applications. Typical actions might include installing, modifying, and making administrative changes to the application. `AdminApp` commands can also be run locally when the server is down. |
| **AdminTask** | Used to run administrative commands. Also has a local mode which, when invoked, allows `AdminTask` commands to be run locally when the server is down. |
| **Help** | Used to get help on available administrative commands from the other four main scripting objects. |

The wsadmin tool can be run in different modes, depending on the requirement. The following table explains the different modes:

| Mode | Description |
|---|---|
| Run scripting commands interactively | The wsadmin tool is run and commands are entered by the user interactively and are run inside the wsadmin interface. |
| Run individual scripting commands | Single commands are executed as command-line parameters (arguments) to the main `wsadmin.sh` command. |
| Run scripting commands in a script file | The most common method is where commands are entered into a file and run by the `wsadmin` tool. Similar to running any batch file process or shell script. |
| Run scripting commands in a profile script | These scripts are run before the wsadmin script executes and can be used to set up environments or perform pre-script actions. |

As already mentioned, the scripting interface for **WAS** is called the **wsadmin** tool. The tool is called by the `wsadmin.sh` script (`wsadmin.bat` for Windows), which is located in the `bin` directory of an Application Server profile, for example, `<was_profile_root>/bin`.

During the remaining chapters of the book, we will refer to this tool as wsadmin. The wsadmin tool is run from a command line and can also be called from other external scripts. In fact, any application that calls an OS script can call wsadmin, which allows administrators to include WAS-specific administration as part of other OS management scripts. There are several ways in which wsadmin can be run. We will cover each method in the following sections.

# Interactive commands

1.  To run the wsadmin tool in interactive mode, log on to your machine on which WAS is installed, and navigate to the `<was_profile_root>/bin` directory (for example, `/apps/was8/profiles/appsrv01/bin` and type the following command:

    ◦   For Linux:

        `./wsadmin.sh -lang jython`

    ◦   For Windows:

        `wsadmin.bat -lang jython`

     You may need to supply the administrative username and password if global security is turned on. If you use the username and password command-line options, you will not be prompted with a username and password dialog box.

    Once the wsadmin tool has loaded, you will see the following on-screen prompt:

    ```
    WASX7209I: Connected to process "server01" on node LocalhostNode01
    using SOAP connector;  The type of process is: UnManagedProcess
    WASX7029I: For help, enter: "$Help help"
    wsadmin>
    ```

2.  Type the following command and hit the *Enter* key:

    `Hello World`

    You will see the text **Hello World** printed to the stdout (the shells screen).

3.  Now, type the following command and hit *Enter*:

    `print Help.help()`

4.  You will see that `help` objects are listed on your screen as shown:

    `wsadmin>print Help.help()`

    WASX7028I: The `Help` object has two purposes:

    ◦   First, provide general help information for the the objects supplied by wsadmin for scripting—`Help`, `AdminApp`, `AdminConfig`, `AdminControl` and `AdminTask`.

○ Second, provide a means to obtain interface information about MBeans running in the system. For this purpose, a variety of commands are available to get information about the operations, attributes, and other interface information about particular MBeans.

The following commands are supported by `Help`:

| | |
|---|---|
| **attributes** | Given an MBean, returns help for attributes |
| **operations** | Given an MBean, returns help for operations |
| **constructors** | Given an MBean, returns help for constructors |
| **description** | Given an MBean, returns help for description |
| **notifications** | Given an MBean, returns help for notifications |
| **classname** | Given an MBean, returns help for classname |
| **all** | Given an MBean, returns help for all the preceding commands |
| **help** | Returns this help text |
| **AdminControl** | Returns general help text for the `AdminControl` object |
| **AdminConfig** | Returns general help text for the `AdminConfig` object |
| **AdminApp** | Returns general help text for the `AdminApp` object |
| **AdminTask** | Returns general help text for the `AdminTask` object |
| **wsadmin** | Returns general help text for the wsadmin script launcher |
| **message** | Given a message ID, returns explanation and user action message |

More detailed information about each of these commands is available by using the help command of Help and supplying the name of the command as an argument.

5. If we wish to drill down into more information on a particular scripting object, we can use the help command. The syntax is as follows:

```
Print Help.<command_object>()
```

For example, to list more details for the `AdminConfig` object, type the following command:

```
print Help.AdminConfig()
```

As a result, you will get a detailed listing of the available commands supported by the `AdminConfig` object. There are many commands listed for each of the main objects. We will not list them here, however, if you wish to see them for yourself, you can run the following four commands from an interactive wsadmin console to list all commands available:

- ° `print Help.AdminConfig()`
- ° `print Help.AdminControl()`
- ° `print Help.AdminApp`
- ° `print Help.AdminTask()`

If you wish to get detailed help for a specific method contained within a particular command object you can use the syntax `print <command_object>.help('<sub_command>')`

For example, to see details of the `list` method (sub-command) of the `AdminConfig` object, type the following command:

**`print AdminConfig.help('list')`**

6. Once you have finished using the interactive console, type `Exit` to leave the wsadmin tool.

# Individual commands

You can execute single wsadmin commands from the command line. This is an easy and effective way of making simple calls. It is not as useful as the interactive command script option. However, there could be situations where you may want a shell script to call a single wsadmin method as a part of some exceeded administrative, monitoring, or reporting function.

1. To call wsadmin via the command line, you use the wsadmin tool with the `-c` option. Ensure that you are in the `<was_profile_root>/bin` folder and type the following command:

   - ° For Linux:

     **`./wsadmin.sh -lang jython -c 'AdminApp.list()'`**

   - ° For Windows:

     **`wsadmin.bat -lang jython -c 'AdminApp.list()'`**

2. The result will list the applications installed on the server which is shown in the following sample output:

```
WASX7209I: Connected to process "server01" on node LocalhostNode01
using SOAP connector;  The type of process is: UnManagedProcess
```

```
'DefaultApplication\r\nHRListerEAR'
```

As you can see from the preceding example, the output is raw text and you will need to process this raw text and separate out the results as required by the calling script.

## Linux command-line example

In the preceding example, you can see that a string of the current applications is returned. Since the output string is not presented in a humanly readable form, you could use a shell script command to parse the line into a more readable format. An example could be that you want a shell script to call a wsadmin command and parse the results for a report or feed as an input parameter to another script. To demonstrate a Linux shell script that calls a wsadmin command, complete the following three steps:

1. Create a file called `scripts_home>/linux/listapps.sh` and copy in the following code:

```
#!/bin/bash
export var=`<was_profile_root>/bin/wsadmin.sh -lang jython -c
'AdminApp.list()'`
export raw_apps=$(echo $var|cut -f 2 -d \')
export parsed_apps=$(echo ${raw_apps} | sed 's/\\n/ /g')
for app in $parsed_apps
do
 echo $a
done
```

2. After saving the file, change the permissions to 755 to make the `listapps.sh` script executable. To change permissions, use the `chmod` Linux command from within the `<scripts_home>/linux` folder, as follows:

```
./chmod 755 ./listapps.sh
```

3. Run the `listapps.sh` script by typing the following command:

```
<scripts_home>/linux/listapps.sh
```

The results of the script will look similar to the following listing:

```
DefaultApplication
```

```
HRListerEAR
```

# Windows command-line example

Using a similar approach to the preceding Linux example, it is also possible to use VBScript to execute and parse the result from the wsadmin command line. To try the example on Windows, follow these steps:

1.  Create a file called `listapps.vbs` in an appropriate folder such as `<scripts_home>\Windows\listapps.vbs` and type in the following code:

```
Dim RegEx, WSH, myList,app,item
Set RegEx = New RegExp
Set WSH = CreateObject("WScript.Shell")
Set oExec = WSH.Exec("<was_profile_root>bin\wsadmin.bat -username
wasadmin -password wasadmin -lang jython -c AdminApp.list()")
RegEx.Pattern ="'.*'"

Do Until oExec.Status = 0
 WScript.Sleep 100
Loop

Do Until oExec.StdOut.AtEndOfStream
 Line = oExec.StdOut.ReadLine
 result=line
 If RegEx.Test(Line) Then myList = replace(RegEx.Replace(Line,
result),"'","")
Loop

resultArray = split(myList,"\r\n")

for each item in resultArray
  app= item & vbCR
  WScript.Echo app
next
```

2.  To execute the VBScript, run the following command within a Windows command prompt:

    **cscript.exe //Nologo <scripts_home>\windows\list.vbs**

3.  The results will be as follows:

    **DefaultApplication**

    **HRListerEAR**

    As you can see from the preceding two command-line examples, you can combine OS scripts and wsadmin commands to produce outputs that can be used to feed into other scripted processes.

# Profile scripts

A profile script is a script that runs before any other Jython script, or before entering interactive mode. You can use profile scripts to set up a scripting environment that is customized for the user or the installation. Often, this is used to set up common global environment variables/settings used by many scripts. For our example, we are going to create a profile script that gets the WAS cell name before entering interactive mode:

1. Create a script called `<scripts_home>/jython/profilescript.py` and enter the following code:

   ```
   #Get cell name
   cellName = AdminControl.getCell()
   print "Cell name = " + cellName
   ```

2. Save the file and run it from `<was_profile_root>`, using the following command:

   - For Linux:

     ```
     ./wsadmin.sh -lang jython -username wasadmin -password
     wasadmin -profile <scripts_home>/jython/profileScript.py
     ```

   - For Windows:

     ```
     wsadmin.bat -lang jython -username wasadmin -password
     wasadmin -profile <scripts_home>\jython\profileScript.py
     ```

3. Before wsadmin enters the interactive mode, it will run the `profilescript.py` Jython script. The results will be something similar to the following output:

   ```
   WASX7209I: Connected to process "server01" on node node01 using
   SOAP connector; The type of process is: UnManagedProcess

   Cell name = s15418557Node01Cell

   WASX7031I: For help, enter: "print Help.help()"wsadmin>
   ```

# Command script files

Using wsadmin with individual commands can be difficult when you want to run multiple commands and use variables to store transient data. Also, wsadmin doesn't have a history of the previous command executed. It is recommended that you run all your scripts via a command file. A command file is just a text-based file containing the Jython commands you wish to execute. A scripted command file contains Jython commands and is passed to wsadmin via the command line. We can harness the power of wsadmin to run complex administrative scripts by using a command file.

# Listing installed applications with Jython

We will now demonstrate our first command file script:

1. Create a folder called `jython` in your `<scripts_home>` folder.

2. Take the following code and paste it into a new file called `listApplications.py` and save:

```
#This Jython code will list all the applications installed on your
WebSphere server.
print AdminApp.list()
```

3. Run the script by typing the following command:
    - For Linux:
      ```
      <was_profile_root>/bin/wsadmin.sh -lang jython -f <scripts_
      home>/jython/listApplications.py
      ```
    - For Windows:
      ```
      <was_profile_root>\bin\wsadmin.bat -lang jython -f <scripts_
      home>\jython\listApplications.py
      ```

The result of running the script will be a listing of the installed applications on your WebSphere server. If you have not uninstalled any applications since the second chapter, you will get the listing shown as follows:

```
WASX7209I: Connected to process "server01" on node node01 using SOAP
connector; The type of process is: UnManagedProcess

DefaultApplication

HRListerEAR
```

# Installing an application using Jython

We have used the wsadmin tool a few times and have seen how it is used. What we will do now is cover how to deploy an application using Jython. We will create two Jython script files to be called by the wsadmin tool. One script will install (deploy) an application and the other will uninstall it.

1. Create a file called `<scripts_home>/jython/uninstallApp.py`.

2. Copy in the following code:

```
#Uninstall the application
deployEAR="<deploy_home>/HRListerEAR.ear"
appName="HRListerEAR"
AdminApp.uninstall(appName);
#save
AdminConfig.save();
```

3. Save the `uninstallApp.py` file.

4. To run the installation, type the following command:

   ° For Linux:

   ```
   <was_profile_root>/bin/wsadmin.sh -username wasadmin -
   password wasadmin -lang jython -f <scripts_home>/jython/
   uninstallHR.py
   ```

   ° For Windows:

   ```
   <was_profile_root>\bin\wsadmin.bat -username wasadmin -
   password wasadmin -lang jython -f <scripts_home>\jython\
   uninstallHR.py
   ```

5. The result of the preceding script will be similar to the following:

   ```
   WASX7209I: Connected to process "server01" on node node01 using
   SOAP connector;  The type of process is: UnManagedProcess

   ADMA5017I: Uninstallation of HRListerEAR started.

   ADMA5104I: The server index entry for WebSphere:cell=s15418557Node
   01Cell,node=node01 is updated successfully.

   ADMA5102I: The configuration data for HRListerEAR from the
   configuration repository is deleted successfully.

   ADMA5011I: The cleanup of the temp directory for application
   HRListerEAR is complete.

   ADMA5106I: Application HRListerEAR uninstalled successfully.
   ```

   We have now uninstalled the `HRLister EAR` file. We want to reinstall it using a different script containing Jython to install an application.

6. Create a file called `<scripts_home>/jython/installApp.py`.

7. Copy in the following code:

   ```
   #install the application
   deployEAR="<scripts_home/deploy>/HRListerEAR.ear"
   appName="HRListerEAR"
   attr="-appname " + appName + " "
   AdminApp.install(deployEAR, "["+attr+"]" );
   #save
   AdminConfig.save();
   ```

8. Save the `installApp.py` file.

9. To run the installation, type the following command:

   ° For Linux:
   ```
   <was_profile_root>/bin/wsadmin.sh –username wasadmin -
   password wasadmin -lang jython -f <scripts_home>/jython/
   installHR.py
   ```

   ° For Windows:
   ```
   <was_profile_root>\bin\wsadmin.bat–username wasadmin -
   password wasadmin -lang jython -f <scripts_home>\installHR.
   py
   ```

10. The result will be similar to the following screen output:

   ```
   WASX7209I: Connected to process "server01" on node node01 using
   SOAP connector;  The type of process is: UnManagedProcess

   ADMA5016I: Installation of HRListerEAR started.

   ADMA5058I: Application and module versions are validated with
   versions of deployment targets.

   ADMA5005I: The application HRListerEAR is configured in the
   WebSphere Application Server repository.

   ADMA5053I: The library references for the installed optional
   package are created.

   ADMA5005I: The application HRListerEAR is configured in the
   WebSphere Application Server repository.

   ADMA5001I: The application binaries are saved in /var/apps/was8/
   profiles/appsrv01/wstemp/Script12ee94c8510/workspace/cells/
   s15418557Node01Cell/applications/HRListerEAR.ear/HRListerEAR.ear

   ADMA5005I: The application HRListerEAR is configured in the
   WebSphere Application Server repository.

   SECJ0400I: Successfully updated the application HRListerEAR with
   the appContextIDForSecurity information.

   ADMA5005I: The application HRListerEAR is configured in the
   WebSphere Application Server repository.

   ADMA5113I: Activation plan created successfully.

   ADMA5011I: The cleanup of the temp directory for application
   HRListerEAR is complete.

   ADMA5013I: Application HRListerEAR installed successfully.
   ```

If you are getting tired of typing `-lang Jython` to specify that wsadmin should use the Jython language, you can change the `wsadmin.properties` file in WebSphere to make Jython the default language for scripting. The `wsadmin.poperties` file is located in the `<was_profile_root>/properties/` folder. Edit the file and change the `com.ibm.ws.scripting.defaultLang=jacl` line to `com.ibm.ws.scripting.defaultLang=jython` and save the changes to ensure that wsadmin uses Jython by default.

# Querying application status

Suppose you wanted to iterate through all the applications installed on your WAS instance and query each application to find their running status. We know from our previous interactive script that we can run `AdminApp.list()`. What we have not covered is that Jython returns list items. We can make calls to specific MBeans methods such as the `list()` method of `AdminApp`, which can use the returned list object to iterate through elements returned by the list object.

1. To demonstrate iteration, we will create a file called `<scripts_home>/jython/iterateApps.py` and copy in the following code:

```
print "Getting Application Status..."
apps = AdminApp.list().splitlines();
for app in apps:
 #print app
 appObj=AdminControl.completeObjectName('type=Application,name='+a
pp+',*')
   if appObj != '' :
     appStatus = 'running';
   else :
     appStatus = 'stopped';
 print 'Application:'+app+'='+appStatus
```

The preceding script gets a list of applications installed and, for each application found, it queries the presence of the application's MBean to find out whether the application is running.

The following table explains key lines of the preceding Jython code:

| Code Element | Description |
|---|---|
| `apps = AdminApp.list().splitlines();` | The apps variable is assigned the Jython string as returned by the call to the `AdminApp.List()` function. However, the function returns a Jython string object, which is essentially a list; we wish to separate the list into individual string elements. By using the `splitlines()` method, we can convert the string list to an array of strings, which we can then iterate. Each element of the apps array contains one single application name. |
| `for app in apps:` | The apps variable is a Jython list and, since it is like an array of strings, we can iterate through the list object. The `for` command allows us to move through the apps Jython list one element at a time, assigning the value to the app variable each time. |
| `appObj=AdminControl.completeObjectName('type=Application,name='+app+',*')` | Now that we have an actual variable name as a string, we can make a call to the `AdminControl()` method called `completeObjectName`, which queries WAS to return the application's internal MBean information. |
| `if appObj != '' :`<br><br>`  appStatus = 'running';` | We use the `if` condition to evaluate the string and, if it is not null, that is if it is not an empty string, then the application has a running MBean, so we know the application has been started. |
| `else :`<br><br>`  appStatus = 'stopped';` | The `else` condition evaluates the opposite of the `if` condition and sets the appStatus variable to the value of stopped, meaning that MBean is not running for the application. |
| `print 'Application:'+app+'='+appStatus` | At the end of each iteration of the `for` loop, we print out a string response that contains the application name and its runtime status. |

You will notice that certain lines are indented with one single space. Jython uses indentation to separate program elements. The amount of space is not important as long as they are consistent indentations. If you have issues with pasting in this code, you can download a correctly-formatted version of the script from http://www.packtpub.com.

2. To run the Jython script, run the following command:

   ◦ For Linux:

   ```
   <was_root>/bin/wsadmin.sh -lang jython -f /home/wasscripts/
   iterateApps.py
   ```

   ◦ For Windows:

   ```
   <was_root>\bin\wsadmin.bat -lang jython -f <scripts_home>\
   iterateApps.py
   ```

3. A typical result of running the script is shown in the following sample output:

   ```
   WASX7209I: Connected to process "server01" on node node01 using
   SOAP connector;  The type of process is: UnManagedProcess

   Getting Application Status...

   Application:DefaultApplication=running

   Application:HRListerEAR=stopped
   ```

Now that we have covered the basics on how to use wsadmin with a command file, we will look at how to create more advanced Jython and learn how to change the configuration of WAS. In *Chapter 2, Installing WebSphere Application Server* we manually created a J2C JAAS connection, using the Administration console. To recap, a J2C JAAS is a Java authentication and authorization service alias which, in simple terms, is a database user name and password resource that can be changed independently from the actual data source itself. What we are going to do is look at how to write a script that will change the configuration of WAS using a script.

Create a file called `<scripts_home>/jython/J2CManager.py` and copy in the following code:

```
import sys
import java.util as util
import java.io as javaio
class JDBCUtil:
  def __init__(self,fullPropsPath):
      self.fullPropsPath=fullPropsPath


#-------------------------------------------------------------
# Create / Modify J2C Java Authentication and Authorization Service
(JAAS)
  def J2CAuthentication(self,props1):
      updJAAS = props1.get("updJAAS")
      JAASAlias = props1.get("JAASAlias")
      JDBCName=props1.get("JDBCName")
```

```
        cellName = AdminControl.getCell()
        JAASConfigID = AdminConfig.getid("/Cell:"+cellName+"/Security:/
JAASAuthData:/" )
        JAASDescription = props1.get("JAASDescription")
        JAASUserId = props1.get("JAASUserId")
        JAASPassword =  props1.get("JAASPassword")
        JAASAttr = [["alias", JAASAlias], ["description",
JAASDescription], ["userId", JAASUserId], ["password", JAASPassword]]
        existingJAASList = AdminConfig.getid("/Cell:"+cellName+"/
Security:/JAASAuthData:/" )
        #Tidy up list and remove blank lines
        JAASItems=existingJAASList.splitlines();
        print "INFO: Looping through Existing JAAS Alias"
        updateJAASFlag="false"
        for JAASItem in JAASItems:
            print JAASItem
            existingJAASAlias = AdminConfig.
showAttribute(JAASItem,"alias")
            print "INFO: ExistingJAASAlias=%s" % existingJAASAlias
            if (cmp(existingJAASAlias, JAASAlias) == 0):
                print "INFO: JAASAuthInfo Exists, Updating
Alias:"+existingJAASAlias+" ......"
                AdminConfig.modify(JAASItem, JAASAttr )
                print "    Modified!"
                updateJAASFlag = "true"
                #Exit the foor loop, now we have updated our match
                break
            #end if
        #end For
        if (cmp(updateJAASFlag, "false") == 0):
            print "INFO: Creating new JAASAuthInfo Alias: "+JAASAlias+"
login/password ......"
            security = AdminConfig.getid("/Cell:"+cellName+"/Security:/"
)
            print "security=%s" % security
            AdminConfig.create("JAASAuthData", security, JAASAttr )
            print "INFO: J2C Authentication Created Successfully!"
        #end if
#-------------------------------------------------------------
# Save Configuration
#-------------------------------------------------------------
        print "Saving configuration..."
                AdminConfig.save()
                print "Complete!"
#-------------------------------------------------------------
```

```
# Load properties File
#----------------------------------------------------------
  def loadproperties(self):

       print "------load properties %s " % self.fullPropsPath
       properties = util.Properties()
       source = javaio.FileInputStream(fullPropsPath)
       bis = javaio.BufferedInputStream(source)
       props = util.Properties()
       props.load(bis)
       print "Properties file has been loaded"
       return props
#----------------------------------------------------------
# Main entry point
#----------------------------------------------------------
fullPropsPath = sys.argv[0]
print "fullPropsPath=%s" % fullPropsPath
dsObj = JDBCUtil(fullPropsPath)
props1=dsObj.loadproperties()
dsObj.J2CAuthentication (props1)
```

Essentially, the preceding code uses a Jython class to create the main function, which does the configuration work. In this example, we have used Java packages that demonstrate the ability to use Java calls inside Jython. Using these Java functions, we enable access to a configuration file that contains configurable properties made available to the Jython code.

The following table explains the code line-by-line:

| Code Element | Description |
| --- | --- |
| import java.util as util | Imports the java.util package which contains Java methods, which give the script ability to access settings contained in an external property file. |
| import java.io as javaio | Imports the java.io package, which gives Jython the ability to access the file system and read the properties file. |
| class JDBCUtil: | To demonstrate that Jython is an object-oriented language, we have declared a class called JDBCUtil, which we will use to create a custom Jython object that has properties and methods. |

| Code Element | Description |
| --- | --- |
| `def __init__ (self,fullPropsPath):` | Declares the constructor of the Jython class. A constructor is called when we create an instance of a class called an object. Essentially, this is the first method called when we instantiate an object of type `JDBCUtil` later in the main entry point of the code. |
| `def J2CAuthentication(self,pro ps1):` | Defines a method (member function) of the `JDBCUtil` class. The `J2CAuthentication` method takes two variables: `self` passes in the object and `props1` passes in the props file object. |
| `updJAAS = props1.get("updJAAS")`<br><br>`JAASAlias = props1. get("JAASAlias")`<br><br>`JDBCName=props1.get("JDBCName")` | These lines get values from the properties file and assign them to local variables. |
| `cellName = AdminControl. getCell()` | This line uses the `AdminControl. getCell()` method to query WebSphere and get the `cellName`. |
| `JAASDescription = props1. get("JAASDescription")`<br><br>`JAASUserId = props1. get("JAASUserId")`<br><br>`JAASPassword = props1. get("JAASPassword")` | These lines get values from the properties file and assign them to local variables. |
| `JAASAttr = [["alias", JAASAlias], ["description", JAASDescription], ["userId", JAASUserId], ["password", JAASPassword]]` | This line builds up an attribute string, which we will use in the creation and modification of the JAAS alias. |
| `existingJAASList = AdminConfig. getid("/Cell:"+cellName+"/ Security:/JAASAuthData:/" )` | This line builds a configuration ID of the JAASAuthData Mbeans, which returns a string of the current JAASAuthData that exists in the WebSphere configuration. |
| `JAASItems=existingJAASList. splitlines();` | This line splits the string into a list that we can iterate through to query for JAASAuthData alias names. |

| Code Element | Description |
|---|---|
| `updateJAASFlag="false"` | Here, we set a flag that we will use to determine if the JAAS alias we are trying to create already exists. |
| `for JAASItem in JAASItems:` | Here, we loop through the list (array) of currently-existing JAAS aliases and assign each one, in turn, to the variable called `JAASItem`. |
| `existingJAASAlias = AdminConfig.showAttribute(JAASItem,"alias")` | This line uses the `JAASItem` string and queries `JAASAuthData` to return the JAAS alias name, which we will use for comparison. |
| `if (cmp(existingJAASAlias, JAASAlias) == 0):` | If we find a match between the alias name we wish to create and one from the list of existing aliases, we will modify it; otherwise, we will create a new one as it doesn't exist. |
| `AdminConfig.modify(JAASItem, JAASAttr )` | This line is executed when there is a match found, so we begin to set up the ability to update an existing alias. |
| `updateJAASFlag = "true"` | We set the flag so that the following code knows we have been modifying an existing alias and do not want to create a duplicate. |
| `if (cmp(updateJAASFlag, "false") == 0):` | If there is no match, it means we are creating the alias for the first time. |
| `security = AdminConfig.getid("/Cell:"+cellName+"/Security:/" )` | This line sets up the correct `config id` for the creation of a new `JAASAuthData` item. |
| `AdminConfig.create("JAASAuthData", security, JAASAttr )` | Here, we call `AdminConfig.create()`, passing the MBean configuration ID. |
| `AdminConfig.save()` | We save the changes we have made in order to retain them in the internal WAS XML configuration files. |
| `def loadproperties(self):` | Defines the `loadproperties()` method. We pass in the instantiated `JDBCUtil` object so we can refer to internal properties. |
| `properties = util.Properties()` | This line creates a Java properties object, which will contain our properties file information. |
| `source = javaio.FileInputStream(fullPropsPath)` | This line creates a `FileInputStream`, which allows us to access the physical properties file. |

| Code Element | Description |
| --- | --- |
| `bis = javaio. BufferedInputStream(source)` | Here, we use a `BufferedInputStream`, which makes efficient use of serializing the file into a usable string that we can assign to the in-memory `props` object, which is of type `util.properties`. |
| `props = util.Properties()` | This line creates the `props` object, which contains the properties file. |
| `props.load(bis)` | Here, we load the file into the `props` object. |
| `return props` | This line returns the newly-created `props` object, which contains the values pairs of the properties file. |
| `fullPropsPath = sys.argv[0]` | This line gets the path to the properties file on disk. The path is passed as a command-line argument to the `wsadmin.sh` tool and shows how Jython can use command-line parameters for organization and configurability of your Jython variables. |
| `dsObj = JDBCUtil(fullPropsPath)` | This line creates an instantiation of the `JDBCUtil` class, creating an object called `dsObject`. |
| `props1=dsObj.loadproperties()` | This line calls the `loadproperties()` method of `dsObj` to load the properties file into an object called `props1`. |
| `dsObj.J2CAuthentication (props1)` | This line calls the `J2CAuthentication()` method of `dsObj`, passing in the properties file as `props1`, which then allows variables in the `J2CAuthentication()` method to be assigned values by name from the properties file. |

Once you have crafted the Jython file, you can now create a new file called `<script_home/jython/J2CManager.properties` and paste in the following code and save:

```
#J2C Authentication Alias Properties
JAASAlias=HR2
JAASDescription=HR Application JAAS #2
JAASUserId=HR
JAASPassword=HR
```

To run the Jython script and pass in the location of the properties configuration file, type the following command:

- **For Linux:**

```
<was_profile_root>/bin/wsadmin.sh -lang jython -username wasadmin
-password wasadmin -f <scripts_home>/jython/J2CManager.py ./
J2CManager.properties
```

- **For Windows:**

```
<was_profile_root>\bin\wsadmin.bat -lang jython -username wasadmin
-password wasadmin -f <scripts_home>\jython\J2CManager.py
J2CManager.properties
```

The result of running this script is as follows:

```
WASX7209I: Connected to process "server01" on node node01 using SOAP
connector;  The type of process is: UnManagedProcess

WASX7303I: The following options are passed to the scripting environment
and are available as arguments that are stored in the argv variable: "[./
jdbcManager.properties]"

fullPropsPath=./jdbcManager.properties

------load properties ./jdbcManager.properties

Properties file has been loaded

INFO: Looping through Existing JAAS Alias

(cells/s15418557Node01Cell|security.xml#JAASAuthData_1300995314935)

INFO: ExistingJAASAlias=HR

INFO: Creating new JAASAuthInfo Alias: HR2 login/password ......

security=(cells/s15418557Node01Cell|security.xml#Security_1)

INFO: J2C Authentication Created Successfully!

Saving configuration...

Complete!
```

The result of running this script will be to add a new J2C Authentication alias just like we created in *Chapter 3, Deploying your Applications*. However, this time we used automation, as opposed to using the Administrative console. The following screenshot shows our new alias:

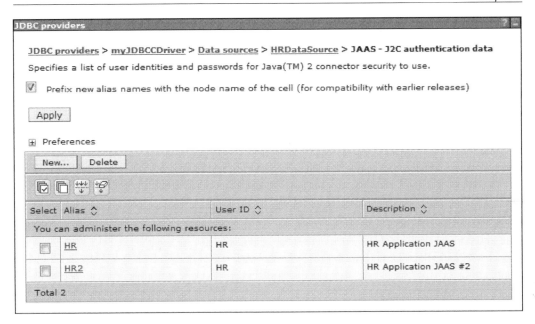

The preceding script contains several key concepts used in enterprise Jython scripting for WAS automation. We cannot cover all the various possibilities of what can be done with Jython, however, the basic principles of using Jython have been covered to help you begin administrative scripting. To give you a helping hand in advanced Jython scripting, a full JDBC management Jython script, called jdbcManager.sh, has been provided. The script and its related properties file, called jdbcManager.properties, can be downloaded from http://www.packtpub.com.

Using scripts is the way forward for efficiently administering WAS. Any investment of time and effort spent developing automation scripts is worth it.

# Configuring the wsadmin tool

The wsadmin tool comes with a properties file that can be used to configure certain runtime options. The file is called wsadmin.properties and is located in the <was_root>/properties folder. You will find the option com.ibm.ws.scripting. defaultLang=jacl, which means that wsadmin is set to use JACL by default and that is why we have been passing the command line option -jython to all of our scripts. By changing this property to com.ibm.ws.scripting.defaultLang=jython, wsadmin will use Jython as the default language instead.

All the properties available in the `wsadmin.properties` file are listed in the following table:

| Property | Description |
|---|---|
| **com.ibm.ws.scripting.connectionType** | • The `connectionType` determines what connector is used. It can be SOAP or RMI.<br>• The default is SOAP. |
| **com.ibm.ws.scripting.port=8880** | • The port property determines what port is used when attempting a connection.<br>• The default SOAP port for a single-server installation is `8880`. |
| **com.ibm.ws.scripting.host=localhost** | • The host property determines what host is used when attempting a connection.<br>• The default value is `localhost`. |
| **com.ibm.ws.scripting.ipchost=localhost** | • The `ipchost` property determines what host is used when attempting a connection with the IPC connector. Use the host name or IP address of the loopback adapter that the IPC connector is listening to, such as `localhost`, `127.0.0.1`, or `::1`.<br>• The default value is `localhost`. |
| **com.ibm.ws.scripting.defaultLang=jacl** | • The `defaultLang` property determines what scripting language to use.<br>• Supported values are `jacl` and `jython`.<br>• The default value is `jacl`. |

| Property | Description |
|---|---|
| **com.ibm.ws.scripting.echoparams=true** | • The echoparams property determines whether parameters or arguments are output to STDOUT or to the wsadmin traceFile. The user has the ability to disable this property so as to not output parameters to STDOUT or to the wsadmin traceFile, for security purposes.<br>• The default value is true. |
| **com.ibm.ws.scripting.traceFile=$(was.install.root)/logs/wsadmin.traceout** | • The traceFile property determines where trace and logging output are directed. If more than one user will be using wsadmin simultaneously, different traceFile properties should be set in the user's properties files.<br>• The default is that all tracing and logging goes to the console. |
| **com.ibm.ws.scripting.validationOutput=** | • The validationOutput property determines where validation reports are directed. If more than one user will be using wsadmin simultaneously, different validationOutput properties should be set in the users' properties files.<br>• The default is wsadmin.valout in the current directory. |
| **com.ibm.ws.scripting.traceString=com.ibm.*=all=enabled** | • The traceString property governs the trace in effect for the scripting client process.<br>• The default is no tracing. |
| **com.ibm.ws.scripting.appendTrace=false** | • The appendTrace property determines whether tracefile appends to the end of the existing log file. The user can disable the property to not append to the log file.<br>• The default value is false. |

| Property | Description |
|---|---|
| com.ibm.ws.scripting.profiles=$(was.install.root)/bin/securityProcs.jacl;$(was.install.root)/bin/LTPA_LDAPSecurityProcs.jacl | • The `profiles` property is a list of profiles to be run before running user commands, scripts, or an interactive shell.<br>• `securityProcs` is included here, by default, to make security configuration easier. |
| com.ibm.ws.scripting.emitWarningForCustomSecurityPolicy=true | • The `tempdir` property determines what directory to use for temporary files when installing applications.<br>• The default is what the JVM decides—`java.io.tmpdir`. |
| com.ibm.ws.scripting.validationLevel= | • The `validationLevel` property determines what level of validation to use when configuration changes are made from the scripting interface.<br>• Possible values are: `NONE`, `LOW`, `MEDIUM`, `HIGH`, and `HIGHEST`.<br>• The default is `HIGHEST`. |
| com.ibm.ws.scripting.crossDocumentValidationEnabled= | • The `crossDocumentValidationEnabled` property determines whether the validation mechanism examines other documents when changes are made to one document.<br>• Possible values are: `true`, `false`.<br>• The default is `true`. |
| #com.ibm.ws.scripting.classpath= | • The `classpath` property is appended to the list of paths to search for classes and resources.<br>• There is no default value. |

# Configuring applications using properties files

Now that we have learned about wsadmin and Jython scripting we can discuss how to configure applications using properties files. WAS 7 introduced to administrators the ability to use application properties files to install enterprise application files on a server or cluster, update deployed applications or modules, or uninstall deployed applications or modules. WAS 8 has extended the feature set to give administrators more functionality and control. There is a caveat, however; an enterprise application file must conform to **Java, Enterprise Edition (Java EE)** specifications to be able to configured using properties files.

 There are recommended Java blueprints on how to design applications correctly, as specified by the JEE specifications.

We will use the **HR Lister application** presented in *Chapter 3*, *Deploying your Applications,* to demonstrate the steps involved in installing, updating, and deleting an application, using properties files.

# Extracting properties from an existing application

Since it can take time to prepare a properties file for property-based application configuration, WAS provides the ability to speed up the process by extracting application properties. Extracting application properties generates a template, giving you insights into property syntax. You can then use the extracted properties in your administration scripts.

## Extracting properties using wsadmin

Using the `PropertiesBasedConfiguration` command group for the wsadmin `AdminTask` object, you can extract the configuration attributes and values to a properties file. We will demonstrate by extracting the properties from the HR Lister application. The following steps assume you have the HR Lister application installed. If you do not have the application installed, please install using your preferred method of installation, either manually or using scripting as learned earlier in the chapter.

1. Start the wsadmin scripting tool using the command mentioned previously in the chapter.

2. Use the `extractConfigProperties` command to extract the object configuration, as the following Jython example demonstrates:

    ° For Linux:

    ```
    AdminTask.extractConfigProperties('[-propertiesFileName /
    tmp/hrLister.props -configData Application=HRListerEAR]')
    ```

    ° For Windows:

    ```
    AdminTask.extractConfigProperties('[-propertiesFileName c:\
    temp\hrLister.props -configData Application=HRlisterEAr]')
    ```

3. The result will be a detailed properties file called `hrLister.props`, which will be located in the specified output folder. The actual contents of the resulting extracted properties file is too verbose to list here. However, a few snippets of what would be expected to be found in the output are as follows:

```
#
#Properties
#
taskName=MapWebModToVH
row1={HRLister HRLister.war,WEB-INF/web.xml default_host}
mutables={false false true} #readonly
row0={webModule uri virtualHost} #readonly


#
#Properties
#
taskName=CtxRootForWebMod
row1={HRLister HRLister.war,WEB-INF/web.xml hrlister}
mutables={false false true} #readonly
row0={webModule uri web.contextroot} #readonly


#
#Properties
#
taskName=MapResRefToEJB
row1={14 24 HRLister "" HRLister.war,WEB-INF/web.xml jdbc/
mydatasource javax.sql.DataSource AppDeploymentOption.No jdbc/
hrdatasource "" "" Container "" false ""}
mutables={false false false false false false false true true true
true false true false false} #readonly
row0={AppVersion ModuleVersion module EJB uri referenceBinding
resRef.type oracleRef JNDI login.config.name auth.props resAuth
dataSourceProps injection.requested lookup.name} #readonly
```

These properties can then give you an outline and serve as a guide to what syntax would be expected during the creation your own property files. We will now cover some simple examples of how to manage the HR Lister application using the properties file approach. The first example will be deleting the HR Lister application. This example assumes you have installed the HR Lister application.

# Deleting an application using a properties file

The following steps are required to delete an application using a property file:

1. Create a properties file called `hrlister_delete.props` in a folder called `<scripts_home>/props`. Within the `props` file, identify the application and specify properties such as the following to uninstall an Application configuration object called `HRListerEAR` (note the `DELETE=true` option):

```
#
# Header
#
ResourceType=Application
ImplementingResourceType=Application
DELETE=true
ResourceId=Cell=!{cellName}:Deployment=!{applicationName}

# Properties
Name=!{applicationName}
#
#Environment Variables Section
#
applicationName=HRListerEAR
cellName=s15418557Node01Cell
serverName=server01
nodeName=node01
```

2. Run the `applyConfigProperties` command from an interactive wsadmin prompt to remove the application, as shown in the following text:

   ○ For Linux:

   ```
   AdminTask.applyConfigProperties(['-propertiesFileName
   <scripts_root>/props/hrlister_delete.props -reportFileName
   <scripts_root>/props/delete_report.txt '])
   ```

   ○ For Windows:

   ```
   AdminTask.applyConfigProperties(['-propertiesFileName
   <scripts_root>\props\hrlister_delete.props -reportFileName
   <scripts_root>\props\delete_report.txt '])
   ```

3. Because we have added the `-reportFileName` option, a report will be generated detailing the actions performed. You must restart the application server for the changes to be made visible in the Administrative console. Once the server has restarted the HR Application will no longer exist.

# Installation using a properties file

The following steps are required to install an application using a property file:

1. Create a file called `<scripts_home>/props/hrlister_install.props` and specify the following properties. Ensure that you replace the appropriate `Cell name`, `serverName`, and `nodeName` as required. Note: you can also get values for `Cell`/`server`/`node Name`, and so on, from the extracted properties file we created earlier.

```
#
# Header
#
ResourceType=Application
ImplementingResourceType=Application
CreateDeleteCommandProperties=true
ResourceId=Deployment=

# Properties
Name=!{applicationName}
TargetServer=!{serverName}
TargetNode=!{nodeName}
EarFileLocation=<path_to_file> HRListerEAR.ear

#
# Environment Variables Section
#
applicationName=HRListerEAR
cellName=s15418557Node01Cell
serverName=server01
nodeName=node01
```

2. Run the `applyConfigProperties` command from an interactive wsadmin prompt to install the application as shown in the following text:

   ○ For Linux:

```
AdminTask.applyConfigProperties(['-propertiesFileName
<scripts_root>/props/hrlister_install.props -reportFileName
<scripts_root/props/install_report.txt ']);

AdminConfig.save();
```

○ For Windows:

```
AdminTask.applyConfigProperties(['-propertiesFileName
<scripts_root>\props\hrlister_install.props -reportFileName
<scripts_root>\props\install_report.txt ']);
```

`AdminConfig.save();`

3. The end result will be the installation of the HR Lister EAR file.

 If you wish to save the changes, you must ensure you run the wsadmin command `AdminConfig.save()`. If you do not save when using the wsadmin Jython command, the installation will not be saved to the underlying WebSphere configuration files.

# Updating applications using a properties file

Using the same concepts as before, we can also reconfigure existing applications. To learn the types of tasks that can be used it is recommended that you first install an application and then extract a template props file as a form of reference. For our example, we are going to change the HR Lister application's context root from hrlister to hrlister_new.

 Context roots are explained in *Chapter 3, Deploying your Applications,* where we cover application deployment.

The steps to update an application's context root are as follows:

1. Create a new props file called `<scripts_root>/props/ hrlister_ context_root.props`. Edit application properties in the properties file as shown in the following code. Note that the ResourceID property value is very specific. This syntax is located within a sample extracted properties file:

```
#
# Header
#
ResourceType=Application
ImplementingResourceType=Application
ResourceId=Cell=!{cellName}:Deployment=!{applicationName}:Applicat
ionDeployment=ID#ApplicationDeployment_1304178427702:WebModuleDepl
oyment=ID#WebModuleDeployment_1304178427703
#
#Properties
#
taskName=CtxRootForWebMod
```

```
row1={HRLister HRLister.war,WEB-INF/web.xml hrlister_new}
mutables={false false true} #readonly
row0={webModule uri web.contextroot} #readonly


#
#Environment Variables Section
#
applicationName=HRListerEAR
cellName=s15418557Node01Cell
```

2. Run the `applyConfigProperties` command from an interactive wsadmin prompt to update the deployed application.

   ○ For Linux:

   ```
   AdminTask.applyConfigProperties(['-propertiesFileName
   <scripts_root>/props/hrlister_context_root.props
   -reportFileName <scripts_root>/props/cr_report.txt ']);
   ```

   ```
   AdminConfig.save();
   ```

   ○ For Windows:

   ```
   AdminTask.applyConfigProperties(['-propertiesFileName
   <scripts_root>\props/hrlister_context_root.props
   -reportFileName <scripts_root>\props/cr_report.txt ']);
   ```

   ```
   AdminConfig.save();
   ```

3. The result will be as follows:

   ```
   ADMG0820I: Start applying properties from file /
   tmp/1304789667189___###__hrlister_context_root.props
   ```

   ```
   ADMG0811I: Changing value for this property row1. New value
   specified is HRLister,HRLister.war,WEB-INF/web.xml,hrlister_new,.
   Old value was HRLister,HRLister.war,WEB-INF/web.xml,hrlister,.
   ```

   ```
   ADMG0821I: End applying properties from file /
   tmp/1304789667189___###__hrlister_context_root.props.
   ```

4. The HR Lister application can now be launched using the URL, `http://<host_name>:9080/hrlister_new/listtable`, as opposed to `http://<host_name>:9080/hrlister/listtable`.

# Configuring monitored deployment with properties

A new feature of WAS 8 is the ability to configure—or reconfigure—applications deployed using the monitored deployment process, as covered in *Chapter 3, Deploying your Applications*. Now that we have seen how to use a property file to manage an application, it is worth a quick note to explain some key points about using properties files as part of monitored deployments.

You do not need to start wsadmin or enter any commands to deploy the application or module. Simply add a properties file to a monitored directory. The product runs the `wsadmin applyConfigProperties` command for you. We can use the exact same methods to install, update, and delete a deployed application or module contained in an application. The server must be running so that the product can detect changes to files in its monitored directory.

> This procedure, listed in the following text, assumes that you use a graphical file browser to drag or copy the properties file. Alternatively, you can use operating system commands to copy a file into a monitored `DeployableApps/deploymentProperties` folder.

# Creating a properties file for monitored deployment

Create a properties file that defines the deployment task you want to complete. The properties files that you use in monitored directories are like the properties files described in the preceding sections, using application properties files to install, update, and delete application files. However, properties files that are used for monitored directories differ slightly. You do not need to specify statements such as `CreateDeleteCommandProperties=true` in the header. You only specify application resource type operations such as `ImplementingResourceType=Application`, in the properties file. If the properties file contains a non-application resource type such as `ImplementingResourceType=Server`, the product will return an error message and won't perform the operation on the resource type.

> You can use an edited properties file to install or update an application. To extract the properties file of a deployed enterprise application to edit or use as a template, run the `extractConfigProperties` command, as discussed earlier.

# Managing system configuration using properties files

Since WAS 7, it has been also possible to administer an application server using the wsadmin tool and special properties files to manage system and runtime configurations. Using this approach, it is possible to use properties files to manage your environment and configuration. The main reason for using property files as opposed to wsadmin scripting is that properties files are portable. You can extract a properties file from one cell, modify some environment-specific variables at the bottom of the extracted properties file, and then apply the modified properties file to another cell. This is a great feature allowing a template approach to standard WAS cell configurations.

It can be difficult to learn all the syntax required to write properties files that can modify your system configurations. To make this easier, WAS provides the ability to extract configuration objects in simple properties file format, modify the extracted properties file, and apply the modified properties file to update the system configuration. File base configuration is useful when a non-programming approach is required.

In addition to updating system properties, you can do the following:

- Extract properties required to run an administrative command.
- Run an administrative command using an extracted properties file.
- Extract or modify properties for any WCCM object type:

  The acronym **WCCM** stands for **WebSphere Common Configuration Model**, although this term is not usually used in the product documentation/ messages. All the files (documents) in a profile/configuration directory tree (like `sib-engines.xml`, in this case) contain persisted configuration data. As the configuration is object-based, these files contain instance data for objects whose types are defined in the WCCM (such as servers, nodes, clusters, messaging engines, and so on).

- Delete or remove a property and modify a property using a single properties file.
- Delete a configuration object in the same properties file that is used to create or modify properties.

- A properties file extracted from a configuration contains the following information about the configuration:
  - Required properties for creating a new object of any type
  - Default values for a property
  - Range of values for a property

We will not be detailing how to use properties files for configuring WAS as it is a large subject. However, using the same principles as learned from configuring applications, you will be able to make a decision on whether the properties-based approach to WAS configuration is useful to you as an administrator.

To learn more about property configuration see `http://publib.boulder.ibm.com/infocenter/wasinfo/v8r0/topic/com.ibm.websphere.base.iseries.doc/info/iseries/ae/txml_property_configuration.html`.

# Command assistance

A really useful feature within the Administrative console is the ability to turn on command assistance. When command assistance is turned on, configuration changes in the Administrative console are recorded and displayed within a link in the right-hand navigation panel of the console. You can then refer to the Jython recorded to understand what wsadmin command is used for a particular configuration change. It is also possible to turn on command logging, which will create a log file containing the recorded configuration changes. To turn on command assistance, follow these steps:

1. Click on the **Console Preferences** link located in the **System administration** section within the left-hand side navigation panel:

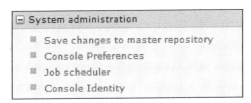

2. Within the **Console Preferences** page you can toggle **Administration console preferences**. Check the **Enable command assistance notifications** option to have the console display the commands as configurations are made. Check the **Log command assistance commands** option to instruct the console to log the equivalent Jython commands that represent the configuration changes. The Jython commands are logged to a file within the application server's log file location. For example, `<was_profile_root>/logs/<servername>`:

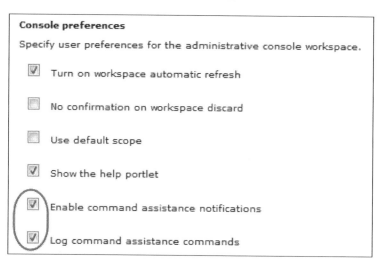

3. Click **Apply** to save the changes.

When configuration changes are made within the Administrative console, a link titled **View administrative scripting commands for last action** will appear in the right-hand side of the console:

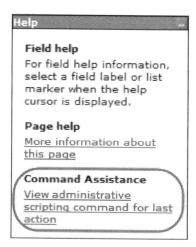

The feature is very useful to gain ideas on which specific wsadmin command objects are required to perform the same action using Jython scripting. You can then search the IBM Information Center for these wsadmin commands to learn more about the methods and properties available. Using this technique can help save time locating the right wsadmin commands required to automate WAS configuration.

# Summary

In this chapter, we learned that WAS has several tools for use in automation. Scripts can be run to either configure WAS or manage the runtime process, such as stopping and starting servers and/or applications.

We looked at the two most common tools used in WAS automation—wsadmin and ws_ant. We explained that ws_ant is based on Apache Ant and can be used for basic deployments and installs, however, it is really only suited for development environments. The wsadmin tool, however, can be used to configure all elements of WebSphere and provides an extensive set of methods that can configure the internals of WebSphere. Larger enterprises typically implement Jython using wsadmin, as opposed to ws_ant. however, both tools have their uses. wsadmin using Jython stretches across both development and production environments.

We were also shown how to create a more advanced Jython script, which included a class. We used this class to change WAS configuration via the command line. We also extended our knowledge about monitored deployments and completed the topic of using properties files to administer application deployments. In the next chapter, we will cover details of the underlying WAS file system and look at some key concepts for WAS administration, including log management and the all-important topic of class loaders.

# 6
# Server Configuration

This chapter covers a number of key areas and topics that are crucial to the administration and functioning of WAS and its deployed applications. Among others, we will look into topics like logging and class loading, and explain the several levels of class-loader settings available to your application server and applications.

In this chapter, we will cover:

- WAS file structure
- XML configuration files
- Logs and trace
- NSCA and the HTTP logging feature
- High Performance Extensible Logging (HPEL)
- Java Virtual Machine (JVM) settings
- Class loading

## WAS file structure

Thus far, we have installed WAS, deployed a few applications, run some administrative scripts, and even changed some security options using the WAS Administrative console. All configuration changes to WAS are saved in configuration files, and it is important for you to understand the WAS filesystem and where configuration files, repositories, and log files are located.

There are several main categories of files that we need to cover:

- XML configuration files
- XML repositories
- Log files
- Properties files

Before we delve into the types of files, we will first cover the WAS filesystem and explain the file structure and layout, identifying key folders and file locations along the way.

# The WAS filesystem

Like almost any other software product, WAS uses a filesystem which contains both runtime files, that is, the **product binaries** and also **configuration files**. Configuration files are XML files which are read at runtime. The Administration console modifies these XML files when you save changes. There are many folders and directories in the WAS folder structure. We will explain the structure in two sections. The first section will cover the key folders of the main product installation folders, and the second section will cover the key folders within a profile.

> We cannot cover all the configurations of WAS in this chapter and so we have covered the most important folders. If you wish to investigate further, you can consult the online WebSphere Application Server Information Center, located at the following URL: `http://publib.boulder.ibm.com/infocenter/wasinfo/v8r0/index.jsp`.

## Product binaries file structure

The folders within a WAS installation contain the files and binaries which form the basis of the WAS product. All WAS profiles utilize and refer to these core files, so it is important to understand key folders and what they are used for. The following screenshot shows the `<was_root>` folder for a WAS instance:

Following is a table of the key directories located on the WAS root path, which we had previously referred to as `<was_root>`:

| Folder name | Description |
| --- | --- |
| bin | Contains the core product runtime binaries, tools, and scripts which are used to run and administer WAS. |
| logs | Contains the main product installation and configuration logs. Very useful for debugging product installation issues and administrative tools when they are not working. |
| samples | If you opted to install samples, then this folder will exist and contain sample code and applications. |
| scriptLibaries | This folder contains a vast amount of re-usable Jython functions, which can be used to fully automate WAS configuration and application deployment. |
| profileTemplates | When you create a profile, WAS uses the XML files in this folder as templates. In WebSphere Application Server, we have two main templates—the management template is used for creating a management profile and the default template is used to define an Application Server profile. |
| properties | Contains product-level configurations, for example, a registry of the current installed profile(s) and other product-level settings. This folder is often never changed by administrators. |
| uninstall | This folder contains the script and executables to cleanly uninstall WAS. |

# The profile file structure

As we have learned in *Chapter 2, Installing WebSphere Application Server*, WebSphere uses profiles to determine the makeup of an application server. A WebSphere profile determines and controls the configuration of the actual application server. Most of the WebSphere administration activities are centered on the profile, so understanding the underlying filesystem within a profile is very important. The following screenshot shows the `<was_profile_root>` folder for a WAS instance:

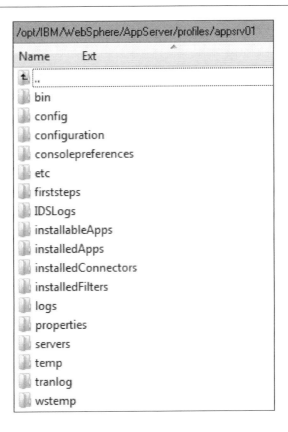

The following table outlines the key folders and subfolders of a profile:

| Folder name | Description |
| --- | --- |
| bin | Contains the scripts used to administer your application server from a command line. Most of the scripts in the `<was_profile_root>` reference and call scripts are located in the `<was_root>` folder. |
| config | Contains the XML files which store (persist) all the configurations made through the Administrative console. We will cover these in detail later in this chapter. |
| firststeps | As we have seen in *Chapter 2, Installing WebSphere Application Server*, this folder contains the first steps console that is available when using graphical installations. Not important for post-install administration. |

| Folder name | Description |
| --- | --- |
| installableApps | Contains default WAS applications which can be installed depending on the type of installation options used in the WAS install process. This is where `defaultApplication.ear` will be located which contains snoop, as seen in *Chapter 3, Deploying your Applications*. |
| installedApps | Contains the on-disk structure of the deployed applications as installed into WAS. This is a very important folder and is used extensively for administrative support of applications. |
| logs | Contains the log files pertinent to WAS runtime. Most debugging of administrative and application issues are achieved through the help of the logs contained in this folder. |
| properties | Contains key properties files which contain settings that can be used to change behaviors, for example, security for the `wsadmin` tool. |
| samples | Contains some portions of the sample applications required for runtime components — if the samples have been installed. |
| temp | Contains runtime temporary files. For example, if JSPs within applications are converted into Java classes at runtime, then the `temp` folder will contain these Java classes. |
| tranlog | If an application contains distributed transactions, then the `tranlog` folder will contain transactional logs which can be used for rollback. We will not be covering this topic in this book. |
| wstemp | Used by WAS during the deployment of applications as a temporary staging area and also contains in-transit configurations before console changes are saved. |

# XML configuration files

The entire WAS configuration is saved and persisted within XML files. When we use the Admin console to configure WAS, certain XML files are updated with the appropriate settings relating to each type of configuration. It is important that an administrator understands the key XML files and what they are used for. When there are configuration or runtime issues, knowing these files and their locations can help with problem-solving. Following is a list of the most important configuration files that a WAS administrator should be aware of. It must be noted that some files exist more than once in different **Scopes**, that is, **cell level**, **node level**, and **server level**.

**Scope** is very important for the WebSphere Application Server Network Deployment (WAS ND) product, which is not covered in this book. However, it must be noted that WAS ND has an additional Scope called cluster level. WAS ND Scopes are cell level, node level, cluster level, and server level. Many WAS configurations, such as **Java Naming Directory Interface (JNDI)**, incorporate the concept of Scope for determining efficiency in resource lookups. JNDI scope is covered in *Chapter 7, WebSphere Messaging*.

# Cell level XML files

Following is a list of the key XML configuration files found at the scope of the cell level:

Located in /<was_profile_root>/config/cells/<cell_name>/

- resources.xml
    - Defines operating cell scope environmental resources, including JDBC, JMS, JavaMail, URL end point configuration, and so on

- security.xml
    - Contains security data, including all user ID and password information

- virtualhosts.xml
    - Contains virtual host and Multipurpose Internet Mail Extensions (MIME)-type configurations

- variables.xml
    - Contains cell level WAS variables

- admin-authz.xml
    - Contains the roles set for administration of the Admin console
    - <was_profile_root>/config/cells/<cell_name>

- wimconfig.xml
    - Contains the federated repository configurations for global security
    - <was_profile_root>config/cells/<cell_name>/wim/config/

- profileRegistry.xml
    - Contains a list of profiles and profile configuration data

# Node level XML files

Following is a list of the key XML configuration files found at the scope of the node level:

Located in: /<was_profile_root>/config/cells/<cell_name>/nodes /<node_name>/

- `variables.xml`
  - ○ Contains node level WAS variables

- `resources.xml`
  - ○ Defines node scope environmental resources, including JDBC, JMS, JavaMail, URL end point configuration, and so on

- `namestore.xml`
  - ○ Provides persistent JNDI namespace binding data

- `serverindex.xml`
  - ○ Specifies all the ports used by servers on this node

# Server level XML files

Following is a list of the key XML configuration files found at the scope of the server level:

Located in: /<was_profile_root>/config/cells/<cell_name>nodes /<node_name>/servers/<server_name>/

- `variables.xml`
  - ○ Contains server level variables

- `server.xml`
  - ○ Contains application server configuration data

- `resources.xml`
  - ○ Contains the configuration of resources, such as JDBC, JMS, JavaMail, and URL end points at server scope

As an administrator, you should rarely ever have to edit these files, and if you do feel at some point that you need to, remember that you can seriously damage your WAS installation if you do not fully understand the influence of changes to these files. All administration should be done through the Admin console or with administrative scripts. It is not recommended that you edit these files directly.

# Important properties files

As an administrator, it is important that you understand the `soap.client.props` and `sas.client.props` files located in the `<was_profile_root>/properties` folder. If you enable security for a WebSphere Application Server cell, you will have to manually enter in the username and password every time you run the `wsadmin` tool. By editing the `sas.client.props` and the `soap.client.props` files, you can specify the username and password you have configured for global security so that you are not prompted to enter the username and password every time you run administrative scripts.

# The soap.client.props file

When global security is enabled in the cell and you have chosen to use **SOAP** as the communication protocol for the `wsadmin` tool (SOAP is the default communication protocol for `wsadmin`), then you will need to update the following properties in the `soap.client.props` file with the appropriate values, as shown next. Doing so will ensure that the `wsadmin` tool does not prompt for a username and password:

```
com.ibm.SOAP.securityEnabled=<true>
com.ibm.SOAP.loginUserid=<username>
com.ibm.SOAP.loginPassword=<password>
Optionally, set the following property:
com.ibm.SOAP.loginSource=none
```

# The sas.client.props file

When global security is enabled in the cell and you change `wsadmin` to use a **Remote Method Invocation (RMI)** connector (RMI is not the default protocol), you need to set the following properties in the `sas.client.props` file with the appropriate values, as shown next. Doing so will ensure that the `wsadmin` tool does not prompt for a username and password:

```
com.ibm.CORBA.loginUserid=
com.ibm.CORBA.loginPassword=
Also, set the following property:
com.ibm.CORBA.loginSource=properties
```

The default value for this property is prompted in the `sas.client.props` file.

 If you leave com.ibm.CORBA.loginSource and com.ibm.CORBA. loginSource to the default values, a dialog box appears with a password prompt. If the script is running unattended, it appears to hang; this is quite a common issue when a WebSphere Application Server has been set up for the first time.

# Encoding property files

When changes are made to property files, it is recommended that the passwords be encrypted. WAS provides a command-line tool called `PropFilePasswordEncoder` which can be used to encode named setting within property files. An example might be that you have altered `soap.client.props` and added a password to the `com.ibm.SOAP.loginPassword` setting to stop server startup scripts from prompting for a username and password. Encoding the password will ensure that the password is not stored in clear text.

To encode a property file, use the following syntax:

- **For Linux:**

```
PropFilePasswordEncoder.sh file_name password_properties_list
  [-Backup/-noBackup]
```

- **For Windows:**

```
PropFilePasswordEncoder.bat file_name password_properties_list
   [-Backup/-noBackup]
```

> When using `PropFilePasswordEncoder` to encode property files, it is recommended that you use the backup option or make a copy of the file, so you can revert if there are any issues.

# Logs and trace

A WebSphere Application Server uses logs to record what is happening during server runtime. Administrators can use the logs to determine the application server runtime status. Logs are also very useful during problem determination when issues arise with WAS. The main log folder is the application server's `logs` directory, which is found in the `<was_profile_root>` folder. Following is a screenshot of a typical logs directory:

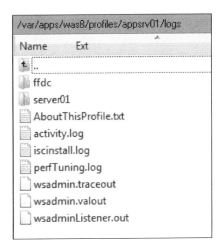

In the previous screenshot, you will see that the application server instance is located in a profile named `appsrv01`, which is located in the `profiles` directory. The `logs` folder is located in the `<was_profile_root>` folder, which we will refer to as the `logs` folder. Logs will always be here unless you override log locations within the Administrative console.

# JVM log files

The main logs for a WebSphere Application Server are contained in a folder with the same name as the application server. In our example, our application server instance is called server01, so the log files are contained in the server01 directory located within the logs directory, which is within the <was_profile_root> folder. Following is an example of the logs that are typically generated by a WebSphere Application Server:

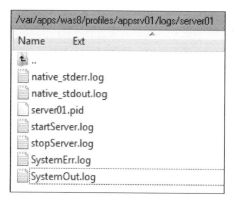

You can see in the previous screenshot that it is typical for a running server instance to have generated several logs during server runtime. Not all the logs will exist immediately; some are spawned when certain conditions occur.

The following table explains what each log is for and what you might expect to find in the log:

| Log name | Description |
|---|---|
| native_stderr.log and native_stdout.log | stdout and stderr streams are redirected to log files at application server startup, which contain text written to the stdout and stderr streams by native modules, that is Linux Modules, and so on. In normal error-free operations, these logs files are typically empty. |
| startServer.log | This log file is named startServer.log and is created in your logs directory when the server starts up. This log is very useful to determine JVM parameters used in the start-up process, the server's process ID, and also the date and time in which the server was started. If there are errors experienced during the start-up (for example, security configuration errors where the application server cannot start), then log information will exist for problem determination. |

| Log name | Description |
| --- | --- |
| stopServer.log | This file logs the fact that the server was stopped via a command line. If the server has trouble stopping, then Java stack traces will be written to the log which can be used in determining why a given application server failed to stop. |
| SystemErr.log | This log file contains Java exceptions and stack traces. |
| | An empty SystemErr.log file does not necessarily indicate a successfully running application server JVM. You may need to consult the other logs in this directory. |
| SystemOut.log | This log file contains messages as generated by the JVM during runtime. Some messages are informational, some are warnings, and some are status updates. Applications can be configured to write to the log and so it is very common for the SystemOut.log to be your first port of call in application debugging. You will find that SystemOut.log is the log you will review most often. |
| | Both this log file and the SystemErr.log file should be checked after starting an application server to confirm that both the server and applications have started correctly. |
| SystemOut_<date_time_stamp>.log | This filename style is an example of a log file roll-over due to the log being full. WAS can be configured to roll over in a different style, which will be covered later in the chapter. |
| <server_name>.pid | This file contains the process ID of the server. In Linux, this is the actual process ID assigned to the JVM process. |
| activity.log | IBM service log (activity.log) contains WAS messages that are written to the System.out stream along with special messages that contain extended service information that can be important when analyzing problems. There is one service log for all WAS JVM's on a node. |
| | The IBM Service log is maintained in a binary format. Use the Log and **Trace Analyzer** or the **Showlog** tool to view the activity.log. |

# Configuring logs and trace

JVM logs can be configured in the Administrative console. Log configuration is specific to each Application Server JVM. To change the JVM logs and trace configurations, log in to the Admin console and navigate to the **Troubleshooting** section in the left-hand-side navigation panel, and click on **Logs and trace**, as shown in the following screenshot:

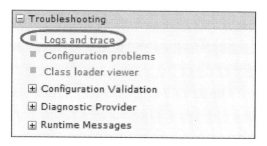

You will then be presented with a list of Application Server JVMs. In our example, we only have one. Click on the **server01** JVM (Application Server) and you will be presented with a list of options, as shown in the following screenshot:

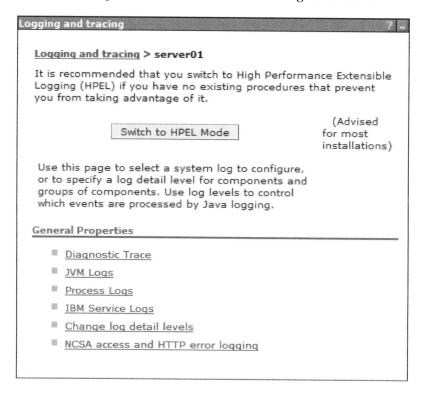

A notable new feature of WAS 8 is the ability to switch to the **HPEL (High Performance Extensible Logging)** mode, which sets WAS to use the new high performance logging techniques. The benefit of using HPEL is that the application server runtime performance increases due to using a binary approach to logging. You can now configure the server to use the HPEL log and trace infrastructure instead of using the SystemOut.log, SystemErr.log, trace.log, and activity. log files. If choosing to use HPEL, you can access your entire log and trace information using the **LogViewer** command-line tool from your server profile bin directory. HPEL configuration details are discussed at the end of this section. The reason we left HPEL until last is that we first need to understand traditional log and trace settings and what log files are used before we switch over to using HPEL.

## Diagnostics trace

The diagnostic trace configuration settings allow trace and state information to be gathered for a server process (JVM process). You can also change many of the trace service properties or settings while the server process is running. To demonstrate an example of server tracing, we will configure the trace settings to output detailed JNDI naming information from the HR Lister application. The HR Lister application uses JNDI to lookup the JDBC data source. To enable a trace to log JNDI information immediately without a server restart, use the following steps:

1. Click **Troubleshooting | Logs and trace** in the console navigation tree, then click **<server_name> | Diagnostic Trace**.

2. Click **Runtime**.

3. Select whether to directly trace output to either a file or an in-memory circular buffer. We will use the default which is **File**. The trace log file will be created in ${SERVER_LOG_ROOT}/trace.log, for example, <was_profile_root>/appsrv01/logs/server01/trace.log, as in the case of server01.

Different components can produce different amounts of trace output per entry. Naming and security tracing, for example, produces a much higher trace output than web container tracing. Consider the type of data being collected when you configure your memory allocation and output settings.

If the in-memory circular buffer is selected for the trace output, you can also set the size of the buffer, specified in thousands of entries. This is the maximum number of entries that will be retained in the buffer at any given time.

If a file is selected for trace output, set the maximum size in megabytes to which the file should be allowed to grow. When the file reaches this size, the existing file will be closed, renamed, and a new file with the original name reopens. The new name of the file will be based upon the original name with a timestamp qualifier added to the name. In addition, you can specify the number of history files to keep.

4. Select the desired **Trace Output Format** for the generated trace. In this example, we will leave the default setting (which is **Basic (Compatible)**) which will generate a human-readable log. You can see an example of the configuration in the next screenshot.

5. To change log level details, you can either click on the link called **Change log level details**, located in the **Additional Properties** section, or you can click **Apply** and then **Save** to save the configuration:

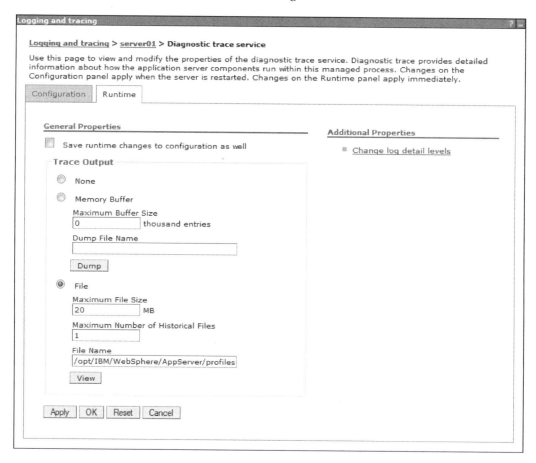

6. If you chose to save, you will be re-directed back to the logs and trace section again. We assume you have clicked **Save** in the **Diagnostics and trace service** screen, as shown previously.

7. We will now change the logging level. Click **server01** and then **Change log detail levels** to configure the level of logging detail.

8. You will now be presented with a tree listing of the different types of trace groups. Scroll down and expand the **com.ibm.websphere.*** group and click on the **com.ibm.websphere.naming.*** group.

9. You will be presented with a context menu. Select the **Message and Trace Levels** menu option to be presented with a drop-down list of log message levels or trace levels.

10. Select **All Messages and Traces** from the list, as shown in the following screenshot:

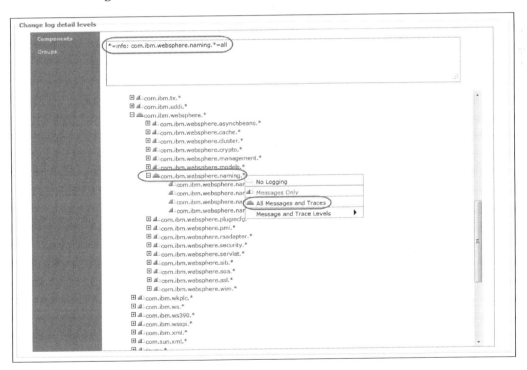

11. Select **Apply** and then **Save**. Note it is also possible to type the trace information directly into the trace field, as shown previously.

Following is a table explaining the log message and trace levels which can be selected. Depending on what trace information you need for your analysis, you can set log tracing levels of information. WAS will then only log information that meets the message log level definition:

| Level | Content/Significance |
| --- | --- |
| Off | No events are logged. |
| Fatal | Task cannot continue and component cannot function. |
| Severe | Task cannot continue, but component can still function. |
| Warning | Potential error or impending error. |
| Audit | Significant event affecting server state or resources. |
| Info | General information outlining overall task progress. |
| Config | Configuration change or status. |
| Detail | General information detailing subtask progress. |
| Fine | Trace information—General trace. |
| Finer | Trace information—Detailed trace + method entry/exit/return values. |
| Finest | Trace information—A more detailed trace—Includes all the details needed to debug problems. |
| All | All events are logged. If you create custom levels, 'All' includes your custom levels and can provide a more detailed trace than Finest. |

You do not need to restart the server for the new trace configuration to take effect. If you look in the SystemOut.log, you will now see WAS reporting that tracing is now set as follows:

**TRAS0017I: The startup trace state is \*=info: com.ibm.websphere.naming.\*=all.**

A `trace.log` file will also exist in the same location as `SystemOut.log`. Looking at this log, we will see trace information pertaining to JNDI naming lookups. If you load the HR Lister's `listtable` servlet, as shown in *Chapter 3, Deploying your Applications*, you will see detailed trace information from the application's JNDI lookup. An example of this tracing information is shown in the following screenshot:

```
root@localhost:/opt/IBM/WebSphere/AppServer/profiles/appsrv01/logs/server01
[7/22/11 16:35:58:632 BST] 00000022 ManagerAdmin  I   TRAS0018I: The trace state has changed. Th
e new trace state is *=info:com.ibm.websphere.naming.*=all.
[7/22/11 16:35:58:670 BST] 00000022 WsnInitialCon >  <init> Entry
[7/22/11 16:35:58:671 BST] 00000022 WsnInitialCon <  <init> Exit
[7/22/11 16:35:58:671 BST] 00000022 WsnInitialCon >  getInitialContext Entry
                            env={java.naming.factory.initial=com.ibm.websphere.naming.WsnIn
itialContextFactory, java.naming.provider.url=corbaloc:rir:/NameServiceServerRoot, java.naming.f
actory.url.pkgs=com.ibm.ws.naming:com.ibm.ws.runtime:com.ibm.iscportal.jndi:com.ibm.ws.naming, o
sgi.service.jndi.bundleContext=com.ibm.osgi.jndi.fep.GatewayBundleContextProxy@39825a3}
[7/22/11 16:35:58:671 BST] 00000022 WsnInitialCon >  initInstance Entry
[7/22/11 16:35:58:671 BST] 00000022 WsnInitialCon <  initInstance Exit
[7/22/11 16:35:58:671 BST] 00000022 WsnInitialCon <  getInitialContext Exit
[7/22/11 16:35:58:737 BST] 00000022 WsnInitialCon >  <init> Entry
[7/22/11 16:35:58:737 BST] 00000022 WsnInitialCon <  <init> Exit
```

Configuring trace can be slightly laborious, so this is a great time to get your Jython-scripting hat on and create a script to turn tracing on and off using the `wasadmin` scripting techniques learned in *Chapter 5, Administrative Scripting*.

In the previous example, we chose to use the **Runtime** tab of the logging and tracing screen. If you use the **Configuration** tab, your trace settings will be applied permanently to the application server the next time it is restarted.

# JVM logs

Within the **JVM Logs** section, it is possible to change the log locations:

1. Click on the **JVM Logs** option and you will be presented with a configuration form allowing you to change the location where the JVM will create logs. You can also change the style in which the application server JVM will log information.

2. To change the log file location, you can use the log configuration page, as shown in the next screenshot, and change the **File Name** field to specify the location within the filesystem where you want your logs located.

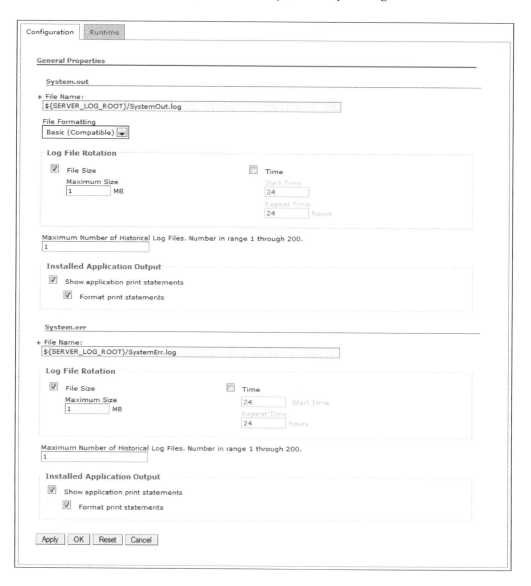

3. In the previous screenshot, you will notice that there is a system variable called **SERVER_LOG_ROOT** that identifies the root location of the logs. You can override system variables by navigating to the **Environment** section located in the right-hand navigation panel of the Admin console and selecting the **WebSphere variables** link:

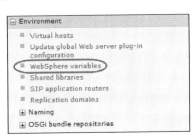

4. When you access the **WebSphere variables** page, you will see a list of configured WAS variables. There are many variables listed depending on the selected **Scope**. Select server scope.

5. Once the screen is reloaded, take a look at the following screenshot and you will see the variable called **SERVER_LOG_ROOT**. This variable is used to define the filesystem path for the location of server01's log files. By changing this location, you can set a different filesystem location for the server01 logs. As you can see, the **SERVER_LOG_ROOT** has a value of **${LOG_ROOT}/server01**. What this demonstrates is that you can nest variables within variables. The **${LOG_ROOT}** variable declaration is actually the application server profile's log folder:

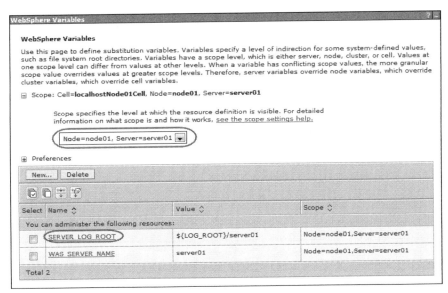

As an administrator you can re-configure environment variables to define specific settings and locations, as required.

## Changing log styles

As explained previously, the **Logging and Tracing | server01 | JVM Logs** page is used to change log settings. In addition to log locations, we can also change the style in which logs are written. Often there may be several applications installed on one single JVM, so there could be loads of messages being generated by both WAS internal runtime processes and the application(s), and hence the log files will increase over time. It is important not to let your logs grow so large that they invariably fill up your operating system's disk space. Using the setting on the **JVM Logs** page, an administrator can control the size and style of logging. This is also very important when problem-solving, where application(s) are configured to write debug statements to SystemOut.log and thus they can generate very large log files. To make logs more manageable, we can change the log size and the number of log files. By using a combination of the **File Size**, **Time**, and **Maximum Number of Historical Log Files** fields, we can control the sizes of our logs. The following table shows some typical log requirements and what settings you would use from this page to configure the logs:

| Scenario | Settings required on the log configuration page |
|---|---|
| Ensure logs are no larger than 2 MB in size. | In the **Log File Rotation** section, tick the **File Size** field and set the **Maximum Size** to **2**. |
| Roll the logs over every day. | Uncheck the **File Size** field and check the **Time** field. |
| Roll logs every 5 MB and ensure we always have 100 MB of historical log files at any time. | Check the **File Size** field, set the **Maximum Size** field to **5**, and type 20 in the **Maximum Number of Historical Log Files** field. |

During debug, it is very important that you configure log sizes to manageable sizes because if they get too large, then log files will become unmanageable for downloading and for debugging purposes and will fill up your filesystem. If logs are left to rollover without control, then historical log information can be lost. It is critical that you think about logs and how you will manage logging in production systems.

# Process logs

This page is used to view or modify settings to specify the files to which the `standard out` and `standard error` streams write. The process logs are created by redirecting the standard out and standard error streams of a process to certain log files. Native code writes to the process logs. These logs can also contain information that relates to problems in native code or diagnostic information written by the JVM. One set of process logs is created for each application server and all of its applications. Changes made in the Administrative console panel apply when the server is restarted. Changes on the **Runtime** panel apply immediately. The two process logs, `native_stderr.log` and `native_stdout.log`, are explained previously in the log definition table located within the *JVM log files* section of this chapter.

# IBM service logs

This page is used to configure the IBM **service log**, also known as the **activity log**. The IBM service log contains both the application server messages that are written to the `System.out` stream, and special messages that contain extended service information that you can use to analyze problems. One service log exists for all JVMs on a node. The IBM Service log is maintained in a binary format. To view an IBM service log, you can use the **Log Analyzer** which can be downloaded from IBM from the following location:

```
https://www-304.ibm.com/support/docview.wss?uid=swg21330148
```

Alternatively, you can use the WAS `Showlog.sh` tool. The settings available are log location, log file size, and the enabling or disabling of the activity log.

 If your organization has a paid support subscription with IBM, then IBM support will often ask, for example, for activity logs to help with debugging support tickets. You would raise an IBM **Problem Management Report (PMR)** in situations where you may have issues with WAS that you cannot resolve using your team's knowledge and experience. We will cover the Log Analyzer tool and Showlog tool in *Chapter 8, Monitoring and Tuning*, where we will cover application server tuning.

# NCSA access and HTTP error logging

Use this page to configure the global HTTP error log, and **National Center for Supercomputing Applications (NCSA)** access log settings for an HTTP inbound channel. The NSCA and HTTP logging feature is new in WAS 8. Administrators who have experience with Apache will already be familiar with this log format.

1. To change NCSA settings, click **Servers | Server Types | WebSphere application servers | <server_name>**.

2. Under **Troubleshooting**, click **NCSA access and HTTP error logging**. Within this page, there are two sections for each type of logging.

3. **Enable logging service at server start-up**:

   Select this option if you want any of the following loggings to start when the server starts:

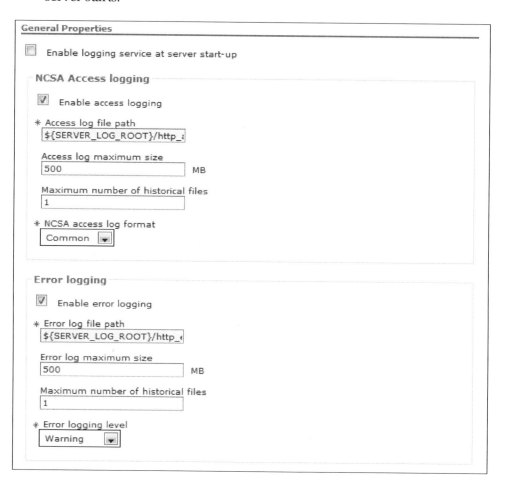

# NCSA access logging

The **NCSA** access log contains a record of all inbound client requests that the HTTP transport channel handles. All of the messages that are contained in an NCSA access log are in NCSA format. The NCSA log formats are based on NCSA HTTPd, and are widely accepted as standard among HTTP server vendors.

- **Enable NCSA access logging**:

  When selected, a record of inbound client requests that the HTTP transport channel handles is kept in the NCSA access log.

- **NCSA access log file path**:

  It specifies the directory path and name of the NCSA access log. Standard variable substitutions, such as `$(SERVER_LOG_ROOT)/http_access.log`, can be used when specifying the file-path where the log will be located.

- **NCSA access log maximum size**:

  Specifies the maximum size, in megabytes, of the NCSA access log. When the content of the NCSA access log reaches the specified maximum size limit, a `log_name.1` archive log is created. The current content of the NCSA access log is then copied to this archive log. The next time the content in the NCSA access log reaches the specified maximum log size, the content of the NCSA access log is rolled over and copied to the `log_name.1` archive log, replacing it if it already exists, with the latest log information.

- **Maximum number of historical files**:

  It specifies the maximum number of historical versions of the NCSA access log file that are kept for future reference.

- **NCSA access log format**:

  Specifies which NCSA format is used when logging client access information. If you select **Common**, then the log entries contain the requested resource and a few other pieces of information, but do not contain referral, user agent, and cookie information. If you select **Combined**, then referral, user agent, and cookie information is included.

# Error logging

The HTTP error log contains a record of HTTP processing errors that occur. The level of error logging that occurs is dependent on the value that is selected for the **Error log level** field.

- **Enable error logging**:

  When selected, HTTP errors that occur while the HTTP channel processes client requests are recorded in the HTTP error log.

- **Error log file path**:

  Specifies the directory path and the name of the HTTP error log. Standard variable substitutions, such as $(SERVER_LOG_ROOT)/http_error.log, can be used.

- **Error log maximum size**:

  Specifies the maximum size, in megabytes, of the HTTP error log. When the content of the HTTP error log reaches the specified maximum size limit, a log_name.1 archive log is created. The current content of the HTTP error log is then copied to this archive log. The next time the content in the HTTP error log reaches the specified maximum log size, the content of the HTTP error log is rolled over and copied to the log_name.1 archive log, replacing it if it already exists with the latest log information.

- **Maximum number of historical files**:

  It specifies the maximum number of historical versions of the error log file that is kept for future reference.

- **Error log level**:

  Specifies the type of error messages that are included in the HTTP error log. Options are detailed in the following table:

| Error logging level | Description |
| --- | --- |
| Critical | Only critical failures that stop the Application Server from functioning properly are logged. |
| Error | The errors that occur in response to clients are logged. These errors require Application Server administrator intervention if they result from server configuration settings. |
| Warning | Information on general errors (such as socket exceptions that occur while handling client requests) is logged. These errors do not typically require Application Server administrator intervention. |

| Error logging level | Description |
|---|---|
| Information | The status of the various tasks that are performed while handling client requests is logged. |
| Debug | More verbose task status information is logged. This level of logging is not intended to replace application logging techniques for debugging problems, but does provide a steady status report on the progress of individual client requests. If this level of logging is selected, you must specify a large enough log file size in the **Error log maximum size** field to contain all of the information that is logged. |

## NCSA and HTTP error log considerations

After you configure the HTTP error logs, NCSA access logs, and FRCA logs, you must explicitly enable each type of logging on the settings page for the HTTP channels for which you want specific types of logging to occur.

To view the settings page of an HTTP channel, click **Servers | Server Types | WebSphere application servers | <server_name> | Web Container Settings | HTTP inbound channel | Web container transport chains**.

# FFDC logs

In the `logs` folder, you will see a folder representing the name of the application server JVM. In our example, the folder is called `server01`, as this is the default name given to our server in our initial installation in *Chapter 2, Installing WebSphere Application Server*. You will also notice a folder called `ffdc` which stands for **First Failure Data Capture (FFDC)**. This folder contains detailed logs of exceptions found during the runtime of the WebSphere Application Server. The FFDC feature preserves the information that is generated from a processing failure and returns control to the affected engines. FFDC is intended primarily for use by IBM Support. Captured data is saved in a log file for analyzing the problem. FFDC instantly collects events and errors that occur during the product runtime. The information is captured as it occurs and is written to a log file that can be analyzed by IBM Support personnel. If you have knowledge of Java, such as Java programming/debugging experience, you can use FFDC to drill-down into low-level Java errors, which may help with resolving a WAS or Application issue.

# Viewing JVM logs

There are several ways in which we can view logs. We can view them via the Admin console or via the filesystem.

# Viewing logs in the Administrative console

To view the logs via the Admin console, go to **Logging and Tracing | server1 | JVM Logs** in the Admin console, and you will be presented with the JVM logs configuration page, as discussed earlier. Once you are in the **JVM Logs** page, click on the **Runtime** tab to see options to **View** the SystemOut.log and SystemErr.log files, as shown in the following screenshot:

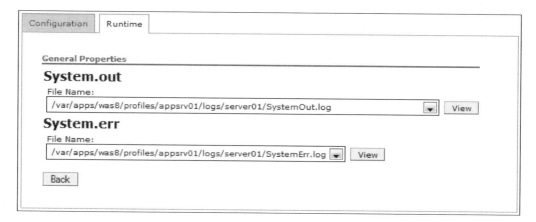

 The downside of using the Admin console to view logs is that you need to continually refresh the screen to get updated log information. When logs grow very large in size, using the Admin console logs can be cumbersome as it can take time to load the new updated log information.

# Viewing logs on the filesystem

The best way to view the JVM logs is via the operating system. However, scanning log files can be arduous if there are lots of logs with verbose log information.

If Linux is chosen as your preferred OS, you can use special Linux commands to search log files for keywords, phrases, and error codes. Two commands commonly used for searching and viewing log file information are grep and tail.

In Windows, it is much more difficult to view and search continuously growing log files using native Windows command-line tools. However, it is possible to download a free Open Source equivalent of the Unix/Linux grep and tail commands.

The specific details of using such commands like grep and tail are beyond the scope of this book.

# High Performance Extensible Logging (HPEL)

We have covered the traditional approach to logging, which uses human-readable log files. However, with WAS 8, a new feature has been introduced called **High Performance Extensible Logging (HPEL)**. HPEL uses an efficient binary file approach to logging, which improves server runtime performance.

To enable HPEL, use the following steps:

1. Click on the **Logs and trace** link located in the **Troubleshooting** section of the left-hand navigation panel of the Admin console. The **Logging and tracing** screen will display a list of servers:

| Server ◇ | Node ◇ | Host Name ◇ | Version ◇ | Type ◇ |
|---|---|---|---|---|
| You can administer the following resources: | | | | |
| server01 | node01 | localhost | Base 8.0.0.0 | servers |
| Total 1 | | | | |

2. Select the server, for example, **server01**, to open the **General properties** screen.

3. In the **General properties** screen, click on the button labeled **Switch to HPEL mode** and click **Save**.

4. Three new links will appear in the **General Properties** section, as seen in the following screenshot:

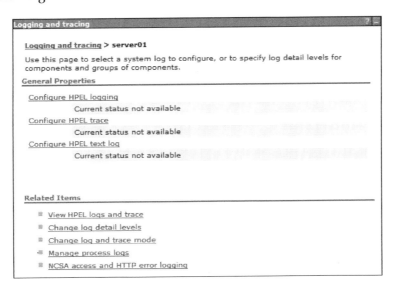

# Configure HPEL logging

The HPEL log configuration screen presents several options for log configuration. If the server is in a running state, then important log configuration values are displayed below the link. These values summarize the current runtime values being used by the server:

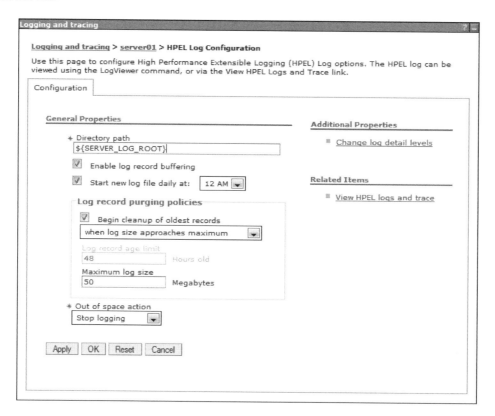

Immediately following is a full description of each of the field settings, as depicted in the previous screenshot. Common descriptions are found in the *Common HPEL settings* section at the end of these explanations.

- **Directory path**:

  Specifies the directory to which log files are written. A subdirectory (log data) is created in this directory, and the log files are written to this location.

- **Begin cleanup of oldest records**:

  It sets the action to be performed when the log's file size approaches a certain threshold.

- **Maximum log size**:

  It defines the maximum file size of the log file.

- **Out of space action**:

  It specifies the action to be performed if the filesystem becomes full.

# Configure HPEL trace

This page is used to configure trace options:

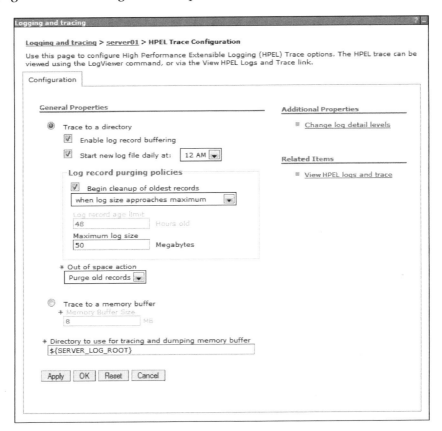

Immediately following is a full description of each of the field settings, as depicted in the previous screenshot. Common descriptions are found in the Common HPEL settings section at the end of these explanations.

- **Trace to a directory**:

  It specifies that the tracing system writes trace records to the trace directory, as they are created by the server.

- **Trace to a memory buffer**:

  It specifies that the tracing system writes trace records to a memory buffer. You can write the memory buffer contents to the trace directory from the **runtime** tab.

- **Memory buffer size**:

  Specifies the amount of memory the tracing system allocates in the server to contain trace records. In cases where the memory buffer is full when a new trace record is created, the oldest entry from the memory buffer is deleted to make space.

- **Directory to use for tracing and dumping memory buffer**:

  Specifies the directory to which trace files are written. A subdirectory, trace data, is created in this directory, and the trace files are written to this location.

# Configure HPEL text log

This page is used to configure HPEL text log options:

Immediately following is a full description of each of the field settings, as depicted in the previous screenshot. Common descriptions are found in the Common HPEL settings section at the end of these explanations.

- **Enable Text Log**:
    - Enables writing log and trace records into the text log file.
    - Specifies that in addition to writing log and trace records in binary format, the logging system writes them in a text format as well. You can configure the text log to be formatted in either of the formats that the basic mode `SystemOut.log` file uses.
    - Enabling the text log degrades performance for applications that frequently create logs or trace entries.

- **Directory path**:
    - Specifies the directory to which log files are written.
    - Text log filenames have the following format: `TextLog_<yy.mm.dd>_<hh.mm.ss>`, where `TextLog_` is a fixed prefix, `<yy.mm.dd>` is a date (year, month, date) of the first record in the file, and `<hh.mm.ss>` is the time (hour, minute, second).

- **Text Output Format**:
    - Specifies the format to use in the text log file.
    - There are two options outlined in the following table:

| Option | Description |
| --- | --- |
| Basic | Select Basic to specify a shorter, one-line-per-record format. |
| Advanced | Select Advanced to specify a longer format using the full logger name and more details about each record. |

- **Include trace records**:
    - Specifies whether trace records are included in the text log file, as well as log records.

# Common HPEL settings

The following field explanations are common to all three HPEL log type configuration screens:

- **Enable log record buffering**:
  - Specifies that the tracing system avoids writing to disk each time a trace record is created. The tracing system creates a buffer that can hold a number of trace records, and writes the buffered events when the buffer is full. The tracing system also writes the buffered events after a few seconds have passed, even if the buffer is not full.
  - Selecting this setting significantly improves tracing performance. However, if the server stops unexpectedly, the contents might not be written to the trace repository.
  - It is an IBM-recommended best practice to enable trace record buffering in almost all cases. Only disable trace record buffering when your server is failing unexpectedly and cannot write buffered content to the disk before stopping.

- **Start new log file daily at <time>**:
  - Enables the tracing framework to close the trace file and start a new file at the specified time of day. Closing the file makes it easy to copy the file to an archive.

 It is an IBM-recommended best practice to set up your backup program to copy files after the time you configured for new files to be started. Configure the backup to occur at least 10 minutes after the time configured for new files to be started to ensure that the server has closed the previous file.

- **Begin cleanup of oldest records**:
  - Specifies the log cleanup settings to be used to automatically purge the oldest log records, or log records that no longer fit in the configured space, from the text log directory.
  - There are three options, as detailed in the following table:

| Option | Description |
| --- | --- |
| When log file approaches maximum | Select this option when the log size approaches maximum to automatically initialize log file cleanup when the total size of the text log files approaches the configured maximum size. |

| Option | Description |
| --- | --- |
| When oldest records reach age limit | Select this option to configure automatic log file cleanup to begin when log content reaches the age limit specified. |
| When either age or size restriction is met | Select this option to determine log file cleanup to begin when either age or size restriction is met. |

- Regardless of the selection chosen, text log files are deleted from the text log directory in the order in which they were written.

- **Log record age limit**:
  - Specifies the lifespan, in hours, that log records can remain in the text log directory before the log records can be automatically deleted by the server. When all records in a text log file have existed longer than the age limit specified, then that file is targeted for deletion by the server.

- **Maximum log size**:
  - Specifies the maximum total size, in megabytes, that the server allows the text log files to reach. When the total size of the text log files approaches this size limit, the server deletes the oldest text log file from the text log directory to make space for new log records.

- **Out of space action**:
  - Specifies how the server reacts to an inability to add content to the text log directory.
  - There are three options, as detailed in the following table:

| Option | Description |
| --- | --- |
| Stop server | Select 'Stop server' to specify that the server stops when the server is unable to write to the text log directory. |
| Purge older records | Select 'Purge older records' to specify that the server continues to run and that the file containing the oldest log records is immediately removed when the server is unable to write to the text log directory. |
| Stop Logging | Select 'Stop logging' to specify that the server continues to run, but that the server cannot continue to write to the log when the server is unable to write to the text log directory. |

- **Save runtime changes to configuration as well**:
  - ° Specifies that changes are made to both the dynamic state of the running server, and the server configuration, which takes effect on the next restart. If this checkbox is not selected, the server does not copy the settings into the server configuration.

# HPEL summary

When HPEL is enabled, there is a quick summary available. To access the quick summary, navigate to the **Troubleshooting** section of the Admin console's left-hand navigation panel and click **Logs and trace** and then **<server_name>**. You will then see a summary similar to the following screenshot:

| General Properties | |
| --- | --- |
| **Configure HPEL logging** | |
| Directory | /var/apps/was8/profiles/appsrv01/logs/server01 |
| For cleanup, delete records older than | Disabled |
| For cleanup, maximum size of logs | 50 Megabytes |
| **Configure HPEL trace** | |
| Directory | /var/apps/was8/profiles/appsrv01/logs/server01 |
| For cleanup, delete records older than | Disabled |
| For cleanup, maximum size of trace | 50 Megabytes |
| **Configure HPEL text log** | |
| Current status: | Enabled |
| Directory | /var/apps/was8/profiles/appsrv01/logs/server01 |
| For cleanup, delete records older than | Disabled |
| For cleanup, maximum size of text log | 50 Megabytes |

# HPEL log location

Once you have enabled HPEL, a new set of folders will be created, as per your HPEL configurations discussed previously.

An example of the HPEL default logging directory might be:
```
/var/apps/was8/profiles/appsrv01/logs/server01/
logdata/1304273261962_16941_server01
```

Contained within this folder are binary files, as per your configuration. An example of a binary logging file found in the `logdata` folder for standard HPEL logging would be:

```
-rw-r--r-- 1 root root 125012 May 1 18:11 1304273261962.wbl
```

If you have not changed the default location, the HPEL tracing log is located in a folder called `/var/apps/was8/profiles/appsrv01/logs/server01/tracedata`.

The contents of this directory will be a tracing lock file similar to the following:

```
-rw-r--r-- 1 root root  0 May  1 18:07 1304273261949_16941_server01.lock
```

Since these log files are not human-readable, you can use the `logViewer.sh/logViewer.bat` command-line tool to read the logs. As a WAS administrator, this could be quite a change for you and it will take some getting used to. Traditionally, text logs have been used by WAS administrators, and many of their scripts and tools assume text files. Turning on HPEL may require some planning and changes to log management. It might be a good to time to remind you that it is possible to output the standard text files (mentioned earlier in this section), but the enhanced WAS 8 high performance logging is compromised.

# Viewing HPEL logs

There are two ways to view HPEL logs:

## View the JVM logs from the Administrative console

1. Click **Troubleshooting | Logs and Trace** in the left-hand navigation panel of the Admin console. To view the logs for a particular server, click on the server name to select it and then click **JVM Logs**.

2. Select the **runtime** tab.

3. Click **View** corresponding to the log you want to view.

# View the JVM logs in the machine that they are stored in

1. Go to the machine where the logs are stored.

2. Navigate to the `<was_profile_root>/bin` folder.

3. Run the `logViewer.sh` command-line tool (`logViewer.bat` for Windows).

By default, the **LogViewer** will output all records in the repository in a basic format. It is possible to use options to control what is included in the LogViewer output to format the output or to direct where the output is sent.

Example Usage:

```
logViewer.sh -repositoryDir dir_path [-options]
```

(where `-repositoryDir` defines the path to the HPEL binary log repository location you want LogViewer to extract information from.)

# JVM settings

An important part of configuring your application server JVM is through the use of JVM parameters. Since an application server is based on the Java Virtual Machine (JVM), we can pass certain parameters to the JVM to set specific runtime settings. To view and change the JVM configuration for an application server's process, use the Java Virtual Machine page of the Administrative console.

 It is also possible to use the `wsadmin` tool with Jython to change JVM configuration through scripting. However, this is beyond the scope of this book.

# Changing JVM settings using the Administrative console

1. In the Administrative console, go to **Servers | Server Types | WebSphere application servers | <server_name>**.

2. Then, under **Server Infrastructure**, go to **Java and process management |
   Process definition**, select **Java Virtual Machine** (application server), and
   then set the field values for the JVM settings as required and click **OK**:

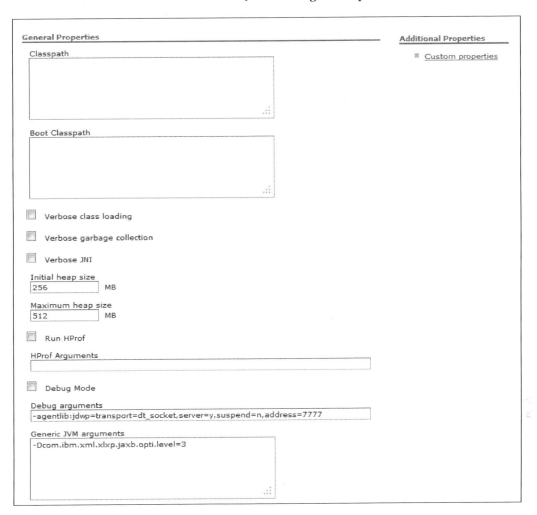

3. Click **Save** to retain the changes. You must restart the application server for
   all JVM parameter changes to take effect.

Following is a table of common JVM settings that an administrator might want to set:

| JVM parameter | Description |
| --- | --- |
| Verbose class loading | Turns on verbose debug output for class loading. The default is not to enable verbose class loading. |
| Verbose garbage collection | Sets verbose debug output for garbage collection. The default is not to enable verbose garbage collection, as it involves a performance hit on the application server. |
| Verbose JNI | Specifies verbose debug output for native method invocation. This is only used if you wish to understand what is happening with external libraries that your application may be calling. |
| Initial heap size | Size in Megabytes of the minimum memory allocated to the JVM's heap. |
| Maximum heap size | Size in Megabytes of the maximum JVM heap size. |

Regarding memory management using the previous JVM setting, remember that tuning a JVM is not easily discussed without a great amount of detail. Therefore, we have not provided a recommended initial/maximum heap size as this will depend on the nature of the application installed. As a rule of thumb, there should be no need to set your JVM maximum heap size to be greater than 1024 Megabytes, and if you are required to do so, it is most often due to application requirement. For more detailed recommendations for tuning your JVM, you can consult the Info Center at the following URL:

```
http://publib.boulder.ibm.com/infocenter/wasinfo/v8r0/topic/com.ibm.
websphere.base.iseries.doc/info/iseries/ae/tprf_tunejvm_v61.html.
```

If the previous URL does not supply enough information, you can search the WAS 8 Information Center using the JVM keyword as your search word, and many documents are available containing the information required to learn about tweaking WAS JVMs. It is also possible to find information about the Java Virtual Machine on Oracles' website. Understanding how JVMs work in principle will help you as a WAS administrator. However, it is beyond the scope of this book to cover the many facets of JVMs.

You can also set custom properties via the additional properties link found in **Application servers | <server_name> | Process definition | Java Virtual Machine**. Custom properties are often used by applications for externalizing configurations options. An example of using custom properties could be an application which implements **Log4j**, an Open Source logging system. In an application that uses Log4j, a configuration file called the `log4j.xml` file is required to allow the configuration of log levels and log file locations. By using a custom property, you could make use of a JVM parameter which can be configured by an administrator at deployment time to specify the location where the Log4j log files will be written. This means that the location of the Log4j log file(s) are not hardcoded into the `log4j.xml` file and the location can be changed by the administrator, rather than making an application change which would be required due to the fact that the `log4j.xml` file is contained within the EAR, and thus saves possible re-deployments.

# Class loaders

**Class loaders** are an integral part of the JVM code and are responsible for finding and loading class files both for the application server itself, and for applications. It is important that you understand class loaders and how they affect the JVM and deployed applications. Application developers and administrators must understand and consider the location of Java classes and Java resource files, and the class loaders used to access those files must also be able to make the appropriate class files available to deployed applications. The configuration of class loaders also affects the packaging of applications and their runtime behavior. In this book, we cannot completely cover all the issues and intricacies of class loaders. However, we will explain the essentials of class loading and what configuration elements you can use in the Administrative console to change class loading behavior.

## Class loading basics

A simple and easy way to understand class loaders is to use the concept of a parent/child hierarchy. When a class loading request is presented to a class loader at whatever level, it first asks its parent class loader to fulfill the request. The parent class loader, in turn, asks its parent for the class until the request reaches the top of the hierarchy. If the class loader at the top of the hierarchy cannot fulfill the request to load a class, then the child class loader that called it is responsible for loading the class. If the child is also unable to load the class, the request continues back down the hierarchy until a class loader fulfills it, or a `ClassNotFoundException` is produced by the last class loader at the bottom of the parent/child hierarchy.

The following simple diagram shows the class loading hierarchy of WAS:

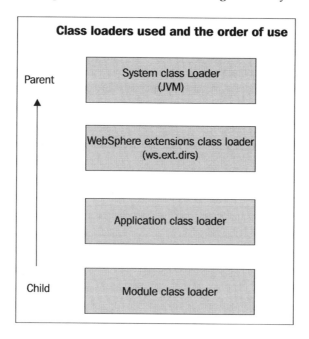

The design and packaging of an application will determine the behavior of class loading. This means that each EAR file can have many **Java Archives (JARs)** and **Web Archives (WARs)** inside it, which will influence the class loading requirements. It really comes down to what Java packages, custom or not, have been included in the applications code base. Because class loading can cause issues, WAS provides the ability to influence class loading behavior.

# WAS class loaders

In WAS, there are several ways to configure class loaders for applications and modules to ensure that they access the Java classes and Java resources packaged within.

Following is a list of the three main class loaders which can be configured via the Administration console:

- Application server class loader:

  The application server class loader policy affects all applications that are deployed on the server.

- Enterprise application class loader:

  An application class loader is the parent class of an Enterprise application archive (EAR) and all modules within it. An application class loader groups Enterprise JavaBean (EJB) modules, shared libraries, and dependency Java Archive (JAR) files associated with an application. Dependency JAR files are JAR files that contain code that can be used by both enterprise beans and servlets.

- Web module class loader:

  A web module has its own Web application archive (WAR) class loader to load the contents of the web module, which are in the WEB-INF/classes and WEB-INF/lib directories.

## Application server class loader

Essentially, this option is setting a single class loader for all applications in the entire application server. The application class loader policy controls the isolation of applications that run in the system (on the server). An application class loader groups together Enterprise JavaBean (EJB) modules, shared libraries, and JAR files that contain code which can be used by both enterprise beans and servlets. The application class loader policy controls whether an application class loader can be shared by multiple applications or is unique for each application.

## Configuring server class loaders

To change an application server's class loader using the Admin console, click **Servers | Server Types | WebSphere application servers | <server_name>** to open the application server settings page. Looking at the page, you can see the section labeled **Server-specific Application Settings**:

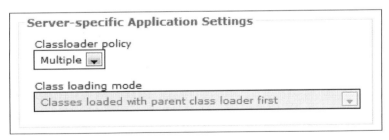

This previous screenshot shows two pick lists, which are explained in the following tables.

# Classloader policy

The following table explains the **Classloader policy** field, as found in the **Server-specific Application Settings** section:

| Option | Description |
| --- | --- |
| Single | Applications are not isolated from each other. Uses a single application class loader to load all of the EJB modules, shared libraries, and JAR files which are contained in all applications installed into the JVM. |
| Multiple | Applications are isolated from each other. Gives each application its own class loader to load the EJB modules, shared libraries, and JAR files. |

# Class loading mode

The following table explains the **Class loading mode** field, as found in the **Server-specific Application Settings** section:

| Option | Description |
| --- | --- |
| **Classes loaded with parent class loader first** | Sets the loading of classes to its parent class loader before attempting to load the class from its local class path. This is the default value for **Class loading mode** and is often referred to in discussion as "Parent first." |
| **Classes loaded with local class loader first (parent last)** | Tells the class loader to start with loading classes from its local class path before asking its parent. In simple terms, it means the application can use its own version of a class that its parent would normally have loaded. Often referred to as "Parent last". |

Often, you will leave the **Class loading mode** field as is. However, it could happen that several applications from different vendors installed on the same JVM might conflict with each other, or even WebSphere Application Server's own internal class loading could conflict with an application's class loading, and so understanding this setting is important.

# Application class loader

An enterprise application is a grouping of one or more web, EJB, or application client modules. Enterprise applications can also override settings within the contained modules deployment descriptors to combine or deploy them in a more useful way. By placing JAR files in the enterprise application instead of the global class path of an application server, they are also within the application and thus they get deployed along with the application. The idea is that an EAR file encapsulates all its required resources and hence it can be pre-configured using a manifest file to specify how it will load its internal classes. A quick Internet search will help you to understand more about how manifest files work.

# Configuring application class loaders

To configure an application's class loading settings, you need to look at the settings of an installed application. To look at an application class loading settings, click **Applications | Application Types | WebSphere enterprise applications | <application_name> | Class loading and update detection** to access the page for configuring an application class loader. Following is an example of the relevant fields from an application class loader:

General Properties

Class reloading options

☐ Override class reloading settings for Web and EJB modules

Polling interval for updated files

[_____] Seconds

Class loader order

◉ Classes loaded with parent class loader first
○ Classes loaded with local class loader first (parent last)

WAR class loader policy

◉ Class loader for each WAR file in application
○ Single class loader for application

You can see in the previous screenshot that there are two sections. One section defines the class loader order and the second the class loader policy. The following tables explain these options.

## Class loader order

The following table explains the **Class loading order** field found in the **General Properties** section:

| Option | Description |
| --- | --- |
| **Classes loaded with parent class loader first** | Sets the loading of classes to its parent class loader before attempting to load the class from its local class path. |
| **Classes loaded with local class loader first (parent last)** | Tells the class loader to start with loading classes from its local class path before asking its parent. |

## WAR class loader policy

The following table explains the class loader options for a WAR file(s) in an EAR file:

| Option | Description |
| --- | --- |
| **Class loader for each WAR file in application** | A separate class loader is assigned to each WAR file. |
| **Single class loader for application** | One class loader is assigned to all WAR files. |

# Web module class loader

Each web module has two folders for Java code—one is called WEB-INF/classes and the other WEB-INF/lib. The classes' folder may contain Java classes within the web application. We can specify a class loader which looks at this folder, so that if changes are made to the classes, they are automatically reloaded by the application server. The lib folder may contain JAR files that the web application also uses. You should place third-party JAR files and other utility JAR files in this folder. However, if other Web or EJB modules use the JAR files, move them into the Enterprise Application's class path, which is global to the application.

# Configuring module class loading

Within an EAR file, we know that we can have more than one WAR file module. WAS allows each module to be configured for class loading. To configure a WAR class loader, you need to drill down into EAR file modules. To do this, follow the following sequence in the Admin console. Click **Enterprise Applications | <application name> | Manage Modules | <module_name>** and you will then be able to see the **Class loader order** field in the **Manage Module** page:

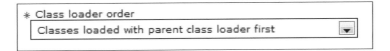

## Class loader order

The following table explains the options of the **Class loader order** field, shown previously:

| Option | Description |
| --- | --- |
| **Classes loaded with parent class loader first** | If set, the class loader searches the application's class loader for the class. |
| **Classes loaded with local class loader first (parent last)** | If set, the class loader searches within the WAR class loader first to load a class. |

# Class loading isolation

Essentially, we can group class loading into three isolation types. By using combinations of the settings in the application server and application class loader configurations, we can produce three different class loading isolations. Following is a table which explains the three types of isolation that are achieved by combinations of the previously explained class loading types:

| Isolation type | Application server class loader policy | WAR class loader policy |
| --- | --- | --- |
| Full | Multiple | WAR (Module) |
| Partial | Multiple | Single (Application) |
| Minimal | Single | Single (Application) |

When the application server policy is **Single**, it indicates a single class loader for all applications installed in the application server. **Multiple** indicates multiple class loaders. A class loader is assigned for each application so that each application becomes isolated from all other applications installed in the same JVM. The WAR class loader policy is simply either **WAR (Module)** or **Single (Application)**. **Single (Application)** indicates a single class loader for the entire application, no matter how many WAR files are included. **WAR (Module)** indicates a class loader for each web module.

 Choosing **Single (Application)** for the application server policy and **WAR (Module)** for the WAR module policy is essentially ignored, as once you set a server to use a Single class loader, there is only one class loader for the entire application server.

# Summary

In this chapter, we learned that all configurations done in the Administrative console are ultimately saved into XML files in the underlying WAS file structure. On startup, WAS reads these files to determine its configuration. We learned there are some important XML files which you should be familiar with to help with troubleshooting, WAS configuration, and runtime issues. We also learned that when global security is turned on, it is possible to edit special property files to disable login prompts when issuing server stop commands.

We covered WAS logging, where application logs are located, and the types of logs used by WAS. We also covered the new WAS 8 High Performance Extensible Logging (HPEL) logging system, which allows WebSphere Application Server to run more efficiently using binary logging information, as opposed to logging to text files.

In this chapter, we also covered the important topic of class loaders, which is very important in the running of both servers and applications. It is the responsibility of a WAS administrator to configure WAS to ensure that an application's required classes are loaded correctly without any problem.

In the next chapter, we will be covering how to configure WAS messaging, covering both the **Java Message Service (JMS)** and **WebSphere MQ (WMQ)** messaging integration.

# 7
# WebSphere Messaging

Applications which require messaging are common, and you should understand what WAS can do for Java Messaging and/or WebSphere MQ (**WMQ**)-based messaging. There are various ways in which WAS can be configured to support the messaging needs of applications. In this chapter, we will learn how to configure WAS to support typical messaging requirements. We will cover how to administer the **Java Message Service (JMS)** through creating **Queue Connection Factories (QCF)** and **Queue Destinations (QD)**. We will also cover how to configure WAS so that an application can communicate with a remote WMQ queue, giving an example along the way of how WMQ can be used as part of your WAS messaging implementation.

In this chapter, we will cover the following topics:

- Java messaging
- JMS API
- WebSphere messaging
- SiBus message reliability
- WebSphere MQ Messaging
- Disabling WebSphere MQ
- WebSphere MQ link
- Configuring MQ link

# Java messaging

Before we can look at what is required to administer JMS within WebSphere, we will cover some basics of **Java Message Service (JMS)**. JMS is the JEE method of communication between software components or applications. A messaging system is often peer-to-peer. This means that a messaging client can send messages to and receive messages, from any other messaging client. Each client connects to, a messaging service that provides a system for creating, sending, receiving, and reading messages. So why do we have Java messaging? Messaging enables distributed communication that is loosely-coupled. What this means is that a client sends a message to a destination and the recipient application can retrieve the message from this destination.

A key point of Java messaging is that the sender and the receiver do not have to be available at the same time in order to communicate.

> The term **communication** can be understood as an exchange of messages between software components. In fact, the sender does not need to know anything about the receiver, nor does the receiver need to know anything about the sender. The sender and the receiver need to know only what message format and which destination to use.

Messaging also differs from e-mail. Messaging is used for communication between software applications or software components. Java messaging attempts to relax tightly coupled communications, such as TCP network sockets, CORBA, or RMI, thus allowing software components to communicate indirectly with each other.

# Java Message Service

**Java Message Service (JMS)** is an Application Program Interface (API), which is a part of the JEE specification. JMS provides a common interface for standard messaging protocols and special messaging services in support of Java programs. Messages can involve the exchange of crucial data between systems and contain information such as event notification and service requests. Messaging is often used to coordinate programs in dissimilar systems or applications written in different programming languages. By using the JMS interface, a programmer can invoke the messaging services such as IBM's WMQ, formerly known as **MQSeries**, and other popular messaging products, such as Microsoft Message Queuing, Apache ActiveMQ, Tibco, and SonicMQ. In addition, JMS supports messages that contain serialized Java objects and messages that contain XML-based data.

JMS application is made up of the following parts:

- A **JMS provider** is a messaging system that implements the JMS interfaces and provides administrative and control features.

- **MS clients** are the programs or components written in the Java programming language that produce and consume messages.

- Messages are the objects that communicate information between JMS clients.

- Administered objects are preconfigured JMS objects created by an administrator for the use of clients. The two kinds of objects are **Destination** and **Connection Factory** (CF):

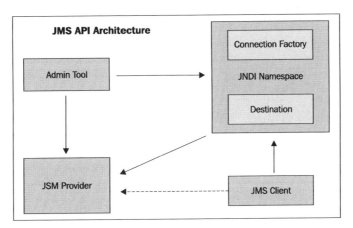

Administrative tools contained in a JEE application server's implementation allow you to create destinations and connection factory resources. Resources are bound to a **Java Naming and Directory Interface (JNDI)** namespace. A JMS client can then look up resources, which are administered objects, using a JNDI name. Once a resource is located from within the namespace, the application code can establish a logical connection to the resource objects through the JMS provider.

JMS is an API, but not an actual implementation. What this means is that an application can use the JMS messaging features provided by an application server without knowing how the messaging sub-system works. This allows programmers to design applications that can run without re-coding, even when the underlying message transport has changed. It is the application server's responsibility to provide the underlying messaging transport layer. A WebSphere Application Server is a JMS provider.

# JMS features

Application clients, **Enterprise JavaBeans** (EJB), and Web components can send or receive JMS messages. A special kind of enterprise bean, the **Message-Driven Bean (MDB)**, enables the asynchronous consumption of messages. A JMS message can also participate in distributed transactions.

# JMS concepts

The JMS API supports two models:

## Point-to-point or queuing model

As shown in the following diagram, in the point-to-point or queuing model, the sender posts messages to a particular queue and a receiver reads messages from the queue. Here, the sender knows the destination of the message and posts the message directly to the receiver's queue. Only one consumer gets the message. The producer does not have to be running at the time the consumer consumes the message, nor does the consumer need to be running at the time the message is sent. Every successfully processed message is acknowledged by the consumer. Multiple queue senders and queue receivers can be associated with a single queue, but an individual message can be delivered to only one queue receiver:

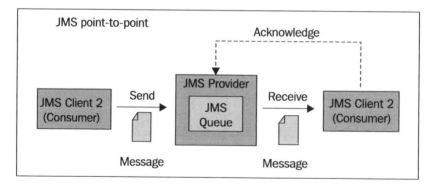

# Publish and subscribe model

As shown in the following diagram, the publish/subscribe (**PubSub**) model supports publishing messages to a particular message topic. Unlike the point-to-point messaging model, **PubSub** messaging allows multiple topic subscribers to receive the same message. JMS retains the message until all topic subscribers have received it; however, these messages can expire if required. The PubSub messaging model supports durable subscribers, allowing you to assign a name to a topic subscriber and associate it with a user or application. Subscribers may register interest in receiving messages on a particular message topic. In this model, neither the publisher, nor the subscriber know about each other:

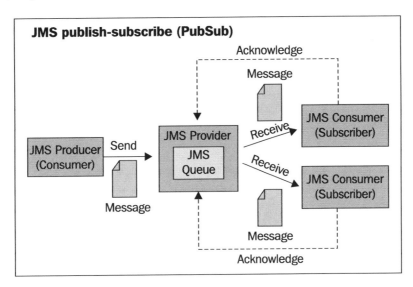

JMS provides a way of separating the application from the transport layer. The application only needs to be concerned with the creating, sending, and receiving of messages without worrying how the underlying transportation is implemented. JMS is designed to make development more portable, and so an application can use the same Java classes to communicate with different JMS providers by using the JNDI information, as managed by an application server, which provides access to a provider.

The application code does not need to know how the connection is actually made. This is the job of the application server to implement the appropriate Java code to communicate with destinations. The Java classes within the application code first use a connection factory to connect, and then they are able read or write to queues or topics. Once messages have been populated, they send or publish the messages. On the receiving side, the clients receive or subscribe to the messages using the appropriate receiving Java classes within the code. The application will not know which JMS provider is being used, as the application server manages the JMS provision.

# JMS API

The JMS API is provided in the Java package `javax.jms`. Following are the main interfaces that are provided:

| Interface | Description |
|---|---|
| **ConnectionFactory interface** | This is a WebSphere-configured resource object that a client uses to create a connection to the JMS provider. JMS clients access the connection factory through interfaces, so the application code does not need to be changed if the underlying JMS implementation changes. Administrators configure the connection factories, which have JNDI names, so that JMS clients can look them up. These resources in WebSphere are known as **JMS Resource references**. |
| **Connection interface** | Once a connection factory is obtained, a connection to a JMS provider can be created. A connection represents a communication link between the application and the messaging system. Depending on the connection type, connections allow users to create sessions for sending and receiving messages from a queue or topic. |
| **Destination interface** | This is a WebSphere-configured resource object that serves as the identity of a message destination, it is where messages are delivered and consumed. It is either a queue or a topic. The WebSphere administrator creates these resource references, and client applications discover them using JNDI lookups. |
| **MessageConsumer interface** | This is a Java object created by a session. It receives messages sent from a destination. The consumer can receive messages synchronously or asynchronously for both queue- and topic-type messaging. |
| **MessageProducer interface** | This is a Java object created by a session that sends messages to a destination. The user can create a sender for a specific destination or create a generic sender that specifies the destination at the time the message is sent. |

Messaging applications use the previous listed interfaces within the Java code to implement JMS.

# WebSphere messaging

WebSphere Application Server provides two main messaging sub-systems:

- The default messaging provider, which is internal to WebSphere and implements the JMS API
- The WebSphere MQ messaging provider, which uses WebSphere MQ

First, we will cover the default messaging provider, which is implemented by using the WebSphere **Service Integration Bus (SiBus)**. Then, we will move onto the WebSphere MQ messaging provider.

To demonstrate the use of the SiBus and the default messaging provider, we will deploy an application, which will use JMS through the SiBus. Before we deploy the application, we will need to set up the JMS resources required for the application to implement Java messaging using the **Java Message Service (JMS)**.

# Default JMS provider

Applications can choose to use JMS. They can use **Connection Factories (CF)** to connect to a service integration bus, which hides the actual JMS implementation from the application. Applications then use queues within the SiBus to send and receive messages. An application sends messages to a specific queue and those messages are retrieved and processed by another application listening to that queue.

In WAS, JMS queues are assigned to queue destinations on a given SiBus. A queue destination is where messages can be persisted over time within the SiBus. Applications can also use topics for messages.

Applications publish messages to the topics. To receive messages, applications subscribe to topics. JMS topics are assigned to topic spaces on the bus. The JMS topics are persisted in the SiBus and accessed through appropriate connection factories, which applications use to gain access to the bus.

The following table gives a quick overview of the types of resources available for configuring JMS resources for the Default JMS provider running in the SiBus:

| JMS resource type | Description |
| --- | --- |
| **JMS provider** | A JMS provider enables messaging based on the **Java Message Service (JMS)**. It provides JEE (Java Enterprise Edition) connection factories to create connections for JMS destinations. |
| **JMS activation specification** | A JMS activation specification is associated with one or more message-driven beans and provides the configuration necessary for them to receive messages and is specific to the SiBus implementation. |
| **JMS connection factory** | A JMS connection factory is used to create connections to the associated JMS provider of JMS destinations, for both point-to-point and PubSub messaging. |
| **JMS queue connection factory** | A JMS queue connection factory is used to create connections to the associated JMS provider of JMS queues, for point-to-point messaging. |
| **JMS queue** | A JMS queue is used as a destination for point-to-point messaging. |
| **JMS topic connection factory** | A JMS topic connection factory is used to create connections to the associated JMS provider of JMS topics, for publish/subscribe messaging. |
| **JMS topic** | A JMS topic is used as a destination for publish/subscribe messaging. |

# WebSphere Service Integration Bus

WebSphere provides a highly available messaging infrastructure through a support layer called the **Service Integration Bus (SiBus)**. Highly available or **High Availability (HA)** is the term given to a system that is resilient and has measures in place to stop the system from going down due to a single point of failure. Before our applications can be installed and set up to use the default messaging provider contained with WAS, we must create a **Service Integration Bus (SiBus)**. In a way, the SiBus provides the backbone for JMS messaging and provides default JMS services by a default JMS provider and no third-party software is required to utilize the SiBus. A service integration bus supports applications using both message-based and service-oriented architectures. A bus is a group of interconnected members made up of servers and clusters that have been added as members of a common bus.

Applications connect to the bus and communicate with messaging engines associated with the bus. Some members of the bus produce messages; other members consume and process these messages. Message destinations within the SiBus provide for both asynchronous and synchronous messaging, and also provide high-availability. It is important to note that in the context of pure JMS usage, as opposed to integration with the likes of IBM MQ messaging, the SiBus can be referred to as a message bus.

The SiBus not only provides for message routing within a cell, but can also provide inter-cell messaging and supports communicating with external messaging systems through gateways.

> An example of a messaging gateway is that some queue destinations do not exist within the WebSphere SiBus. The SiBus needs to communicate with an external message network. A foreign WebSphere MQ network is a good example where a SiBus would communicate with a gateway Queue Manager, thus allowing the flow of messages from WMQ to WebSphere, and vice versa.

When multiple members exist in the SiBus, only one **Message Engine (ME)** is active. Each SiBus member contains a component called a messaging engine that processes messaging, send and receive requests, and can host destinations.

When you add an application server or a server cluster as a bus member, a messaging engine is automatically created for this new member. This ensures that messages are consumed in the correct order.

For highly-available messaging needs, it is possible to configure many message engines to load balance message persistence, processing, and so on. What we mean here is that when multiple servers and/or clusters are added to a SiBus, they work together to ensure reliance.

A SiBus supports the following types of messaging:

- Sending messages asynchronously
    - Asynchronous messaging does not need the consumer to be available at the time of sending a message

- Sending messages synchronously
    - As explained earlier, the consumer needs to be available for synchronous messages

- Publishing messages
    - Notifications and events can be published by the SiBus itself

# Creating a SiBus

The following steps cover the process for creating a WebSphere Application Server Service Integration Bus (SiBus):

1. To create a **Service Integration Bus (SiBus)**, login to the Administrative console and navigate to the **Service integration** section within the left-hand-side panel.

2. Click on **Buses**, as shown in the following screenshot:

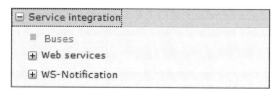

3. Click **New** to enter the **Create a new Service Integration Bus.** page, where we will begin our SiBus creation.

4. Type **InternalJMS** in the **Enter the name for your new bus.** field and uncheck the **Bus security** checkbox as shown. Then Click **Next**:

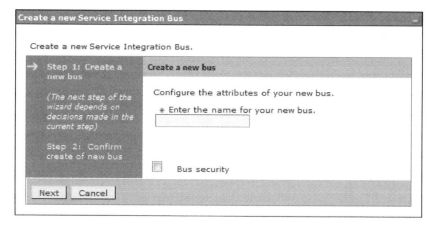

5. On the next screen, you will be prompted to confirm your SiBus settings. Click **Finish** to complete the creation of the SiBus.

6.  Once the wizard has completed, click **Save** to retain your configuration change. You will be returned to a screen which lists the available SiBuses installed in your WAS configuration.

7.  Now that the SiBus has been created, you can click on the SiBus name to configure settings and operation of the SiBus.

> We will not be covering all the detailed facets of managing a SiBus in this book, as it is beyond our scope. All we need to do is create a SiBus so we can demonstrate an application using the default JMS provider, which requires a SiBus to operate.

# Bus members

A bus needs to contain members which are servers or clusters. When bus members are added to the bus, a separate underlying **Message Engine** is created for each cluster member (for clusters), and one for every individual non-clustered server. Members can be deleted and added to the bus dynamically.

> If all members are removed; applications that require the use of the bus will lose message services and subsequently, could stop functioning. WebSphere only uses one ME at any given time. Depending on the design of your SiBus there may be many MEs; however, WebSphere manages the active ME and hardly ever has a single instance running to preserve the message order.

# Adding bus members

To complete the configuration of the SiBus, we must add an existing server as a member to the SiBus so that we have a facility for message persistence. The SiBus is just a service integration bus, almost like a connecting conduit; however, we need actual members, which in our case will be our application server called **server01**, which contains the actual implementation for the message store.

1.  To add a server as a bus member, click on the bus name called **InternalJMS** in the SiBus list, and then navigate to the **Topology** section and click **Bus members**, as shown in the following screenshot:

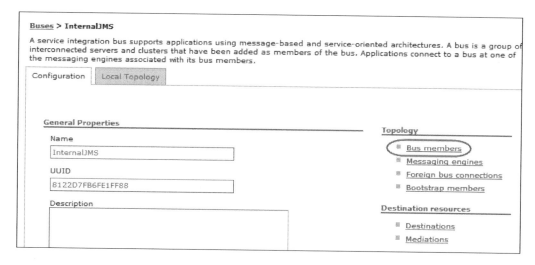

2.  You will now be presented with a screen where you can add bus members. Click **Add** and you will be able to select the server you wish to add as a member to the bus. You will notice that the server is already pre-selected, as shown in the following screenshot:

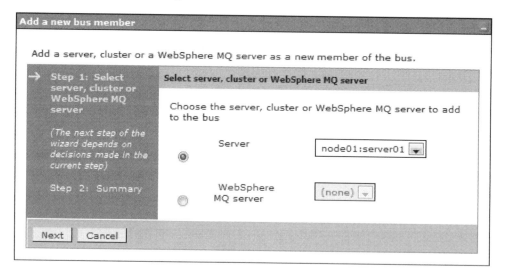

3. Click **Next** to proceed to the final screen, where you will select the **File store** option from the option group field labeled **Choose type of message store for the persistence of message state**.

4. Click **Next** to view the next configuration page where we will use the page defaults.

5. Click **Next** to enter the **Tune performance parameters** page, here also we will use the defaults.

6. Clicking **Next** again will take you to the final summary page, where you will click **Finish** to finalize adding the application server as a bus member.

7. Click **Save** to retain the changes. You will now see the application server called **server01** listed as a bus member.

At this point, the server must be restarted to start the SiBus message engine. Now we can move on to configure the JMS resources.

# Configuring JMS

Once a SiBus has been created, we can configure JMS resources, which are served by the bus. The types of resources we need to create depend entirely upon the application being deployed. In our example, we have a JMS-ready application. With the demo application, we are going to demonstrate putting a message on a queue using a sending Servlet, which places messages on a queue (known as the **sender**), and then demonstrate receiving a message on the receiving Servlet, known as the **receiver**. The sample application is called the **JMS Test Tool,** and before we can deploy the application, we need to create and configure appropriate JMS resources for the application to function. We will need to create a queue connection factory and destination queue as part of the application's requirement to function. To do this, we will set up a queue connection factory, which the application will use to connect to a message queue, and then we will create an actual queue, which the application will send messages to and receive messages from.

# Creating queue connection factories

Follow these steps to create a QCF:

1.  To create a queue connection factory, navigate to the **Resources** section of the left-hand-side panel in the Administrative console and click **Queue connection factories** from the **JMS** category, as shown in the following screenshot:

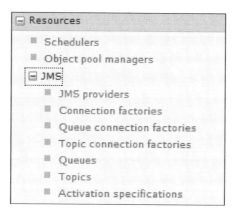

2.  Select a scope of cell from the cell-scope pick-list and then click **New** to create a new QCF.

3.  In the **Select JMS resource provider** screen, as shown in the following screenshot, select **Default messaging provider** from the available provider options, and click **OK**:

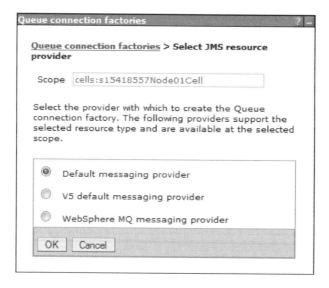

4. On the next page, you will be asked to fill in the configuration settings for the QCF. We will only need to fill in a few fields. As shown, type **QCF.Test** in the **Name** field, **jms/QCF.Test** in the **JNDI name** field, and select the bus called **InternalJMS** from the **Bus name** field, as shown in the following screenshot:

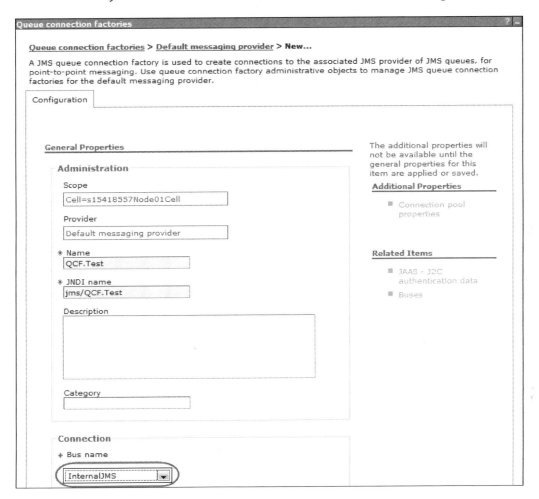

5. Click **Apply** and then **Save** when prompted to do so in order to retain the changes. You will now see the QCF listed in the list of configured QCF.

# Creating queue destinations

To create a queue, we will follow a similar process to creating a QCF:

1. Select **Queues** from the JMS category located in the **Resources** section found in the left-hand-side panel of the Administrative console.

2. Select **Default messaging provider** from the list of messaging providers and then click on **OK** to enter the queue configuration page.

3. On the queue configuration page, enter **Q.Test** in the **Name** field and **jms/Q. Test** in the **JNDI name** field.

4. Select **InternalJMS** from the **Bus name** field found in the **Connection** section, and select **Create Service Bus destination** from the **Queue name** field and click **Apply**. You will then be prompted to create a queue destination.

5. In the **Create a new queue for point-to-point messaging** screen, type **QD.Test** in the **identifier** field and click **Next**. In the following screen of the wizard labeled **Assign the queue to a bus member**, you will see that **server01** is already pre-selected in the field called **Bus member**.

>  The bus mentioned in the **Bus member** field is where the actual queue destination will be created.

6. Clicking **Next** will present you with the final step, a summary screen where you can click **Finish** and then **Save** to retain your queue configuration.

## Reviewing the queue destination

1. To view your queue destination, you need to select the bus called **InternalJMS** from the list of buses.

2. The list of buses is found by navigating to the **Service integration** section of the left-hand-side panel from the Administrative console, and then clicking **Buses**. You will recognize this screen as the main bus configuration page we used when we created the SiBus.

3. Click the **Destinations** link located in the **Destination resources** section shown in the **Destinations** page, as shown in the following screenshot:

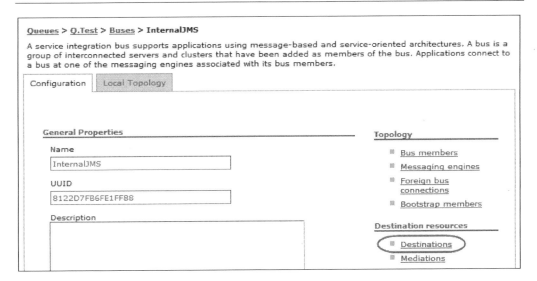

4. You will then be presented with a list of queue destinations in the SiBus:

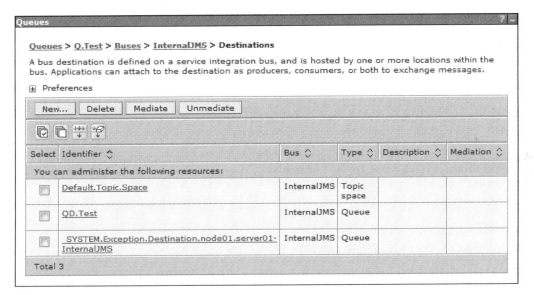

# Creating topic connection factories and destinations

To create **Topic Connection Factories** (TCF) and **Topic Destinations** (TD) for PubSub messaging, you can follow a similar process. You can use the process defined for creating QCF and QD as an example for how to create TCF and TD.

# Installing the JMS demo application

To demonstrate the use of QCF and QD in the SiBus, we will manually deploy an EAR file, which contains two servlets that can be used to test JMS configurations.

The **JMS Test Tool** application is a web application which provides a controller servlet that will process requests from an input page, which allows a user to put a simple message on a queue and then get the message. The application is not industrial strength; however, it goes a long way to demonstrate the basics of JMS.

 The sample application can be downloaded from www.packtpub.com and it also contains all the source code, so you can look into the mechanics of simple JMS programming.

After you have downloaded the `JMSTester.ear` file to your local machine, use the Administrative console to deploy it using the instructions in *Chapter 2, Installing WebSphere Application Server*, as a guide. Now let's go through the process step-by-step to ensure that you correctly configure the appropriate resources as part of the installation.

1.  When you start the installation (deployment) of the EAR file, ensure you select the option called **Detailed** from the **How do you want to install the application?** section, which is located within the **Preparing for the application installation** screen, as shown in the following screenshot. Doing this will provide additional configuration steps required by the EAR file. Otherwise, you will be given the default JMS configuration, and you might not understand how JMS has been configured in the application. Another good reason for selecting the **Detailed** option is that the wizard will present extra screens, which will allow you to optionally override the JNDI mappings for resource references:

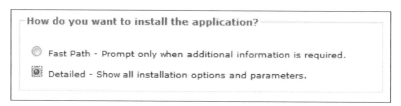

2.  On the **Install New Application** screen, change the application name to **JMS Test Tool**, and then keep clicking **Next** until you come to the **Bind message destination references to administered objects** page.

3.  When you get to the **Bind message destination references to administered objects** page, type `jms/Q.Test` in the **Target Resource JNDI Name** field.

This indicates that you want to bind the application's internal resource reference called jms/Queue to the WebSphere-configured JMS queue destination called jms/Q.Test (which we created earlier), as shown in the following screenshot:

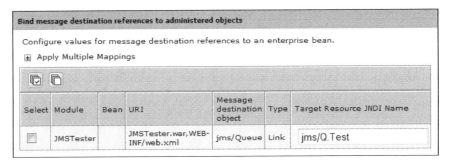

Using this level of JNDI abstraction means that the application does not need to know the actual JMS implementation technology, which, in this case happens to be the internal WebSphere Default JMS provider. The benefit of JNDI abstraction allows the underlying JMS messaging system to be replaced without the application needing to be re-coded.

4. Click **Next** to proceed to the next step of the wizard. The next screen of the wizard will be the **Map resource references to resources** screen where you will be given the option of binding the application's JNDI resource declarations to the actual JNDI implementation, as configured in WebSphere.

5. In the following screenshot, you can see that the application has been configured to point to a QCF called jms/QCF. However, in our configuration of WebSphere, we have called our connection factory jms/QCF.Test. Type jms/QCF.Test into the **Target Resource JNDI Name** field:

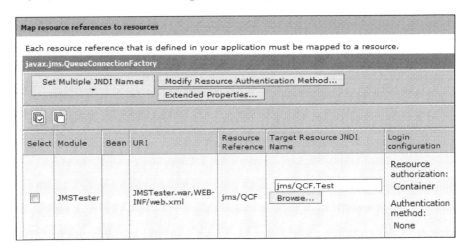

A new feature of WebSphere 8 introduces a browse button enabling you to select a JNDI resource from the JNDI namespace. This saves time and ensures that the JNDI name selected is spelt correctly.

This concept of abstraction, which WebSphere offers to JEE applications that utilize indirect JNDI naming, is a very powerful and important part of configuring enterprise applications. Using indirect JNDI allows the decoupling of the application from the application server's actual implementation of JMS. The application's resource is then pointed to the JNDI name, which it will use to look up the actual resource reference that has been configured in WebSphere. So, to put simply, the administrator decides what messaging sub-system the application will be using:

1.  We have now completed the configuration elements that require user intervention, so we can keep clicking **Next** until the application wizard is complete. If you get any warning, you can ignore it. The warnings come up due to WebSphere telling you that you have configured the QCF and queue destinations at cell level, and that other applications could be referencing them as well. This is useful to know to re-confirm that you have chosen the correct scope for the application's JNDI lookups. If multiple applications are using cell scope, there could be a JNDI naming conflict.

2.  Click **Continue** to move on to the next steps.

3.  When you come to the **Context root** page, take note that the EAR file has been configured to use JMSTester as the web application's context root. We will leave this as default for our demonstration. However, you could override it by typing in another context root.

4.  When you get to the **Summary** page of the wizard, click on **Finish** and **Save** to retain the application's deployment configuration.

# JMS Test Tool application

The **JMS Test Tool** application provides a simple test harness to send and receive messages to and from queues. The application can be downloaded from http://www.packtpub.com. To launch the deployed application, you can use the following URL: http://<host_name>:9080/JMSTester.

If the application is deployed and has started error-free, you will be presented with the JMS Test Tool interface, which is a set of three HTML frames, as shown in the following screenshot:

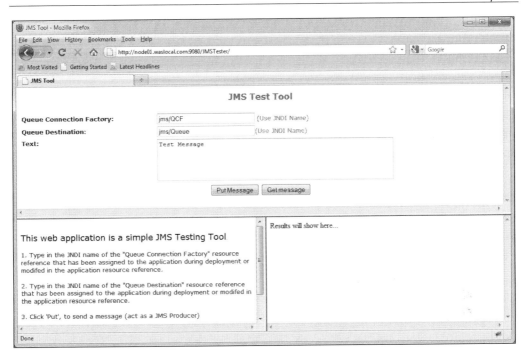

The main frame is the top-most frame where you enter a test message, as shown in the next screenshot. The left-hand-side bottom frame provides help on how to use the tool, and the right-hand-side frame will show the results of a **Put Message** or **Get Message** action:

If you click **Put Message**, you will see that the left-hand-side bottom frame displays the status of the message being sent, as shown in the next screenshot. Each time you click **Put Message**, a new message will be put on the queue:

```
INFO: Producing a message
MESSAGE:
Test Message

INFO: Message put on queue.

JMS Message ID=ID:35b416bf0522526d4b1188f3110a134f0000000000000001
```

If you click **Get Message**, you will see that the left-hand-side bottom frame displays the contents of a given message retrieved from the queue, as shown in the following screenshot:

```
INFO: Consuming a message
INFO: Message found on queue.
MESSAGE:
Test Message
```

Each time you click **Get Message**, the next message will be read from the queue until there are no more messages:

```
INFO: Consuming a message
INFO: No message found on queue!
```

You can use this application in any of your WebSphere environments to verify whether the JMS point-to-point messaging is setup correctly or not.

Now that you know how to use JMS and the default messaging provider, we will move on to discover how WebSphere can be configured to allow applications to communicate with WebSphere MQ, as opposed to JMS.

# SiBus message reliability

In production environments it is important to keep WAS messaging running and to ensure minimum disruption to message services. Previously, we configured the SiBus to use a file store for its local message persistence mechanism. What we mean by persistence is the ability to store messages in a non-volatile way; for example, the messages will remain on queues and topics even if the WAS is restarted. However, in reality, you must decide whether to use a file store or a data store for your messaging engine, by considering the advantages of each type:

| File store advantages | Data store advantages |
|---|---|
| • With the file store you can achieve even better performance without having to use a separate database server. | • Message data can be viewed using SQL administration techniques. |
| • The file store can be used in environments without a database server. | • A data store can be used to remove a level of responsibility from the WAS administrator about ensuring that the message store's persistence is highly-available. |
| • The file store combines high throughput with little or no administration. This is suitable if there are no concerns about where the messaging engine is storing its recoverable data. The file store improves on the throughput, scalability, and resilience of Apache Derby. | • Access to a database is secured by using a user ID and password, not maintained by the WAS admin, and may be pertinent for security policies. |
| | • Logical and physical separation of your database server can also be used to improve the overall security of your data. |
| • Use of a data store might require database administration to configure and manage your messaging engines and so it involves more teams. | • Using a data store means some JEE applications can share JDBC connections and benefits from one-phase commit optimization. |

| File store disadvantages | Data store disadvantages |
|---|---|
| • Requires a filesystem setup to cater multi-node cells. | • Using a data store is inherently slower as the database is often remote to the WebSphere server. |
| • A filesystem can be accidentally deleted by other system administrators working at the operating system level. | • It involves another level of overall system administration complexity when other teams are responsible for systems that are required by WAS. |

Using a file store has a distinct disadvantage when WAS environments consist of many nodes. For a single WAS instance, using the file store is OK as there is only one application server node. Using the principles of WAS, it is possible that you may decide to use WebSphere ND for your actual production environments.

As discussed in *Chapter 1, WebSphere Application Server 8.0: Product Overview*, WAS ND allows the clustering of many WAS nodes. We are not covering clustering in this book; however, it is important to note that using a file store when multiple nodes and clusters exist, administration can be more complex.

What we mean by complex is that you will have to ensure that the file store exists on many physical servers' filesystems. Relying on filesystems is prone to accidental folder deletions as they may be forgotten about. So, if you do decide to use an RDBMS for message persistence, we will now cover the steps for backing the SiBus with an RDBMS otherwise known as creating a data store as opposed to a file store.

Some organizations prefer to use a data store because it uses their existing resources more effectively. For example, this might be the case for a company with a strong team of database specialists, or a stable database infrastructure.

# Preparing a data store

Before you can configure SiBus members to use a data store, you need to decide which type of database you are going to use, then create the DB and populate it with special tables required by the SiBus message engine. Once the database has been created within the RDBMS, (for example DB/2, Oracle, or even the local Derby database as discussed in *Chapter 3, Deploying your Applications*), then special command-line tools or GUIs need to be used to generate the SQL for the message store tables. Depending on your environment, you will require the services of your organization's database administrator to help you prepare the required databases.

## Generating the SQL to create data store tables

To enable your database administrator to create the data store tables manually, you must generate SQL in the form of a set of Data Definition Language (DDL) statements. To do this, we use a tool called sibDDLGenerator, which generates the required SQL statements.

## Steps for generating DDL

1.  Open a command prompt on your operating system and execute the following command:

    **For Linux:**

    ```
    <was_root>/bin/sibDDLGenerator.sh -statementend ; > ddl.sql
    ```

    **For Windows:**

    ```
    <was_root>\bin\sibDDLGenerator.sh -statementend ; > ddl.sql
    ```

> You can use the -help command line argument to display other options for sibDDLGenerator. Options are available for defining the database name, schema name, and even user names for table ownership. Also, an optional parameter is available to control the format of the DDL statements. For example, whether each SQL statement in the DDL should be terminated with a semicolon.

2.  Send the resulting generated DDL file to your database administrator to process the DDL statements that are generated into the appropriate RDMS as required.

> Your database administrator can modify the DDL statements, but must not modify the table names or the column names in any way because doing so might prevent the messaging engine from starting.

# Creating a JDBC datasource

Now that you have a RDBMS prepared, you will need to create a JDBC provider and a JDBC datasource to allow bus members to connect to the data store. Detailed steps on how to create a JDBC provider and JDBC datasource can be found in *Chapter 3, Deploying your Applications*.

# Configuring the SiBus to use a data store

Once a JDBS datasource is available, you can use the following steps to configure a bus member to use a data store:

1.  Create a SiBus using the steps explained earlier in the chapter.

2. When it comes to adding members to the SiBus, choose **Data store** instead, as shown in the following screenshot:

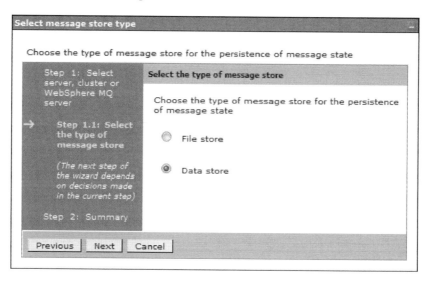

3. Click **Next**. You can choose to use the **Create default data source with generated JNDI name** option, which uses a WAS pre-configured JDBC datasource and JDNI names, or you can select a JDBC provider/datasource that you have previously set up:

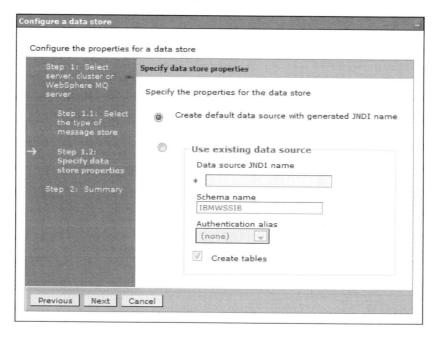

4. Note, if you choose **Use existing data source**, you will need to create/assign the appropriate J2C authentication alias using the correct RDBMS username and password to access your RDBMS schema. If you do choose the default option, you will see a Derby JDBC datasource created for you, as shown in the following screenshot:

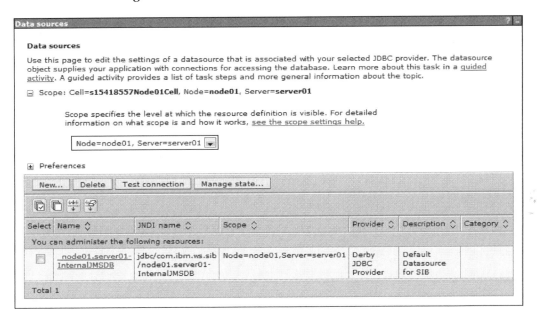

5. The Derby datasource uses the embedded version of the Derby installation provided with WebSphere. This is not suitable for a production data store, you should use an RDMS.

6. Click **Next** to set any tuning settings, then click **Next** to review the summary, and Click **Finish** and **Save**.

We have now completed how to configure a SiBus to use a data store. We will now move on to WebSphere MQ Messaging, where we will learn how to configure WAS to connect to WebSphere MQ.

# WebSphere MQ Messaging

WebSphere MQ, formerly known as MQ Series, is IBM's enterprise messaging solution. In a nutshell, WMQ provides the mechanisms for messaging in both point-to-point and PubSub; however, it guarantees to deliver a message only once. This is important for critical business applications which implement messaging. A good example of a critical system is a banking payments system, where messages pertain to money transfers between banking systems, so guaranteeing delivery of a debit/credit is paramount in this context. Aside from guaranteed delivery, WMQ is often used for messaging between dissimilar systems, and the WMQ software provides programming interfaces in most of the common languages, such as Java, C, C++, and so on. If you are using WAS, then it is common to find that WMQ is often used with WAS when it is hosting message-enabled applications. It is important that you understand how to configure WAS resources so that an application can be coupled to MQ queues.

# WMQ case study in action

To demonstrate messaging using WebSphere MQ, we are going to re-configure the previously deployed JMS Tester application so that it will use a connection factory, which communicates with a queue on a WMQ queue manager, as opposed to using the default provider, which we demonstrated earlier.

## Installing WebSphere MQ

Before we can install our demo messaging application, we will need to download and install WebSphere MQ 7.0.1.3, a free 90-day trial which can be found here:

```
http://www.ibm.com/developerworks/downloads/ws/wmq
```

As with downloads mentioned in *Chapter 1, WebSphere Application Server 8.0: Product Overview*, you will be prompted to register as an IBM website user before you can download the WebSphere MQ Trial. Once you have registered and logged in, the previous download link will take you to a page which lists the available downloads for different operating systems. We will not be covering how to install WebSphere MQ on Windows; instead, we will only be covering a Linux install of WMQ. The entire WebSphere-related configuration is unrelated to the platform on which WMQ is installed. If you have chosen to install WMQ for Windows, then you can still use the same MQ configuration commands listed in the following exercises.

Once you have logged in and found the WMQ trial downloads page, select **WebSphere MQ V7.0.1.3 Trial for Linux on x86 64 Multilingual** from the list of available options. The following screenshot shows the download version correct at the time of writing; so, select the latest version that suits your requirements. We have chosen to download the Linux x86 64-bit version; your download choice will depend on whether you are using a 32-bit platform or a 64-bit platform:

WebSphere MQ V7.0.1.3 Trial for Linux on x86 64 Multilingual     ⬇ Download now
CZRW3ML.tar.gz (470 MB)

Just like in *Chapter 1, WebSphere Application Server 8.0: Product Overview*, remember that if you are downloading to a local workstation/laptop, make sure you use the IBM HTTP Download director as shown previously. This will ensure that your download will resume even if your Internet connection is lost. Alternatively, you can right-click on the HTTP link to find out the full URL of the download you have chosen and use a command-line download as well, such as **wget**, to download directly into an appropriate directory for your server.

We have chosen to use /apps/wmq_install on our Linux machine as the location for the WMQ download; however, any location is suitable. The file downloaded is called CZRW3ML.tar.gz. Once you have the file available on your Linux server, you can then decompress the file and run the installer to install WebSphere MQ.

## Running the WMQ installer

Now that you have the trial de-compressed on your Linux machine, you can follow these steps to install WMQ:

1. Before we can run the WMQ installations, we need to accept the license agreement by running the following command:

   ```
   ./mqlicense.sh -accept
   ```

2. To run the WebSphere MQ installation, type the following commands:

   ```
   rpm -ivh MQSeriesRuntime-7.0.1-3.x86_64.rpm

   rpm -ivh MQSeriesServer-7.0.1-3.x86_64.rpm

   rpm -ivh MQSeriesSamples-7.0.1-3.x86_64.rpm
   ```

3. As a result of running the MQSeriesServer installation, a new user called `mqm` is created. Before running any WMQ command, we need to switch to this user using the following command:

`su - mqm`

4. Then, we can run commands such as the `dspmqver` command, which can be run to check that WMQ was installed correctly. To check whether WMQ is installed, run the following command:

`/opt/mqm/bin/dspmqver`

5. The result will be the following message:

**Name:    WebSphere MQ**
**Version:   7.0.1.3**
**CMVC level: p701-7013TRIAL**
**BuildType:  IKAP - (Production)**

# Creating a queue manager

Before we can complete our WAS configuration, we need to create a WMQ queue manager and a queue, and then we will use some MQ command-line tools to put a test message on an MQ queue and get a message from an MQ queue.

1. To create a new queue manager called TSTDADQ1, use the following command:
`crtmqm TSTDADQ1`

2. The result will be as follows:

**There are 90 days left in the trial period for this copy of WebSphere MQ.**

**WebSphere MQ queue manager created.**

**Directory '/var/mqm/qmgrs/TSTDADQ1' created.**

**Creating or replacing default objects for TSTDADQ1.**

**Default objects statistics : 65 created. 0 replaced. 0 failed.**

**Completing setup.**

**Setup completed.**

3. We can now type the following command to list queue managers:
`dspmq`

4. The result of running the `dspmq` command is shown as follows:
**QMNAME(TSTDADQ1)          STATUS(Ended normally)**

5. To start the queue manager (QM), type the following command:

   `strmqm TSTDADQ1`

6. The result of starting the QM will be similar to the following:

   **There are 90 days left in the trial period for this copy of WebSphere MQ.**

   **WebSphere MQ queue manager 'TSTDADQ1' starting.**

   **5 log records accessed on queue manager 'TSTDADQ1' during the log replay phase.**

   **Log replay for queue manager 'TSTDADQ1' complete.**

   **Transaction manager state recovered for queue manager 'TSTDADQ1'.**

   **WebSphere MQ queue manager 'TSTDADQ1' started.**

7. Now that we have successfully created a QM, we now need to add a queue called `LQ.Test`, where we can put and get messages.

8. To create a local queue on the `TSTDADQ1` QM, type the following command:

   `runmqsc TSTDADQ1`

9. You are now running the MQ scripting command line, where you can issue MQ commands to configure the QM.

10. To create the queue, type the following command and press *Enter*:

    `define qlocal(LQ.TEST)`

11. Then, immediately type the following command:

    `end`

12. Press *Enter* to complete the QM configuration, as shown by the following screen output:

    **5724-H72 (C) Copyright IBM Corp. 1994, 2009. ALL RIGHTS RESERVED.**

    **Starting MQSC for queue manager TSTDADQ1.**

    **define qlocal(LQ.TEST)**

    **1 : define qlocal(LQ.TEST)**

    **AMQ8006: WebSphere MQ queue created.**

    **end**

    **2 : end**

    **One MQSC command read.**

    **No commands have a syntax error.**

    **All valid MQSC commands were processed.**

13. You can use the following command to see if your LQ.TEST queue exists:

```
echo "dis QLOCAL(*)" | runmqsc TSTDADQ1 | grep -i test
```

14. You have now added a local queue called Q.Test to the TSTDADQ1 queue manager:

```
runmqsc TSTDADQ1
DEFINE LISTENER(TSTDADQ1.listener) TRPTYPE (TCP) PORT(1414)
START LISTENER(TSTDADQ1.listener)
End
```

15. After creating a listener definition, it is recommended that you restart the queue manager using the endmqm and strmqmq commands, as shown here:

```
endmqm TSTDADQ1
```

**Quiesce request accepted. The queue manager will stop when all outstanding work is complete**

```
strmqm TSTDADQ1
```

**WebSphere MQ queue manager 'TSTDADQ1' starting.**
**5 log records accessed on queue manager 'TSTDADQ1' during the log replay phase.**
**Log replay for queue manager 'TSTDADQ1' complete.**
**Transaction manager state recovered for queue manager 'TSTDADQ1'.**
**WebSphere MQ queue manager 'TSTDADQ1' started.**

16. The listener will have started along with the Queue Manager; you can now type the following command to ensure that your QM listener is running:

```
ps -ef | grep mqlsr
```

17. The result will be similar to the following:

**mqm      4321 3603 0 12:04 ?       00:00:00 /opt/mqm/bin/runmqlsr -r -m TSTDADQ1 -t TCP -p 1414**

18. To create a default channel, you can run the following MQSC commands using the runmqsc command line tool:

```
runmqsc TSTDADQ1

DEFINE CHANNEL(SYSTEM.ADMIN.SVRCONN) +
CHLTYPE(SVRCONN) +
TRPTYPE(TCP) +
DESCR('Server connection for WebSphere MQ') +
REPLACE

End
```

19. We can now use a sample MQ program called `amqsput`, which we can use to put and get a test message from a queue to ensure that our MQ configuration is working before we continue to configure WebSphere.

20. Type the following command to put a test message on the `LQ.Test` queue:

    `/opt/mqm/samp/bin/amqsput LQ.TEST TSTDADQ1`

21. Then you can type a test message `Test Message` and hit *Enter* (twice); this will put a message on the `LQ.Test` queue and will exit you from the `AMQSPUTQ` command tool.

    **/opt/mqm/samp/bin/amqsput LQ.TEST TSTDADQ1**

    **Sample AMQSPUT0 start**
    **target queue is LQ.TEST**
    **Test Message**
    **Sample AMQSPUT0**
    **end**

22. Now that we have put a message on the queue, we can read the message by using the MQ Sample command tool called `amqsget`. Type the following command to get the message you posted earlier:

    `/opt/mqm/samp/bin/amqsget LQ.TEST TSTDADQ1`

23. The result will be that all messages on the `LQ.TEST` queue will be listed, and then the `amsget` tool will timeout after a few seconds, as shown:

    **/opt/mqm/samp/bin/amqsget LQ.TEST TSTDADQ1**

    **Sample AMQSGET0 start**

    **message <Test Message>**

    **no more messages**

    **Sample AMQSGET0 end**

24. We need to do two final steps to complete this process. The first step is to add the root user to the mqm group. This is not a standard practice in an enterprise, but we have to do this because our WAS installation is running as root. If we don't, we would have to reconfigure the user which the WAS process is running under and then add the new user to MQ security. To keep things simple, ensure that root is a member of the mqm group by typing the following command:

    `usermod -a -G mqm root`

25. The second step, is to change WMQ security to ensure that all users of the mqm group have access to all the objects of the TSTDADQ1 queue manager. To change WMQ security to give access to all objects in the QM, type the following command:

```
setmqaut -m TSTDADQ1 -t qmgr -g mqm +all
```

Now we are ready to re-continue our configuring of WebSphere, and create the appropriate QCF and queue destinations to access WMQ from WebSphere.

# Creating a WMQ connection factory

Creating a WMQ connection factory is very similar to creating a JMS QCF. However, there are a few differences, which will be explained in the following steps.

1. To create a WMQ QCF, log in to the Administrative console, and on the left-hand-side panel of the console, click on **Queue connection factories**.

2. Select the **Cell** scope and click on **New**.

3. You will be presented with an option to select a message provider. Select **WebSphere MQ messaging provider** as shown in the following screenshot and click **OK**:

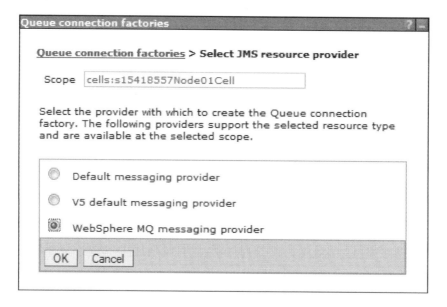

4. You will then be presented with a wizard that will ask you for the name of the QCF. Type **QCF.LQTest** in the **Name** field and type **jms/QCF.LQTest** in the **JNDI name** field:

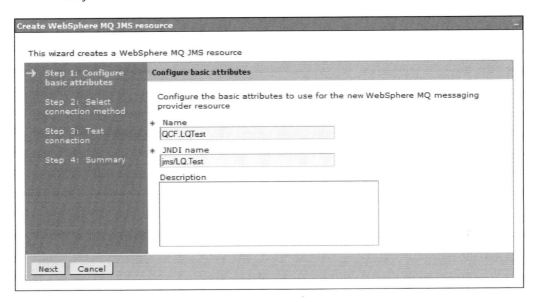

5. Click on **Next** to progress to the next step of the wizard, where you will decide how to connect to WMQ.

6. Select the **Enter all the required information into this wizard** option and then click on **Next**:

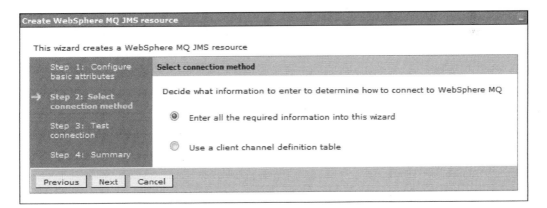

7. In the **Supply queue manager details** screen, you will need to type TSTDADQ1 into the **Queue manager or queue sharing group name** field and click on **Next**:

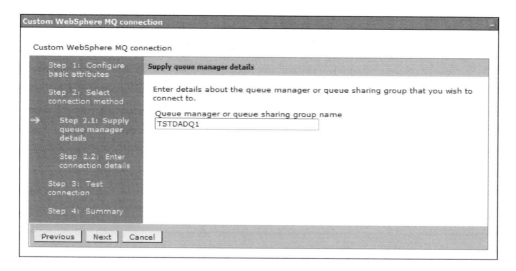

8. On the next screen of the wizard, you will be asked to fill in some connection details. Ensure that the **Transport** field is set to **Bindings, then client**.

9. Type **localhost** in the **Hostname** field and then add the value **1414** to the **Port** field, and type **SYSTEM.ADMIN.SVRCONN** into the **Server connection channel** field, as shown in the next screenshot.

10. Click on **Next** to move to the next step of the wizard:

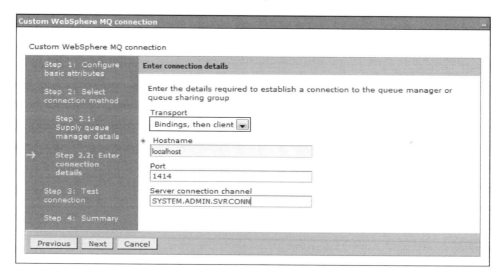

11. On the next page, you will be presented with a button to test your connection to WMQ. If you have set up WMQ correctly, then you will be able to connect and a results page will be displayed confirming a successful connection to WMQ. Once your test is successful, click on **Next** to move on to the final **Summary** page, which will list your QCF configuration.

12. On the final page of the wizard, click **Finish** to complete the WMQ QCF configuration and click **Save** to retain the changes. You will now see two QCF configurations, one for JMS and one for WMQ, as shown in the following screenshot:

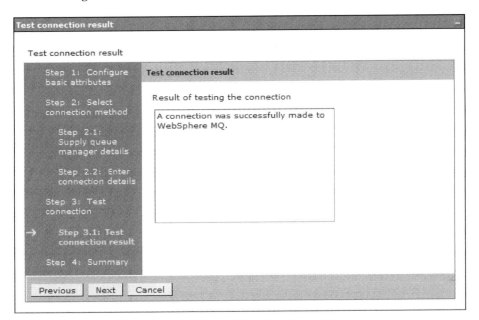

# Creating a WMQ queue destination

The next step after creating a QCF is to create a queue destination. We will use the queue named LQ.Test, which we created on the TSTDADQ1 queue manager.

1. To create a new queue, navigate to the **JMS** category of the **Resources** section in the left-hand-side panel of the Administration console and click **Queues**.

2. Click on **New** to start the queue creation wizard.

3. In the provider selector screen, select **WebSphere MQ messaging provider** and click on **Next**.

4. You will then be presented with a page that allows you to specify settings for the queue. In the **Name** field, type **LQ.Test**, and then type **jms/LQ.Test** in the **JNDI name** field.

5. In the **Queue name** field, type **LQ.TEST**, which is the actual name for the underlying queue, as shown in the following screenshot:

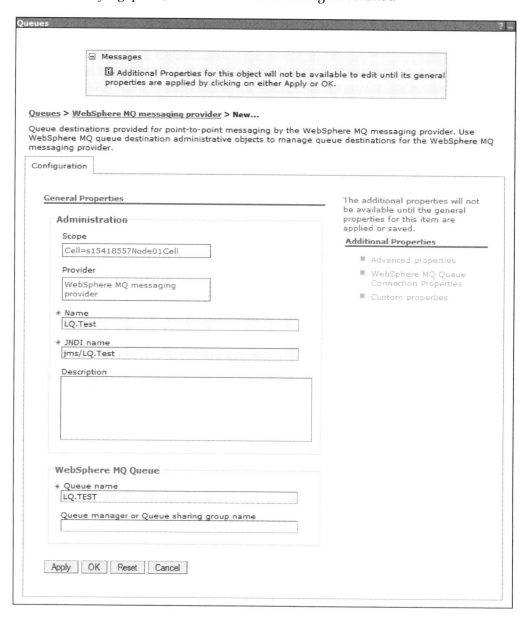

6.   Click on **Apply** to submit the changes, and then click on **Save** to retain. You will then be presented with a list of queues, as shown in the following screenshot:

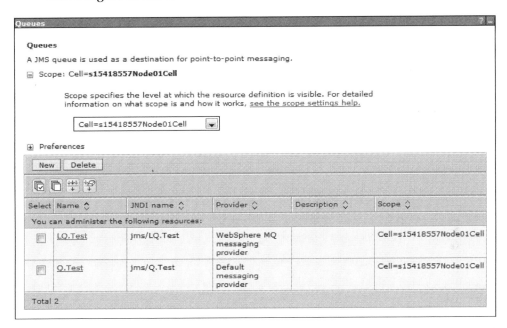

We have now configured a WebSphere MQ queue connection factory and a WebSphere MQ queue destination, which our test application will use to send and receive messages from WMQ.

# Reconfiguring the JMS application

Now that we have created a QCF and queue destination using WMQ as the message provider, we will need to reconfigure the **JMS Test Tool** application to point to the WMQ JNDI names, as opposed to the Default Provider JNDI names. When we deployed the application, the installation wizard allowed us the option of redirecting the JNDI names. This was because the application's deployment descriptor declared resource references, which the installation wizard picked up and presented as configurable options in the installation wizard. Even after a deployment is complete, it is possible to reconfigure an application at any time by drilling down into the application configuration. For our example, we need to change the JNDI names the application is using for the QCF and queue destination. The change is required to redirect the QCF to use the JNDI names for the WMQ QCG as opposed to the previous JMS QCF. This re-mapping of the application's JNDI will allow it to use WMQ instead of JMS through the SiBus.

We are going to alter the following JNDI names:

jms/QCF.Test to jms/QCF.LQTest

and

jms/Q.Test to jms/LQ.Test

1.  To change the application's resource references, click **Applications** in the left-hand-side panel of the Administrative console, and then expand the **Application Types** section and click **WebSphere enterprise applications**.

2.  Click on the JMS Test Tool (or appropriate application name if you have changed it) from the application list.

3.  You will then be presented with the main application configuration panel. Look for a section called **References** as shown in the following screenshot:

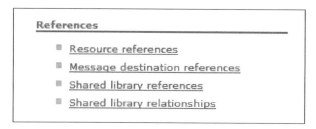

4.  Click on the **Resource references** link and change the **Target Resource JNDI Name** field to **jms/QCF.LQTest** as shown in the following screenshot, and then click on **OK** to return to the previous page:

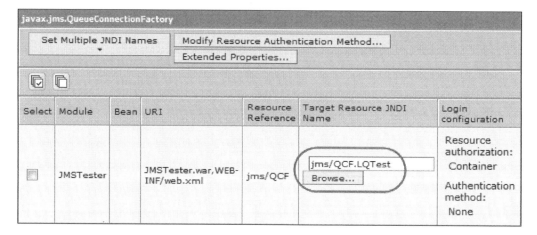

5. Click on **Continue** if you get any warnings. We have now redirected the application's QCF reference to the new WMQ QCF configuration.

6. To change the queue destination, we click on the **Message destination references** link and change the **Target Resource JNDI Name** field to **jms/LQ.Test**.

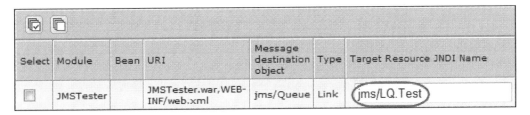

| Select | Module | Bean | URI | Message destination object | Type | Target Resource JNDI Name |
|---|---|---|---|---|---|---|
| ☐ | JMSTester | | JMSTester.war,WEB-INF/web.xml | jms/Queue | Link | jms/LQ.Test |

7. We have now completed the re-mapping of resources. Click on **Save** to make the changes permanent and restart the application server.

When you next use the **JMS Test Tool** application, the sending and receiving of messages will be using WMQ instead of the Default Messaging Provider.

You can use the following command to show the messages sitting on the LQ.TEST queue if you wish to see the queue depth (how many messages are on the queue):

```
echo "dis ql(*) curdepth where (curdepth gt 0)" | runmqsc
TSTDADQ1
```

# Disabling WebSphere MQ

A new feature available to WebSphere 8 is the ability to disable the internal WebSphere MQ messaging provider. Disabling WMQ, when it is not required, improves WAS performance. In the previous section, we demonstrated how an application deployed in WebSphere can use JNDI to communicate with a WMQ queue which exists on an external WMQ queue manager. If your applications have no need for WMQ, then you can disable the loading of WebSphere MQ. Disabling WMQ improves server startup time and saves on JVM memory utilization. There are three ways in which WMQ can be disabled.

- Through the Administrative console
    - In a standalone install, WMQ can be disabled at server scope. For WebSphere ND, WMQ can be disabled at different scopes; for example, Cell, Node, cluster, and Server scope.

- The `manageWMQ wsadmin` command
  - ○ Use the `manageWMQ` administrative command with the `disableWMQ` flag. This command is useful for scripted Jython configurations.

- MQ Java client
  - ○ By using `com.ibm.ejs.jms.disableWMQSupport=true` it is possible for a Java application client to disable WMQ. (We will not be covering this option).

# Disabling MQ through the Administrative console

To disable WMQ using the Administrative console, follow these steps:

1. Select the **JMS Providers** link from the **JMS** category of the **Resources** section in the left-hand-side navigation panel of the Administrative console:

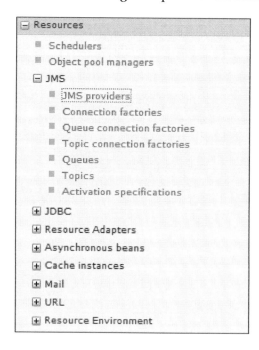

2. On the **JMS providers** screen, select the appropriate server scope from the scope's selection list, as shown in the following screenshot. This action will load all JMS providers set to server scope:

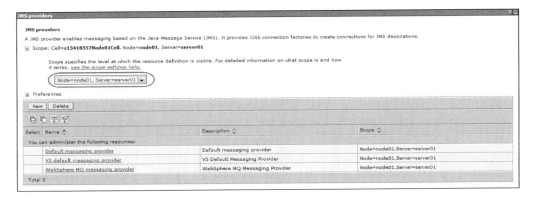

3. Click on the **WebSphere MQ messaging provider** link as shown previously, and on the next screen, as shown in the following screenshot, check the **Disable WebSphere MQ** checkbox. Then click the **Save** button.

A server restart is needed for the setting to take effect:

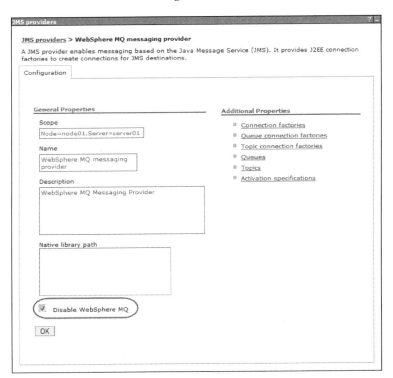

Once the server has been restarted, you will see the following message in the `SystemOut.log` for your server:

**[13/03/11 15:56:50:425 GMT] 00000000 JMSRegistrati I  WMSG1720I: All WebSphere MQ functionality on this server has been disabled.**

# Disabling WMQ using wsadmin

There is now a new `wsadmin` command available for configuration scripting using `wsadmin`. The new command is called `manageWMQ`. We will demonstrate the use of the command using a Jython script file using techniques we learned in *Chapter 4, Security*.

Follow these steps to manually disable WMA using `wsadmin`:

1. Create a file called `disableMQ.py` and save it in a folder that you can reference using the `wsadmin` command.

2. Once the file has been created, paste in the following code:

```
#Get cell name
cellName = AdminControl.getCell()
print cellName
nodeName = AdminControl.getNode()
print nodeName
serverName="server01"
print serverName
#Get List of J2C Resource Adapters
ras = AdminUtilities.convertToList(AdminConfig.
list('J2CResourceAdapter'))

#Iterate through [Built In WebSphere MQ Resource Adapter]s and
find server01, then set MQ as disabled
for ra in ras :
  desc = AdminConfig.showAttribute(ra, "description")
  if desc.find("Built In WebSphere MQ Resource Adapter") > 0:
  print "Match found"
  if ra.find(serverName) > 0:
    print serverName + ": found in adapter list"
    AdminTask.manageWMQ(ra, '[-nativePath -disableWMQ true ]')
    AdminConfig.save()
    print "WMQ has been disabled for server01"
  #end if
  #end if
#end for
```

3. To run the script using `wsadmin` through the command line, use the following command:

Linux

```
./wsadmin.sh -lang jython -f /<script_path>/disableWMQ.py
```

Windows

```
wsadmin.bat -lang jython -f c:\<script_path>\disableWMQ.py
```

4. The result of running the script will be similar to the following lines:

**WASX7209I: Connected to process "server01" on node node01 using SOAP connector; The type of process is: UnManagedProcess**

**s15418557Node01Cell**

**node01**

**server01**

**WMQ has been disabled for server01**

To print help information specifically for the `manageMQ` command, use the `print AdminTask.help('manageWMQ')` command.

To list other `wsadmin` commands available for managing WMQ with Jython, use the `print AdminTask.help('WMQAdminCommands')` command.

# Enabling MQ

To enable MQ Messaging, you can use a script or manually enable a WebSphere MQ messaging provider.

- To do this manually, navigate to **JMS providers | WebSphere MQ messaging provider** in the Administrative console and uncheck the **Disable WebSphere MQ** option

- To enable through script, edit the script we used to disable WMQ and set `disableWMQ` to `true`

You will be required to start WebSphere after making the changes.

# WebSphere MQ link

WebSphere MQ link allows you to connect the WebSphere Application Server or any WAS-based product, such as WebSphere ESB, to an external WebSphere MQ server. From the perspective of WMQ, WAS/ESB messaging engine appears to be just another WMQ server. From the perspective of WAS/ESB, WMQ appears to be a foreign bus. Thus, "foreign destinations" (WAS/ESB) and "remote queues" (WMQ) can be involved in message exchange with WAS using the MQ link.

Both point-to-point and PubSub style messaging can be used, and the MQ link maps corresponding message features as closely as possible. This is particularly useful for **ESB** (**Enterprise Service Bus**) designs, as it allows it to mediate messages from and to an MQ queue using JMS bindings.

A new feature of WebSphere 8 supports better provision of high availability for a WebSphere MQ queue manager that is connected to a WebSphere Application Server. High availability is configured by specifying multiple connection names in your WebSphere Application Server definition for the WebSphere MQ link sender channel. If the active gateway queue manager fails, the service integration bus can use this information to reconnect to a standby gateway queue manager.

# Configuring MQ link

A WebSphere MQ link connects one service integration messaging engine, called the gateway messaging engine, to one WebSphere MQ queue manager or queue-sharing group, called the gateway queue manager.

All messaging engines in the service integration bus use the gateway messaging engine to route messages to and from the WebSphere MQ network; all queue managers and queue-sharing groups in the WebSphere MQ network use the gateway queue manager to route messages to and from the service integration bus.

Typically, a WebSphere MQ link consists of two TCP/IP connections:

- The WebSphere MQ link sender channel, which carries messages from a SiBus to WebSphere MQ

- The WebSphere MQ link receiver channel, which carries messages from WebSphere MQ to a SiBus

 WebSphere MQ calls these TCP/IP connections message channels: a receiver channel, which connects to the WebSphere MQ link sender channel; and a sender channel, which connects to the WebSphere MQ link receiver channel.

The following diagram shows an example, with a WebSphere MQ link sender channel called **BUS01.TO.QM01** and a WebSphere MQ link receiver channel called **QM01.TO.BUS01**. We will now cover how to configure this scenario:

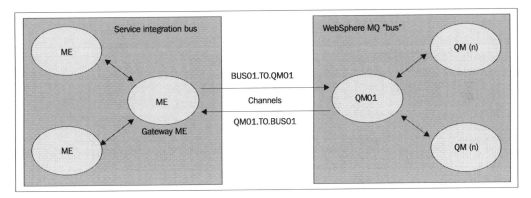

# Configuring a SiBus for MQ link

1. Using the instructions outlined previously in this chapter, create a new SiBus called BUS01. Note that during the SiBus creation wizard, ensure that the **Require clients use SSL protected transports** field is unchecked.

2. Assign server01 as a member of BUS01. A member called node01:server01 will appear as a bus member after you have added server01 as a member. Essentially, this member is the gateway message engine.

# Creating a queue destination for testing

To test our MQ link, we need to ensure that there is a JMS queue destination that can receive messages form WMQ.

1. Create a queue-type bus destination called DestinationQueue01, which is one of the destinations in BUS01. Select **Resources | JMS | Queues** from the Administrative console.

2. Select the **Server** scope, and then click **New**.

3. Choose **Default messaging provider** from the available messaging providers and click **OK** to progress.

4. In the new queue destination properties screen, type `DestinationQueue01` in the name field. Type `jms/DestinationQueue01` as the JNDI name. Select **BUS01** for the **Bus** field and then select **Create service integration bus destination** from the **Queue name** select-list.

5. In the **Create new** queue screen, type `DestinationQueue01` as the identifier and click **Next**.

6. Now we are asked to assign the queue to a bus member that will store and process the messages for the queue. Choose **Server01** from the **Bus member** select-list. Click **Next** to move onto the summary screen.

7. Click **Finish** and you will be returned to the queue destination screen.

8. Review and **Save**. The result will be a new queue destination, as shown in the following screenshot:

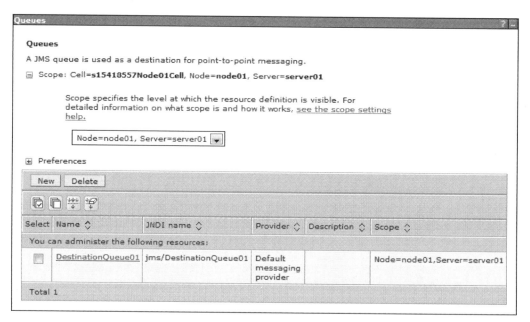

# Creating a foreign bus and MQ link connection

Next, we need to create a foreign bus definition for WMQ. A foreign bus definition provides details for WebSphere Application Server to connect to WebSphere MQ. The following steps outline the process of creating a foreign bus:

1. Click on **Service Integration | Buses** from the left-hand-side navigation panel of the Administrative console. From the list of available buses, select the new bus you created earlier called **BUS01**.

2. Locate the **Topology** section and click **Foreign bus connections**. A foreign bus connection allows communication with another bus. The foreign bus can represent another Service Integration Bus, an instance of WebSphere MQ, or an indirect connection to another foreign bus.

3. Click **New** to start the foreign bus creation wizard. In the **Bus connection type** screen, select **Direct connection** as the **Bus connection type**.

4. Click **Next** to enter the **Foreign bus type** screen. Choose **WebSphere MQ** as the foreign bus type.

5. Click **Next** to move on to the **Local bus details** screen. The **node01-server01-BUS01** message engine will already be selected by default. If you have more than one message engine, then you can choose which message engine will host the connection. Type BUS01 in the **Virtual queue manager name** field. The foreign MQ network will know the message engine by this name. It is recommended practice that you use the bus name.

6. Click **Next** to complete the **WebSphere MQ details** screen as seen in the next screenshot. In this screen, type the value **QM01** in the **Foreign bus name** field. It is good practice to use the name of the gateway queue manager. Type the value **TO.QM01** in the **MQ link name** field. It is good practice to use a name that explains what the MQ link is for.

7. Ensure that the **Enable Service integration bus to WebSphere MQ message flow** checkbox is checked.

8. Type **BUS01.TO.QM01** in the **WebSphere MQ receiver channel name** field. Note that this name is the name of the sender channel as defined in the QM01 queue manager. The idea here is to pair the MQ link receiver channel with the WMQ sender channel. For the **Host name** field, type **localhost** as the hostname. Type the value **1420** in the **Port** field.

9. Ensure that the **Enable WebSphere MQ to Service integration bus message flow** checkbox is checked. In the **Websphere MQ sender channel name** field, type **QM01.TO.BUS01**. This value matches the receiver channel defined in WMQ:

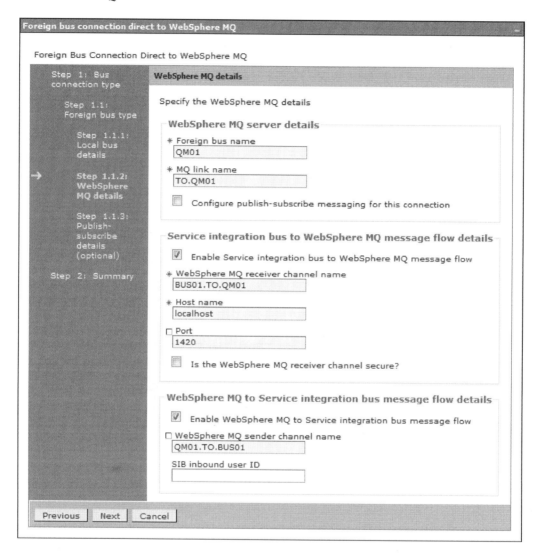

10. Click **Next** to view the summary, click **Finish**, and then click **Save**.

11. You will be returned to the **Foreign bus connections** screen, where the **QM01** foreign connection will appear:

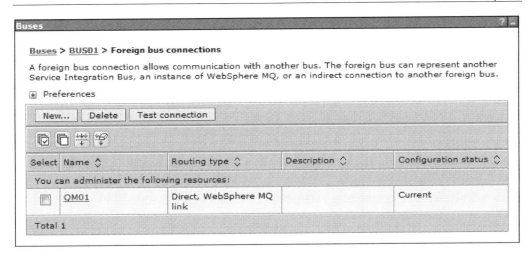

# Viewing MQ link details

To view the specifics of the MQ link, as created by the wizard, click on the foreign bus link called **QM01**. In the **Foreign bus properties** screen, locate the **Related items** section and click **WebSphere MQ links** link. You will be presented with a screen detailing the status of the MQ link:

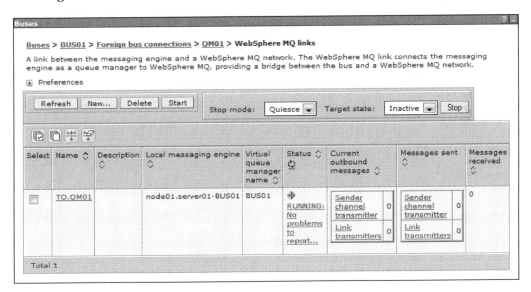

# Viewing channel definitions

To view the sender and receiver channel configurations, click on the MQ link called **TO.QM01**. Once the MQ link properties screen has loaded, locate the **Additional properties** section and you will see two links: **Receiver Channel** and **Sender Channel**.

- The receiver channel is the one that receives messages from the gateway WebSphere MQ queue manager. The receiver channel communicates with a WebSphere MQ sender channel on the gateway queue manager and converts MQ format messages to service integration bus messages.

- The sender channel is the one that sends messages to the gateway queue manager. The sender channel communicates with a WebSphere MQ receiver channel on the gateway queue manager and converts service integration bus messages to MQ format messages.

# Preparing WMQ for MQ link

Now that we have created a new SiBus and foreign bus with an MQ link definition, we need to create a WMQ Queue Manager with appropriate channel definitions. We know that our foreign bus definition has both a sender and receiver channel defined. The following steps provide the details required for the WMQ configuration to test our MQ link.

1. Create a new QM called QM01 using the following MQ command script:

   ```
   crtmqm QM01
   ```

2. Start the queue manager using the following command:

   ```
   strmqm QM01
   ```

3. Once the QM01 Queue Manager is running, create queues, channels and appropriate settings by running the following MQSC commands:

   ```
   runmqsc QM01
   ```

   ```
   *Add the SVRCONN channel to allow MQ explorer to manage this queue
   DEFINE CHANNEL(SYSTEM.ADMIN.SVRCONN) +
      CHLTYPE(SVRCONN) +
      TRPTYPE(TCP) +
      DESCR('Server connection for WebSphere MQ')


   *create a QM listener
   ```

```
DEFINE LISTENER(QM01.listener) TRPTYPE (TCP) PORT(1420)


*start the listener
START LISTENER(QM01.listener)


*WebSphere MQ command to configure the sender channel
DEFINE CHL(QM01.TO.BUS01) +
    CHLTYPE(SDR) +
    TRPTYPE(TCP) +
    CONNAME('localhost(5558)') +
    XMITQ(BUS01)


*WebSphere MQ command to configure the receiver channel
DEFINE CHL(BUS01.TO.QM01) +
    CHLTYPE(RCVR) +
    TRPTYPE(TCP)


*Define a transmission queue, which is used by the sender channel
DEFINE QL(BUS01) +
        USAGE(XMITQ)


*define a local queue for testing
DEFINE QLOCAL('WMQ01') +
    DESCR('My Test Queue') +
    DEFPSIST(YES)   +
    SHARE DEFSOPT(SHARED) +
    MAXDEPTH(100000)


*define a remote queue definition for the SiBus destination
 DEFINE QREMOTE(RQ1) +
    DESCR('Remote queue for BUS01') +
    PUT(ENABLED) +
    XMITQ(BUS01) +
    RNAME(DestinationQueue01) +
    RQMNAME(BUS01)
```

The lines prefixed with * are comments. You will notice that we have defined the port 1420 as the listener port and that the sender channel (QM01.TO.BUS01) communicates with port 5558. Port 5558 is the port defined in the server ports list and is known as the `SiBus_MQ_ENDPOINT_ADDRESS` port value.

# Sending a message to WebSphere from WMQ

To test our new configuration, we will put a message on the `RQ1` queue, which will then appear on the `DestinationQueue01` queue destination defined in the SiBus.

To put in a test message, type the following MQ command:

```
/opt/mqm/samp/bin/amqsput RQ1 QM01
```

1. Then you can type a test message: `Test Message` and hit *Enter* (twice); this will put a message on the `RQ1` remote queue and will exit you from the `AMQSPUTQ` command tool.

2. Navigate to the **Service integration | Buses | BUS01 | Foreign bus connections | QM01** screen.

3. Then click **WebSphere MQ links**, which is located within the **Related items** section of the foreign bus properties screen.

4. You will then be presented with an MQ link page and one message will be showing in the message received column, as shown in the following screenshot:

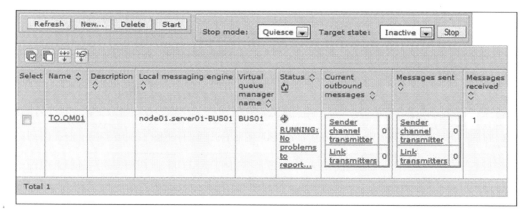

You may need to set inbound and outbound user ID's in the WebSphere MQ link routing properties for the foreign bus connection.

5. To set the inbound and outbound user IDs, click **Service Integration | Buses | BUS01 | Foreign bus connections | QM01**.

6. Locate the **Additional Properties** section and click **WebSphere MQ link routing properties**.

7. Type **wasadmin** in the **Inbound user Id** field and **mqm** in the **Outbound user Id** field as shown in the next screenshot. This will ensure that messages will flow using the correct user credentials at each side of the connection:

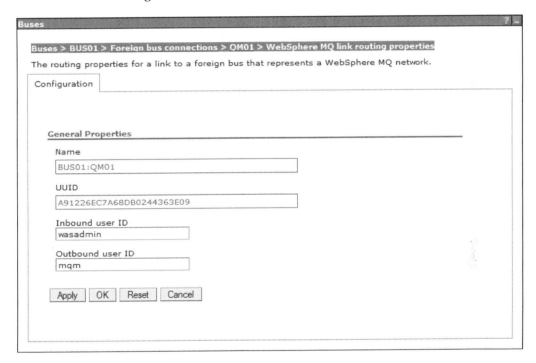

We have now demonstrated a message flow from WMQ to WebSphere Application Server.

# Summary

In this chapter, we learned that WebSphere Application Server provides a level of abstraction to messaging configuration by allowing resources to be referenced by JNDI. We deployed a message-enabled application, which required a queue connection factory and queue destination, which it used to send and receive messages. Also, in this chapter, we discussed how to configure SiBus members to use either a file store or a data store and outlined the pros and cons of each.

We then covered how to install WebSphere MQ and learned how to create a queue manager and a queue. We then covered how to re-map our application's resource references to re-point the application to use MQ messaging subsystem, as opposed to the internal messaging subsystem.

There are many uses of messaging in enterprise applications and we have covered the key areas for configuring WAS to facilitate resources for message-enabled applications.

MQ link was explained through an example demonstration. We learned how to configure a foreign bus connection to allow WAS to receive messages from WMQ. In this case, WebSphere appears as a WMQ Queue Manager to other WMQ managers, this allows WMQ to route messages through to a WebSphere SiBus.

We also covered a new feature of WAS 8, which allows WMQ to be disabled; increasing server performance due to the fact that the underlying MQ Java classes are no longer loaded into memory.

In the next chapter, we will be covering monitoring and tuning to ensure that WAS is running at its best.

# 8
# Monitoring and Tuning

Keeping your WebSphere Application Server (WAS) system well-oiled is paramount to keeping your environment as trouble-free as possible. In the software world, for some strange reason, things break and they stop running. This can be due to software bugs, network traffic, server load, and so on. By tuning your environment, you will ensure your applications perform as well as possible and, by monitoring them, you will be able to keep an eye on your systems to ensure that they run error-free.

In this chapter, we will cover the following topics:

- Using Tivoli Performance Viewer (TPV)
- Request metrics and PMI
- Dynamic caching
- **Java Virtual Machine (JVM)** parameters
- Java core dumps
- Java heap dumps
- Basic JVM tuning

Before we look at how to tune WAS configuration, we will need to look at some of the tools that are provided within WAS itself, which can be used to view runtime metrics and monitor the state of deployed applications. We will then discuss some of the key JVM and configuration settings, which can be used to improve performance.

# Using Tivoli Performance Viewer

IBM includes a tool for monitoring and tuning a WebSphere Application Server called **Tivoli Performance Viewer (TPV)**. This tool is embedded in the admin console. For a quick look at TPV history. In Version 4.0 of WAS, TPV was originally named the Resource Analyzer. In Version 5.0, TPV was implemented as a standalone Java application. In Versions 6.0.x and onwards, TPV is embedded in the Administrative console and provides a graphical display to show live activity.

By using TPV, you can view summary reports, or log **Performance Monitoring Infrastructure (PMI)** performance data in real time. You can also save logging data as XML files. You can later play back the logged data (saved XML files) through the TPV to see what happened during a recorded logging session over a particular time period.

It must be said that JVM tuning, in general, requires effort to get right. However, by applying common sense, and using the monitors that TPV provides, you can monitor the health of your WebSphere Application Server and identify areas where simple tuning can improve performance. TPV provides metrics, which can be selected for a given report and the data logged can be viewed graphically or as a table.

 It must be noted that you cannot only view current activity or log PMI performance data from WAS, but can also log data for other installed products or applications that have implemented PMI.

TPV monitoring can be broken down into three main categories, as shown as follows:

- System resources:
    - ○ JVM memory usage
    - ○ CPU utilization
    - ○ Monitor sessions
    - ○ Server response time
    - ○ PMI metrics
    - ○ Custom Application MBeans (**Java Management Extensions (JMX)**) attributes
- WebSphere pools and queues:
    - ○ Monitor thread pools
    - ○ Monitor DB (JDBC) connection pools

- Application data:
  - ○ User sessions and details
  - ○ **Enterprise JavaBeans** (EJBs)
  - ○ Metrics of all web applications
  - ○ Servlet response times

# Enabling Tivoli Performance Viewer

To access Tivoli Performance Viewer, navigate to the **Monitoring and Tuning** section located in the left-hand side navigation panel of the Administrative console as shown in the following screenshot:

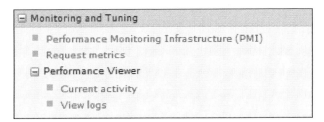

Now expand the **Performance Viewer** category and click on the **Current activity** link located underneath, which will take you to a page that lists available servers to be monitored, as shown in the following screenshot:

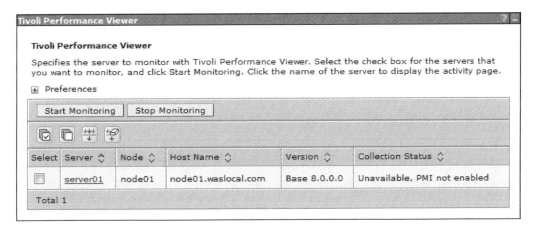

You will notice in the preceding screenshot that the **Collection Status** column is telling us that, for **server01**, PMI is not enabled.

# Enabling PMI

Follow the ensuing steps to enable PMI if it is disabled or to change PMI settings:

1. To enable PMI, click on the **Performance Monitoring Infrastructure (PMI)** link located in the **Monitoring and Tuning** section of the left-hand side panel in the Administrative console, which will take you to a page that lists the servers which can be configured for PMI.

2. We are using WebSphere base, so we only have one server. Click on **server01** to enter the PMI configuration page as shown in the following screenshot:

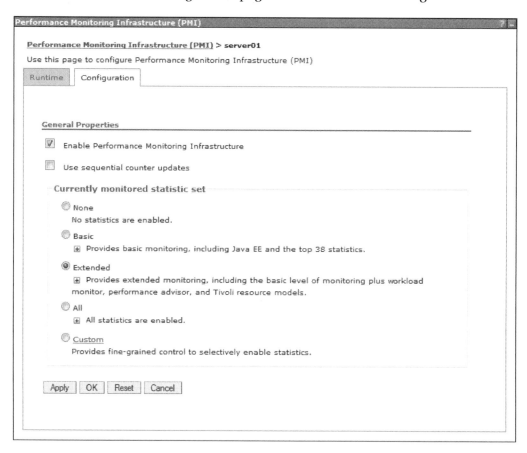

3. In the PMI configuration page, you will see several options. Check the **Enable Performance Monitoring Infrastructure** checkbox to turn on PMI. You can opt to select the **Use sequential counter updates** checkbox for more precise monitoring, but you might find that there is a performance hit if this option is used.

4. In the next section, called **Currently monitored statistic set**, you will see that the **Basic** option is the default selection. We will change this to **Extended**, which will give more reporting modules to use in TPV reports. Click on **Apply** and then **Save**. Restart the application server to apply the changes.

 Often external monitoring tools such as IBM Tivoli Composite Application Manager for WebSphere and HP SiteScope will require the **Extended** option to be turned on to allow full monitoring of WAS.

If you view the application server's `SystemOut.log` located in the `<was_profile_root>/logs/<server_name>` folder, you will notice that PMI is now enabled as shown:

```
[25/05/11 11:36:17:354 BST] 00000000 PMIImpl      A   CWPMI1001I: PMI is enabled
```

To explore TPV functionality, you should remove unnecessary applications from the server where you are going to use to test TPV. This will ensure TPV is not listing too many modules, especially servlets which can make the summary report pages very long. For this section, you should only have the HR Lister (*Chapter 3, Deploying your Applications*) and JMS Tester (*Chapter 7, WebSphere Messaging*) applications remaining.

We will now go to the **Current activity** link and, this time, we will click on **server01** and enter the **Tivoli Performance Viewer** main page.

The main TPV page is split into two sections: the left-hand side contains a tree-based control from which you select objects to monitor, and the right-hand side shows a reporting panel, which is currently set, by default, to the summary report called **Servlets Summary Report**.

Let's walk through the options available on the left-hand panel. The panel lists a number of **Performance Modules**, as shown in the following screenshot:

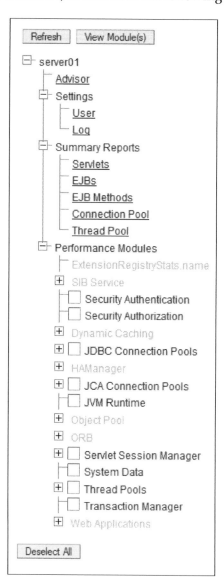

# Key TPV categories

The following table describes the TPV categories, as seen in the preceding screenshot:

| Module section | Description |
| --- | --- |
| Advisor | You can use **Advisor** to examine data while your application is running and it also provides advice to help tune systems for optimal performance using the PMI data collected. There are several tables listed in the **Advisor** panel.<br><br>The first table represents the number of requests per second and the response time in milliseconds for the web container. You will also notice that there is a pie graph in the left-hand-side of the **Advisor** panel displaying the CPU activity.<br><br>Another table displays average thread activity for the different resources like the web container. Data is shown as the number of threads that are busy or idle.<br><br>The last table is an **Advice** table where WebSphere will list **Messages Suggestion Tuning**. Select the message you want to view to determine if you wish to follow the advice. |
| Settings | This section allows you to adjust several settings:<br><br>• The refresh rate of how frequently TPV gathers statistics. The default is 30 seconds.<br>• The in-memory buffer size of data being collected<br>• The view data, which controls how stats are displayed. The options are:<br>　○ **Raw Value**: Displays the actual value.<br>　○ **Change in Value**: Displays the change in the current value from the previous value.<br>　○ **Rate of Change**: Displays the result of calculation determining the rate of change between value changes. |
| Log settings | **Log** settings control is what happens when **Start Logging** is clicked. There are controls such as **Duration, Maximum File Size, Maximum Number of Historical Files**, and so on. |
| Summary Reports | **Summary reports** are available for each application server. This list of reports is covered in a separate table in the section titled **Summary Reports**. |
| Performance Modules | Performance modules provide graphics and charts of various performance data on system resources, such as CPU utilization, database connection pools and other custom PMI as set by applications. The types of modules are covered in a separate table titled **Key Performance Modules**. |

# Summary reports

The following table describes the types of reports available in the **Summary Reports** section of TPV:

| | |
|---|---|
| **Servlets** | The **Servlets** report shows the total number of requests, average response time, and multiplication of total requests by average response time for all the servlets in a table layout. The **Servlets** option provides a table column sorting feature to help you find which servlet is the slowest or fastest, and which servlet is called most frequently. |
| **EJBs** | Enterprise JavaBeans (**EJBs**) show the total number of method calls, average response time, and multiplication of total method calls by the average response times for all the Enterprise beans. The data is presented in a table layout. The **EJBs** table provides a sorting feature to help you find which EJB is the slowest or fastest and which EJB is called most frequently. |
| **EJB Methods** | The **EJB Methods** report shows the total number of method calls, average response time, and multiplication of total method calls by average response time for the individual EJB methods, and the data is displayed in a table layout. **EJB Methods** provide a table column sorting feature; for example, you can sort by average response time to help you find which EJB method is the slowest or fastest and which EJB method is called most frequently. |
| **Connection pool** | **Connection Pool** shows a chart of pool size and the pool in use for each data source. |
| **Thread pool** | **Thread Pool** shows charts of pool size, active threads, average response time, and throughput in the thread pool. |

# Key performance modules

Each performance module has several counters associated with it and these counters are displayed in a table underneath the data chart or table. Selected counters are displayed in the chart or table on the right-hand side of the TPV screen. You can add or remove counters from the chart or table by selecting or deselecting the checkbox displayed next to each counter from the list of available counters as listed in the navigation tree.

Depending on your WAS configuration, the number of applications, and actual application design, you will be able to view different counters. Some counters are always available and these can be considered as the default counters. However, if your application incorporates custom PMI counters, these will also be listed. Since there are numerous performance counters that can be used, for the purpose of this chapter, we will name a few of the most common counters. You will invariably use these in most tuning exercises. They are as follows:

- JDBC connection pools
- JVM runtime
- Servlet session manager
- System data
- Thread pools
- Transaction manager
- Web applications

When you wish to monitor your server or applications, you will most probably use the counters in the preceding list to help you determine the success or failure of tuning WebSphere or applications. Choosing which counters to use will depend on requirement. Tuning for performance is subjective, meaning that there are no hard and fast rules. Using the tools presented here will give you a range of options and help you determine the effect of changes you make when you are debugging slow performance or making changes to enhance performance.

A key point for tuning is to start from a known reference. There is often a misunderstanding that if you know all of the settings of WebSphere Application Server, then you can use them all to gain best performance. Yes, it is true that particular settings can be recommended for certain situations, however, it depends on the **Operating System (OS)**, the version of WebSphere, fix pack levels, application design, code design, and server load.

It is important to note that there is no magic answer, just knowledge and experience from trial and error. Hopefully, every time you go through performance testing and analysis, you will document lessons learned, which can be applied to known issues or configurations in your environments, over time. Often these experiences can be used as a baseline for other situations in other environments in the future.

Here's a useful hint. If you experience an error similar to **Data Not Available** being displayed when trying to access the TPV graphing utility, you are prompted to download the Adobe SVG dll. If, after download, the graphical interface still fails to work, visit the Adobe SVG Zone web site at http://www.adobe.com/svg/main.html to test your **Adobe SVG Viewer**. You can also download the most recent version of the Adobe SVG Viewer, view the release notes, and report any bugs with the Adobe SVG Viewer from this website.

# Starting Tivoli Performance Viewer

What we will do now is look at how to start monitoring and look at some of the ways we can use TPV.

Ensure that you have opened the **Current activity** screen in the administrative console. You can do this by clicking **Monitoring and Tuning | Performance Viewer | Current activity** from the left-hand-side panel of the Admin console. The TPV current activity collection page is displayed. Click on **Start Monitoring** to start logging the current activity of the server you want to monitor, as shown in the following screenshot:

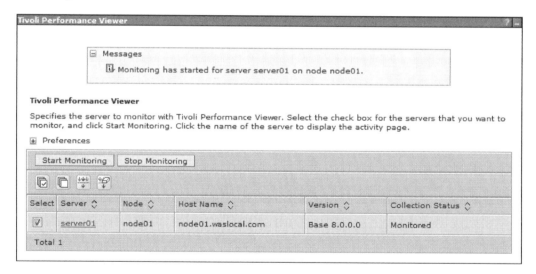

The **Collection Status** column will be updated to display a status of **Available**.

# TPV console panel

The following steps will take you through how to use the TPV console:

1. Click on the server name (in our case it is **server01**). The TPV console panel will be displayed, providing a navigation tree on the left and a view of real-time data for the server you have selected. We now can select which parts of the server activity data we want to view by checking options from the navigation tree.

2. We wish to find out the state of the JBDC connection pools in our server. To do this, check the **JDBC Connection Pools** performance module, as shown in the next screenshot. We are presented with a graph and a table underneath showing the counters which can be added to the graph. The default internal refresh is 30 seconds, so the graph will refresh after every 30 seconds.

The right-hand panel contains two sections. The top section is the graph and the table in the bottom section contains the list of possible counters for the currently selected performance modules. Previously, when we set PMI to use extended data, it was so that we could see more counters displayed in the left-hand tree than if we had set PMI to basic.

# Monitoring example

To demonstrate connection pool monitoring we need to ensure that the HR Lister application has been restarted and contains no open database connections.

For **JDBC Connection Pools**, we will focus on three counters—**CreateCount**, **CloseCount**, and **AllocateCount**. These counters refer to the number of created connections. It shows how many have been created and closed, and how many are currently allocated.

The next screenshot shows a sample graph before we open any sessions of the HR Lister application:

[ Note: Ensure that the **JDBC Connection Pool** module
is selected and click **View Modules**. ]

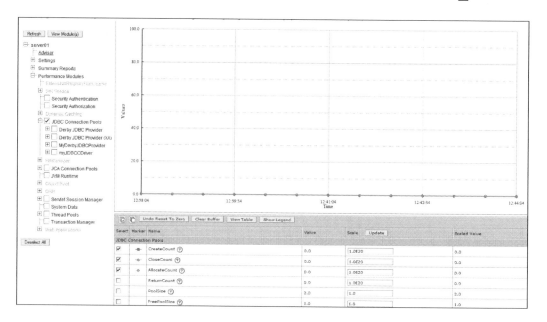

You can see in the preceding screenshot, that there are currently no connections.

Open a browser to the HR Lister application using the URL `http://<host_name>:9080/hrlister`. A database connection will be made and we will see the **CreateCount** and **AllocateCount** counter values increase. After opening a session to the HR Lister application, using a browser, we will see the graph update over time. However, to see the change more clearly, we may need to change the scale of the counters by a factor of 10, so that we can see the single connection more clearly. The following screenshot shows the updated graph, several minutes after we have made a database connection:

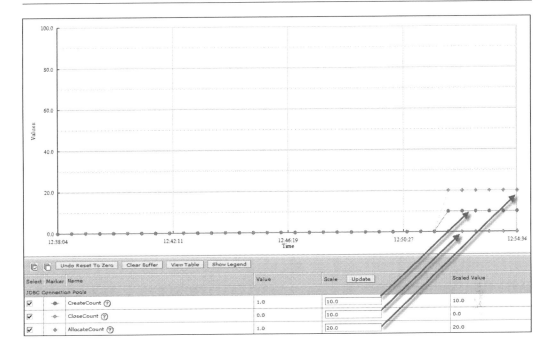

It is possible to change the scale of counters to allow you to see overlapping values. In the preceding screenshot, the **CreateCount** counter has a scale of 10 and so it is showing that there has been one connection created. **AllocateCount** counter has been set with a scale of 20 which means there is one allocated connection.

If you now open a second browser session to the same URL, you will see that another connection is established. If you refresh your browser several times, thus making more database calls, you will see that TPV shows the counters increasing as more JDBC connections are opened. In our example, we continued and opened four browser sessions to the HR Lister application over a period of a few seconds and the following screenshot shows the allocated count increasing as we opened more sessions, creating more database connections:

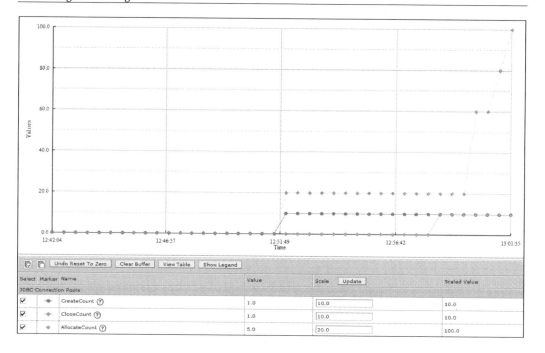

If you click on **Show Legend**, you will see labels appear on the graph for each counter you have chosen to display, as shown in the following screenshot:

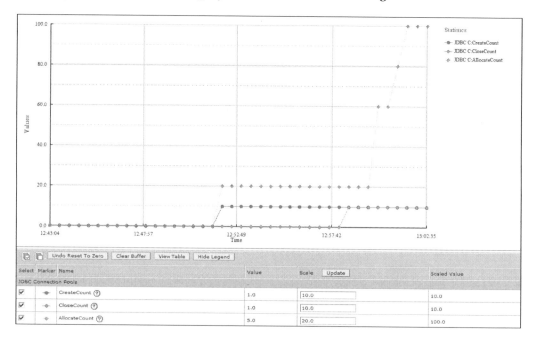

Closing the browser sessions will not necessarily release all the DB connections; this will depend on your code and the underlying DB. When testing a DB connection, you will need to understand what connection timeouts will apply to your particular JDBC data source configuration.

We can review the default properties of data source we created in *Chapter 2, Installing WebSphere Application Server*. We do this by navigating to **JDBC providers | MyJDBCDriver | Data sources | MyDataSource | Connection pools**. We can see that the **unusedTimeout** field is set to **1800** seconds, which specifies the maximum number of seconds that an idle connection can remain in the pool before being discarded by the maintenance thread. This means that if we close all our browser sessions, after 30 minutes the connections in the connection pool will be discarded. Thus, it might take time for your graph to report no connections. Whilst database tuning is out-of-scope for this book, this demonstrates how TPV can be used to monitor, and identify potential performance issues. Recorded PMI metrics can be used to help make decisions for which configuration settings might need to be adjusted for optimal performance.

# TPV Logging

Before we finish discussing TPV, we must mention that, by clicking on the **Start Logging** button at the top of the graph, the counter metrics will be saved to an XML file, which can be played back later. You can set the location of the log files by clicking the **Log** link in the **Settings** category in the right-hand side navigation panel of the TPV page as shown in the following screenshot:

You can set several settings such as **Duration, Maximum File Size**, how many times the log file will roll over, and even the name for the file.

The log files will be saved to the `<was_profile_root>/logs/tpv` folder and a typical log file would be named as follows: `tpv_server1_1238601424024_1.xml`

To view logged data, follow the ensuing steps:

1. Navigate to the **Monitoring and Tuning | Performance Viewer** section of the left-hand side panel in the **Administration** console and click **View logs**:

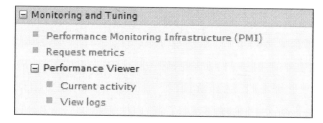

You will then be able to browse for a previously-logged XML file and play back the recorded data through the viewer. You can browse the server's file system and look for the XML file you wish to play back as shown in the following screenshot:

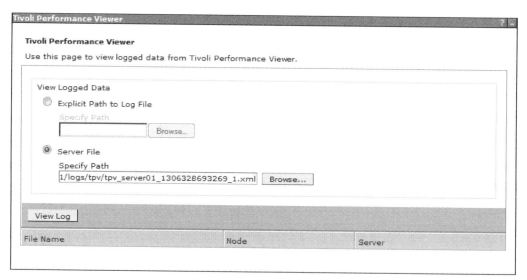

2. Once you have selected the file you want, and selected **View Log**, as shown in the preceding screenshot, the result is as follows:

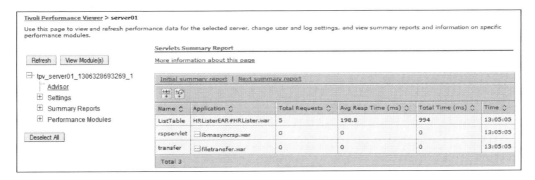

3. Expand the **Performance Modules** category, and select the **JDBS Connection Pools** counters and click **View Modules**. The main panel will refresh and TPV player buttons will appear. Use the player buttons to play back the TPV log and watch the graph change as the data is played back:

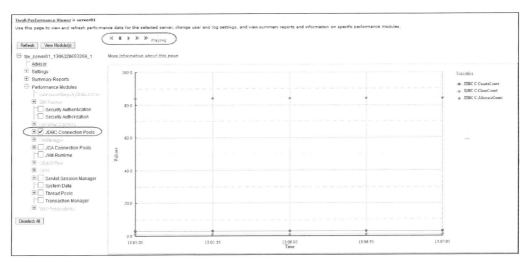

As shown in the preceding screenshot, you do not have to view all the counters which were logged during logging. You can review the counter metrics, as required, by selecting additional counters and the graph will display the data by time sequences.

This is a great feature to use during performance analysis as you can build a log of XML files that can be saved as an audit trail to indicate that analysis was done and can serve as a baseline of results of particular configurations.

# PMI for external monitoring

If you decide to use third-party tools to monitor WAS, then the following list will serve as a quick guide to the PMI you should be monitoring to ensure the health of your system:

- Average response time: Response time statistics indicate how much time is spent in various sections of WebSphere Application Server and might quickly indicate where the problem is.

- Number of requests (transactions): Enables you to look at how much traffic is processed by the WebSphere Application Server, helping you to determine the capacity that you have to manage.

- Number of HTTP sessions: The number of live HTTP sessions reflects the concurrent usage of your site.

- Web server and EJB thread pools: Thread pools might constrain performance due to their size.

- Database and connection pool size: The thread pools setting can be too small or too large, therefore, causing performance problems.

- **Java Virtual Memory (JVM)**: Use the JVM metric to understand the JVM heap dynamics, including the frequency of garbage collection.

- CPU, I/O, and System paging: CPU, I/O, and paging to handle the workload capacity.

# Request metrics

The WebSphere Application Sever also provides a request metrics facility that allows you to track the processing time of transactions and key WAS components. Once enabled, the metrics can be sent to third-party monitoring agents like **Application Response Measurement (ARM)** agents, and can also be saved to log files.

ARM is an industry-standard API that is used to monitor the availability and performance of applications. This monitoring is done from the perspective of the application itself, so it reflects those units of work (transactions) that are important from the perspective of measurement. We cannot cover how third-party tools, such as IBM Tivoli Composite Application Manager for WebSphere, which use this information via ARM, do this, as it is beyond the scope of this book. However, we can describe how to configure WAS for products which use ARM.

Once enabled in WAS, the request metrics subsystem tracks individual transactions in a given piece of work, that is, a transaction as it is flowing through WAS. The information logged can be used to map a picture of what happened during the transaction. This is often used to track timings of individual components when you want to monitor if your system is running within performance thresholds; it is also a great way to help find bottlenecks in throughput during performance troubleshooting exercises. Some of the reasons why metrics are useful are listed in the following list. This is not a comprehensive list; however, it will serve as a guide to understand why request metrics may be considered important to your WAS service:

- Hung transactions: The application may hang in certain situations and you may wish to monitor when and for how long a transaction hangs.

- Failing transactions: You may wish to monitor when key transactions fail as it may mean other subsystems have also failed.

- Response times: Often an application or service will need to meet a service-level commitment like number of transactions per second.

- Application usage: Sometimes, application usage may need to be monitored to justify features or provide feedback for improvements and removal of redundant code or processes.

# Enabling request metrics

To turn on request metrics, navigate to the **Monitoring and Tuning** section of the left-hand side of the Administrative console and click on the **Request Metrics** link to open the **Request Metrics** configuration page, as shown in the following screenshot:

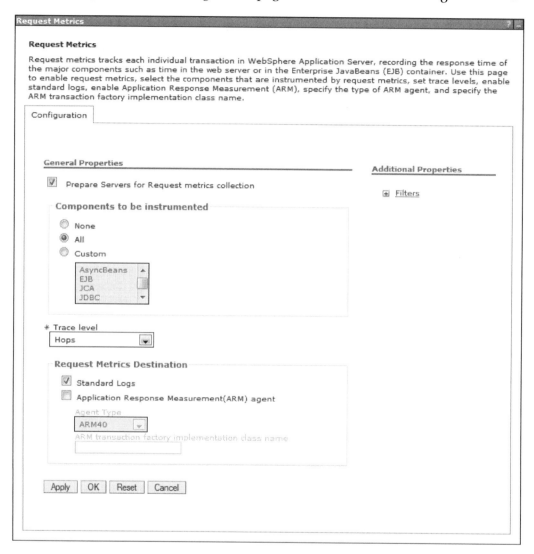

# Components to be instrumented

By default, **Request Metrics** is enabled. However, there may not be any actual logging of component metrics. You have three options to choose the appropriate components to be measured — **None**, **All**, or **Custom**. To enable all request metrics, choose **All** from the **Components to be instrumented** field. You also have a choice to select specific components by selecting **Custom**. The components that can be measured are listed below.

- **EJB**
- **JCA**
- **JDBC**
- **JMS**
- **JNDI**
- **Portlet**
- **SIB**
- **Servlet**
- **Servlet filter**
- **WebServices**

For our demonstration, we are going to select **All**.

# Trace level

The **Trace level** field is used to specify how much trace data to accumulate for a given transaction. Please select **Performance debug.**

# Request metrics destination

There are two possible destinations; you can select both or just one. As mentioned before, we can allow the request metrics to be sent to an ARM Agent, or a log file or both. For the purpose of our exercise, we are going to send the metrics to the standard log files, which means the metrics will be sent to the `SystemOut.log` file.

Click on **Apply**, save your reconfiguration and restart the application server.

When the application restarts, you will see extra metrics information written out to the standard JVM logs, for example, `SystemOut.log`.

# Request metrics in SystemOut.log

Once you have enabled request metrics and have restarted your application server, you can open the HR Lister program. To run the HR Lister program, use the URL mentioned in the *Starting Tivoli Performance Viewer* section, where we discussed TPV, to open the HR Lister application in a browser. Once the application has opened in a browser and has generated some log information, we can review the logs.

The following log is an example of request metrics found in `SystemOut.log` when the HR Lister application has been opened in a browser. The actual numbers in the list are not important; they are only to show you what kind of data you get when RM is enabled.

## Example log messages and meanings

The following entry shows how long it took to get a JDBC connection factory; in this case it was instantaneous as it says 0 milliseconds.

Note: Due to connection pooling, the first connection always takes longer and subsequent connections come from the pool. In this example, the application had previously made a connection. So, a connection that was already open was reused.

```
[4/3/11 7:41:04:334 BST] 00000028 PmiRmArmWrapp I  PMRM0003I:   pa
rent:ver=1,ip=192.168.0.94,time=1238738901071,pid=8712,reqid=41
19,event=1 - current:ver=1,ip=192.168.0.94,time=1238738901071,p
id=8712,reqid=4120,event=1 type=JDBC detail=javax.resource.spi.
ManagedConnectionFactory.createConnectionFactory(ConnectionManager)
elapsed=0
```

The following entry shows it took a lot longer to actually create a connection to the Oracle Database. In this line, it took 1 millisecond.

```
[4/3/11 7:41:04:346 BST] 00000028 PmiRmArmWrapp I  PMRM0003I:   pa
rent:ver=1,ip=192.168.0.94,time=1238738901071,pid=8712,reqid=41
19,event=1 - current:ver=1,ip=192.168.0.94,time=1238738901071,p
id=8712,reqid=4122,event=1 type=JDBC detail=javax.resource.spi.
ManagedConnection.getConnection(Subject, ConnectionRequestInfo)
elapsed=1
```

The following entry shows that it took 12 milliseconds to run the query to get the list of tables:

```
[4/3/11 7:41:04:361 BST] 00000028 PmiRmArmWrapp I  PMRM0003I:   pa
rent:ver=1,ip=192.168.0.94,time=1238738901071,pid=8712,reqid=41
19,event=1 - current:ver=1,ip=192.168.0.94,time=1238738901071,p
id=8712,reqid=4123,event=1 type=JDBC detail=java.sql.Statement.
executeQuery(String) elapsed=12
```

As you can see in the preceding table, when request metrics are enabled, there will be request metrics information in the log, which is very useful to help you tune performance by analyzing intervals and durations.

# Retrieving performance data with PerfServlet

WebSphere provides an EAR file called `PerfServletApp.ear` located in the `<was_root>/installableApps` directory. Within the application is a servlet called PerfServlet, which allows HTTP access to performance metrics across an entire server. The servlet provides the data in XML format and, since it is served via HTTP, it can be accessed across firewalls. The XML data is provided in an industry format known as the JEE Performance Data Framework.

To install the PerfServlet, follow the instructions we learned in *Chapter 3, Deploying your Applications* and deploy the `PerfServletApp.ear` file. After you have deployed the application, you will need to configure security within the servlet as it has a role that needs to be mapped to users to allow access to the applications.

To set security on the `PerfServletApp` application, follow these steps:

1.  Navigate to the **Applications | Application Types | WebSphere enterprise applications** link and click to get the list of installed applications. Look for the name of the application (it will be **perfServletApp**, if you have not changed the name) and click to enter the applications configuration page.

2.  Click on the **Security role to user | group mapping** link to enter the screen from where you can map security roles. Select the **monitor** role and click the **Map Users** button.

3.  In the **Search and Select Users** section, type `wasadmin` in the **Search string** field and click on the **Search** button. Then, when you see the **LDAP** name of `wasadmin` appear, you can click the right arrow to move the `wasadmin` user to the **Selected** field

4.  Click on **OK** and then click **Save** the configuration.

Once you have competed assigning a security role, start the application. When the application has been started, you can use the following URL to launch the main data presentation servlet which is called `perfservlet`:

`http://<host_name>/wasPerfTool/servlet/perfservlet`

The following screenshot is an example of the XML data the servlet produces, which third-party tools can use to get to metrics via HTTP:

http://node01.waslocal.com:9080/wasPerfTool/servlet/perfservlet

- <Stat name="JDBC Connection Pools">
  - <Stat name="Derby JDBC Provider">
    - <Stat name="jdbc/com.ibm.ws.sib/node01.server01-InternalJMSDB">
        <CountStatistic ID="1" count="2" lastSampleTime="1306330308498" name="CreateCount" startTime="1306330306828" unit="N/A"/>
        <CountStatistic ID="2" count="1" lastSampleTime="1306332288527" name="CloseCount" startTime="1306330306828" unit="N/A"/>
        <CountStatistic ID="3" count="79" lastSampleTime="1306330308958" name="AllocateCount" startTime="1306330306828" unit="N/A"/>
        <CountStatistic ID="4" count="78" lastSampleTime="1306330308958" name="ReturnCount" startTime="1306330306828" unit="N/A"/>
        <BoundedRangeStatistic ID="5" highWaterMark="2" integral="4541526.0" lastSampleTime="1306332869719" lowWaterMark="0" lowerBo
        <BoundedRangeStatistic ID="6" highWaterMark="1" integral="1979639.0" lastSampleTime="1306332869719" lowWaterMark="0" lowerBo
        value="0"/>
        <RangeStatistic ID="7" highWaterMark="0" integral="0.0" lastSampleTime="1306332869719" lowWaterMark="0" mean="0.0" name="Wait
        <CountStatistic ID="8" count="0" lastSampleTime="1306330306828" name="FaultCount" startTime="1306330306828" unit="N/A"/>
        <RangeStatistic ID="9" highWaterMark="100" integral="5123774.0" lastSampleTime="1306332869719" lowWaterMark="98" mean="1.999
        <TimeStatistic ID="12" lastSampleTime="1306330308958" max="248" min="0" name="UseTime" startTime="1306330306828" totalTime="86
        <TimeStatistic ID="13" lastSampleTime="1306330306829" max="0" min="0" name="WaitTime" startTime="1306330306829" totalTime="0" u
        <CountStatistic ID="21" count="0" lastSampleTime="1306330306829" name="PrepStmtCacheDiscardCount" startTime="1306330306829" uni
        <TimeStatistic ID="22" lastSampleTime="1306332869191" max="162" min="0" name="JDBCTime" startTime="1306330306829" totalTime="
      </Stat>
        <CountStatistic ID="1" count="2" lastSampleTime="1306330308498" name="CreateCount" startTime="1306330306828" unit="N/A"/>
        <CountStatistic ID="2" count="1" lastSampleTime="1306332288527" name="CloseCount" startTime="1306330306828" unit="N/A"/>
        <CountStatistic ID="3" count="79" lastSampleTime="1306330308958" name="AllocateCount" startTime="1306330306828" unit="N/A"/>
        <CountStatistic ID="4" count="78" lastSampleTime="1306330308958" name="ReturnCount" startTime="1306330306828" unit="N/A"/>
        <BoundedRangeStatistic ID="5" highWaterMark="2" integral="4541526.0" lastSampleTime="1306332869719" lowWaterMark="0" lowerBou
        <BoundedRangeStatistic ID="6" highWaterMark="1" integral="1979639.0" lastSampleTime="1306332869719" lowWaterMark="0" lowerBou
        <RangeStatistic ID="7" highWaterMark="0" integral="0.0" lastSampleTime="1306332869719" lowWaterMark="0" mean="0.0" name="Waiting
        <CountStatistic ID="8" count="0" lastSampleTime="1306330306829" name="FaultCount" startTime="1306330306828" unit="N/A"/>
        <RangeStatistic ID="9" highWaterMark="100" integral="5123774.0" lastSampleTime="1306332869719" lowWaterMark="0" mean="1.999216
        <TimeStatistic ID="12" lastSampleTime="1306330308958" max="248" min="0" name="UseTime" startTime="1306330306828" totalTime="860"
        <TimeStatistic ID="13" lastSampleTime="1306330306829" max="0" min="0" name="WaitTime" startTime="1306330306828" totalTime="0" unit
        <CountStatistic ID="21" count="0" lastSampleTime="1306330306829" name="PrepStmtCacheDiscardCount" startTime="1306330306828" unit="
        <TimeStatistic ID="22" lastSampleTime="1306332869191" max="162" min="0" name="JDBCTime" startTime="1306330306828" totalTime="61
      </Stat>

# Dynamic caching

By enabling the dynamic cache service, you can improve performance. The dynamic cache service improves performance by caching the output of servlets, commands, web services, and **JavaServer Pages (JSP)** files. The dynamic cache service works within the application server JVM, intercepting calls to cacheable objects. For example, it intercepts calls to a servlet and serves the response (Java objects) either from the cache or it caches the object once it has been created, allowing the cached version to be called on the next call.

To enable the dynamic cache service, open the Administrative console and click **Servers | Application Servers | server | Container Settings | Dynamic cache service** as shown in the following screenshot:

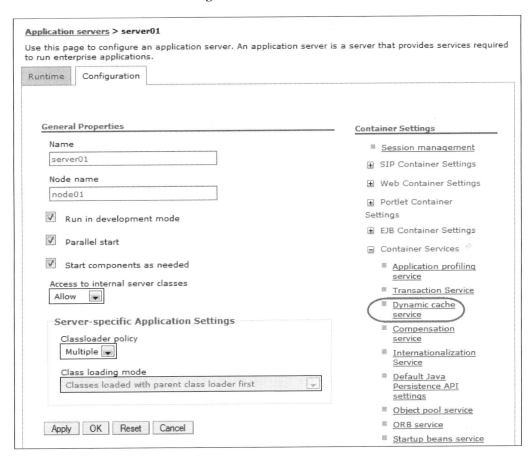

There is a penalty associated with caching, as the first time an object is cached it can take some time to store the object in the cache. During first use, the application might suffer performance degradation, until all objects are cached.

 It is recommended that during performance-tuning exercises, tests should be performed to determine whether this option offers benefit to application performance and ultimate end-user experience.

# JVM tuning

Tuning the application server is recommended as opposed to just using the default values assigned during an application server install. If the heap size is not managed or tuned, you may see the symptoms of poor memory management, which can vary from intermittent performance problems to the periodic failure and automatic restarts of the JVM, which may not generate a core dump or error.

What we can do is set JVM arguments to ensure that Java core dumps are executed when the JVM crashes. A Java core dump is similar to a Linux core dump, which contains processes and state of the OS system. However, a Java core dump only contains the processes and state of the JVM itself.

A JVM may crash due to hung threads or other internal JVM issues; it could be faulty code such as a bug, or many other scenarios like deadlocked code. A Java core dump is essentially a set of Java stack traces at the moment the error occurs, or when the core dump is manually issued. We cannot cover all the scenarios which can cause a JVM crash, but we can cover some configurations to help you catch debug information which you can use in your investigations to find the root cause of a JVM crash.

If we set the JVM to core dump, we will get a core dump file which can be reviewed. If a JVM crashed because it did not have enough memory, the core dump would say so. It is important that every administrator knows how to use settings and debug the resulting core dump file.

First, we will look at how to generate a Java core dump, and then we will look at how to analyze core dumps.

# JVM core and heap dumps

There are several ways in which core dumps can be initiated. Core dumps and heap dumps can be generated by the JVM when it gets to a point where the JVM crashes, for example, when a memory leak is detected and heap dumps are generated. However, we can also set up the JVM to generate core and heap dumps on request. This is a feature of JVMs.

# Requesting a Java core dump using Jython

There are several ways to generate core dumps. First, we will create a simple Jython script which we can run to generate Java core dump information. The steps to do so are as follows:

1. Create a file on your WAS server filesystem called `threadDump.py` and paste the following code:

```
jvmObject = AdminControl.completeObjectName('type=JVM,process=serv
er01,*')
AdminControl.invoke(jvmObject, 'dumpThreads')
```

2. Save the file and run it using the following command:

```
<was_profile_root>/wsadmin.sh -lang jython -f <path_to_file>/
threadDump.py
```

Running this script will create a thread core dump file with thread information. The actual core dump will be located in the `<was_profile_root>` directory and will be named something similar to `javacore.20090403.221606.8712.0001.txt`.

# Requesting a heap dump using Jython

To generate a heap dump instead, the steps are as follows:

1. Change the script to the following:

```
jvmObject = AdminControl.completeObjectName('type=JVM,process=serv
er1,*')
AdminControl.invoke(jvmObject, 'generateHeapDump' )
```

2. The resulting heap dump will be located in the `<was_profile_root>` directory and will be named something similar to `heapdump.20090403.222239.8712.0002.phd`.

# Analyzing a Java core (thread) dump

In this section, we are going to use a custom EAR file called `ThreadLock.ear`. The **ThreadLock** application contains a single servlet which we can call to create a thread lock. Once we have triggered a thread lock situation, we can use Jython to generate a Java core (thread) dump and demonstrate the usefulness of the free IBM Thread and Monitor Dump Analyzer tool to diagnose the problem.

Download the `ThreadLock.ear` file from `http://www.packtpub.com` and manually deploy the application. The default to call the thread locking servlet will be

`http://<host_name>:9080/ThreadLockWEB/DoThreadLock.`

Once the servlet has been loaded, it will report two locks, which will cause a thread deadlock situation. You can generate a thread dump using the Jython code as discussed in the *Requesting a Java core dump* section

# IBM Thread and Monitor Dump Analyzer for Java

IBM provides a tool called **IBM Thread and Monitor Dump Analyzer for Java (JCA)**, which allows you to analyze core dump files. You can download the tool from the IBM alphaWorks web site at the following URL:

`http://www.alphaworks.ibm.com/tech/jca/download`

 **Helpful hint**: A Java thread dump is one of the traces/dumps that the JVM provides to help diagnosis of a hang, deadlock which can often be the result a contention issue. A resulting thread dump contains diagnostic information related to the JVM and the Java application captured at a point during runtime execution.

# Installing the JCA tool

JCA is for Windows only and is designed to be run on a Windows client. To install the JCA tool, follow the instruction as listed on the download page mentioned in the preceding text. Essentially, all you have to do is unzip the ZIP file into an appropriate location like `C:\temp`. Ensure that you have JRE installed and listed in the Windows path, as the application is a Java application and requires JRE to run.

# Generate a Java core dump to view the thread lock

If you have not already deployed the ThreadLock application to WAS, do so using the instructions mentioned previously in the *Analyzing a Java core (thread) dump* section in this chapter. When you have loaded the servlet and created the thread lock situation, you can generate a thread dump using the Jython code as discussed in the *Requesting a Java core dump* section. Once the core dump has been requested, run the JCA tool, as shown in the following command line, to view the thread dump. Download the generated thread dump to your Windows desktop machine into the `C:\temp` folder for analysis.

Run the JCA tool from a command line using the following syntax:

```
java -Xmx[heapsize] -jar jca<Thread and Monitor Dump Analyzer for Java
version>.jar
```

Once loaded, you can open the generated thread dump file as shown in the following screenshot:

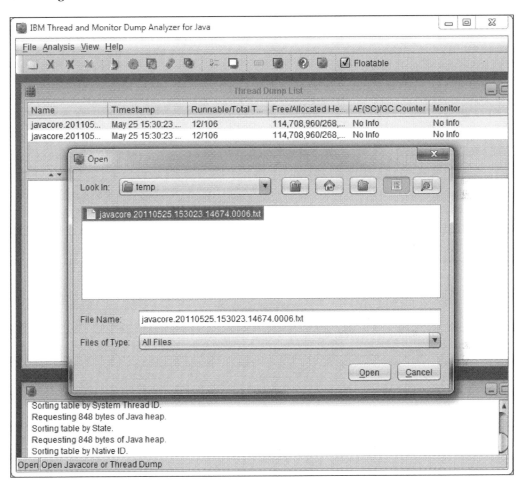

Once the thread dump has been loaded, you can double-click on an actual thread dump entry and an information window will load detailing the thread dump:

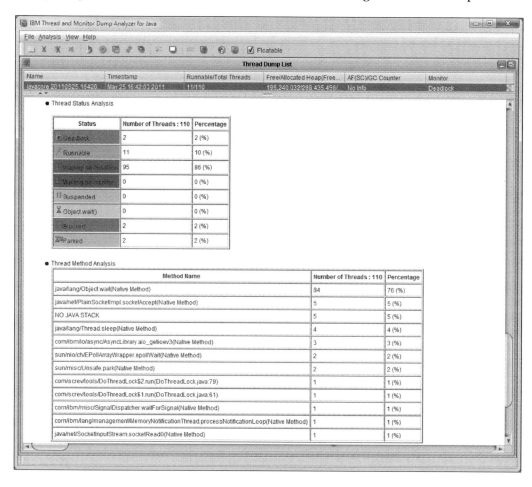

By using the **Analysis** menu option, you can open separate windows which detail different aspects of the thread dump. We will select the **Thread Detail** menu option:

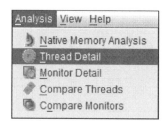

A new thread detail window will appear, which you can scroll through to view thread information that was generated at the time of the thread dump, as shown in the following screenshot. You can see that this tool provides a legend of colors to highlight different types of thread information. This is very useful in determining the cause of a system-generated core dump; it can also be used to look at thread data that has been dumped upon request:

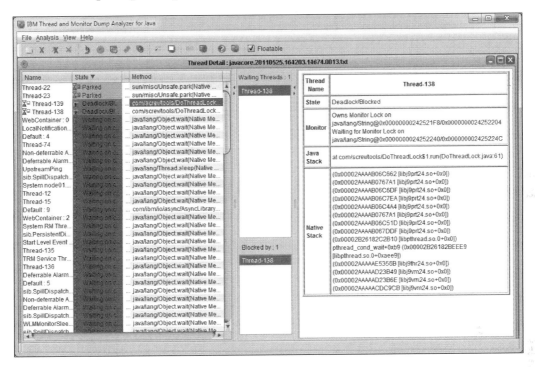

In the preceding example, threads have been sorted by state. What we can see is that there are two threads that have been blocked. Clicking on a particular thread will load details of what thread is blocking the currently-selected thread.

Looking at the Java stack trace for **Thread-138**, as shown in the preceding screenshot, we can see that the code has a Java object that is most probably in a mutual lock with another thread, which also has a lock on the same object; thus, these threads are in a deadlock situation.

To fully understand what the problem is, you would then speak to an application developer from your development team. By showing the developer the stack trace from the preceding screenshot, you can quickly see that it is most probably due to an error related to code in the `com.screv.tools.DothreadLock.java` file. The developer could use this information to help track down the root cause in the actual code.

Using this tool is very simple and, as you can see from the basic example given, this tool from IBM is very useful in problem determination when your JVM unrepentantly core dumps.

# Other analysis tools

There are many more tools available to help you with troubleshooting and problem analysis. The following table lists the tools that IBM makes available on `http://www. alphaworks.ibm.com`:

| Tool | Description and download URL |
| --- | --- |
| Web Services Validation Tool for WSDL and SOAP | An analysis tool for Web service artifacts, including WSDL and SOAP messages. |
| | Download URL: |
| | `http://www.alphaworks.ibm.com/tech/wsvt` |
| HeapAnalyzer | A graphical tool for discovering possible Java heap leaks. |
| | Download URL: |
| | `http://www.alphaworks.ibm.com/tech/heapanalyzer` |
| IBM Pattern Modeling and Analysis Tool for Java Garbage Collector | A tool that parses verbose GC trace, analyzes Java heap usage, and recommends key configurations based on pattern modeling of Java heap usage. |
| | Download URL: |
| | `http://www.alphaworks.ibm.com/tech/pmat` |
| IBM Trace and Request Analyzer for WebSphere Application Server | A tool that detects delays and hangs in WebSphere(R) trace and HTTP plug-in trace. |
| | Download URL: |
| | `http://www.alphaworks.ibm.com/tech/tra` |
| IBM Web Server Plug-in Analyzer for WebSphere Application Server | A tool that detects improper or ill-advised WebSphere Application Server plug-in configurations and corresponding HTTP request/response failures. |
| | Download URL: |
| | `http://www.alphaworks.ibm.com/tech/wspa` |

| Tool | Description and download URL |
|------|------------------------------|
| Database Connection Pool Analyzer for IBM WebSphere Application Server | A tool that analyzes problems in JDBC connection pools on WebSphere Application Server.<br><br>Download URL:<br><br>`http://www.alphaworks.ibm.com/tech/jcp` |
| Performance Analysis Tool for Java | A tool that automatically detects Java threads that consume unanticipated, large amounts of system resources.<br><br>Download URL:<br><br>`http://www.alphaworks.ibm.com/tech/pat4j` |
| Processor Time Analysis Tool for Linux | A tool to detect Java threads that consume most of the processor resources on Linux.<br><br>Download URL:<br><br>`http://www.alphaworks.ibm.com/tech/ptat` |

# Setting the initial and maximum heap sizes

By default, an application server will take as much memory as it needs. A good tip to keep in mind is that you should start up your application with the minimum heap size that it needs to function. When the application starts up, the Garbage Collector will often run efficiently as the heap is small. By implementing a maximum heap size, you limit the amount of memory the application can take. If you set the minimum heap size to be too large, the heap is most likely to be very fragmented when a heap compaction occurs. Compacting the heap is a very expensive operation, so it is important to help prevent heap fragmentation to maximize your JVM performance.

## Tuning your heap size

We covered JVM settings in *Chapter 5, Administrative Scripting*, where we learned we can use the Admin console to change the JVM Initial heap size and Maximum heap size using the field in the JVM configuration page. It is important to realize that these settings are standard JVM arguments, called `-Xms` and `-Xmx` respectively. To tune JVM memory, refer to the following best practice:

- Start with a small heap. Set `-Xms` far lower than `-Xmx`

- The default `-Xms` size is `256MB` in WebSphere and, since it is a low value, it is a good starting point

- To tune your JVM memory, increase the maximum heap size (`-Xmx`) over time to see how the application behaves

- You can use TPV to monitor the JVM memory usage and, by using verbose garbage collection settings, you can monitor the JVM memory to help your tuning

**Helpful hint**: Note that the tuning recommendations in the preceding list might not avoid fragmentation in all cases. It is recommended that you use Google to research JVMs to understand what other experts do to tune JVMs. IBM also offers advice in the WebSphere Application Server, Version 7.0 Information Center located at the following URL: `http://publib.boulder.ibm.com/infocenter/wasinfo/v8r0/index.jsp`.

# Summary

WebSphere administrators are often asked questions like "What is the best configuration for performance and tracking so that WebSphere, and the applications installed within, are tuned to perform, along with an optimal configuration?" The answer to this question is much like the classic response to "How long is a piece of a string?" However, using the tools and options explained in this chapter, you will be able to apply different techniques by using the facilities provided by the administrative console, so you can, over time, tune your system for best performance.

TPV can be used to watch an application during runtime and, along with request metrics, you can see what is happening and measure transaction durations so that you can create baselines that can be used to compare the best settings required for each situation.

Once you have found key areas where there is degradation in a particular component, you can then tune that component by altering WAS settings that influence the underlying JVM, by allowing more threads, more memory, better connection pooling, or some other setting.

Tuning is a hands-on subject, not a theoretical exercise. You need to ensure that your applications go through performance testing, where you test your applications against known configurations and which allows you to determine the best configuration for your applications. It is important to realize that performance tuning involves a triangular relationship between the following three activities:

- Measuring system performance and collecting performance data
- Locating a bottleneck
- Eliminating a bottleneck

Whichever methods and tools you use, you need to follow the cyclic path of monitor, tune, and test.

Enterprise application architecture can be challenging on most days. Often, application development loses sight of the bottom-line that applications need to perform. Performance and response times are critical factors to the real-world success of application deployment. Using the tools provided by IBM, you can help developers ensure that applications and WAS are tuned for best performance.

In the next chapter, we will look into the Administrative Agent and also cover how to install and configure an IBM HTTP Server and a WebSphere plugin.

# 9
# Administrative Features

The administrative agent is a new feature since WAS 7. It provides a single interface to administer multiple standalone application servers. The administrative agent can manage multiple nodes (an application server registered to a **WebSphere Application Server (WAS)** cell is called a node) and provides a common Administrative console to administer the registered nodes. Using this method reduces the need to have separate Administrative consoles for each application server. In this chapter, we will also cover IBM HTTP Server and the WebSphere plugin. The plugin allows **IBM HTTP Server (IHS)** to be used in web application architecture designs, where you may want static web content to be served by a web server (IHS) and requests for dynamic context, such as servlets, to route to the application server.

In this chapter, we will cover the following topics:

- The administrative agent
- Removing the administrative agent
- IBM HTTP Server (IHS)
- WebSphere plugin
- Configuring SSL for IHS and the WebSphere plugin
- Configuring virtual hosts

# The administrative agent

You can use the administrative agent to remotely install applications on application servers, change application server configurations, stop and restart application servers, and create additional application servers from a single administrative console. This is a concept similar to the approach that **WebSphere 8 Network Deployment (WAS ND)** takes. However, WAS 8 provides some of the WAS ND administrative features without the cost and complexity associated with WAS ND.

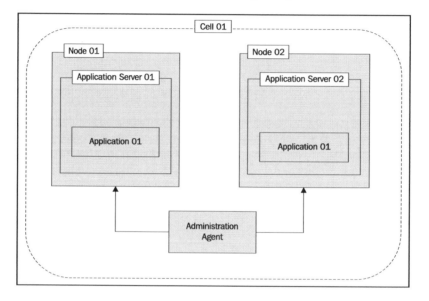

Before we continue, we will need to reconfigure our current WAS installation to create an administrative agent profile and another application server profile. Then, we will be able to use a single Administrative console to manage two application servers, as shown in the preceding image.

Before we can demonstrate the working of the administrative agent, we need to complete the following tasks:

- Create a management profile for the administrative agent
- Use the `registerNode` command to register at least one application server node with the administrative agent

# Creating an administration profile

We created an application server profile in *Chapter 2, Installing WebSphere Application Server*. To create a new management profile we have two options: we can either install manually using the graphical installer or we can use the command line. To ensure you grasp the concepts of the process, we are going to use the graphical installation method.

## Profile Management Tool

As in *Chapter 2, Installing WebSphere Application Server*, we are going to use the **Profile Management Tool** (**PMT**) to create our profiles. A management profile defines the administrative agent. The following steps will guide you through creating a management profile:

1. To start the PMT, navigate to the following folder: `<was_root>\bin\ ProfileManagement`

2. Type the following command:

    ○ For Linux:

       `./pmt.sh`

    ○ For Windows:

       `pmt.bat`

3. Once the **Profile Management Tool** has loaded, you will notice our current application server profile (**appsrv01**), which we created in *Chapter 2, Installing WebSphere Application Server*, as shown in the following screenshot:

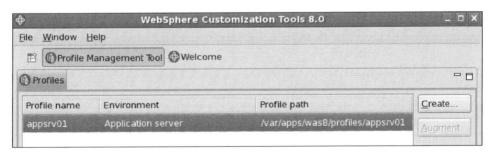

4.  To start the creation of a management profile, click on the **Create** button to start the creation of the new profile. Select **Management** from the list of profile types, as seen in the following screenshot, and click **Next**:

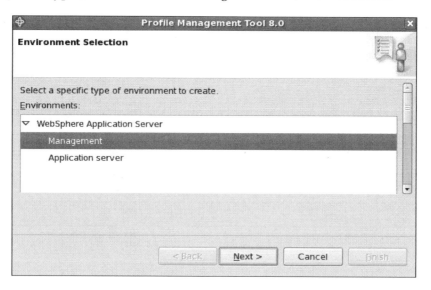

5.  On the next screen, click **Advanced Profile Creation**, then click **Next** to proceed to the next screen:

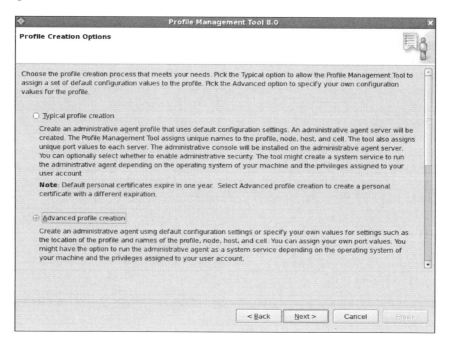

6. You will now be asked if you wish to install an Administrative console. Ensure that the **Deploy the administrative console (recommended)** check-box is checked.

7. Click **Next** to continue to the **Profile Name and Location** screen. Type `adminagent01` in the **Profile name** field and type `<was_root>/profiles/adminagent01` in the **Profile directory** field, as shown in the following image. We will refer to this profile's path as `<admin_profile_root>`:

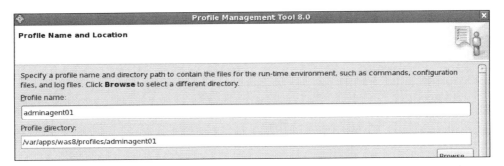

8. On the next screen, you will be given the opportunity to change the node and host names. Type values in the **Node name** and **Host name** fields as required:

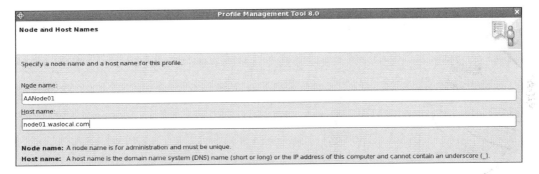

 Take note of the **Node name** you assign as this will be required later to select a specific node when we login to the Administrative console.

9. Click on **Next** to go to the **Administrative Security** page. Turn on administrative security by checking the **Enable administrative security** check-box and type `wsadmin` for both the **User name** and **Password** fields.

10. Click **Next** to enter the **Security (Part 1)** page; accept the defaults and click **Next**. On the **Security (Part 2)** page, click **Next** again to move on to the **Port Values Assignment** page.

11. On the **Port Values Assignment** screen, accept the recommended ports, as shown in the following screenshot. WAS automatically detected the presence of an existing profile; because we had already installed an application server before on this node, and port **9060** has already been assigned. The wizard has automatically suggested alternative port numbers and you will notice that the ports have been automatically incremented by a value of 1:

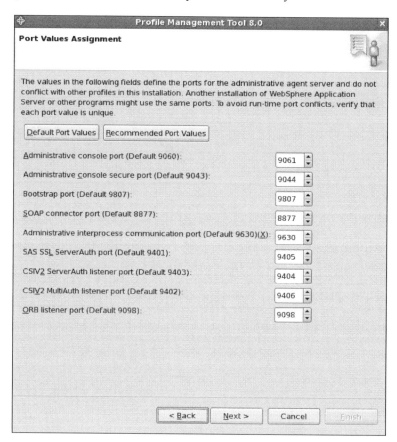

 If you wanted to make your Administrative console use the default WAS ports, you would have to remove the original application server's profile. Also be aware that, though possible, it is not recommended that two profiles use the same ports; otherwise, a port conflict will occur.

12. Click **Next** to move on to the **Linux service definition** screen. We don't need to automatically have our management profile restarted on server boot-up, so, we can accept the default and click on **Next**.

13. In the final summary screen, verify that your settings are correct and click on **Create** to start the profile creation. When the installation is complete, you can optionally choose to use the first step console to test your installation. Close the wizard window or click **Finish**, and you will be returned to PMT. You should see the new **Management** profile listed, as seen in the following screenshot:

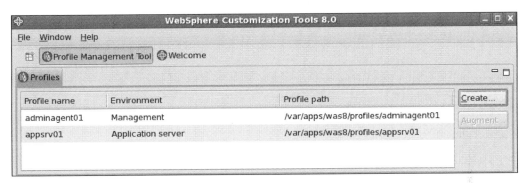

>  You may notice that the application server profile shown in the preceding screenshot is stored in the **Profiles** folder. When you start using the administrative agent, it is recommended that you use a separate folder for each node's profile so that you can clearly identify them at the filesystem level and navigate between them.

14. Close the PMT tool.

# Starting the administrative agent

To start the administrative agent, navigate to the folder `<was_root>/profiles/adminagent01/bin` and then type the following command:

- **For Linux:**

  ```
  ./startServer.sh adminagent
  ```

- **For Windows:**

  ```
  startServer.bat adminagent
  ```

**Note**: To stop the administrative agent, issue the following command:

- **For Linux:**

  ```
  ./stopServer.sh adminagent
  ```

- **For Windows:**

  ```
  stopServer.bat adminagent
  ```

> Once the administrative agent (`adminagent`) has started, we can log in to the `adminagent` console, the URL for which will be `http://<host_name>:9061/ibm/console`
>
> If you access the non-secure 9061 port, the console will redirect you to the secure URL, as follows: `https://<host_name>:9044/ibm/console/logon.jsp`.

Log in to the console using `wasadmin` as your username and password.

# Administrative agent console

When you log in to the Administration console of the administrative agent, you will notice that it is similar to the Administration console for an application server. However, there are fewer options available. The way the administrative agent console works is that you can register nodes (standalone application server profiles) to be administered from a central interface. We will briefly look at the **Administrative agent** section.

Navigate to the **System administration** section of the left-hand-side main navigation panel and click **Administrative agent**, as shown in the following screenshot:

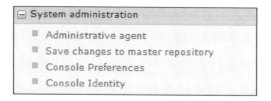

The **Administrative agent** page is very similar to that of a standalone application server configuration page. Here, you can view port information and JVM settings pertaining to the actual administrative agent itself.

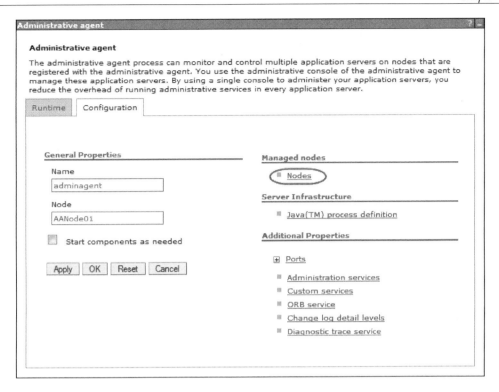

Click on the **Nodes** link in the **Managed Nodes** section, as seen in the preceding screenshot, to view the nodes that have been registered with the cell for administration. As shown in the following screenshot, we have not yet registered any application server nodes:

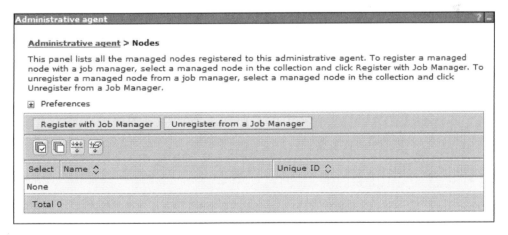

We will now cover how to register application servers and register with the WAS cell.

# Registering an application server node

To register nodes to be administered centrally by the admin agent, we need to go to the application server profile, which we created in *Chapter 2, Installing WebSphere Application Server* and run the `<admin_profile_root>registerNode.sh` command. An example path for the admin agents profile root would be something like `/var/apps/was8/profiles/adminagent01/bin`.

The syntax of `registerNode.sh` is as follows:

```
Usage: registerNode -profilePath <path to the base profile to be
registered>
        [-host <adminagent host>] [-connType <SOAP | RMI | JSR160RMI |
IPC>]
        [-port <adminagent JMX port>] [-name <managed node name>]
        [-openConnectors <SOAP,IPC,...>] [-username <adminagent user
name>]
        [-password <adminagent password>] [-nodeusername <base node
user
        name>] [-nodepassword <base node password>] [-profileName
        <adminagent profile name>] [-portsFile <jmx ports filename>]
        [-trace] [-help]
```

The following steps detail how to register an application server node:

1. To register our original application server, and register with the admin agent's cell, type the following command:

    ° For Linux:

      ```
      <admin_profile_root>/bin/registerNode.sh -profilePath <was_
      profile_root>/appsrv01 -username wasadmin -password wasadmin
      ```

    ° For Windows:

      ```
      <admin_profile_root>\bin\registerNode.bat -profilePath <was_
      profile_root>\appsrv01 -username wasadmin -password wasadmin
      ```

   The result of running the command to register our existing application server profile is shown in the following screenshot:

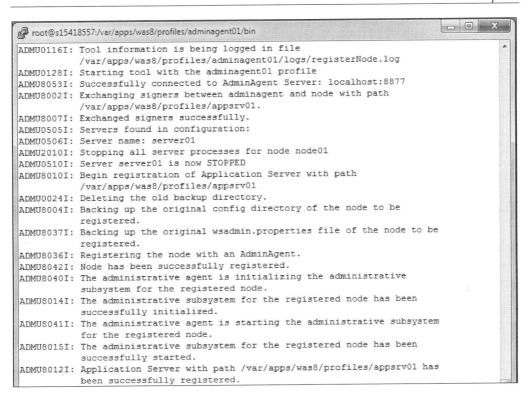

```
root@s15418557:/var/apps/was8/profiles/adminagent01/bin
ADMU0116I: Tool information is being logged in file
           /var/apps/was8/profiles/adminagent01/logs/registerNode.log
ADMU0128I: Starting tool with the adminagent01 profile
ADMU8053I: Successfully connected to AdminAgent Server: localhost:8877
ADMU8002I: Exchanging signers between adminagent and node with path
           /var/apps/was8/profiles/appsrv01.
ADMU8007I: Exchanged signers successfully.
ADMU0505I: Servers found in configuration:
ADMU0506I: Server name: server01
ADMU2010I: Stopping all server processes for node node01
ADMU0510I: Server server01 is now STOPPED
ADMU8010I: Begin registration of Application Server with path
           /var/apps/was8/profiles/appsrv01
ADMU0024I: Deleting the old backup directory.
ADMU8004I: Backing up the original config directory of the node to be
           registered.
ADMU8037I: Backing up the original wsadmin.properties file of the node to be
           registered.
ADMU8036I: Registering the node with an AdminAgent.
ADMU8042I: Node has been successfully registered.
ADMU8040I: The administrative agent is initializing the administrative
           subsystem for the registered node.
ADMU8014I: The administrative subsystem for the registered node has been
           successfully initialized.
ADMU8041I: The administrative agent is starting the administrative subsystem
           for the registered node.
ADMU8015I: The administrative subsystem for the registered node has been
           successfully started.
ADMU8012I: Application Server with path /var/apps/was8/profiles/appsrv01 has
           been successfully registered.
```

2. Now that we have successfully registered the application server defined by the `appsrv01` profile, which contains our JVM called **server01**, we need to restart the administrative agent and then log back in to the administration agent's Admin console to see the registered application server.

3. Type the following commands to restart the admin agent:

   ○ For Linux:

   ```
   ./stopServer.sh adminagent
   ./startServer.sh adminagent
   ```

   ○ For Windows:

   ```
   stopServer.bat adminagent
   startServer.bat adminagent
   ```

**Note**: Since administrative security has been turned on, you will be presented with a prompt to type in the username and password. You can refer to *Chapter 4, Security*, to learn how to edit the `soap.client.props` file to stop the security prompt occurring when the server starts and stops. You can also pass the `-username` and `-password` options via the command line, for example, `./stopServer.sh adminagent -username wasadmin -password wasadmin`.

4. Once the admin agent server has restarted, log back in to the console using the URL `https://<host_name>:9044/ibm/console/`.

You will now see that the login page of the Admin console has changed, as shown in the following screenshot:

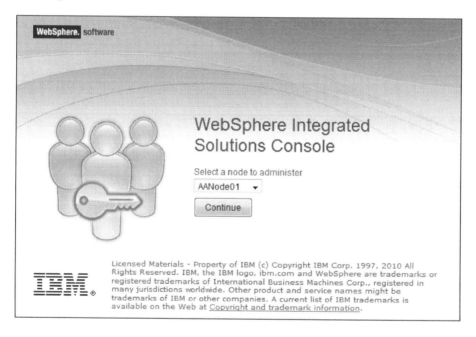

You will notice that we have two nodes. The first node is the new admin agent node that we created earlier, and **AANode01** is the node name of our application server, which we created in *Chapter 2, Installing WebSphere Application Server*.

It is recommended that consistent naming conventions be adopted in your use of the admin agent. When using the command line, using naming conventions will help you clearly see, at a glance, which profile is being administered.

Select **AANode01** from the **Select a node to administer** radio options and click on
**Continue**. You will be presented with a login screen to log in to the application
server's Admin console. It is important to note that you can now start and stop your
application server and still maintain access to an Administrative console. Since the
application server is now registered with the admin agent, the application is no
longer connected to the Admin console. (The application server's Admin console
is now de-coupled from the application server.) You can no longer log in to the
application server's Admin console directly. At any time, you can also de-register the
application server from the admin agent by using the `deregisterNode.sh` command
found in the `<admin_profile_root>/bin` directory.

Using the administrative agent is a very powerful administration feature of
WAS 8. We will now create a second application server profile so we demonstrate
how to administer two application servers independently of each other, using the
same common Administration console.

# Creating a second application server node

Now, we are using the admin agent, we can register as many application server
profiles as required. All servers can be administered from a common interface. To
demonstrate this, we will now create a new application server profile, using PMT.

1. Navigate to the `<was_root>/bin/ProfileManagement` folder, and type the
   following command:

   ° For Linux:

     `./pmt.sh`

   ° For Windows:

     `pmt.bat`

2. Create another profile called `appsrv02` by selecting **Application server** from
   the create profile wizard.

3. Click **Next** and select the **Advanced profile creation** option when asked.

4. Click **Next** again to enter the **Optional Application Deployment** screen. On
   this screen, please make sure that all radio options are deselected. We do
   not need sample applications. We also don't want the default application
   at this stage and we don't require an Administration console as we will be
   registering this application server with the admin agent.

5.  Click on **Next** to go to the **Profile and Location** screen. Type `appsrv02` in the **Profile name** field and type `<was_root>/profiles/appsrv02` in the **Profile location** field, as seen in the following screenshot:

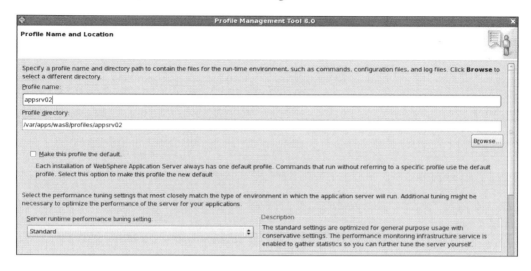

6.  Click on **Next** to go to the **Nodes and Host Names** screen and type `node02` in the **Node name** field; type `server2` for the **Server name**. The **Host name** field will automatically be filled in with the `<host_name>` you entered last time you used the PMT; you can change this as required:

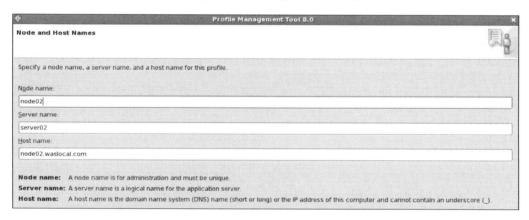

7.  Click **Next** to go to the **Administrative Security** screen and enter `wasadmin` as the username and password. Click **Next** twice to skip the SSL certificate generation as we wish to use self-signed certificates.

8. Once you get to the **Port Values Assignment** screen, you will notice that the Admin console ports are grayed out as we are not using them. Also note, once again, that all the ports have been incremented by 1 from the port numbers used in the `appsrv01` profile, that is, the `server01` JVM.

9. Click on **Next** and skip the **Linux service definition** page.

10. On the following screen, you will be presented with a screen to create a Web Server definition. If we had IBM HTTP Server installed, we could allow the wizard to automatically create a Web Server definition; the admin agent can administer the IHS server. We will skip this section as we will be creating this manually once we have installed IBM HTTP Server, later on in the chapter.

11. Click on **Next** to continue to the summary screen, and then click on **Create** to start the creation of the `appsrv02` profile, which will contain the new application server called `server02`.

12. When the wizard is complete, click **Finish** and close the **First steps** console window.

13. On the PMT screen, you will now see that there are three profiles listed, as shown in the following screenshot:

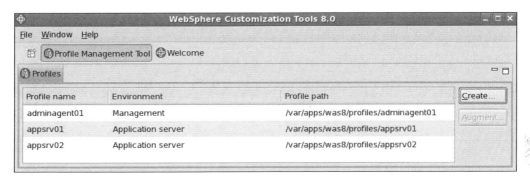

14. Close the PMT.

15. We now have to register the new profile with the admin agent. Type the following command to register the `appsrv02` profile:

   ° For Linux:

   ```
   <admin_profile_root>/bin/registerNode.sh -profilePath <was_
   pofile_root>/appsrv02 -username wasadmin -password wasadmin
   ```

   ° For Windows:

   ```
   <admin_profile_root>\bin\registerNode.bat -profilePath <was_
   pofile_root>\appsrv02 -username wasadmin -password wasadmin
   ```

16. Once the registration has completed, restart the administrative agent using the stop and start commands we learned earlier. When you try to log in to the admin agent's console the next time, you will see that there are now two servers you can administer. An immediate benefit is we can now start and stop each application server instance independently.

17. Select **node02** from **Select a node to administer**, log in using `wasadmin` as the username and password, and navigate to the **Servers | Server Types** section and click **WebSphere application servers**. You can now start **server02** by selecting **server02** from the list and clicking **Start**, as shown in the following screenshot:

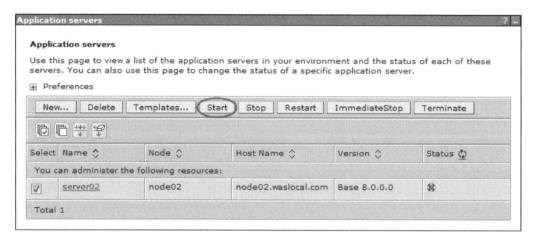

18. Now that we have created and registered two application server profiles, log out of any application server Admin consoles you might be in and re-log in to the admin agent console. Once you have logged in, we can list the nodes administered by the admin agent by navigating to the **System administration** section of the left-hand-side main navigation panel and clicking the **Administrative agent** link. Then click the **Nodes** link located in the **Managed nodes** section of the **Administrative agent** page. You will be presented with a list of registered application servers (nodes), as shown in the following screenshot:

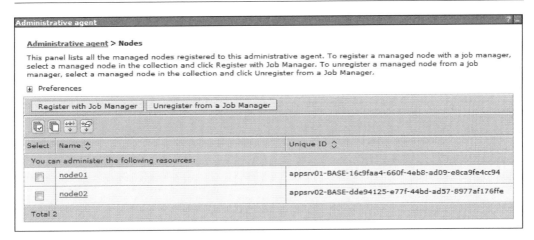

We have now demonstrated registering multiple nodes, which can be centrally managed.

# Removing the administrative agent

To remove the administrative agent, we will need to unregister each application server from the administrative agent and then delete the unwanted profiles. Our goal is to be left with the single application server we started with at the beginning of this chapter.

The command we are going to use is the `deregisterNode.sh` command:

```
Usage: deregisterNode -profilePath <path of profile to be deregistered>
[-host
        <adminagent host>] [-connType <SOAP | RMI | JSR160RMI | IPC>]
[-port
        <adminagent JMX port>] [-username <adminagent user name>]
[-password
        <adminagent password>] [-nodeusername <registered node user
name>]
        [-nodepassword <registered node password>] [-profileName
<adminagent
        profile name>] [-trace] [-help]
```

To unregister each server, navigate to the Admin agents bin directory `<agent_ profile_root>/bin` and type the following commands:

- **For Linux:**

  ```
  ./deregisterNode.sh -profilePath <was_profile_root>/profiles/
  appsrv01 -username wasadmin -password wasadmin

  ./deregisterNode.sh -profilePath <was_profile_root>/profiles/
  appsrv02 -username wasadmin -password wasadmin
  ```

- **For Windows:**

  ```
  deregisterNode.bat -profilePath <was_profile_root>\profiles\
  appsrv01 -username wasadmin -password wasadmin

  deregisterNode.bat -profilePath <was_profile_root>\profiles\
  appsrv02 -username wasadmin -password wasadmin
  ```

Once an application server profile has been unregistered, you will see a report similar to the following screenshot:

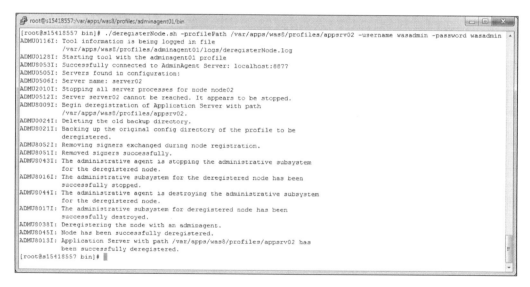

Now that we have successfully removed both application server profiles from the admin agent, we can stop the admin agent and remove its profile.

1.  To stop the admin agent, type the following command:

    ◦  For Linux:

        `<admin_profile_root>/bin/stopServer.sh adminagent`

    ◦  For Windows:

        `<admin_profile_root>\bin\stopServer.bat adminagent`

2.  Once the admin agent server has stopped, navigate to the `<was_install_root>/bin` folder and type the following command to list the currently-installed profiles:

    ◦  For Linux:

        `./manageprofiles.sh –listProfiles`

    ◦  For Windows:

        `manageprofiles.bat –listProfiles`

3.  You will get the following list: `[appsrv01, adminagent01, appsrv02]`

4.  Type the following command to remove the `adminagent01` profile:

    ◦  For Linux:

        `./manageProfiles.sh -delete -profileName adminagent01`

    ◦  For Windows:

        `manageProfiles.bat -delete -profileName adminagent01`

5.  Once the admin agent's profile has been removed, we can remove the `appsrv02` profile as well, using the same process as before. Once you have finished removing the `appsrv02` profile, we can re-run the `listProfiles` option of the manage profiles script. You should get the following list of profiles: `[appsrv01]`

    You should now have only one profile called `appsrv01` remaining, as shown in the fifth step.

# IBM HTTP Server

IBM HTTP Server is based on the Apache HTTP Server (`httpd.apache.org`), developed by the Apache Software Foundation. In this section, we are going to install **IBM HTTP Server (IHS)**, which will receive our web requests and allow a web application running on WAS to be served over port 80, as opposed to the web container port; for example, use port 80 instead of port 9080. The following diagram depicts the configuration we are going to achieve:

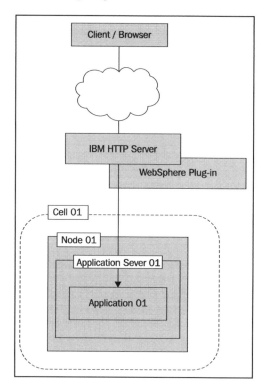

As shown in the preceding diagram, we will install **IBM Http Server (IHS)** and the WebSphere plugin to route HTTP requests to a single application server. In our example, we will be using the latest version of IHS (version 7.0), which can be downloaded from the IBM web site (`http://www-01.ibm.com/software/webservers/httpservers/`).

Download IBM HTTP Server 7.0.0.0 as your preferred platform. For example, the Windows download is called `ihs.7000.windows.ia32.zip` (115 MB). Once you have downloaded it, upload the installer to your server machine.

You will be able to use the same user ID that you registered on IBM's website when you downloaded WebSphere Application Server in *Chapter 2, Installing WebSphere Application Server.*

Once you have uploaded the IHS installation to your server, follow these steps to install IHS:

1.  Type the following command to run the IHS installer:

    ○   For Linux:

        ```
        <ihs_installer_root>/IHS/install
        ```

    ○   For Windows:

        ```
        <ihs_installer_root>\IHS\install
        ```

2.  Once the graphical installer has loaded, click **Next**, accept the license, and click **Next** again to move on to the **System Prerequisites check** page. Then, click **Next** again after the prerequisites have been passed and enter your installation location in the **Product install location** field. This location will be known as `<ihs_install_root>`.

3.  Click on **Next** to move on to the **Port Values Assignment** page, where you will leave the defaults, as shown in the following screenshot:

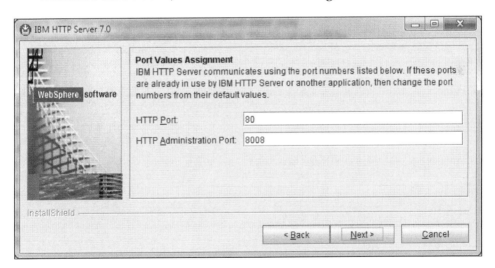

4.  Click on **Next** to enter the **Service definition** page, where you can optionally choose to set IHS to start automatically upon an OS restart. **Note**: If you are installing on Windows, it is recommended that you enable the **IBM HTTP Server 7.0 Window service**.

5. Click **Next** to move onto the **HTTP Administration Server Authentication** page. Here, you will be asked to optionally enter **Username** and **Password** for IHS administration from WAS. Type `wasadmin` for both the **Username** and **Password**.

6. Click **Next** to review the summary and click on **Next** to begin the IHS installation. When the installation has finished, click on **Finish** to close the wizard.

If you have any trouble with the wizard configuring IHS, you can use the following commands from the `<ihs_install_root>/bin` directory.

The first command creates a clear-text password that is used by a file called `admin.conf`, which WAS uses to connect to remote web servers:

```
./htpasswd -cpb <ihs_install_root>/conf/admin.passwd
wasadmin wasadmin
```

The second command creates the `admin.conf` file used for remote administration of IHS:

```
./setupadm -create -usr ihs -grp ihs -cfg /apps/ihs/
conf/httpd.conf -adm <ihs_install_root>/conf/admin.
conf
```

By definition, IHS is local to your server, but it is good to know how the wizard would configure IHS for remote administration, for situations when IHS is not installed on the same machine as the WebSphere Application Server instance. You can find more about IHS 7 at the following URL: `http://publib.boulder.ibm.com/infocenter/wasinfo/v7r0/index.jsp?topic=/com.ibm.websphere.ihs.doc/info/welcome_ihs.html`.

# Starting IBM HTTP Server

To start IHS using Linux, navigate to the `<ihs_install_root>/bin` folder and type the following command:

```
./apachectl start
```

**Note**: To start IHS on Windows use the IBM HTTP Server 7.0 Windows service. You can access the **Windows Services** applet from the **Windows Control Panel** to start/stop services.

If you have any issues with starting IHS, you can check the logs located in the `<ihs_install_root>/logs` folder.

To test if IHS is running, open the following URL:

```
http://<host_name>:80.
```

If you see the following page, you know that you have successfully installed and started IHS:

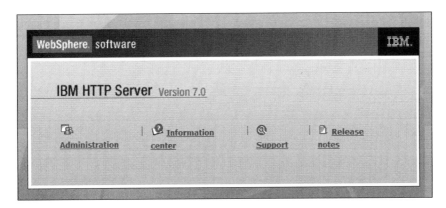

Now that we have installed IHS, we need to download and configure the WebSphere plugin.

# The WebSphere plugin

The WebSphere plugin provides the mechanism for IHS to route requests to WebSphere Application Server and holds configuration information that directs HTTP traffic to applications running in WAS.

The WebSphere plugin can be downloaded from the following URL:

```
http://www14.software.ibm.com/webapp/download/search.
jsp?go=y&rs=wspwas.
```

To locate the WebSphere plugin download, look for references to "Web Server Plugin for WebSphere Application Server". Once again, you will need to use the IBM user ID you registered when you first downloaded WAS in *Chapter 2, Installing WebSphere Application Server*. Download the installer as required for your preferred OS and upload your server. We will refer to this folder as `<plug-in_installer_root>`.

# Installing the WebSphere plugin

Once you have expanded the WebSphere plugin installation files, you can follow these steps to perform the installation:

 If you want to learn more about the various plugin installation scenarios, you can consult the locally-installed documentation located in the folder `<plug-in_install_root>`/plug-in/ `plg.plgmain.pak/repository/image.plug-in.roadmap/` `roadmap/index_roadmap_en.html`.

1. Navigate to the `<plug-in_installer_root>`/plug-in folder and type the following command:

    ○ For Linux:

    `./install`

    ○ For Windows:

    `install`

2. You will then be presented with the WebSphere plugin installation wizard. De-select all the checkboxes, click on **Next**, and accept the license.

3. Click on **Next** until you reach the following screen and select **IBM HTTP Server v7** from the available server types, as shown in the following screenshot:

 If you only wish to install the plugin binaries, you can choose **None** and no automatic IHS configuration will occur. However, you will need to manually configure the `httpd.conf` file. Instructions on how to manually configure IHS and the plugin are covered in a later section.

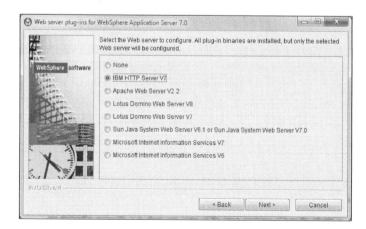

4.  Click **Next** to choose the installation scenario. Select the **WebSphere Application Server machine (local)** option. In our example, WAS and IHS are on the same machine and so the wizard will automatically configure the plugin by altering the IHS `httpd.conf` file:

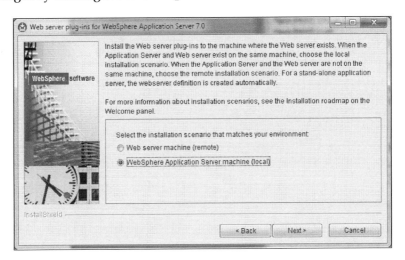

5.  Click on **Next** to specify the location where the plugin will be installed. Type the `<ihs_install_root/Plugins>` path into the **Product install location** field and click on **Next**.

6.  On the following screen, you will be prompted for the location of your local WAS installation. Type the path to the root of your WAS installation. Click **Next**.

7.  On the next screen, you will be asked to define the location of the `httpd.conf` file. The installation will modify this file with appropriate plugin settings. Type in the path to your IHS `httpd.conf` file, which is located in the `<ihs_install_root>/conf` folder. A typical path on Windows might be something like the following: `d:\ihs7\conf\httpd.conf`.

8.  Click **Next** to specify the name of a Web server definition. For WAS, IHS, and the plugin to work together, a web server definition must be created. We will discuss this in more detail in the following sections. Type `webserver01` in the **Specify a unique web server definition name** field and click **Next**.

9.  Confirm the settings and then click **Next** again to begin the installation; click on **Finish** when it is complete.

If you did choose to automatically configure IHS as per the preceding instructions, then the `httpd.conf` file will contain the appended lines similar to the following:

```
LoadModule was_ap22_module "d:\ihs7\Plugins\bin\mod_was_ap22_http.
dll"
WebSpherePluginConfig "d:\ihs7\Plugins\config\webserver01\plugin-
cfg.xml"
```

# Accessing an application via IHS

We now need to install the default application to test our configuration using the snoop servlet. As instructed in *Chapter 3, Deploying your Applications*, install the default application EAR file. However, when you get to the **Map modules to servers** screen, ensure that the application is mapped to the web server, as shown in the following screenshot:

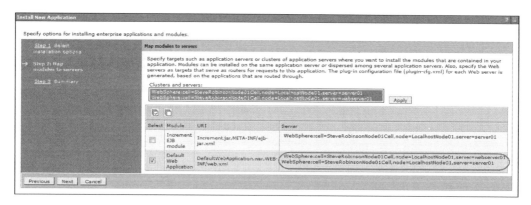

Once the default application EAR has been installed and you have mapped the web server definition, save your changes and start the application.

Now, we must inform the plugin of the configuration changes.

# Updating plugin-cfg.xml

Any changes to the applications web module mappings or context root changes will require a regeneration of the plugin `cfg.xml` file. To do this, go to the web server definition and click the **Generate Plug-in** button, and then the **Propagate Plug-in** button, as shown in the following screenshot:

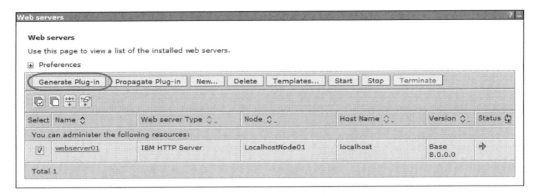

Once the `plugin-cfg.xml` has been updated, you can restart IBM HTTP Server. Once IHS has been restarted, you will be able to open the snoop servlet in the browser using the URL `http://<host_name>/snoop`.

Notice how we no longer need to specify `port 9080`, as we did in *Chapter 3, Deploying your Applications*. We can now use the default HTTP port 80, which means that the request is being routed through IHS. Because we mapped the default application (EAR file) to both the application server and the web server, we can also use the application server web container port using the URL `http://<host_name>:9080/snoop`.

If we don't want this to happen in future, we can go into the application settings and remap the application web module to `webserver01` and restart the application server. Regenerate the `plugin-cfg.xml` file and propagate it to IBM IHS. Then, IHS will have no path to find the application via port 80.

 Since the plugin was automatically configured as part of the plugin installation, we still need to know how to do this manually for situations where an automatic install and configuration is not possible or not suitable. In the next section, we will review how to manually configure the plugin configuration and explain more about the `plugin-cfg.xml` file.

# Manually configuring the plugin

Assuming you have opted to only install the plugin binaries and have not used the automatic configuration options, we can log in to the Admin console, review the web server definition, and understand more about the configuration and subsequent propagation of the `plugin-cfg.xml` file to IHS. The `plugin-cfg.xml` is used to tell IHS what **URI paths** are available to applications running in the application server.

# Manually creating a web server definition

If you require to manually create a web server definition, follow these steps:

1.  Log in to the console, navigate to the **Server | Server types** category in the left-hand-side navigation panel. Click on **Web servers**. You will then be presented with the option to configure existing web server definitions or set up new ones.

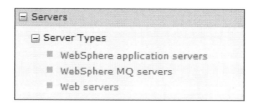

2.  Click the **New** button to enter the **Create new Web server definition** screen. Type a unique web server definition into the **Server name** field, ensure that the **Type** field has **IBM HTTP Server** selected, type the **Host name** or IP address of your server, and select the appropriate **Platform**, as shown in the following screenshot:

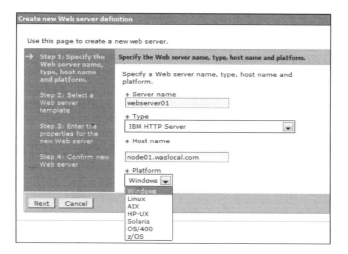

3.  Click **Next** and skip the next screen to move on to the **Enter the properties for the new Web server** screen. Type the location of your IHS installation into the **Web server installation location** field and type the location of your plugin installation path in the **Plug-in installation location** field. Use wasadmin as the value for both the **Username** and **Password** fields, as shown in the following screenshot. This screenshot depicts what the paths might look like for a Windows installation:

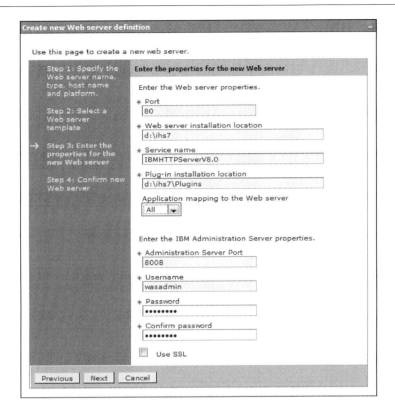

4. Click **Next** to proceed to the summary screen and click **Finish** to complete the wizard. Once the configuration has been made, click **Save** in order to retain the web server definition.

   Now, we can go back to the web server definition list screen, for example, **Server | Server Types | Web servers**. Update the configuration of the web server definition we created earlier to ensure that the `plugin-cfg.xml` file can be propagated correctly to IHS. The following steps outline how to re-generate the `plugin-cf.xml` file.

5. Locate the **webserver01** link to enter the web server definition configuration page.

6. Click on the **Plug-in properties** link and you will be able to see the location in which the web server definition expects IHS to find the `plugin-cfg.xml`.

7. Typically, the `plugin-cfg.xml` file is configured to be propagated to the `<ihs_install_root>/Plugins/config/webserver01` folder. What you need to do now is edit the IHS `httpd.conf` file, which tells IHS where the plugin binaries and plugin files are located.

8. To edit the `httpd.conf` file, navigate to the IHS file system, to the `<ihs_install_root>/conf/` location, and edit the `httpd.conf` file by appending the following two lines and saving the file:

```
LoadModule was_ap20_module <ihs_install_root>/Plugins/bin/mod_was_
ap20_http.so
WebSpherePluginConfig <ihs_install_root>/Plugins/config/
webserver1/plugin-cfg.xml.
```

9. Save the `httpd.conf` file and restart the IBM HTTP Server using the following commands (for Linux):

```
<ihs_install_root>/bin/apachectl stop
```

```
<ihs_install_root>/bin/apachectl start
```

For Windows installations, restart the IBM HTTP Server 7.0 Windows service.

# Configuring SSL for IHS and the WebSphere plugin

So far, we have only covered how to configure the HTTP port 80 for use with IHS, the plugin, and WAS. In production systems, it will most probably be a requirement that HTTP/S port 443 be enabled. The following steps outline how to configure SSL for IHS and the plugin.

## Creating a self-signed SSL certificate

1. First, we need to generate a new self-signed certificate that requires the use of the **ikeyman** utility shipped with IHS.

2. Run the following command to start the ikeyman utility:
    ◦ For Linux:
        ```
        <ihs_install_root>/bin/ikeyman.sh
        ```
    ◦ For Windows:
        ```
        <ihs_install_root>\bin\ikeyman.bat
        ```

    When the **IBM Key Management** tool has loaded, click **Key Database File | New** from the menu, as shown in the following screenshot:

3. Select **CMS** as the **Key database type**:

4. Click **OK** and you will be prompted for a **Password** to secure your new key ring, as shown in the following screenshot. You can use any password you wish. Check the **Stash password to a file** option:

5. Click **OK** and you will be reminded that a stash file has been created. This file will be used later by IHS to gain access to the key ring.

6. To create a new self-signed certificate, you need to select **Personal Certificates** from the **Certificate Type** drop down, as shown in the following screenshot, and then click the **New Self Signed** button to begin the creation of a new self-signed certificate:

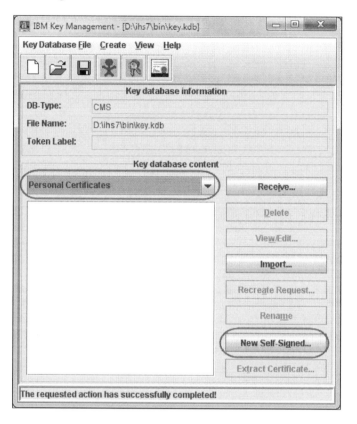

7. You will now be prompted to fill in the certificate details, as seen in the next screenshot. Ensure you use a label that you can recognize (if there were more than one in your key ring). We will refer to this label in the IHS `httpd.conf` file later:

 If you do not want the certificate to expire in one year, add another 0 to make the **Validity Period** 3650 **Days**.

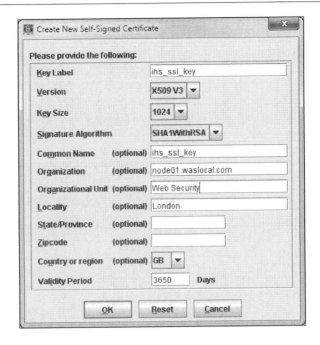

8. Click **OK** to generate the certificate; you will see it listed when you return to the main panel.

 As shown in the following screenshot, it is a good habit to ensure that you have saved the current password to your stash file before exiting the key ring:

9. You can now exit the ikeyman tool.

# Adding SSL to the IHS virtual host configuration

What we now need to do is add a virtual host to the IBM HTTP Server configuration so that we can use SSL.

1. Stop IHS, using the commands learned earlier in the chapter.

2. Add the following configuration to the bottom of your `<ihs_install>/conf/httpd.conf` file, just above the plugin configuration details. Ensure that you replace the words `%ihs_install_root%` with the location of your IHS install. Also ensure that you specify the correct value for the **SSLServerCert** option. This value will be the same value you used as the **Key label** during the creation of your self-signed SSL certificate, which we created earlier.

>  **Note:** The document root is where static HTML files are located.

```
Listen 0.0.0.0:443
<VirtualHost *:443>
SSLEnable
SSLProtocolDisable SSLv2
SSLServerCert ihs_ssl_key
SSLClientAuth None
</VirtualHost>

SSLDisable
KeyFile "%ihs_install_root%\bin\key.kdb"
SSLV3Timeout 1000
```

3. Verify that the SSL modules are uncommented within the `httpd.conf` file. If they do not exist, then add the following lines:

   ○ For Linux:

   ```
   LoadModule ibm_ssl_module modules/mod_ibm_ssl.so
   ```

   ○ For Windows:

   ```
   LoadModule ibm_ssl_module modules/mod_ibm_ssl.so
   ```

Configuring SSL between IHS and WAS Web Container.

We now need to ensure that WAS and IHS will communicate via SSL.

4. Navigate to your **Web server definition** in the Admin console and click to edit the configuration.

5. Locate the **Repository copy of Web server plug-in files** section and click the **Copy to Web server key store directory** button, as shown in the following screenshot:

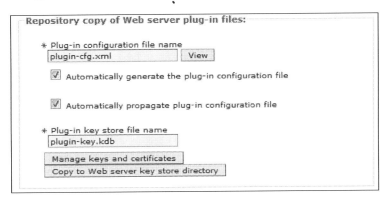

The plug-in key ring file is propagated to IHS and a message similar to the following will be displayed:

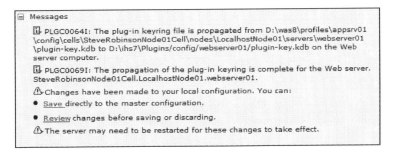

6. Restart the IBM HTTP Server.

7.  Open the snoop via HTTP/S (port 443) using the following URL:

    `https://<host_name>/snoop`. You will get a screen similar to the following:

| **Snoop Servlet - Request/Client Information** | |
|---|---|
| **Requested URL:** | |
| https://localhost/snoop | |
| **Servlet Name:** | |
| Snoop Servlet | |

**Request Information:**

| | |
|---|---|
| Request method | GET |
| Request URI | /snoop |
| Request protocol | HTTP/1.1 |
| Servlet path | /snoop |
| Path info | <none> |
| Path translated | <none> |
| Character encoding | <none> |
| Query string | <none> |
| Content length | <none> |
| Content type | <none> |
| Server name | localhost |
| Server port | 443 |
| Remote user | wasadmin |
| Remote address | 127.0.0.1 |
| Remote host | 127.0.0.1 |
| Remote port | 52193 |
| Local address | 127.0.0.1 |
| Local host | 127.0.0.1 |
| Local port | 9443 |

8.  Note that the server port it **443**, which is the HTTP port for the IHS server. However, if you look further down the image, you will see the local port is **9443**, which is the port that the WAS web container is serving the **Snoop Servlet**.

Congratulations! You have now configured SSL between IBM HTTP Server, the WebSphere plugin, and WebSphere Application server.

# Configuring virtual hosts

When we installed the WebSphere plugin and IBM HTTP Server, we were using port 80. For WAS to receive HTTP requests on ports other than the default HTTP port (9080), virtual host definitions need to be created.

By configuring virtual hosts, you can separate and control which resources are available for client requests by combining multiple host machines into a single virtual host, or by assigning host machines to different virtual hosts.

If any of the following conditions exist, you must update existing HTTP ports or add additional HTTP port numbers associated with the default virtual host:

- Your external HTTP server configuration uses a port other than the default port of 9080, you must define the port that you are using.

- You are using the default HTTP port 9080, but the port is no longer defined. You must define port 9080.

- You have created multiple application servers and these servers use the same virtual host. Because each server must be listening on a different port, you must define a virtual host alias for the HTTP port of each server.

# Updating an existing virtual host definition

To update an existing host alias, follow these steps:

1. From within the Administrative console, click **Virtual hosts**, located in the **Environment** section:

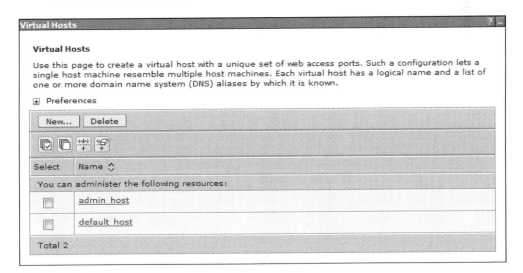

2. Select an existing host alias name such as **default_host**.

3. In the next screen, you can change the **Name** of the virtual host and add **Host Aliases** and **MIME Types**.

4. The host aliases associated with the **default_host** virtual host are set to *
when you install the product. The * (asterisk) indicates that the alias name
does not have to be specified or that any name can be specified. When the
URL for the application is entered into a web browser, the port number
is included. For example, if 9083 is the port number, the specified URL
might look like `http://localhost:9083/<application_context_root/
resource_URI`.

5. Predefined MIME object types and corresponding file names exist. Each entry
specifies a MIME type, which can be application, audio, image, text, video,
www, or x-world. An example value for MIME type is text/HTML.

6. To modify existing host aliases or to select the appropriate virtual host, click
**Host Aliases**:

There must be a virtual host alias corresponding to each port
your HTTP server configuration uses. There is one HTTP port
associated with each web container, and it is usually assigned to
the virtual host named **default_host**. You can change the default
assignment to any valid virtual host.

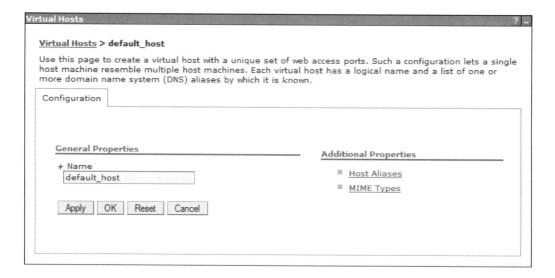

7. You will be presented with a list of aliases. Click **New** to add a new host alias:

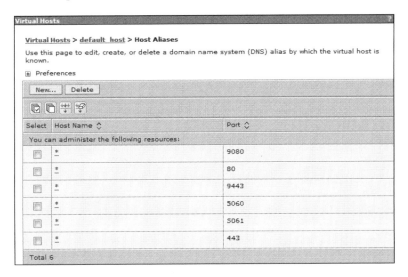

8. If you wish to modify an existing host alias, click the **Host name** of the host alias you wish to change.

9. Specify a host alias name in the **Host Name** field and one of your HTTP ports in the **Port** field:

 You can specify * (asterisk) for the alias name if you want to allow any host name to be specified. If you specify a host name, only requests from that particular host name will be accepted for this port.

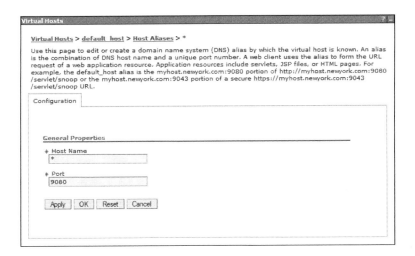

10. Click **OK** and **Save**, to save your configuration change.

11. Optionally, for each required update to MIME entries, navigate to the **MIME type** collection page and click **New** or select an existing MIME type.

12. On the **MIME type** settings page, specify a **MIME type** and **Extension**:

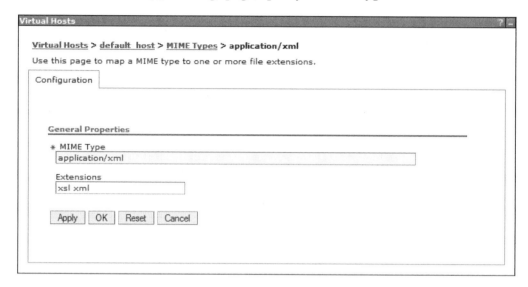

13. Click **OK** and **Save** to save your configuration change.

When changes are made to virtual host settings, a regeneration of the web-server plugin in required. Propagation may also be required. Instructions on how to do this are explained in the *The WebSphere plugin* section, earlier in the chapter.

14. Restart the application server for the virtual host configuration to take effect.

# Summary

In this chapter, we covered the admin agent, which allows the use of a single Administrative console to be used to administer multiple application servers. When a server is registered (federated) to the admin agent, we can start and stop servers without losing access to the Admin console. The admin agent allows us to also configure other aspects of WebSphere Application Server in a centralized fashion.

We also covered a simple example of how to use IHS as a web server in front of the WebSphere Application Server, thus allowing HTTP requests to applications mapped to the web server on port 80, as opposed to going to the web container. We learned that IBM HTTP Server can use the WebSphere plugin, which is the mechanism by which IHS can route requests to the application server. By creating a web server definition, we were able to propagate (copy) a file called `plugin-cfg.xml`, which contains the URI paths (context root and URLs) of all the applications that have web modules mapped to a given web server.

We also covered how to configure SSL between IHS, the WebSphere plugin, and WebSphere Application Server. In the next chapter, we will cover some important administration tools.

# 10
# Administration Tools

In the preceding chapters, we have covered the core concepts of administering **WebSphere Application Server (WAS)**. However, there are a number of other tools available, which we have not yet covered. In this chapter, we will be covering a few of the command-line tools shipped with WAS to help you with problem diagnosis when WebSphere or applications are not running as they should. We will also introduce the IBM Support Assistant, a very powerful WAS support tool, and walk through how to analyze a WAS log file using one of the many ISA add-ons.

In this chapter, we will cover the following topics:

- Dumping namespaces
- EAR expander
- IBM Support Assistant (ISA)

## Dumping namespaces

To diagnose a problem, you might need to collect WAS JNDI information. WebSphere Application Server provides a utility that dumps the JNDI namespace.

The dumpNamespace.sh script dumps information about the WAS namespace and is very useful when debugging applications when JNDI errors are seen in WAS logs. You can use this utility to dump the namespace to see the JNDI tree that the WAS name server (WAS JNDI lookup service provider) is providing for applications.

This tool is very useful in JNDI problem determination, for example, when debugging incorrect JNDI resource mappings in the case where an application resource is not mapped correctly to a WAS-configured resource or the application is using direct JNDI lookups when really it should be using indirect lookups.

For this tool to work, WAS must be running when this utility is run.

To run the utility, use the following syntax:

`./dumpNameSpace.sh -<command_option>`

There are many options for this tool and the following table lists the command-line options available by typing the command `<was_root>/dumpsnameSpace.sh -help`:

| Command option | Description |
|---|---|
| `-host <host>` | Bootstrap host, that is, the WebSphere host whose namespace you want to dump. Defaults to `localhost`. |
| `-port <port>` | Bootstrap port. Defaults to `2809`. |
| `-user <name>` | Username for authentication if security is enabled on the server. Acts the same way as the `-username` keyword. |
| `-username <name>` | Username for authentication if security is enabled on the server. Acts the same way as the `-user` keyword. |
| `-password <password>` | Password for authentication, if security is enabled in the server. |
| `-factory <factory>` | The initial context factory to be used to get the JNDI initial context. Defaults to `com.ibm.websphere.naming.WsnInitialContextFactory` and normally does not need to be changed. |
| `-root [ cell | server | node | host | legacy | tree | default ]` | Scope of the namespace to dump. |
| For WS 5.0 or later: | |
| `cell:` | DumpNameSpace default. Dump the tree starting at the `cell` root context. |
| `server:` | Dump the tree starting at the `server` root context. |
| `node:` | Dump the tree starting at the `node` root context. (Synonymous with **host**) |
| For WS 4.0 or later: | |
| `legacy:` | DumpNameSpace default. Dump the tree starting at the `legacy` root context. |
| `host:` | Dump the tree starting at the bootstrap `host` root context. (Synonymous with **node**) |
| `tree:` | Dump the tree starting at the `tree` root context. |

| Command option | Description |
|---|---|
| For all WebSphere and other name servers: | |
| `default:` | Dump the tree starting at the initial context, which JNDI returns by default for that server type. This is the only `-root` choice that is compatible with WebSphere servers prior to 4.0 and with non-WebSphere name servers. The WebSphere initial JNDI context factory (default) obtains the desired root by specifying a key specific to the server type when requesting an initial CosNaming NamingContext reference. The default roots and the corresponding keys used for the various server types are listed as follows: |
| | • WebSphere 5.0: Server root context. This is the initial reference registered under the key of `NameServiceServerRoot` on the server. |
| | • WebSphere 4.0: Legacy root context. This context is bound under the name `domain/legacyRoot`, in the initial context registered on the server, under the key `NameService`. |
| | • WebSphere 3.5: Initial reference registered under the key of `NameService`, on the server. |
| | • Non-WebSphere: Initial reference registered under the key of `NameService`, on the server. |
| `-url <url>` | The value for the `java.naming.provider.url` property used to get the initial JNDI context. This option can be used in place of the `-host`, `-port`, and `-root` options. If the `-url` option is specified, the `-host`, `-port`, and `-root` options are ignored. |
| `-startAt <some/subcontext/ in/the/tree>` | The path from the requested root context to the top-level context, where the dump should begin. Recursively dumps (displays a tree-like structure) the sub-contexts of each namespace context. Defaults to empty string, that is, root context requested with the `-root` option. |

| Command option | Description |
|---|---|
| `-format [ jndi \| ins ]` | `jndi`: Display name components as atomic strings. |
| | `ins`: Display name components parsed per INS rules (`id.kind`) |
| | The default format is `jndi`. |
| `-report [ short \| long ]` | `short`: Dumps the binding name and bound object type, which is essentially what JNDI `Context.list()` provides. |
| | `long`: Dumps the binding name, bound object type, local object type, and string representation of the local object, that is, Interoperable Object References (IORs) string values, and so on, are printed). |
| | The default report option is `short`. |
| `-traceString <some.package.to.trace.*=all>` | Trace string of the same format used with servers, with output going to the `DumpNameSpaceTrace.out` file. |

# Example name space dump

To see the result of using the namespace tool, navigate to the `<was_root>/bin` directory on your Linux server and type the following command:

- **For Linux:**

  ```
  ./dumpNameSpace.sh -root cell -report short -username wasadmin
  -password wasadmin >> /tmp/jnditree.txt
  ```

- **For Windows:**

  ```
  ./dumpNameSpace.bat -root cell -report short -username wasadmin
  -password wasadmin > c:\temp\jnditree.txt
  ```

The following screenshot shows a few segments of the contents of an example `jnditree.txt` file which would contain the output of the previous command.

In your example, you should be able to see the JNDI names for the JDBC data sources we created for the application in *Chapter 3*, *Deploying your Applications*, and the JNDI names for the JMS and MQ connection factories and destination we created in *Chapter 7*, *WebSphere Messaging*:

```
=================================================================
Name Space Dump
   Context factory: com.ibm.websphere.naming.WsnInitialContextFactory
   Provider URL: corbaloc:iiop:localhost:2809
   Requested root context: cell
   Starting context: (top)=localhostNode01Cell
   Formatting rules: jndi
   Time of dump: Sun Jul 24 09:23:48 BST 2011
=================================================================



=================================================================
Beginning of Name Space Dump
=================================================================


   1  (top)
   2  (top)/nodes                                  javax.naming.Context
   3  (top)/nodes/node01                           javax.naming.Context
   4  (top)/nodes/node01/cell                      javax.naming.Context
   4     Linked to context: localhostNode01Cell
   5  (top)/nodes/node01/node                      javax.naming.Context
   5     Linked to context: localhostNode01Cell/nodes/node01
   6  (top)/nodes/node01/nodename                  java.lang.String
   7  (top)/nodes/node01/persistent                javax.naming.Context
   8  (top)/nodes/node01/domain                    javax.naming.Context
   8     Linked to context: localhostNode01Cell
   9  (top)/nodes/node01/servers                   javax.naming.Context
  10  (top)/nodes/node01/servers/server01          javax.naming.Context
```

# EAR expander

Sometimes during application debugging or automated application deployment, you may need to enquire about the contents of an Enterprise Archive (EAR) file. An EAR file is made up of one or more WAR files (web applications), one or more **Enterprise JavaBeans (EJBs)**, and there can be shared JAR files as well. Also, within each WAR file, there may be JAR files as well. The EARExpander.sh utility allows all artifacts to be fully decompressed much as expanding a TAR file.

Usage syntax:

```
EARExpander -ear (name of the input EAR file for the expand
operation or name of the output EAR file for the collapse operation)
-operationDir (directory to which the EAR file is expanded or
directory from which the EAR file is collapsed) -operation (expand |
collapse) [-expansionFlags (all | war)] [-verbose]
```

To demonstrate the utility, we will expand the `HRListerEAR.ear` file we installed in *Chapter 3, Deploying your Applications*. Ensure that you have uploaded the `HRListerEAR.ear` file to a new folder called `/tmp/EARExpander` on your Linux server or an appropriate alternative location and run the following command:

- **For Linux:**

```
<was_root>/bin/EARExpander.sh -ear /tmp/HRListerEAR.ear
-operationDir /tmp/expanded -operation expand -expansionFlags all
-verbose
```

- **For Windows:**

```
<was_root>\bin\EARExpander.bat -ear c:\temp\HRListerEAR.ear
-operationDir c:\temp\expanded -operation expand -expansionFlags
all -verbose
```

The result will be an expanded on-disk structure of the contents of the entire EAR file, as shown in the following screenshot:

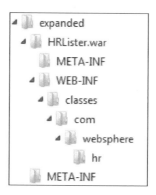

An example of everyday use could be that `EARExpander.sh` is used as part of a deployment script where an EAR file is expanded and hardcoded properties files are searched and replaced. The EAR is then re-packaged using the `EARExpander -operation collapse` option to recreate the EAR file once the find-and-replace routine has completed. An example of how to collapse an expanded EAR file is as follows:

- **For Linux:**

```
<was_root>/bin/EARExpander.sh -ear /tmp/collapsed/HRListerEAR.ear
-operationDir /tmp/expanded -operation collapse -expansionFlags
all -verbose
```

- **For Windows:**

```
<was_root>\bin\EARExpander.bat -ear c:\temp\collapsed\HRListerEAR.
ear -operationDir c:\temp\expanded -operation collapse
-expansionFlags all -verbose
```

In the previous command line examples, the folder called EARExpander contains an expanded HRListerEAR.ear file, which was created when we used the -expand command example previously.

To collapse the files back into an EAR file, use the -collapse option, as shown previously in the command line example. Collapsing the EAR folders results in a file called HRListerEAR.ear, which is created by collapsing the expanded folder contents back into a single EAR file.

# IBM Support Assistant

IBM Support Assistant can help you locate technical documents and fixes, and discover the latest and most useful support resources available. IBM Support Assistant can be customized for over 350 products and over 20 tools, not just WebSphere Application Server.

The following is a list of the current features in IBM Support Assistant:

- Search Information
    - Search and filter results from a number of different websites and IBM Information Centers with just one click.

- Product Information
    - Provides you with a page full of related resources specific to the IBM software you are looking to support. It also lists the latest support news and information, such as the latest fixes, APARs, Technotes, and other support data for your IBM product.

- Find product education and training materials
    - Using this feature, you can search for online educational materials on how to use your IBM product.

- Media Viewer
    - The media viewer allows you search and find free education and training materials available on the IBM Education Assistant sites.
    - You can also watch Flash-based videos, read documentation, view slide presentations, or download for offline access.

- Automate data collection and analysis
  - ° Support Assistant can help you gather the relevant diagnostic information automatically so you do not have to manually locate the resources that can explain the cause of the issue.
  - ° With its automated data collection capabilities, ISA allows you to specify the troublesome symptom and have the relevant information automatically gathered in an archive. You can then look through this data, analyze it with the IBM Support Assistant tool, and even forward data to IBM support.
  - ° Generate IBM Support Assistant Lite packages for any product add-on that has data collection scripts. You can then export a lightweight Java application that can easily be transferred to remote systems for remote data connection.

- Analysis and troubleshooting tools for IBM products
  - ° ISA contains tools that enable you to troubleshoot system problems. These include: analyzing JVM core dumps and garbage collector data, analyzing system ports, and also getting remote assistance from IBM support.

- Guided Troubleshooter
  - ° This feature provides a step-by-step troubleshooting wizard that can be used to help you look for logs, suggest tools, or recommend steps on fixing the problems you are experiencing.

- Remote Agent technology
  - ° Remote agent capabilities through the feature pack provide the ability to perform data collection and file transfer through the workbench from remote systems. Note that the Remote agents must be installed and configured with appropriate 'root-level' access.

ISA is a very detailed tool and we cannot cover every feature in this chapter. However, for a demonstration, we will install ISA and then update ISA with an add-on called the Log Analyzer. We will use the Log Analyzer to analyze a WAS `SystemOut.log` file.

# Downloading the ISA workbench

To download ISA you will require your IBM user ID, as used in *Chapter 2, Installing WebSphere Application Server*. The download can be found at the following URL:

`http://www-01.ibm.com/software/support/isa/download.html`

It is possible to download both Windows and Linux versions.

# Installing the ISA workbench

To start the ISA workbench installation run the following commands:

- **For Linux:**

  `rpm -ivh support-assistant-4.1.2.00-20101123_1610.i386.rpm`

- **For Windows:**

  `setupwin32.exe`

 In the following example, we are using a Windows installation; however, the process is almost identical for Linux, except that the installation location filepaths will be different. For Linux, the RPM installer will install ISA in the following location: `/opt/ibm/ IBMSupportAssistant_4`.

Follow these steps for the installation wizard:

1. Once the ISA workbench installation wizard has loaded, Click **Next** and then read and accept the **License Agreement** on the following page. Click **Next** again.

2. On the **Destination folder** screen, choose the location where you wish to install the ISA binaries. Click **Next** to continue.

3. On the next screen, you will be given an option to choose the location of where your user data will be stored. Choose an appropriate option to suit your requirement and click **Next** to continue. In our example, we have chosen to use the default location.

4. On the last screen, review your settings and click **Install** to begin the installation.

5. Once the installation wizard has completed click **Finish**.

# Launching ISA

One you have installed ISA, you can launch the ISA workbench application using the following commands:

- **For Linux:**

```
/opt/ibm/IBMSupportAssistant_41/rcp/rcplauncher
```

- **For Windows:**

```
C:\Program Files (x86)\ibm\IBM Support Assistant v41\rcp\
rcplauncher
```

When ISA loads it will present the welcome page:

 The first time the ISA workbench is loaded, it will prompt to inform you that it needs to update the list of available add-ons. The update process runs as a background task to keep ISA up-to-date with available add-ons.

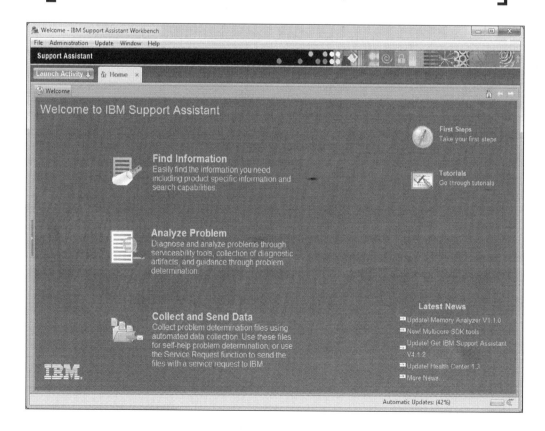

By default, ISA is set to start the update process as a background task every time ISA is launched; however, you may wish to disable automatic updates or simply schedule updates to occur at certain times of the day. Using the **File | Preferences | Updater Preferences** menu, you can enable/disable updates via the **Automatically find new updates and notify me** checkbox option:

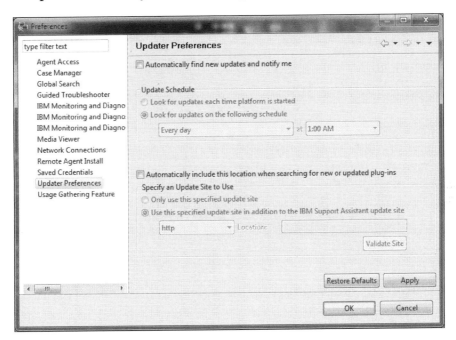

# Adding add-on tools

ISA organizes the downloads of add-on tools, such as the Log Analyzer, Symptom Editor, Memory Analyzer, Garbage Collection and Memory Visualizer, and Dump Analyzer, to name a few, which are all very useful tools for WAS administration. There are many other tools and add-ons constantly being made available.

The following steps explain how to install the Log Analyzer:

1. Ensure you have an Internet connection as ISA will be communicating with IBM remote repositories.

2. From the workbench menu, select **Update | Find New | Tools Add-ons**:

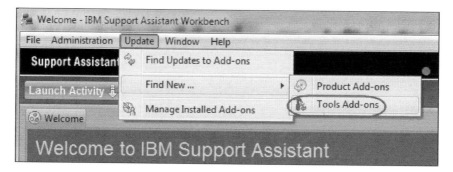

3. A background task will be initiated and ISA will return with a list of the latest available add-ons from IBM.

4. When the **Tool add-ons to install** window appears, expand the **JVM-based tools** option:

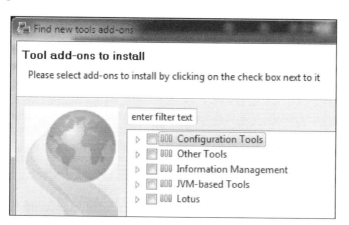

5. Select **Log Analyzer 4.5.0.3** (or the latest version) from the list of available tools:

 It is possible to install several tools at the same time.

6. On the **License of Add-ons to install** screen, read and accept the license agreement and click **Next** to continue.

7. You will now be presented with a summary of the add-ons that will be installed. Click **Install**.

8. After the installation has completed, you will be prompted with a screen summarizing the results of the installation operations:

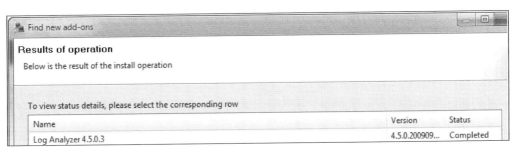

9. Click **Finish** to complete and you will be prompted to restart ISA. Once ISA has been restarted, you can use the Log Analyzer add-on.

# Analyzing log files

Now that we have installed the Log Analyzer, we can import a WAS `SystemOut.log` and analyze it. In our example, we will use a local copy of `SystemOut.log`, which has been copied from a WAS server and is located in `C:\temp`.

> Log Analyzer can analyze all of the WAS log types covered in *Chapter 6, Server Configuration*.

1. To analyze a log file, click on the **Analyze Problem** link on the workbench welcome page:

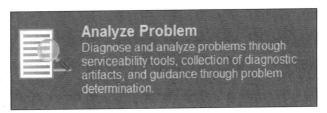

2. From the **Tools Catalog** list, locate **Log Analyzer** and click **Launch**:

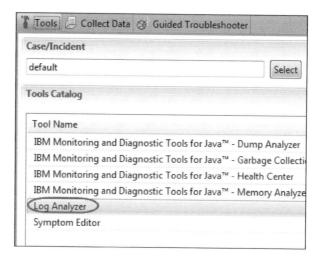

3. Once the Log Analyzer has loaded, select **File | Import Log** from the main menu:

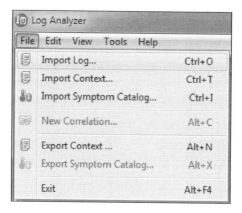

4. On the **Import Log** screen, select the **Import from the local system** option and click **Next**:

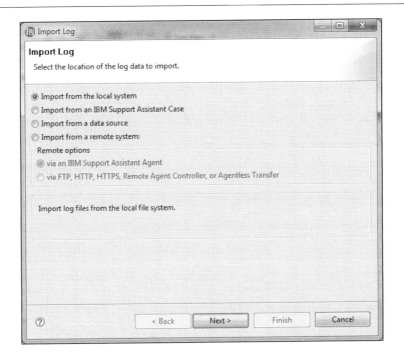

5.  On the **Import from the local system** screen, browse for the log file, then click the **Add** button to add the log to the **Logs to be imported into Log Analyzer** list and click **Finish**. The log will be parsed by the Log Analyzer and imported. The result will be to display the log data as a list of rows in the right-hand panel. In the following screenshot, we see example entries which you might find in a `SystemOut.log` file:

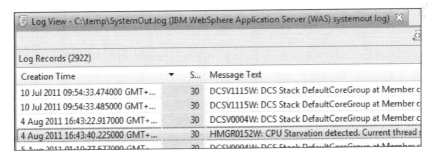

6.  Now you have imported a log file, you can navigate through the log data as a set of rows. Note that there is a toolbar located above the main log panel, as shown in the following screenshot:

7. This toolbar allows you to change the colors of specific error severities and select columns of field data as required. It also allows you to sort columns to make it easier to navigate through the log data in a structured manner.

# Loading symptom catalogs

Just viewing logs is not a useful problem analysis activity until the log is compared against a database of known symptoms and recommended solutions.

A symptom catalog contains three key types of information:

- Symptoms: Common problems or error messages
- Solutions: Reasons why the error may have occurred
- Directives or resolutions: Possible resolutions for the error

Within the example imported log as shown in the previous section, we can see that there is a CPU Starvation detected. We can import a symptom catalogue to get recommended solutions from the IBM support knowledge base.

Use the following steps as a guide to import a symptom catalog:

1. Select **File | Import Symptom Catalog** from the main menu.
2. On the **Import Symptom Catalog** screen, choose an appropriate symptom catalog in the **From remote host** list:

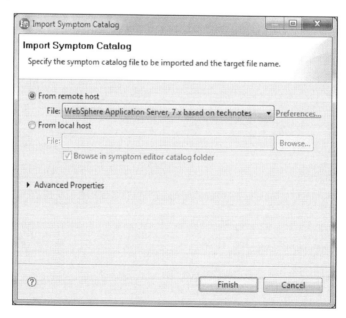

In our example, we are using a WAS 7 symptom catalog as, at the time of writing, there are no WAS 8 symptom catalogs available. Symptom catalogs are continually being added and updated by IBM support on a regular basis. Symptom catalogs are still very useful, even if they are for a previous version of WAS, as many errors are generic and similar across versions.

3. Click **Finish** to import the symptom catalog. The symptom catalog will appear in the **Log Navigator**, as shown in the following screenshot:

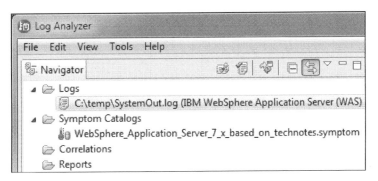

4. Right-click the **SystemOut.log** entry in the **Log Navigator** and select **Analyze**. The result will be a report listing solutions and recommendations for known errors. The report is located in the bottom section of the right-hand log entry panel.

5. Locate the **Symptom Analysis Result** panel and select the symptom you are interested in to view details from IBM Support:

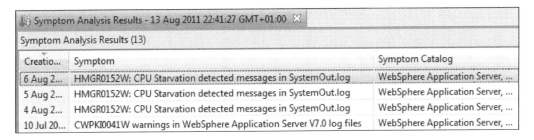

6.  In the previous example, we have selected one of the **CPU Starvation** symptom records. To the right of the **Symptom Analysis Result** panel is another panel called the **Symptom Definition** panel. Here, details such as recommendations and solutions are described for the selected symptom. Often, there is a URL link (within the description field) to an online IBM support page detailing the error and known solutions:

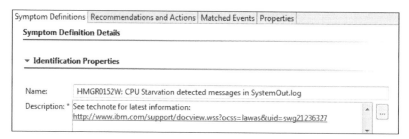

We have now completed a very simple log analysis. The ISA is a very powerful application. By demonstrating just one of the many add-ons, such as Log Analyzer, we see that the ISA is a very important administration tool.

# Summary

In this chapter, we saw that WebSphere Application Server comes with some useful command-line tools. The dumpNameSpace.sh utility can be used to view the JNDI tree of a running application server, which is very useful in helping with debugging the root cause of application failures that involve JNDI resource lookups. Another tool we looked at was the EARExpander.sh utility, which can be used to unpack an EAR file during automated deployments, to manipulate the EAR file, and repackage it on the fly. It can also be used during problem diagnosis if the supplied EAR file has problems during deployment.

We also learned that IBM provides a powerful support tool called the IBM Support Assistant (ISA). ISA provides tools and add-ons that can be used to analyze log files produced by WebSphere Application Server. We also learned how to import a symptom catalog into the Log Analyzer add-on to help find solutions for known errors found in a SystemOut.log file. Once imported, a symptom database offers suggestions from IBM Support on resolving errors; these suggestions are presented by the Log Analyzer to help correct problems with both application and server configurations.

Though we only covered the Log Analyzer add-on, IBM is continually providing new support add-ons for use with ISA. It is recommended that the reader keep abreast with new add-ons as they become available.

In the next and final chapter, we will be covering maintenance and support.

# 11
# Product Maintenance

An important role of a **WebSphere Application Server (WAS)** administrator is to ensure that the product is up-to-date and patched accordingly. IBM frequently makes updates available as they release improvements as part of the product lifecycle. The goal of this chapter is to instruct you on the options available to locate and download product updates, then apply them in the correct manner to your WAS installation.

In this chapter, we will cover the following topics:

- Understanding updates
- Update process overview
- Preparing for updates
- Creating a backup
- Locating updates
- Update installers
- Applying updates
- Verification of updates
- Silent updates
- Logs
- Troubleshooting tips

# Understanding updates

All software products can have defects, often termed as bugs. Product updates are released to address known defects. IBM WebSphere has an aggressive product update strategy to keep your product up-to-date, stable, and secure, which will ensure that applications run without issues introduced by defects in the underlying application server.

Security is also paramount in WebSphere. Since WebSphere is often part of the public-facing web portal solution for many companies, it is important to ensure that the product has no security holes that can be used by hackers to circumvent security.

By understanding how to locate, download, and apply product updates to your WebSphere Application Server, you will need to ensure that, as a product, it is running as error-free as possible.

 Having a good update strategy is paramount. To learn more about IBM's product update strategy, it is recommended you consult the IBM support website located at the following URL: `http://www.ibm.com/support/us/en/`.

# Product update types

Before we continue, it is important to note that there are several types of product updates. You need to be familiar with the terms used in the maintenance of packages, such as fix packs, features packs, interim fixes, and interim features.

The following table explains the different types of product updates in case you come across these terms on websites, installers, and/or documentation:

| Type of update | Description |
|---|---|
| Release | Essentially, a new product version.<br><br>• A new WebSphere Application Server that includes major new functions, such as V8.0<br><br>• This is a separate installation that can coexist with other Application Server releases<br><br>• Full testing of all applications with a new release is recommended |
| Fix pack | A product update that fixes defects.<br><br>• This is the standard delivery for updates—it has been regression tested.<br><br>• A fix pack is a cumulative package of fixes, such as Fix Pack 2 (8.0.0.2).<br><br>• Fix packs also install on top of a previous fix pack, such as applying V8.0.0.2 to V8.0.0.1.<br><br>• Fix packs are cumulative, so V8.0.0.2 includes all fixes in V8.0.0.1.<br><br>• Fix packs uninstall all Interim Fixes applied to the release since the last fix pack was installed. Therefore, it is necessary to check the list of delivered fixes to determine if an interim fix needs to be reinstalled.<br><br>Note: Brief testing of critical functions with the new fix pack is recommended. |
| Feature pack | A new set of features added to your WAS.<br><br>• WebSphere Application Server V8.0 releases feature packs, which are free, downloadable product extensions (on top of V7.0) that provide incremental new features<br><br>Note: Regression testing of critical functions with new feature packs is strongly recommended before you release environments for production use. |

| Type of update | Description |
| --- | --- |
| Fix | Emergency fixes to names and recorded defects. |

- A single published emergency fix, such as PK41267 (sample number).
- A fix is an interim fix or test fix that resolves one or more product defects.
- A fix can be applied to a release or fix pack where applicable.
- Interim fix = IFnnnn (for example, 7.0 IF0001).
- Test fix = TFnnnn (for example, 7.0 TF0002).
- Interim fixes are created when a standalone fix is required between fix packs. They are validated by at least one customer prior to being published by IBM.
- It is recommended that you test functions affected by the WebSphere Application Server component, which is fixed by an interim fix. You do not need to apply interim fixes, unless you have a requirement.
- It is recommended that you frequently visit the WebSphere recommended fixes page (Fix Central) for currently available fixes. When urgent, the fix will also be flashed on IBM Support pages.

# Update process overview

The update process can basically be broken down into the following steps:

1. Read relevant supporting documentation.
2. Locate, download, and install (if required) the latest Update Installer.
3. Locate and download product updates.
4. Verify the current version of WAS using the `versionInfo.sh` command script.
5. Ensure you have stopped all WAS processes.
6. Create a backup.
7. Apply updates.
8. Verify the new version of WAS using the `versionInfo.sh` command script.
9. Restart WAS.
10. Optionally, check WebSphere logs to ensure that there are no installation errors.

We will now step through the previous list, in more detail to explain the process of upgrading WAS 8.0.

# Preparing for updates

Before you apply any updates, you should query your WAS product to see what the current version is. This will help you decide which product updates you may wish to apply. You can use the WebSphere command script `<was_root>/bin/versionInfo.sh`for Linux and `<was_root>/bin/versionInfo.bat` for Windows, to evaluate what has been installed and which updates have already been applied.

The result of running `versionInfo` will be a report similar to the example report, as shown in the following screenshot:

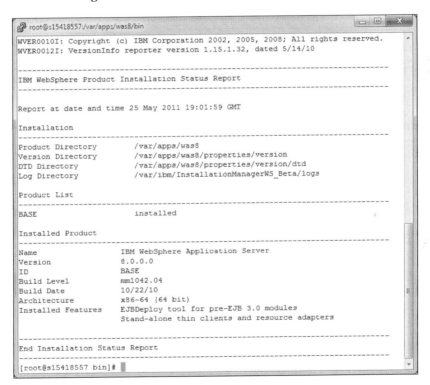

The section of the report that we are most interested in is the **Installed Product** section. This section details the current base version and any applied fix packs or feature packs. By referring to this section of the report, we can see what updates have already been applied. It is also useful for audit purposes to confirm the status of recently applied updates and to confirm that the updates have successfully been registered.

# Creating a backup

Before making any changes to an existing WebSphere installation, it is mandatory practice to make a backup before an upgrade is applied. You can backup WAS using the `backupConfig.sh/bat` command. This will create a ZIP file of your full WAS configuration in case there are problems and you need to resort back to a previously known copy. If you run `backupConfig.sh` without any parameters, it will automatically create a date and time-stamped `.zip` file.

You can get help for the command by typing the following command:

- **For Linux:**

  `./backupConfig.sh -help`

- **For Windows:**

  **backupConfig.bat -help**

  ```
  Usage: backupConfig [backup_file] [-nostop] [-quiet]
  [-logfile<filename>]
              [-replacelog] [-trace] [-username <username>]
  [-password
  <password>]
              [-profileName<profile>] [-help]
  ```

An example of running the `backupConfig.sh/bat` utility is shown in the following screenshot:

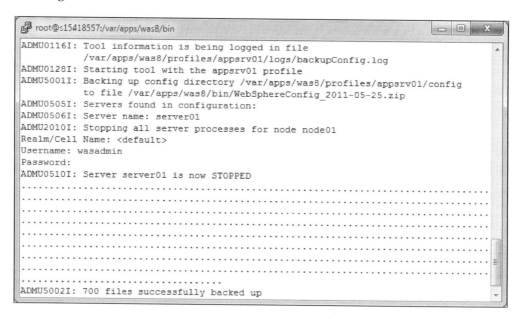

```
root@s15418557:/var/apps/was8/bin

ADMU0116I: Tool information is being logged in file
           /var/apps/was8/profiles/appsrv01/logs/backupConfig.log
ADMU0128I: Starting tool with the appsrv01 profile
ADMU5001I: Backing up config directory /var/apps/was8/profiles/appsrv01/config
           to file /var/apps/was8/bin/WebSphereConfig_2011-05-25.zip
ADMU0505I: Servers found in configuration:
ADMU0506I: Server name: server01
ADMU2010I: Stopping all server processes for node node01
Realm/Cell Name: <default>
Username: wasadmin
Password:
ADMU0510I: Server server01 is now STOPPED
.............................................................
.............................................................
.............................................................
.............................................................
.............................................................
.............................................................
.............................................................
.............................................................
.............................................................
.....................................
ADMU5002I: 700 files successfully backed up
```

During backup, the `backupConfig` stops the WAS processes, so this should be a planned activity to avoid impacting production services.Even though WebSphere provides a profile backup facility, it is recommended that you have a backup of the actual filesystem from an OS point of view. Often it is easier to not use the WebSphere profile backup facility and just TAR/ZIP the WebSphere installation folders, so you have a complete rollback scenario.

We all know that things can go wrong and so having multiple ways to roll back to a known point in time is a good thing.

If you are using WAS on VMWare or similar virtual server technology, you can create a snapshot, which saves the entire state of the virtual machine. If an error occurs at any time during upgrades, you can roll back to a known point of time for the entire virtual machine.

# Locating updates

IBM provides a dedicated web portal called **Fix Central**. Fix Central features an interface that is designed to help you locate your product updates. The WAS product suite is huge and there are many hundreds of product updates available for many releases at any given time.

Fix Central's goal is to help you find your product updates relevant to your particular WebSphere product as easily as possible. In our case, we are only interested in updates for WAS 8.0 and it must be noted that IBM's website is in a constant state of flux and thus, may not look exactly the same when you go to find your updates. The screenshots in this chapter are used to help you see the typical style that IBM uses in its support pages and hopefully serve as a guide going forward; as it is likely that the IBM website pages and processes will change over time.

**Helpful hint**:At the time of writing this book, we came across an article on IBM's website that covers how to use Fix Central located at the following URL:`http://www.ibm.com/developerworks/websphere/techjournal/0711_supauth/0711_supauth.html#seca.`

# Fix Central

Fix Central is located using the following URL:

`http://www-933.ibm.com/support/fixcentral/.`

To find the latest fix packs available for WAS 8, follow these steps:

1. Navigate to the Fix Central URL mentioned earlier. When you open the Fix Central landing page, you will need to select the **Product Group**, **Product**, and **Version** using the pick-lists provided. When you click Continue, you will be taken to a filter page where you can decide what kind of updates you are looking for. Look to see if there are any updates to WAS 8.0.

2. Eventually, you will get to a screen that will list the available updates. Click Continue to move on to the fixes download page.

3. Once you have located the download page, you can choose to use direct HTTP or the IBM Download Director, a reusable downloader supplied by IBM. Using the Download Director is highly recommended to ensure your download continues if there is a loss of connection during your download.

As with WAS binary downloads, WAS fix packs can be very large in size. Depending on your available bandwidth, it can take time for downloads to complete. Using the Download Director can ensure that these large files are downloaded over time even when connections are intermittent.

# Update Installers

Product updates are installed using the **IBM Update Installer for WebSphere Software** tool. Since new updates are made to the Update Installer tool over time, it may be required to download the latest version of the Update Installer.

The Update Installer is a JAVA application and will run on multiple platforms. For each fix pack, IBM will recommend the appropriate version of the Update Installer.

Just like the WAS installer covered in *Chapter 2, Installing WebSphere Application Server*, the Update Installer wizard runs either as a graphical user interface or in silent mode with a response file.

The Update Installer is used to apply Fix packs for WAS, **IBM HTTP Server (IHS)** and also the WebSphere Plug-in.

# Downloading the Update Installer

Fix Central will recommend the latest Update Installer required for each level of Fixpack. During a product's lifecycle, IBM often changes track with their install technology and so it is recommended that you read all supporting documentation made available on the page where the download is located, to understand whether you need to use the Update Installer that comes with WebSphere or download a newer version from IBM.

As mentioned in the *Fix Central* section earlier, you can do a quick search on IBM's Fix Central site to search for the latest Update Installer. Often the actual fix pack download page has a link to the latest Update Installer as well.

For further information on how to use the Update Installer, you can also follow the instructions that are included in the **readme** file, which is available in the install directory:

`<installer_home>/docs/readme_updateinstaller.pdf`.

# Installing the Update Installer

To apply a product update, you must first download, unpack, and install the latest version of the Update Installer.

Once downloaded, decompress the Update Installer binaries into an appropriate folder. An example path could be as follows:

- **For Linux:**

  `/tmp/UpdateInstaller`

- **For Windows:**

  `C:\temp\UpdateInstaller`

1. To begin the installation of the Update Installer, run the following command:

   ○ **For Linux:**

     `./install`

   ○ **For Windows:**

     `install`

If you are using a graphical install on Linux, you will need to ensure that you have an X11server available.

2. When the Update Installer's installation wizard has loaded, you will be presented with a license screen. Read, and accept the license and click on **Next** to continue to the **Installation Directory** screen.

3. It is standard practice to install the Update Installer in the following directory `<was_root>/UpdateInstaller`. We will refer to this path as the `<udi_root>`.

4. To proceed, click **Next** to move on to the installation and follow through the screens until completion of the wizard steps, where you will be presented with a summary screen.

If you have already downloaded a fix pack, you can save time by checking the **Launch IBM Update Installer for WebSphere Software on exit** option and this will automatically launch the Update Installer.

It is also possible to install the Update Installer silently. A silent installation of the Update Installer can be used as part of a completely automated WAS installation and upgrade.

# Downloading updates

The next step is to download the most current version of the fix pack that you wish to apply from the appropriate support site. Copy the fix pack into the Update Installer's maintenance directory.

You can however unpack the update files anywhere. Newer versions of the update installer allow for fix packs to be located through a browse button in the graphical installer during a fix pack installation.

Once the Update Installer has been installed as mentioned in the previous steps, it is recommended practice to copy the downloaded `*.pak` files (for example, `8.0.0-WS-WAS-LinuxX64-FP0000001.pak`) to the maintenance folder within the Update Installer. This will then allow the Update Installer to automatically detect available fix packs, without having to expressly browse the filesystem for them during the fix pack installation process.

Before applying updates, please consider that if you have not already chosen to install the sample applications, they might not work if installed at a later stage after a fix pack has been applied. The best approach is to ensure that all samples and features are installed before fix packs are applied.

# Applying an update using the Update Installer

Before the installation of a fix pack, it is required that you stop all running WAS processes. Once you have ensured that there are no running WAS processes, launch the Update Installer if it is not already running.

1.  Once the Update Installer has loaded, you will be presented with the following screen. Click on **Next** to move on to the **Product Selection** screen.

2.  Once you are in the **Product Selection** screen, select the appropriate path where WebSphere is installed. This is the folder that the fix pack will be applied to. In *Chapter 2, Installing WebSphere Application Server,* we referred to this location as the `<was_root>` path. If you have changed this path, please use the path you used in *Chapter 2.*

3.  Click on **Next** to move on to the **Maintenance Operation Selection** screen. Here, you need to select whether you are applying a fix pack or removing it. Since we are applying a fix pack, we accept the default setting of **Install maintenance package**, and then click on **Next** to view the available fix packs.

4.  The next screen is the **Available Maintenance Package to Install** screen. Here, you can see that the wizard will find the maintenance packages that were placed in the maintenance folder.

5.  Click on **Next** to go to the final **Installation Summary** screen where you will be prompted to choose whether or not you wish to verify that the current user has appropriate permissions to perform the install.

6.  Click **Next** and the installation of the fix pack will occur.

7.  At the end, the Update Installer will report **Success** or **Failure**. Click on **Finish** to complete the fix pack installation.

> **Useful hint:** It is important to know that the Update Installer creates a backup file in the `<was_root>/properties/version/nif/backup` directory. This backup file is used by the uninstall process.

Once you have completed applying the fix pack, it is good practice to verify that it has been installed correctly. Re-run the `versionInfo` command script and evaluate the product list section to ensure the update has been applied.

> The current version of WAS will be reported in the right-hand corner of the welcome screen, which can be seen when you next log in to the Administrative console.

# Silent updates

Instead of using the graphical installer, you can choose to use the **Update Installer for WebSphere Software** in silent mode to install fixes and features. The following is an overview of the tasks required to implement updates through the silent installation process.

Remember, before applying fix packs, install the most recent version of the Update Installer on the WAS server.

 When you run the Update Installer, make sure you run it using the same user which was used to install WAS. Otherwise, file ownership issues can arise and will require correction by the root user.

Download the required interim fix, interim feature, or fix pack from the IBM Fix Central site into the `<udi_root>/maintenance` directory.

A sample response file exists called `install.txt` and will be located in the `<udi_root>/responsefiles` directory. Edit the response file, changing any of the fields as required. The following table explains the two key options, which can be changed as required for the silent install to work correctly.

| Property | Description |
|---|---|
| `-W maintenance.package=` | Specify a single maintenance package full filename, or a semi-colon delimited list, or a folder containing the updates, for example `<udi_root>\maintenance\<file_name>.pak`. |
| `-W product.location=` | Identify the WAS install location that will be updated. |

The options mentioned in the previous table are the two main options that you will need to change. There are other options you can adjust as required. The provided sample response file (`install.txt`) is very descriptive and is self-explanatory.

 Remember to stop all WebSphere processes. It is required that all WAS processes must be stopped so that there are no conflicts with filesystem updates.

Run the Update Installer silently using the following command:

- Linux

  ```
  <udi_root>/update -options <udi_root>/responsefiles/install.txt -
  silent
  ```

- Windows

  ```
  <udi_root>\update -options <udi_root>\responsefiles/install.txt -
  silent
  ```

# Logs

As a general rule, it is wise to check the installer logs after installation of an update to verify that the install is successful. The log can be found in the following folder: `<udi_root>/logs/update/install`.

For reference, following are some key error words you may find in the log, along with their explanations:

| Status | Description |
| --- | --- |
| INSTCONFSUCCESS | The complete installation is a success. |
| INSTCONFPARTIALSUCCESS | The installation is partially successful; refer to the installer log for more details. |
| INSTCONFFAILED | The installation has failed; refer to the installer log for more details. Some of the most common reasons for errors are running out of disk space, folder permissions and environment paths, script syntax, and mismatched versions of update installers. |
| | The best thing to do before any installation is to check you have enough disk space on the filesystem and ensure you have read any notes about the update, often listed on the update's download page. Sometimes it is useful to read the `readme.txt` in the Update Installer, as IBM can often change the update process between versions. |

If the maintenance package is not applied to the WebSphere installation, a log file found in `<udi_root>logs/tempX` will contain the reason(s) for the failure. A log file of the naming sequence `tmpX` will exist to reflect the status of installs. `X` refers to the first available empty directory.

# Troubleshooting tips

Update Installers can sometimes be problematic and often it is hard to deduce the root cause of a fix pack installation failing. The obvious reason for failure is often the amount of disk space left on the filesystem, folder permissions and environment variables, namely system paths. However, there are a few other kinds of errors that are less intuitive. The following is a list of the common problems and their solutions, to help you with problem-solving upgrade failures:

## Problem: Silent Install

When using the silent option of installing a fix pack, the installer may not accurately report the root cause of a failed installation in the logs.

## Resolution: Silent Install

You can opt to try a graphical installation. Using the manual install approach can often shed light on errors that are reported in the GUI, but not in the silent installer.

## Problem: GUI Install

Launchpad installation wizard will not start or fail when using GUI.

## Resolution: GUI Install

Problems starting the launchpad or installation wizard can usually be traced back to missing prerequisite system or application levels, and permissions.

## Problem: Installation wizard fails

The installation fails with INSTCONFPARTIALSUCCESS or INSTCONFFAILED.

## Resolution: Installation wizard fails

- JVM errors can cause the installation to stop and can be due to system paths or permissions. To solve JVM issues related to the installer, you can ensure that you have the correct permissions and your Linux profile has not been altered and is not causing an environmental variable conflict.

- Filesystem errors can mean the installer has not completed. Check disk space, mounting of filesystems, and permissions.

# Problem: Installation wizard hangs

During installation, a progress indicator shows you how far the install has progressed. If there is no change in the progress indicator for a very long time, the installation process could have hung.

## Resolution: Installation wizard hangs

- The most common reason is that system resources are low. Check memory, swap space and filesystem disk space.

- On Linux, another reason can be that X11is running slow, due to network traffic. This can be your workstation being affected by your local desktop's local network and also your desktop's resources. Ensure that your machine has a good network connection and plenty of memory.

For further reading on detailed problems and resolutions, you can consult the IBM Redbooks site using the following URL:

`http://www.redbooks.ibm.com/redbooks.nsf/portals/.`

If you search the Redbooks site using the **Advanced search** option and use the search words "WebSphere Application Server Installation Problem Determination", you will find that many Redbooks and Redpapers are listed, which contain problems and resolutions of typical WebSphere installer issues. At the time of writing this book, there were no WebSphere8 problem determination guides. However, if you check this site every quarter, you will find that there are always new Redbooks and Redpapers available. It is important to know that often referring to Redbooks covering the previous version of WebSphere will frequently provide valuable information, which is still relevant to the next version of WebSphere.

 **Helpful hint**: To keep up-to-date with product updates as they become available, you can subscribe to an e-mail support account on IBM's website. The following URL covers how you can set up notifications:`http://www-01.ibm.com/support/docview.wss?rs=180&uid=swg21159292.`

# Summary

In this chapter, we introduced the need for fix packs and how to locate, download, and apply them using the IBM Update Installer for WebSphere software. We have demonstrated an easy approach to maintenance, and by using these steps you should be confident to prepare for maintenance in your environment.

It is recommended that you plan your update strategy for when you move into production, as it can be a complex task organizing production updates, often due to the fact that change requests are required and change windows may be infrequent for many live environments.

Since there are many releases, updates, and fixes throughout a given product's lifecycle, it is a good idea to schedule time to continually assess and improve your WebSphere estate. During this assessment, you can make decisions if updates should be applied.

It may mean that you need to provide **proof of concept** and/or **test environments** (sand boxes) to ensure that your applications will still work with applied fix packs. Any updates you make should go through the complete lifecycle of testing, just like with application development and deployment cycles.

# Index

request, receiving 191

# D

data access applications
  about 88
  data source, creating 102-107
  data sources 89
  deploying 107
  J2C alias, creating 100-102
  JDBC provider, creating 95-99
  JDBC providers 95
  Oracle, preparing for 89
  Oracle XE, installing 90-94
data access applications, deployment
  about 107, 108
  context routes, mapping for web modules 111
  JSP reloading options providing, for web modules 108
  modules, mapping to server 108
  resource references, mapping to resources 109, 110
  shared libraries, mapping 109
  steps, reviewing 111
  virtual hosts, mapping for web modules 110
Database Connection Pool Analyzer for IBM WebSphere Application Server tool 377
Database Management System. *See* DBMS
data source
  SiBus, configuring 313-315
data store
  advantages 311
  disadvantages 311
  preparing 312
Dblook, command script 114
DBMS 24
DefaultApplication.ear file
  uninstalling 133
default, command option 425
Definition Language (DDL) statements
  about 312
  generating, steps 313
deleteAll, command-line option 73
Delete button 188

delete, command-line option 72
Deploy enterprise beans, option 81
deploying 82
deploymentProperties folder 135
Derby
  about 113
  Derby JDBC 113
  Derby JDBC data source, adding 117
  Derby JDBC data source, creating 119
  Derby JDBC provider, creating 117, 118
  JAAS, creating for Derby data source 119, 120
  managing 114
  starting 114
  tables, creating 115, 116
Destination interface 294
Detailed option 80
detail level 258
development option 54
Directory to install application, option 81
Distribute application, option 81
drag and drop deploy 136
dumpNamespace.sh script 423
dynamic caching
  about 368
  enabling 369

# E

EAR expander
  about 427
  usage syntax 427
EIS 24
EJB container 19, 22
enterprise application 78
enterprise application class loader 283
Enterprise application (EAR) 283
Enterprise Application Resource (EAR) 81
Enterprise Information system. *See* EIS
Enterprise JavaBeans (EJB) 292, 352, 427
environment settings 22
error log level, HTTP error logging
  critical 266
  debug 267
  error 266

networkServerControl, command script 114
node 27, 381
node, command option 424
node level XML files, XML configuration
    files
  namestore.xml 248
  resources.xml 248
  serverindex.xml 248
  variables.xml 248

## O

off level 258
Open Services Gateway initiative. *See* OSGi
Operating System (OS) 47, 353
Oracle Express Edition (Oracle XE)
  about 89
  installing 90-94
OSGi 11
OS versions
  AIX 32 32
  HP-UX 30
  Linux 32 30
  Linux 64 30
  Solaris 32 30
  Solaris 64 30
  Windows 32 31
  Windows 64 32
  z/OS 32 32
  z/OS 64 32
Override class reloading settings for Web
    and EJB modules, option 82

## P

Pages (JSP) files 81
Passport Advantage 41
Performance Analysis Tool for Java tool 377
performance data
  retrieving, with PerfServlet 367
Performance Monitoring Infrastructure. *See*
    PMI
PerfServlet
  performance data, retrieving with 367
plugin-cfg.xml
  updating 406, 407

PMI
  about 346
  enabling 348, 349
  for external monitoring 362
PMT, administration profile
  about 383
  creating, steps 383-387
point-to-point model 292
Port Values Assignment screen 386
Precompile JavaServer Pages files, option
    81
Problem Management Report (PMR) 263
Process ID (PID) 62
Processor Time Analysis Tool for Linux tool
    377
product binaries file structure, WebSphere
    filesystem
  about 242-244
  bin, folder 244
  logs, folder 244
  profileTemplates, folder 244
  properties, folder 244
  samples, folder 244
  scriptLibaries, folder 244
  uninstall, folder 244
production option 54
profile file structure, WebSphere filesystem
  about 244
  bin, folder 245
  config, folder 245
  firststeps, folder 245
  installableApps, folder 246
  installedApps, folder 246
  logs, folder 246
  properties, folder 246
  samples, folder 246
  temp, folder 246
  tranlog, folder 246
  wstemp, folder 246
Profile Management Tool. *See* PMT,
    administration profile
Profile Management Tool (PMT)
  files 61
  logs 60
Profile Management Tool (PMT) 51
profileRegistry.xml, cell level XML files 247

## Thank you for buying
## IBM WebSphere Application Server 8.0
## Administration Guide

# About Packt Publishing

Packt, pronounced 'packed', published its first book "Mastering phpMyAdmin for Effective MySQL Management" in April 2004 and subsequently continued to specialize in publishing highly focused books on specific technologies and solutions.

Our books and publications share the experiences of your fellow IT professionals in adapting and customizing today's systems, applications, and frameworks. Our solution based books give you the knowledge and power to customize the software and technologies you're using to get the job done. Packt books are more specific and less general than the IT books you have seen in the past. Our unique business model allows us to bring you more focused information, giving you more of what you need to know, and less of what you don't.

Packt is a modern, yet unique publishing company, which focuses on producing quality, cutting-edge books for communities of developers, administrators, and newbies alike. For more information, please visit our website: www.packtpub.com.

# About Packt Enterprise

In 2010, Packt launched two new brands, Packt Enterprise and Packt Open Source, in order to continue its focus on specialization. This book is part of the Packt Enterprise brand, home to books published on enterprise software – software created by major vendors, including (but not limited to) IBM, Microsoft and Oracle, often for use in other corporations. Its titles will offer information relevant to a range of users of this software, including administrators, developers, architects, and end users.

# Writing for Packt

We welcome all inquiries from people who are interested in authoring. Book proposals should be sent to author@packtpub.com. If your book idea is still at an early stage and you would like to discuss it first before writing a formal book proposal, contact us; one of our commissioning editors will get in touch with you.

We're not just looking for published authors; if you have strong technical skills but no writing experience, our experienced editors can help you develop a writing career, or simply get some additional reward for your expertise.

## Application Development for IBM WebSphere Process Server 7 and Enterprise Service Bus 7

ISBN: 978-1-847198-28-0        Paperback: 548 pages

Build SOA-based flexible, economical, and efficient applications

1. Develop SOA applications using the WebSphere Process Server (WPS) and WebSphere Enterprise Service Bus (WESB)

2. Analyze business requirements and rationalize your thoughts to see if an SOA approach is appropriate for your project

3. Quickly build an SOA-based Order Management application by using some fundamental concepts and functions of WPS and WESB

## IBM WebSphere Application Server v7.0 Security

ISBN: 978-1-849681-48-3        Paperback: 312 pages

Secure your IBM WebSphere applications with Java EE and JAAS security standards

1. Discover the salient and new security features offered by WebSphere Application Server version 7.0 to create secure installations

2. Explore and learn how to secure Application Servers, Java Applications, and EJB Applications along with setting up user authentication and authorization

Please check **www.PacktPub.com** for information on our titles

## IBM Lotus Sametime 8 Essentials: A User's Guide

ISBN: 978-1-849680-60-8          Paperback: 284 pages

Master Online Enterprise Communication with this collaborative software

1. Collaborate securely with your colleagues and teammates both inside and outside your organization by using Sametime features such as instant messaging and online meetings

2. Make your instant messaging communication more interesting with the inclusion of graphics, images, and emoticons to convey more information in fewer words

3. Communicate with other instant messaging services and users, such as AOL Instant Messaging, Yahoo Instant Messaging, and Google Talk and know how someone's online status can help you communicate faster and more efficiently

## IBM Lotus Notes and Domino 8.5.1

ISBN: 978-1-847199-28-7          Paperback: 336  pages

Upgrade your system and embrace the exciting new features of the IBM Lotus Notes and Domino 8.5.1 platform

1. Upgrade to the latest version of Lotus Notes and Domino

2. Understand the new features and put them to work in your business

3. Thoroughly covers Domino Attachment Object Service (DAOS), Domino Configuration Tuner (DCT), and iNotes

Please check **www.PacktPub.com** for information on our titles